I0884558

Fighters across frontiers

Manchester University Press

Fighters across frontiers

Transnational resistance in Europe, 1936–48

Edited by
Robert Gildea and Ismee Tames

Manchester University Press

Copyright © Manchester University Press 2020

While copyright in the volume as a whole is vested in Manchester University Press, copyright in individual chapters belongs to their respective authors, and no chapter may be reproduced wholly or in part without the express permission in writing of both author and publisher.

Published by Manchester University Press
Altrincham Street, Manchester M1 7JA

www.manchesteruniversitypress.co.uk

British Library Cataloguing-in-Publication Data
A catalogue record for this book is available from the British Library

ISBN 978 1 5261 5124 7 hardback

First published 2020

The publisher has no responsibility for the persistence or accuracy of URLs for any external or third-party internet websites referred to in this book, and does not guarantee that any content on such websites is, or will remain, accurate or appropriate.

Typeset by
Servis Filmsetting Ltd, Stockport, Cheshire
Printed in Great Britain by
TJ Books, Padstow

Contents

Plates

Plates can be found on pages 183–192

Escape lines

Guerrilla fighters in the Balkans

The nationalisation of transnational resistance

Commemoration of Yugoslav International Brigaders

Maps

Contributors

Enrico Acciai is Associate Professor of Modern History at the University of Rome Tor Vergata. Formerly Associate Professor of Modern History at the University of Copenhagen, he co-runs a project on 'Foreign Fighters: Past, Present and Future', funded by the Carlsberg Foundation. His publications include *Antifascismo, volontariato e guerra civile in Spagna: la Sezione Italiana della Colonna Ascaso* (Milan: Unicopli, 2016).

Bojan Aleksov is Associate Professor in Modern Southeast European History in the School of Slavonic and East European Studies (SSEES), University College London. He is co-editor of *Wars and Between: Big Powers and Middle Europe 1918–1945* (forthcoming from CEU Press).

Roderick Bailey is Research Fellow in the History of Medicine at the University of Oxford. His publications include *Target: Italy. The Secret War against Mussolini, 1940–1943: The Official History of SOE Operations in Fascist Italy* (London: Faber & Faber, 2014).

Ginta Ieva Bikše is Scientific Assistant at the Institute of Latvian History, University of Latvia, Riga. Her publications include 'Latvijas un Spānijas attiecības (1936–1940): Spānijas pilsoņu kara konteksts' (Relations between Latvia and Spain (1936–1940) in the context of the Spanish Civil War), in *Latvijas Universitātes Žurnāls VĒSTURE 97*, 2 (2016), 68–88.

Jason Chandrinos is Research Associate at the University of Regensburg and a special researcher at the Jewish Museum of Greece, Athens. Among his publications are 'The Aftermath: Survival, Restitution, Memory', in G. Antoniou and A. Moses (eds), *The Holocaust in Greece* (Cambridge: Cambridge University Press, 2018).

Cristina Diac is Senior Researcher at the National Institute for the Study of Totalitarianism in Bucharest and the author of publications including

Zorii comunismului in România: Ștefan Foriș, un destin neterminat (The dawn of the communist era in Romania: Stephan Foris, an unfinished destiny) (Târgoviște: Cetatea de Scaun, 2014).

Laurent Douzou is Professor of Contemporary History at the Institut d'Études Politiques de Lyon. He is co-editor with Mercedes Yusta of *La Résistance à l'épreuve du genre: hommes et femmes dans la résistance antifasciste en Europe du Sud* (Rennes: Presses Universitaires de Rennes, 2018) and co-author with Sébastien Albertelli and Julien Blanc of *La lutte clandestine en France: une histoire de la Résistance, 1940–1944* (Paris: Seuil, 2019).

Yaacov Falkov is Lecturer in History at Tel Aviv University. Among his publications are *Meragle ha-ye'arot: pe'ilutam ha-modi'init shel ha-parṭizanim ha-Sovyeṭim 1941–1945* (*Forest* spies: the intelligence activity of the Soviet Partisans, 1941–1945) (Jerusalem: The Hebrew University Magness Press and Yad Vashem Press, 2017).

Diego Gaspar Celaya is Juan de la Cierva Postdoctoral Fellow at the University of Saragossa and the author of, among other publications, *La guerra continúa:oluntarios españoles al servicio de la Francia libre (1940–1945)* (Madrid: Marcial Pons, 2015) and '"Premature Resisters": Spanish Contribution to the French National Defence Campaign in 1939/1940', *Journal of Modern European History*, 16.2 (2018), 203–24.

Robert Gildea is Professor of Modern History at the University of Oxford. Among his publications are *Europe's 1968: Voices of Revolt* (edited with Anette Warring and James Mark, Oxford: Oxford University Press, 2013), *Fighters in the Shadows: A New History of the French Resistance* (London: Faber & Faber, 2015; Cambridge, MA: Harvard University Press, 2015) and *Empires of the Mind: The Colonial Past and the Politics of the Present* (Cambridge: Cambridge University Press, 2019).

Megan Koreman, formerly Associate Professor at the University of Michigan, is an independent historian. She is the author of *The Expectation of Justice: France 1944–1946* (Durham, NC: Duke University Press, 1999) and *The Escape Line: How the Ordinary Heroes of Dutch-Paris Resisted the Nazi Occupation of Western Europe* (New York: Oxford University Press, 2018).

Samuël Kruizinga is Senior Lecturer in Contemporary and Military History at the University of Amsterdam. His publications include

'Struggling to Fit In: The Dutch in a Transnational Army, 1936–1939', *Journal of Modern European History*, 16.2 (2018), 192–4.

Jorge Marco is Lecturer in Spanish Politics, History and Society in the Department of Politics, Languages and International Studies at the University of Bath. Among his publications are *Guerrilleros and Neighbours in Arms: Identities and Cultures of Anti-Fascist Resistance in Spain* (Brighton: Sussex Academic Press, 2016).

Zdenko Maršálek is a researcher at the Institute of Contemporary History, Czech Academy of Sciences, Prague, and the author of publications including *'Česká', nebo 'československá' armáda? Národnostní složení československých vojenských jednotek v zahraničí v letech 1939–1945* ('Czech' or 'Czechoslovak' Army? The national composition of Czechoslovak military units abroad in 1939–1945) (Prague: Academia, 2017).

Srđan Milošević is a researcher at the Institute for Recent History, Belgrade. His publications include 'The Role of the Yugoslav Popular Front in Implementing Communist-Style Measures in Yugoslav Rural Areas (1945–1953)' in *Tokovi istorije* (2018).

Olga Manojlović Pintar is Senior Research Fellow at the Institute for Recent History, Belgrade, and the author of publications including *Arheologija sećanja: spomenici i identiteti u Srbiji 1918–1989* (Archaeology of memory: monuments and identities in Serbia 1918–1989) (Belgrade: Udruženje za Društvenu Istoriju, Čigoja Štampa, 2014).

Milovan Pisarri holds a scholarship from the Gerda Henkel Stiftung and is the Director of the Centre for Public History, Belgrade. His publications include *The Suffering of the Roma in Serbia during the Holocaust* (Belgrade: Forum for Applied History, 2014) and *Sul fronte balcanico: guerra e crimini contro la popolazione civile in Serbia tra il 1914 e il 1918* (Novi Sad: Archive of Vojvodina, 2019).

Renée Poznanski is Emerita Yaacov and Poria Avnon Professor of Holocaust Studies in the Department of Politics and Government and head of the Simone Veil Research Centre for Contemporary European Studies, both at Ben Gurion University. Among her publications are *Jews in France during World War II* (Hanover and London: University Press of New England, 2001) and *Propagandes et persécutions: la Résistance et le 'problème juif'* (Paris: Fayard, 2008).

Lennert Savenije is a researcher at Radboud University, Nijmegen, and the author of *Nijmegen, collaboratie en verzet: een stad in oorlogstijd* (Nijmegen: Vantilt, 2018).

Vít Smetana is a lecturer in the Institute of Contemporary History at the Czech Academy of Sciences. He is the author of *In the Shadow of Munich: British Policy towards Czechoslovakia from the Endorsement to the Renunciation of the Munich Agreement, 1938–1942* (Prague: Charles University, Karolinum Press, 2014) and co-editor, with Kathleen Geaney, of *Exile in London: The Experience of Czechoslovakia and the Other Occupied Nations, 1939–1945* (Prague: Charles University, 2018).

Ismee Tames is Programme Leader, War and Society, at the Insitute for War, Holocaust and Genocide Studies (NIOD) in Amsterdam and Professor of the History of Resistance in Times of War and Persecution at Utrecht University. Her publications include *Doorn in het vlees: Foute Nederlanders in de jaren vijftig en zestig* (Thorn in the flesh: Dutch Nazi collaborators after the war) (Amsterdam: Balans, 2013) and 'Over grenzen: liminaliteit en de ervaring van verzet' (About thresholds: liminality and the experience of resistance), her inaugural lecture at Utrecht University (Amsterdam, 2016).

Mercedes Yusta Rodrigo is Professor of the Contemporary History of Spain in the Department of Spanish, University of Paris VIII. She is the author of publications including *Guerrilla y resistencia campesina: la resistencia armada contra el franquismo en Aragón* (Saragossa: Prensas Universitarias de Zaragoza, 2003) and co-editor, with Laurent Douzou, of *La Résistance à l'épreuve du genre: hommes et femmes dans la Résistance antifasciste en Europe du Sud* (Rennes: Presses Universitaires de Rennes, 2018).

Franziska Zaugg is a Swiss National Science Foundation/Amizione postdoctoral fellow at the University of Bern, Switzerland. Formerly a Gerda Henkel Foundation postdoctoral fellow at University College Dublin's Centre for War Studies, she is the author of *Albanische Muslime in der Waffen-SS, von Großalbanien zur Division Skanderbeg* (Paderborn: Schöningh Verlag, 2016).

Abbreviations

ACCPCE	Archivo del Comité Central del Partido Comunista de España/Archives of the Central Committee of the Spanish Communist Party, Madrid
AD	Archives Départementales
AHPCE	Archivo Histórico del Partido Comunista de España/ Historical Archives of the Spanish Communist Party
AK	Armija Krajova/Home Army
AKFD	Antifaschistisches Komitee 'Freies Deutschland'/'Free Germany' Anti-Fascist Committee
AN	Archives Nationales/National Archives, Paris
AoY	Arhiv Jugoslavije/Archives of Yugoslavia, Belgrade
ASF	Archivio di Stato di Firenze/State Archives, Florence
AUSSME	Archivio Ufficio Storico dello Stato Maggiore dell'Esercito, Rome
BArchB	Bundesarchiv, Berlin-Lichterfelde
BArchF	Bundesarchiv-Militärarchiv, Freiburg
BSW	Bratskoe Sotrudnichestvo Voennoplennykh/Fraternal Cooperation of Prisoners of War
CADI	Comité d'Action et Défense des Immigrés/Immigrant Defence and Action Group
CAPM	Centre des Archives du Personnel Militaire/Military Staff Archive Centre, Pau
CDJC	Centre de Documentation Juive Contemporaine/ Contemporary Jewish Documentation Centre, Paris
CFA	Corps Franc d'Afrique/African French Corps
CHPM	Central Headquarters of the Partisan Movement
CNR	Conseil National de la Résistance/National Resistance Council
CPL	Comité Parisien de Libération/Paris Liberation Committee
CSAPOU	Central State Archives of Public Organisations of Ukraine, Kiev

DDR	Deutsche Demokratische Republik/German Democratic Republic (East Germany)
EAM	Ethnikó Apeleftherotikó Métopo/National Liberation Front
EDES	Ethnikos Dimokratikos Ellinikos Syndesmos/National Republican Greek League
EIF	Éclaireurs Israélites de France/French Jewish Scout movement
ELAS	Ellinikos Laikos Apeleftherotikos Stratos/Greek People's Liberation Army
FFIs	Forces Françaises de l'Interieur/French Forces of the Interior
FTP	Francs-Tireurs et Partisans/Sharp Shooters and Partisans
FTP-MOI	Francs-Tireurs et Partisans-Main d'Oeuvre Immigrée/ Sharp Shooters and Partisans of the Immigrant Labour Organisation
GAP	Gruppi di Azione Patriottica/Patriotic Action Groups
GRU	Glavnoye Razvedyvatelnoye Upravlenie/Soviet Military Strategic Intelligence
GTE	Groupes des Travailleurs Étrangers/Foreign Workers' Teams
IB	International Brigades
ITWF	International Transport Workers' Federation
JOC	Jeunesse Ouvrière Chrétienne/Young Christian Workers
KAJ	Katholieke Arbeidersjeugd/Young Christian Workers
KKE	Kommounistikó Kómma Elládas/Greek Communist Party
KPD	Kommunistische Partei Deutschlands/German Communist Party
LNA	Latvian National Archives, Riga
LO	Landelijke Organisatie voor Hulp aan Onderduikers/ National Organisation for the Help of People in Hiding
MDL	Museum of Dutch Literature/Stichting Nederlands Literatuurmuseum en Literatuurarchief, The Hague
MOI	Main d'Oeuvre Immigrée/Immigrant Labour Organisation
NAR	National Archives of Romania
NDH	Nezavisna Država Hrvatska/Independent State of Croatia
NKVD	Narodnyy Komissariat Vnutrennikh Del/People's Commissariat for Internal Affairs
OJC	Organisation Juive de Combat/Jewish Combat Organisation
OMSBON	Otdel'naya Motostrel'kovaya Brigada Osobogo Naznacheniya/Independent Motorised Brigade for Special Assignment

OS	Organisation Spéciale/Special Organisation
OSE	Oeuvre de Secours aux Enfants/Children's Rescue Programme
OSS	Office of Strategic Services
PAI	Polizia dell'Africa Italiana/Italian African Police
PCA	Parti Communiste Algérien/Algerian Communist Party
PCE	Partido Comunista de España/Spanish Communist Party
PCF	Parti Communiste Français/French Communist Party
PCI	Partito Communista Italiano/Italian Communist Party
POW	prisoner of war
PZPR	Polska Zjednoczona Partia Robotnicza/Polish United Workers' Party
RAF	Royal Air Force
RGASPI	Russian State Archive of Socio-Political History, Moscow
RMVE	Régiments de Marche de Volontaires Étrangers/Foreign Volunteers' Infantry Regiments
SED	Sozialistische Einheitspartei Deutschlands/Socialist Unity Party
SHD	Service Historique de la Défense/French Military Archives, Vincennes
SIS	Secret Intelligence Service
SNK	Slovenská Národná Rada/Slovakian National Committee
SOE	Special Operations Executive
SPD	Sozialdemokratische Partei Deutschlands/German Social Democratic Party
STO	Service du Travail Obligatoire/Forced Labour Service
TNA	The National Archives, Kew
USHMM	United States Holocaust Memorial Museum
UPMS	Ukrainian Partisan Movement Staff
VÚA–VHA	Vojenský Ústřední Archiv – Vojenský Historický Archiv/Central Military Archives – Military Historical Archives, Prague

Chronology of events

1936

16 February, victory of Popular Front in Spanish elections
7 March, German forces occupy the demilitarised Rhineland
3 May, victory of Popular Front in French elections
17 July, anti-republican military coup in Spanish Morocco, spreads to Spain
19 July, opening of International Workers' Olympiad, Barcelona
1 August, opening of Olympic Games in Berlin
19 August, opening of first Great Purge trial in Moscow
18 September, Comintern orders formation of International Brigades to defend the Spanish Republic
25 October, formation of Rome–Berlin Axis
6 November, beginning of siege of republican-held Madrid by Nationalist forces
26 November, Anti-Comintern Pact signed by Germany and Japan

1937

23 January, opening of second Great Purge trial in Moscow
26 April, bombing of Basque city of Guernica by German and Italian planes
3 May, rising of anarchists and syndicalists in Barcelona
6 November, Anti-Comintern Pact joined by Fascist Italy

1938

10 February, dictatorship of King Carol II in Romania
12 March, German forces enter Austria: the *Anschluss*
21 September, order to International Brigades to retreat and disband
29 September, Munich conference between Germany, Italy, France and Britain

1 October, Germany occupies Sudetenland of Czechoslovakia
5 October, Czechoslovak President Edvard Beneš resigns and goes into exile
6 October, anti-Semitic legislation passed in Fascist Italy
9 November, *Kristallnacht* anti-Jewish pogrom in Germany and Austria

1939

26 January, capture of Barcelona by Nationalist forces; mass exodus across the Pyrenees to France
15 March 1939, Germany invades Czechoslovakia and occupies Prague
28 March, surrender of republican Madrid to nationalist forces
7 April, Italy invades Albania; Spain joins the Anti-Comintern Pact
22 May, formation of Pact of Steel between Germany and Italy
23 May, White Paper limiting Jewish migration to Palestine approved by British Parliament
23 August, Non-Aggression Pact between Soviet Union and Nazi Germany; partition of Poland follows
3 September, Britain and France declare war on Germany

1940

1 February, Russo-Finnish 'Winter War' begins
9 April, German armies occupy Denmark and Norway
10 April, First Battle of Narvik in Norway
10 May, German armies invade the Netherlands, Belgium, Luxembourg and northern France
10 June, Italy declares war on France and Britain
14 June, German forces enter Paris
22–24 June, German and Italian armistices with France
10 July, French Parliament meeting in Vichy gives full powers to Marshal Pétain
27 September, Tripartite Pact between Germany, Italy and Japan
28 October, Mussolini orders attack on Greece
20–23 November, Hungary and Romania sign Tripartite Pact

1941

25 March, Yugoslav government signs Tripartite Pact
27 March, Yugoslav coup d'état replaces pro-Axis regent and government and installs King Peter II
6 April, Germany, Italy and Bulgaria invade Yugoslavia

17 April, surrender of Yugoslavia, partitioned between Germany, Italy, Bulgaria and Hungary; Croatia becomes fascist German vassal state
26 April, Osvobodilna Fronta – the Liberation Front – formed in Ljubljana
22 June, Operation Barbarossa: Germany invades the Soviet Union
4 July, the Communist Party of Yugoslavia calls for an armed uprising in all its territories
19 September, German armies take the Ukraine capital Kiev
24 September, Germans take Kharkov
25 September, failure of first German offensive against Moscow
16 November, second German offensive against Moscow

1942

20 January, Nazi leaders discuss the Final Solution in Berlin's Wannsee suburb
21 January, Hungarian raid on Serbian city of Novi Said
16–17 July, mass round-up of Jews in Paris
13 September, beginning of Battle of Stalingrad
8 November, Operation Torch: Allied troops land in Morocco and Algeria; Germany occupies Tunisia
11 November, Germany occupies the whole of France
24 December, assassination of Vichy's Admiral Darlan in Algiers

1943

2 February, surrender of German armies at Stalingrad
19 April, Warsaw Ghetto uprising
27 May, secret formation of National Council of Resistance in Paris
3 June, formation in Algiers of French Committee of National Liberation under Generals de Gaulle and Giraud
10 July, Allies invade Sicily
25 July, Mussolini removed from office by the Fascist Grand Council and King Victor Emmanuel III
8 September, armistice between Italy and the Allies
10 September, Germans occupy Rome
15 September, Mussolini sets up an Italian Socialist Republic
1 October, British liberate Naples

1944

17 January, beginning of Battle of Monte Cassino, Italy
27 January, German siege of Leningrad ended by Soviet army

21 February, execution of Manouchian Group in Paris
10 March, formation of Greek Provisional National Liberation Committee
19 March, Germans occupy the territory of former ally Hungary
4 June, liberation of Rome by the Allies
6 June, Allied D-Day landings in Normandy
4 July, Soviet forces cross 1939 border into Poland
20 July, assassination attempt on Adolf Hitler
1 August, beginning of Warsaw uprising
15 August, Allies and French forces land on south coast of France
19 August, beginning of Paris uprising
21 August, restoration of Czechoslovak Republic proclaimed
22 August, foundation of the Antifaschistisches Komitee 'Freies Deutschland/'Free Germany' Anti-Fascist Committee of German Soldiers in Greece
23 August, Romania leaves Axis and sides with the Allies
24–6 August, liberation of Paris
29 August, outbreak of Slovak uprising
2 October, German suppression of Warsaw uprising
4 October, British forces invade Greece
19 October, Spanish republicans invade Franco's Spain
20 October, liberation of Belgrade
27 October, retreat of Slovak fighters to the mountains
3 December, demonstrations in Greece suppressed by Greek police with British backing

1945

1 January, Lublin Committee proclaims itself Poland's provisional government
17 January, Soviet armies enter Warsaw
3 April, provisional government appointed in Czechoslovakia by Eduard Beneš
28 April, Mussolini captured and executed by partisans
30 April, suicide of Hitler
2 May, Soviet army enters Berlin
8 May, surrender of German armies to Allies; Victory in Europe celebrated
24 June, liberation parade in Moscow
19 August, World Jewish Congress in Paris demands admission of a million Jews into Palestine
2 September, surrender of Japan

1946

30 March, outbreak of civil war in Greece
9 May, abdication of King Victor Emmanuel III of Italy
2 June, referendum in Italy replaces monarchy by republic
17 July, execution of Serb royalist leader Draža Mihailović
22 July, Zionist militants blow up British headquarters in King David Hotel, Jerusalem
1 September, referendum in Greece backs restoration of the monarchy

1947

29 March, doctrine against global communist expansion announced by US President Truman
5 May, communist ministers dismissed from French government
18 July, British forces board the *Exodus* carrying over 4,000 Jewish refugees off the Palestinian coast and force it to turn back
29 September, Zionist militants blow up Central Police headquarters in Haifa
5 October, formation of Communist Information Bureau (Cominform) in Warsaw
27 December, Greek government dissolves Greek Communist Party and Council of National Liberation (EAM)
30 December, abdication of King Michael of Romania

1948

25 February, communist coup d'état in Czechoslovakia
21 April, first 'Dachau Trial' of political suspects in Yugoslavia
14 May, declaration of the establishment of the state of Israel
28 June, Yugoslavia expelled from the Cominform
15 December, Polish Workers Party takes over Polish Socialist Party to form Polish United Workers Party under the Stalinist Bolesław Bierut

Acknowledgements

We would like to thank the Leverhulme Trust for the award of an International Network grant. This linked seven research centres – the Oxford Centre for European History, University College Dublin Centre for War Studies, the School of Slavonic and East European Studies (SEES), London, the Institute for War, Holocaust and Genocide Studies (NIOD), Amsterdam, the Institut Universitaire de France, the Institute for Contemporary History of the Academy of Sciences of the Czech Republic, Prague, and the Institute for the Recent History of Serbia, Belgrade. It brought in two visiting fellows, from the Ben Gurion University of the Negev Tel Aviv University, and supported three international workshops in Belgrade (2016), Dublin (2017) and Oxford (2018). Thanks are due to Professors Olga Manojlović Pintar and Robert Gerwarth for generously hosting the Belgrade and Dublin meetings.

We wish to thank the Gerry Holdsworth Special Forces Trust, and especially its secretary, Michael Martin. The Trust provided funding to bring thirteen postdoctoral researchers onto the project, greatly extending its reach and richness, and to finance research trips to key archives in the USA, Europe and Israel. Professor Hew Strachan is to be thanked for putting us in contact with the Trust.

Jeanette Atkinson was a superb administrator, facilitator and source of advice to members of the team. She organised the workshops with military precision, built and populated the website and demonstrated unfailing goodwill.

All translations were provided by the authors themselves. The bibliography was compiled with huge efficiency and goodwill by Alexandra Paulin-Booth.

We would like to thank Manchester University Press for taking up the challenge of publishing this collective work. Not all publishers have such faith in work that can only be crafted by an international research team. We are indebted to the two anonymous readers who reported on the significance of the project as well as the difficulties of pulling it together. Jonathan de Peyer was a wonderful commissioning editor, with vision, enthusiasm and great attention to detail. Editorial Director Emma Brennan expertly saw the project to completion. For their professionalism and good humour we would also like to thank Deborah Smith of the contracts department, Editorial Services Manager Lianne Slavin and Assistant Editor Alun Richards. Fiona Little undertook the copy-editing with immense patience and attention to detail.

Introduction

Robert Gildea and Ismee Tames

In October 1939 Arthur Koestler, the Hungarian-Jewish journalist and former member of the Kommunistische Partei Deutschlands (German Communist Party, KPD), who had been a war correspondent in Spain, found himself in a high-security internment camp on the French side of the Pyrenees. It was full of defeated fighters of the International Brigades (IB), most of them communists or anarchists, together with Spanish republicans who had fled across the mountains from Franco's victorious forces, German anti-Nazis and Jews escaping persecution in Central and Eastern Europe. 'One half of the world regarded them as heroes and saints, the other half loathed them as madmen and adventurers. In reality they were both at once.' The 'scum of the earth' was the phrase he found for the title of his book.[1]

Foreigners, communists and Jews. Many of them, like Koestler himself, were all three rolled into one. They were the vanguard of a small army of about 35,000 volunteers who had travelled across Europe, and even from North America, to take up arms against fascism. Republican Spain, which Franco had tried to overthrow by a military coup and was supported by Mussolini's Italy and Hitler's Germany, was for them the first battlefield of a war of resistance against fascism that would continue for ten years.

When we think about resistance to fascism and Nazism and Europe's liberation from them, certain images come to mind. General de Gaulle calling on the BBC in 1940 for the French to continue the war against Germany and, on 26 August 1944, walking tall down the Champs-Élysées as the head of France's liberating forces. Yugoslav resistance forces, women as well as men, fighting in the mountains and liberating Belgrade in October 1944. The defeat of the German army at Stalingrad and the Red Army liberation parade in Moscow on 24 June 1945. These dramatise stories of national liberation, the remaking of nation-states that had all but been destroyed by the Second World War. The very fact of the near-destruction of these countries made it imperative after liberation for countries to construct narratives of national resistance in order to redefine and reunite them.

It may be that some of the inmates of Koestler's camp found themselves in these victory parades. But it is unlikely. They may have contributed to national liberation, but national liberation was not what they were about. Their resistance was not a national but a transnational endeavour. Most of their resistance activity was undertaken outside their country of origin. They found themselves in a European space which was divided by war and occupation but connected by lines of escape and resistance. They might eventually seek to return to liberate their country of origin, but for the moment they were on the move, resisting far from home.

Transnational resistance: the wider context

Transnational resistance did not spring fully armed across Europe in 1939, or indeed in 1936. It emerged in a mid-century crisis characterised by mass migration and exile, internationalist ideologies, the rise of populism and the shattering of the European state system.

First, individuals were more likely to engage in transnational resistance activity if they were already people on the move, if not on the run, *before* the Second World War. They might be economic migrants, seeking work in countries with shortages of labour. Many Poles, for example, came to seek work in the coalmines of the Ruhr, Belgium or the north-east of France. Many Italians migrated to find work in the iron industry of Lorraine or the vineyards of the south of France. Dutch business people settled in Paris or Lyons, seeking new partners and new markets. Others were on the move as students studying abroad, sometimes because they were not able to study in their country of origin because of a *numerus clausus* introduced against Jewish students. They might be political or religious refugees, fleeing persecution in their own country. Often they would be taking routes and using familial, economic or organisational links that were well established.

Second, being oppressed at home and frequently on the move, they were attracted by ideologies that were not national but international. These were communism and anti-fascism. Many were inspired by the Bolshevik Party, which took power in Russia in 1917, made peace with Germany and in 1919 set up the Comintern, an international communist movement dedicated to the revolutionary overthrow of capitalism and imperialism by the proletariat and peasantry under the leadership of Moscow.[2] The Comintern created the International Brigades in the autumn of 1936 to draw volunteers from all over Europe and also further afield to defend the Spanish Republic that was threatened by a military coup, backed by Nazi Germany and Fascist Italy. An Anti-Comintern Pact was signed by Germany and Japan in 1936 and joined by Fascist Italy and Spain in 1937. The members clamped down on their communist enemies in waves of political and religious persecution, and created waves of exiles who fled first to the democratic republic of Czechoslovakia, and then to the Netherlands, Belgium, France or Britain. These exiles were at the forefront of a transnational anti-fascist struggle.

Communism and anti-fascism overlapped but were not quite the same thing.[3] Within communism there was an inherent contradiction between fomenting world revolution and defending the Soviet Union, which Stalin prioritised as 'socialism in one country'. At its most cynical this resulted in a non-aggression pact with Nazi Germany in August 1939. Communist militants across the world were told overnight that the real enemy was not Nazi Germany but imperialist Britain and France. They had to choose between anti-fascism and communism. Hardline communists swallowed the Nazi–Soviet Pact and did not openly resist fascism until the Third Reich invaded the Soviet Union in June 1941. Anti-fascists who broke with or distanced themselves from communism over the pact, however, were freer to join resistance activities between 1939 and 1941.

Third, the shattering of the European state system before and during the Second World War itself was perhaps the most powerful driver of transnational resistance. After the Nazi seizure of power in Germany Jews fled west to the Netherlands, Belgium, France or Britain. They also fled south and east, and in 1935 some 62,000 Jews left for the British Mandate of Palestine. The German-Austrian *Anschluss* of March 1938 followed by *Kristallnacht* in November 1938 drove 36,000 Jews out of Germany and Austria in 1938 and 77,000 in 1939. The Nazi–Soviet Pact meant the partition of Poland; thousands of Polish Jews fled to the Soviet zone while Nazi troops began the extermination of the communist elite, which was often Jewish, in their zone. The outbreak of war turned Central and Eastern Europe into what Gordon East called a 'shatter zone' vulnerable for centuries to the expansion of Germany on the one side and Russia on the other and what Timothy Snyder, focusing on the Second World War, called 'Bloodlands'.[4] Germany invaded Czechoslovakia in March 1939, forming the Protectorate of Bohemia and Moravia and setting up Slovakia as a puppet state. The partition of Poland in 1939 left a rump General Government under German control that became a laboratory for the destruction of Polish elites, and the ghettoisation and extermination of the Jewish population. In April–June 1940 German armies occupied

Norway, Denmark, Netherlands, Belgium and northern France, driving before them waves of refugees, including Jews who had taken refuge in the Low Countries. France was divided into zones occupied by Germany and Italy, with a rump satellite state governed from Vichy. The Germans took away 1.8 million prisoners of war (POWs) from France and Britain and 65,000 from Belgium.

The advancing juggernaut continued to tear up the existing state system. In the spring of 1941 the Wehrmacht and the Italian armies invaded, occupied and partitioned Albania, Yugoslavia and Greece, forming a puppet state of Croatia under the fascist Ustaša movement. This created another 'shatter zone' in the Balkans, from the Danube to the southern tip of Greece. In June 1941 the Wehrmacht invaded the Soviet Union, capturing 3.5 million POWs. Behind the advancing German lines *Einsatzgruppen* undertook the systematic killing of 'Jewish Bolsheviks'. After the fall of Kiev in September 1941, nearly 34,000 were executed in the nearby ravine of Babi Yar. In the Warsaw Ghetto 400,000 Jews were driven into an area of 1.3 square miles.

In Western Europe, occupation was less catastrophic because the Germans retained the existing state system and encouraged collaboration by national and local authorities. Communities tried to put their lives back together and reach some kind of accommodation with the New Order.[5] The German occupation, however, fragilised the position of many people, not least communists, foreigners and Jews who were seen as the enemy within both by the Germans and the collaborating authorities and were subjected to renewed persecution. In southern and Eastern Europe, where existing states were destroyed and Slav populations were regarded as racially inferior, the Germans set a ratio for collective reprisals of a hundred civilians for every Wehrmacht soldier killed and fifty for every soldier wounded by partisans. Thus when ten soldiers were killed and twenty-six soldiers were wounded at Kragujevac in Serbia in October 1941, more than two thousand men from the surrounding area were shot.[6]

The situation grew worse in 1942, when the implementation of the Final Solution meant the millions of Jews from France to Greece were rounded up and deported to death camps in Poland. Many fled, and some joined resistance organisations. They found that they were fighting what David Erlich, aka David Diamant, a Polish-Jewish worker in Paris and communist resister, called 'the war within the war'.[7]

At the same time, in order to sustain the German war economy, vast numbers of forced workers were recruited from all over Europe to work in German factories. Recruitment was stepped up in 1943, and over the war these totalled 8.4 million foreign workers, including 80,000 Danes, 375,000 Belgians, 475,000 Dutch, 960,000 Italians, 1,050,000 French, 1,600,000

Poles and 2,775,000 Russians. Whereas in Western Europe, state and church authorities largely prevented the labour conscription of women, this was not the case among the *Ostarbeiter*, 50.9 per cent of whom were women. The threat of conscription for forced labour drove thousands of young people underground or to flee to mountains and forests of greater safety. There many of them joined bands of *maquisards* or partisans to wage guerrilla war on the Germans.[8]

A transnational approach to resistance

Resistance activity came in many forms and guises: it might be local, national, international, multinational and, finally, transnational. Local resistance was close to people's everyday concerns. It included bread riots, industrial strikes and giving shelter to Allied servicemen, resisters and Jews on the run. National resistance involved raising the national flag, wearing national colours on historic anniversaries or joining resistance organisations with a national reach. International resistance meant working for international organisations such as communist parties which in theory at least were responsible to Comintern. Multinational resistance was resistance by a national group in a wider multinational organisation, but with very little contact between groups of different nationalities. Transnational resistance meant three things. First, it meant trajectories taken by resisters which led them to resist outside their country of origin. Second, it involved transnational encounters – meeting and cooperating with people of different national origins. Third, at its most developed, it allowed experiences of transnational resistance which in some ways changed a resister's thinking, practice and identity.

This study adopts a transnational approach to explore resistance in Europe, using some of the tools of transnational history that have been developed over the last twenty or so years. These enable us to deal with the three elements of transnational trajectories, encounters and experiences.

While many biographies are limited by a national framework, transnational historians explore the 'transnational lives' of sailors, merchants, engineers, missionaries, convicts, migrants, performers and artists who cross many boundaries, including national ones, in pursuit of wealth, adventure or self-realisation.[9] Encounters, bringing with them exchanges of ideas, skills and goods, have been theorised by apologists of 'connected history' such as Sanjay Subrahmanyam.[10] Here there is an overlap with global history. One of its practitioners, Jürgen Osterhammel, has argued that 'If a plenary assembly of global historians were asked to choose the one central concept defining the field, the majority is likely to vote for "connectivity".'[11] There is also an overlap with microhistory, since 'the new microhistory of connected lives' conceptualised by Emma Rothschild traces trajectories and encounters between individuals and groups in relation to the wider history of Europe and empire.[12]

The most interesting but also the most challenging dimension of the transnational approach is the study of the experience of transnational resistance. Wartime conditions subjected people to radically new circumstances. These included displacements and incarcerations, ruptures of existing ties and the weaving of new ones, the fading of old hostilities and the advent of new ones. How did they adapt? Did they change their name or reinvent their identity? What new skills did they learn? Did they lose one set of beliefs and take up another? In what ways was transnational resistance transformative?

The scope of the study is broad in both time and space. Time-wise, it starts before and finishes after the conventional 1939–45 dates of the Second World War. It begins with the Spanish Civil War in 1936 and the experience of the International Brigades. It tracks key turning points: the defeat of the Spanish Republic in 1939 that led to an exodus of Spanish republicans and International Brigaders, many of whom were interned in French camps; the German *Blitzkrieg* of 1940, which drove armies and refugees *pêle-mêle* before it; the Italian and German invasion of the Balkans and German invasion of the Soviet Union in 1941; the invasion of North Africa by the Americans and British in 1942; Italy's crash out of the war in 1943, leaving its soldiers German prisoners or a resource for the resistance; the liberation movements of 1944–45. The story continues to 1948, following Jewish rescue and resistance organisations' bid to found a Jewish homeland in Palestine, and the onset of the Cold War that froze out transnational resistance as a threat to the new regimes in East and West.

Geographically, the scope is wide too. It begins with the Spanish Civil War and the recruitment of volunteers from Eastern Europe, Palestine and the USA. It traces former International Brigaders and Spanish republicans in the resistance activity as far as the Soviet Union. It untangles escape routes from the Low Countries to the Pyrenees and resistance networks from North Africa to the Eastern Front. The Balkans, occupied by four powers – Italy, Germany, Hungary and Bulgaria – and a destination of Jewish refugees, are a particularly dense theatre of transnational resistance.

While the study is ambitious in time and space it frequently adopts the case study in order to focus on an individual or groups of individuals. These make it possible to explore how resisters adapted to new circumstances, negotiated successive challenges and reinvented themselves at different moments. The case study moves the focus away from institutions or organisations such as the Comintern towards individuals and the networks in which they found themselves, developed or broke away from. It also permits multiple perspectives on resisters by members of the research team with different languages and area expertises. It allows the intersection of several viewpoints on the same character who, for example, appears in the Greek and German or in the French, Yugoslav and Russian archives. This is an articulation of the *histoire croisée* which seeks to exploit the many and intersection positions of different historical observers.[13]

A collective project

This is a collective project by twenty-three scholars, specialising in the Second World War in Spain, France, Italy, the Netherlands, Germany, Czechoslovakia, Yugoslavia, Romania, Russia, Greece and Palestine. The diversity of the research team offered challenges as well as opportunities. Scholars came from different historical traditions, with different assumptions and practices. Narratives of national resistance and national liberation are entrenched in some traditions, and it took time for all to agree on how to grasp and exploit the idea of transnational resistance. Similarly, whereas the notion of 'rewriting history' is unproblematic in some traditions, being purely historiographical, in others it is more difficult, because it is political and generally follows regime change. How to write the individual chapters also posed challenges. A priority was always to write chapters thematically, drawing widely of different case studies and evidence. On the other hand, depth of analysis and a firm line of argument – both within and between chapters – was also required. The solution we found was to appoint a lead writer or writers to each chapter, giving them responsibility for ensuring overall coherence and direction.

Historiography

A transnational approach to resistance in Europe has yet to be attempted. This absence is due, firstly, to the dominant narratives which have shaped understanding of resistance: the national myth, the Cold War and the Holocaust, and secondly, because it was only in the 1990s that transnational approaches to history began to be developed.

In the immediate postwar national narratives of resistance were dominant. These responded to the near-destruction of nation-states in the Second World War and the need to unite traumatised and divided peoples behind a single story of national struggle and liberation. Foreign resisters were excluded as they did not fit this story. This process has been amply demonstrated for France, Belgium and the Netherlands by Pieter Lagrou.[14]

Histories of resistance in Czechoslovakia, Poland, Yugoslavia and Romania have also been dominated by national narratives.

The onset of the Cold War, dividing the 'free' from the communist world, had the effect of demonising transnational resisters as fifth columnists, spies and traitors. In the Eastern bloc 'cosmopolitan' communists who had engaged in resistance abroad beyond Moscow's control were suspected of being Trotskyists, imperialists or Zionists. Many were put on trial for their lives in 1948–52 and their stories erased.[15] In the West, transnational resisters were marginalised and even punished if they had any past dealings with communism. The International Brigaders were *personae non gratae.* Highlighted instead were secret agents parachuted in to work with tight groups of non-communist resisters in support of liberation and the restoration of democracy by the Allies. [16]

Another grand narrative, meanwhile, arrived to overlay stories of transnational resistance. From the time of the Eichmann trial in 1961, the Second World War was increasingly seen through the lens of the Holocaust. This highlighted the fate of the Jews as victims of a unique atrocity and marginalised the study of their resistance as heroes.[17] This way of understanding both the war and the fate of Jews was popularised in the 1970s and 1980s with media sensations such as the American television series *Holocaust* in 1978 and Claude Lanzmann's epic *Shoah* in 1985.

Alternative narratives of transnational resistance found it very difficult to find a hearing. Gradually, however, over time, shoots appeared. During the limited 'thaw' of Stalinism in 1956 celebrations of the International Brigades were held in Yugoslavia. Two international conferences on European resistance were organised in Liège and Milan in 1958.[18] A history of Jewish resistance to Nazism emerged after the 1967 Six Day War which demonstrated that the Israelis were more than capable of fighting back. This gave rise to a number of publications about resistance by Jews, who had not all gone 'like lambs to the slaughter'.[19] Yad Vashem, which promoted Holocaust memory, organised a conference in Jerusalem in 1968 on 'Jewish Resistance during the Holocaust'.[20] After 1968 and the growth of détente and *Ostpolitik* Cold War narratives weakened. There was a critique of Stalinist show trials which had eliminated transnational resisters and some of those who had survived met up with former comrades across the Iron Curtain. The contribution of German anti-Nazis and Romanian communists to the French resistance was now recognised, as was that of communist partisans in Yugoslavia.[21]

There were renewed attempts by historians after 1968 to demonstrate that resistance had been a European phenomenon. Jacques Delperrie de Bayac and Verle B. Johnston published works on the International Brigades.[22] Henri Michel of the French Comité d'Histoire de la Deuxième

Guerre Mondiale, published *La guerre de l'ombre: la résistance en Europe* in 1970.[23] A symposium on 'Resistance in Europe, 1939–1945' was held at the University of Salford in 1973.[24] The Danish historian Jørgen Haestrup published *Europe Ablaze: An Analysis of the History of the European Resistance Movements, 1939–1945* (1978), while Werner Rings, who had fled Hitler's Germany in 1933 into exile in Spain, France and Switzerland, published *Life with the Enemy: Collaboration and Resistance in Europe, 1939–1945* (1982).[25] Although powerful contributions to the debate, these studies either offered simply a typology of resistance movements or examined resistance on a country-by-country basis. At most the analysis was comparative, without a transnational dimension.

The end of the Cold War after 1989 and what appeared as the victory of Western liberalism put paid to the dominant communist narrative of anti-fascist liberation. In the West there was a return of an almost triumphalist pro-Allied narrative of resistance in Europe, in which a key role was played by the American Office of Strategic Services (OSS) and the British Special Operations Executive (SOE), at the expense of the internal resistance.[26] In Eastern Europe and the Baltics, released from the Communist bloc, there was a revival of a nationalist narrative that was now directed more against Soviet domination than against Nazi occupation.[27] Many Western and Western-trained scholars focused on the Warsaw uprising of 1944 and the work of the Armija Krajova or Home Army (AK), not of communist resisters, which Stalin had allowed the Germans to crush.[28]

New connections across Europe after the fall of the Berlin Wall and the collapse of the Soviet Union opened the way to a fresh wave of writing the history of resistance in Europe. Claudio Pavone's work presenting the Italian resistance as a class war and civil war, as well as a war of national liberation, was published in 1991.[29] Tony Judt's *Mediterranean Europe* (1989), Jean-Marie Guillon and Robert Mencherini on southern Europe (1997) and Bob Moore on Western Europe (2000) explored different regional theatres.[30] Other works privileged particular angles. Rab Bennett's study of resistance and collaboration in Europe was billed as a contribution to the ethics of war, while Tim Kirk and Anthony McElligott explored resistance at the level of the local community.[31]

At this point various strands of historical enquiry contributed to what might become a transnational historical approach. First, the role of foreigners in the French Resistance was charted from 1989 by Denis Peschanski working with former Polish-Jewish resister Adam Rayski and Karol Bartosek.[32] Second, a historiography on homecomings and displaced persons after the war provided a focus on deportation and camp life, and suggested that POWs and forced labourers were involved in resistance activity away from home.[33] Third, the proliferation of non-governmental organisations dedicated to issues of human rights, women's rights and the environment since the Tlateloco massacre in Mexico City in 1968 stimulated thinking about transnational advocacy networks by Margaret Keck and Kathy Sikkink while the anti-globalisation movement symbolised by the Battle in Seattle against the World Trade Organization in 1999 influenced research on previous transnational resistance movements by the likes of Sidney Tarrow.[34] Fourth, the history of memory was used by Josie McLellan to demonstrate how the role of German communists in the International Brigades was a controversial presence in East German memory.[35] Fifth, there was a revival of interest in autobiographical accounts and life-history writing which were provided with new theoretical frameworks.[36] This stimulated a greater interest in subjectivity, motives and identities and fed through into eye-catching first-person accounts of persecution, rescue and resistance by former activists who often represented themselves as transnational resisters.[37]

These developments provided fertile ground for historical works adopting a transnational approach and exploring in different ways transnational trajectories, encounters and experiences. Among them were Rémi Skoutelsky's account of French volunteers in the International Brigades, Antonio Arévalo's 2004 collection of testimonies of Spanish fighters in France, Paul Arrighi's 2007 biography of Silvio Trentin, an Italian anti-fascist active in France, Andrea Martocchia's 2011 study of Yugoslavs to the Italian resistance, Enrico Acciai's work on Italian fighters and Gerben Zaagsma's study of Jewish volunteers in Spain.[38] Conferences on 'Antifascism as a Practice and Discourse' in 2011 and on 'Antifascism as a Transnational Phenomenon' in 2013 gave rise to a collection entitled *Rethinking Antifascism* in 2016.[39]

Transnational approaches are in some ways more advanced in the field of fascism. Jochen Böhler and Robert Gerwarth examined the Waffen-SS not as a purely German but as a European phenomenon, while Arnd Bauerkämper and Grzegorz Rossolinski explored the transnational connections and interactions between fascist movements between 1918 and 1945.[40] Three chapters in this book in fact deal with transnational resistance, but the transnational approach is a long way from becoming dominant in the field. Philip Cooke and Ben Shepherd's *European Resistance in the Second World War* (2013) brought together separate single-authored chapters of resistance in ten European countries but made no attempt to trace transnational connections between resisters active across them.[41] Robert Gildea's *Fighters in the Shadows* explores the role of Spanish republicans, Polish Jews, German anti-Nazis and British agents in the French Resistance but indicated that a far wider lens from different European perspectives is required.[42] Olivier Wieviorka's *The Resistance in Western Europe, 1940–1945* is a vertical study of the relations between SOE, OSS and national resistance movements. It says nothing about 'horizontal' relations between resistance fighters on the ground that would permit an exploration of transnational encounters and transformations.[43]

This project was conceived from the outset to explore, experiment with and test transnational approaches to resistance. The study of trajectories begins with a sample of those who volunteered from widely different backgrounds to fight in Spain. After the defeat of the Spanish Republic it follows those resisters across Europe to where they used their expertise to become involved in other resistance movements. Some, however, either lost faith or turned to other contradictory movements. Encounters between individuals were central to the exchange of ideas and practices. These we explore in internment camps, which we see as crucibles of transnational resistance, in often unhappy periods spent in regular armies, in secret services and escape lines for Allied servicemen, resisters and Jews in flight, in rural guerrilla units and in urban uprisings. Lastly, and most challengingly, the project seeks to explore the experiences of resisters who followed these trajectories and made these encounters, thinking about how far their beliefs, practices and even identities were changed. We discover that all was not rosy on the transnational scene. Encounters with other was as likely to provoke misunderstanding and antagonism as discovery and cooperation. The final chapter takes the story beyond the Second World War to trace the afterlives of some of the resisters we have been following and tracing the fortunes of transnational narratives of resistance in competition with other narratives of national resistance, the Cold War and the Holocaust.

1

'For your freedom and ours!': transnational experiences in the Spanish Civil War, 1936–39

Samuël Kruizinga with Cristina Diac, Enrico Acciai, Franziska Zaugg, Ginta Ieva Bikše, Olga Manojlović Pintar and Yaacov Falkov

In July 1936, over six thousand athletes from twenty-two different countries gathered in Barcelona to participate in the International Workers' Olympiad. Less a sporting event than a mass political rally, it was intended by its organisers to attract both more participants and more spectators than the official 1936 Olympic Games that were to be held in Nazi Germany from 1 August. These alternative Olympics were sponsored by the Popular Front government of Spain, made up of a coalition of liberal and leftist parties elected on an anti-fascist platform. The Barcelona Olympiad promised to be the vanguard of a powerful Europe-wide countermovement and drew the eyes of the European left-wing press.[1]

On 19 July, however, the very same day the opening ceremony of the 'People's Olympia' was to take place, Barcelona was rocked by a military revolt. Rebel generals ordered its garrison to take control of the city as part of a coordinated strike against the Popular Front government.[2] In response, many international athletes helped the civilian population to resist, and together they fought off the Barcelona coup. In other Spanish cities, too, military revolts were quickly quelled. Only Seville fell to the rebels on 26 July, but this proved to be a turning point in the history of Spain. Its capture allowed rebel officers to airlift the Army of Africa, which they controlled, from Spanish Morocco to mainland Europe. There they were joined by about half the Spanish territorial army and the vast majority of its officers. The revolt now turned into a full-blown civil war in which the rebels enjoyed the support not only of most of the army and various rightist, monarchist and fascist political organisations but also of Fascist Italy and Nazi Germany. The forces of the Republic nevertheless resisted. Left-wing journalists who had come to cover a sports event became war reporters. News of Spain's resistance against a fascist takeover quickly spread, and socialists, communists and other leftists all over Europe soon pledged their support.[3]

The threat of foreign intervention on both sides of the Spanish Civil War led the governments of Britain and France to propose a non-intervention agreement to localise the conflict and thereby, hopefully, prevent the outbreak of a second World War. While openly agreeing to the principle of non-intervention, however, Germany and Italy secretly continued to supply men, materiel and money to the rebel forces, while the Soviet Union supported the Republic. Joseph Stalin hoped to deter German aggression against the Soviet Union while highlighting the importance of communism in the fight against fascism. In order to entice Western democracies to join an anti-fascist defensive pact he decided against flagrant infractions of the non-intervention agreement, but on 18 September 1936 the Executive Committee of the Communist International (Comintern) instructed its non-Soviet member parties to start recruiting a volunteer force to fight in Spain.[4] Comintern officials travelled to Spain to help create new International Brigades of the loyalist Spanish army, officially formed at Albacete, some 150 miles from Madrid, on 14 October 1936. The base was to be commanded by leading communists, and the Parisian offices of the French Communist Party (Parti Communiste Français, PCF) were designated by the Comintern as the transit point for recruits from all over Europe on their way to Spain. Its importance to international volunteers only increased from February 1937 when, as part of continuing international efforts to localise the Spanish conflict, the Franco-Spanish border was closed and the Spanish coast blockaded by an international fleet. From that moment, volunteers all but required the help of the international Communist Party apparatus to reach Spain.[5]

The International Brigades quickly became the default destination for international volunteers for Spain. Their recruitment drive stressed the fight against fascism as transcending narrow party-political boundaries, and they welcomed anti-fascists of many different creeds among their ranks. However, their creation by the Comintern polarised scholarly opinion on both its organisation, and its membership from the moment the Spanish Civil War ended. Were the Brigades composed of communists fighting to establish a 'Red' Spain? Were they innocent idealists duped by the Comintern into fighting for Moscow? Or were they simply committed, as Eric Hobsbawm put it, to 'the only political cause which, even in retrospect, appears as pure and compelling as it did in 1936', to halt the rise of fascism and Nazism before it was too late? Since the 1990s the opening of archives related to the Civil War has refocused research on the creation of collective biographies of national contingents of International Brigades, particularly those from the United States, France and the United Kingdom, in order to answer these questions.[6]

This chapter, however, seeks to explore another angle, and focuses on the International Brigades as a focal point for the diverse transnational experiences of those who volunteered. In choosing to fight for Spain, anti-fascists from all over the globe came together, each guided by a wide range of expectations and beliefs. On the Spanish battlefields, people came to different understandings of themselves and others, of their role in world affairs and of the meaning of anti-fascism, fascism and communism. Fighting a war far from their home and surrounded by 'otherness', they added new layers to individuals' already complex identities, and were propelled on new paths by the way they navigated the conflict and its confusing aftermath. Moreover, crossing paths in Spain was not always simple. It might also result in failures to communicate, misunderstandings, disappointments and even conflict, the aftereffects of which lingered long after the end of the war.

In order to explore these developments, we will follow eight very different and relatively unknown people who all travelled to Spain from far-flung parts of Europe in order to fight fascism, as they understood it. These were Aureliano Santini from Italy, Clara Thalmann from Switzerland, Galia Sincari from Romania, Žanis Folmanis from Latvia, Ljubo Ilić from Yugoslavia, Jona Brodkin from the British Mandate of Palestine, and Jef Last from the Netherlands. They have been chosen not because they were crucial to the Spanish war effort, were uniquely present at key junctures of its history or are archetypical of different varieties of transnational experience. It is rather because, firstly, these eight have left testimonies which allow us to trace transnational 'lines' and 'nodes': that is, their routes into and through the Spanish conflict, and the hubs of transnational activity where these routes crossed with those of others. These allow us, secondly, to (re)consider key questions of agency and identity within the mass ideological conflicts of the twentieth century. Thirdly, these cases give us insights into the very different geographical and institutional contexts that shaped their anti-fascism, ranging from the Arab–Jewish conflict in Palestine and anti-Semitism in Romania to the experience of exile in Paris and an intellectual's disappointment in Stalin's leadership. Fourthly, their histories provide an implicit commentary on and even a correction to our understanding of the global anti-fascist solidarity movement for Spain which, until now, has been shaped primarily through British, French and American frames of reference.

Pathways to Spain

Anti-fascists broadly understood the Spanish Civil War as a local flash-point in a global war between fascism and its opponents. Victory or defeat would therefore have consequences that far superseded the local Spanish context. Victory might mean that fascists everywhere would be on the defensive, even in Germany and Italy; defeat meant that the fascists would be emboldened, perhaps enough to launch a new world war. The International Brigades' motto, *Por vuestra libertad y la nuestra* ('For your freedom and ours'), reflected this connection between the Spanish struggle, the global ideological battle between fascism and anti-fascism (in whatever guise), and individual brigades' own concerns about their present and future.[7]

Those who joined the International Brigades from an enforced exile, such as the young Italian communist Aureliano Santini, born in 1912, were perhaps most alive to this connection between the local and the global. As a ten-year-old, he saw Benito Mussoloni's Blackshirts burn the socialist party branch headquarters in his native Empoli, in Tuscany. Deeply shaken by this act of violence, Santini yearned for a chance to retaliate against the Blackshirts and at the age of eighteen joined an underground communist cell. After he was twice arrested and imprisoned, Santini decided to join other Italian communists in exile in France. In Paris, which had become the prime European hub for exiles fleeing persecution in the 1930s, the PCF played a key role in helping communists who were fleeing political persecution in countries with right-wing, fascist or Nazi dictatorships to re-establish a working political apparatus. Evidently impressing the leadership of the exiled Italian communists in Paris, Santini was chosen to study at the International Lenin School in Moscow, where the future cadres of the Party were trained. This gave him opportunities for both a Marxist-Leninist education and the practical acquisition of a working knowledge of German and Russian. Letters from the late 1930s to his friends and loved ones back in Italy testify that his separation from them heightened his feelings of urgency and that the struggle against fascism was at once Italian and global. When news of the outbreak of the Spanish Civil War reached him, Santini was among the first to join the Giuseppe Garibaldi Battalion of the International Brigades, composed of Italian exiles.[8] His letters to his girlfriend, who had begged him not to go, detail his belief that going to Spain was his duty as an Italian and a communist. 'Could I be absent from a great fight like the one fought in Spain? No! I am happy to find myself here in the midst of the struggle'.[9]

Santini's words will have sounded familiar to many Germans, Austrians, Yugoslavs and others who had been forced underground or into exile for their political beliefs, and who relished the fight against fascism. In Spain they could both engage their enemies in a fair fight and give their own dictators a bloody nose in the process. This realisation was sometimes not immediate. Ljubomir ('Ljubo') Ilić had voluntarily chosen exile, leaving his native, impoverished Split (in current-day Croatia), where he was born in 1905, to pursue architecture studies in Paris. There he combined a cosmopolitan lifestyle with an interest in left-wing politics. He engaged with communism intellectually rather than emotionally, as Santini did, and in the early 1930s decided to join both the French and the Yugoslav Communist Parties, the latter having its headquarters in Paris because of political repression at home. Following the assassination of King Alexander of Yugoslavia in Marseilles in October 1934, during a state visit to France, Ilić was held for four months by French police and repeatedly beaten. This clearly had a radicalising effect on him, and after his release Ilić was one of the first Yugoslavs to go to Spain. According to his Yugoslav Communist Party file he did not volunteer as such but was ordered to go by the party-in-exile to prepare the ground for other Yugoslavs to follow.[10]

Žanis Folmanis, like Ilić, was an intellectual. An aspiring Latvian poet and writer, born in 1910, he joined a Riga communist cell when in May 1934 a coup installed a right-wing dictatorship led by Kārlis Ulmanis. After the outbreak of the Spanish Civil War Folmanis immediately set his sights on joining the International Brigades in order to defeat fascism both in Spain and internationally. This, however, was far from easy. Latvia's borders were heavily patrolled, and its accession to the international non-intervention agreement heightened government surveillance of potential Spanish volunteers. Folmanis nevertheless obtained a passport and bought a train ticket to Paris with money collected by Latvian chapter of the Comintern-affiliated International Red Aid, under the pretence of visiting the 1937 International Exhibition in Paris. Once there he used the underground 'railway' established by the PCF to shuttle volunteers across the Franco-Spanish border in secret, although for him the 'railway' meant crossing the Pyrenees on foot.[11]

Galia Sincari, by contrast, was far from a devoted anti-fascist, let alone a communist. In her case, it was not personal or ideological convictions, nor any external pressure exerted on her by a political party or organisation that inspired her volunteering for Spain. Born in 1912 into the Jewish minority that lived in Bessarabia, she moved to the interior of Romania and worked as a nurse in a Jewish hospital in the Romanian town of Iași. She associated with communists socially, but a former colleague asserted in 1950 that communist colleagues had a hard time trusting her.[12] What is clear, however, is that early in 1937 she faced disciplinary actions at the hospital for allegedly socialising with communists, and that Iași was threatened by the anti-Semitic violence of the far-right Iron Guard movement. Vulnerable professionally and fearing for her safety, Sincari sought a way out. When she was approached by a communist handler who solicited her aid to fight for Spain, she accepted, although on condition that she could say goodbye to her mother in Bessarabia.[13] She undertook the trip to Paris at roughly the same time as Folmanis and using the same cover story. Sincari later testified that the shared experience of crossing the Pyrenean border brought together her rag-tag group of Europeans, who could not speak each other's language, and resulted in joint celebrations when they finally caught sight of Spain.[14]

Galia Sincari was not the only woman to travel to Spain. About thirty women from Romania alone volunteered for the International Red Aid missions, the medical services of the Republican Army or the International Brigades. But not everybody accepted the contemporary gender norms that a women's place in war was at home or in the hospitals. Clara Thalmann, born in Basel, Switzerland, in 1908, was one of them, although she conceded in later interviews that at the time she scarcely considered herself a trailblazer or even a feminist. Rather, she felt like a political outsider who had fallen out with the Communist Party in 1925 for sympathising with the so-called Left Opposition and its chief ideologue, Leon Trotsky. She was inspired by the powerful Spanish anarcho-syndicalist movement, which advocated a far more radical programme of revolution than the Stalinist Soviet Union. Its inclusion in the Spanish Popular Front government a sign that its economic-political principles might begin to shape the policy of a major European state. Her interests in Spanish ultra-left politics combined with her love of swimming to bring her to Barcelona in July 1936, where she was to compete in the Workers' Olympiad. When war broke out she promptly joined the Durutti Column, a Spanish anarcho-syndicalist militia named after José Buenaventura Durruti Dumange, the anarchist militant who had prevented Barcelona's takeover by rebel officers.[15]

Spanish resistance to fascism, at least to begin with, provided many of those who had become confused or disillusioned by left-wing politics with a simple, pure creed. Jona Brodkin, born in 1901, was another of them. In his unpublished memoirs, as related to and recorded by a relative of his in 1982, he reveals that he had begun to doubt the party line before coming to Spain. Born a Jewish inhabitant of the Ottoman Empire, he became embroiled in the civil strife that rocked Palestine, administered as a mandate by the British nominally on behalf of the League of Nations, in the 1930s. A member of the local Communist Party, he and his fellow members were ordered to support the Arab inhabitants of Palestine in their anti-British and anti-Zionist revolt in early 1936.[16] Faced with the prospect of either having to fight fellow Jews or being thrown out of the Party, many Palestinian-Jewish communists volunteered for what Brodkin called the 'Spanish democracy protection war'. Although his memoirs do not state this explicitly, Brodkin may have been one of many who left

Palestine to fight a good, clean fight and at the same time escape ostracism by the Communist Party.[17]

The disillusionment with Communist Party politics of the Dutch novelist Jef Last, born in 1898, likewise played a crucial role in his decision to embark for Spain. His disappointment originated in the Soviet Union, which he visited a number of times to write propaganda pieces about the miracles of communism for Dutch Communist Party newspapers. In his private diary, however, he confided that the visits had left him with the sense that Stalin had turned the Soviet Union into a virtual dictatorship where his will was law and the overbearing power of the state crushed humanity.[18] He was nevertheless unwilling at this stage to take the ultimate step of leaving the party. In the 1960s, long after he had completed his break with communism, he explained:

> One can simply cancel one's membership of a club or political party when one does not longer believe in what it stands for. But the Communist Party was something else: we felt it was the vanguard of the proletariat, and therefore History's inexorable will made tangible reality. Leaving the Communist Party meant being *extra muros* and nothing you said or did could ever make a real difference again. All you could do is stay within the Party, keep your discontent to yourself, swallow your pride and patiently await the day when the Soviet Union and the Comintern would be democratised.[19]

André Gide, the future Nobel Prize-winning French author and Last's lover, would later claim that Last saw in Spain a form of pure communism, untainted by the blemishes he had seen during his travels across the Soviet Union.[20] As if to underscore his independence from the party, Last used his own transnational connections to get to Spain: Gide introduced him to André Malraux, who was helping to organise the Spanish Republic's air force and managed to secure Last a seat on a plane heading towards the war.[21]

Transnational harmony and discord in Spain

The first volunteers to come to Spain after the outbreak of the Civil War in July 1936 formed volunteer 'columns' or 'centuria' or joined existing Spanish units. After the creation of the International Brigade of the Spanish Republican or People's Army in October 1936, most (but not all) foreign volunteers joined one of their battalions.[22] The Brigade's Comintern-appointed leadership decided from the outset to group soldiers who spoke 'roughly' the same language together.[23] This copied Soviet nationality policy, which held that so long as the content of the message was socialist the language in which was spoken or written was immaterial.[24] It soon

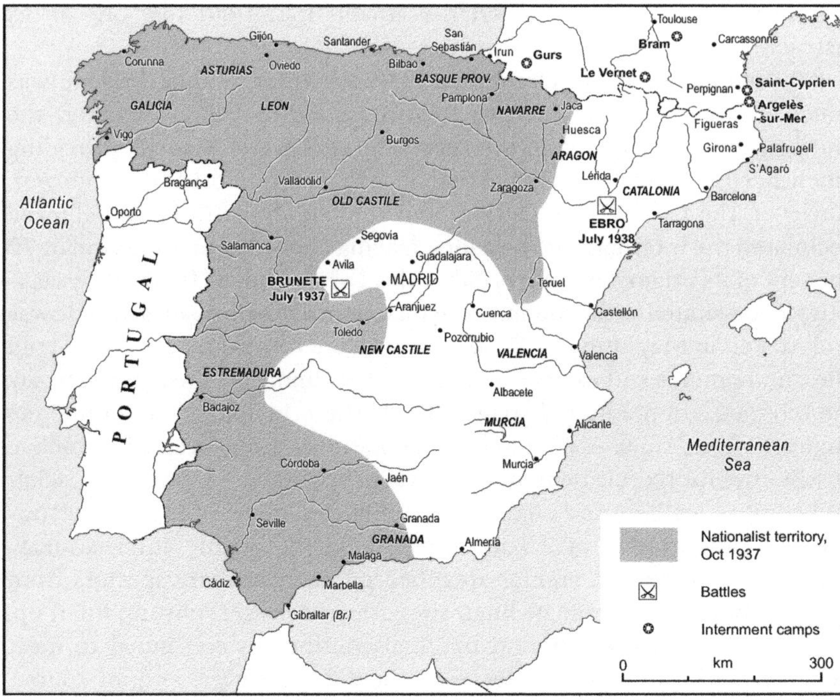

1 Spain during the Civil War, 1937

emerged, however, that the realities of warfare and the uneven flow of recruits prevented gathering 'language groups' or nationalities together. Jona Brodkin was sent by the Brigades' leadership not to a Palestinian or Jewish unit but to the Franco-Belgian 'Bataillon Six-Février', named after the fascist riots against the French Republic on that day in 1934. In other cases, people who spoke the same language were grouped together with others whose language or cultures were thought of as 'similar'. Dutchmen, for example, were put in German and French-speaking Belgian units.[25] Additionally, military necessity often forced transfers of recruits with particular technical and or tactical skills between units regardless of nationality or language concerns.[26] The Latvian writer Žanis Folmanis was one of them: he was assigned to the 3rd Kolarev Battery of the 1st Slavic Heavy Artillery Group because his military service in the Latvian army made him a suitable candidate in the eyes of the International Brigades' leadership.[27] The battery's members came from thirteen different countries. Neither Folmanis or any of the other twelve Latvians in his unit spoke the officers' Bulgarian or the Serbo-Croatian that was used by his instructors in topography and trigonometry – essential skills in artillery spotting. Common ground was found, however, when Folmanis found out that one of his instructors, like him, spoke German.[28]

Between October and December 1936, the International Brigade was joined by three others; a fourth followed early in 1937. Together, the four brigades participated in the successful defence of Madrid, providing much-needed enthusiasm, tangible signs of global support and manpower. However, the Civil War raged on, and the bloody battles that followed decimated the International Brigades, leaving about fifteen thousand or 70 per cent of its original members either dead or wounded. These mass casualties necessitated a thorough reorganisation of the brigades which was undertaken in May–June 1937. New units were formed from depleted old ones, and officers and experts were moved around.[29] At least theoretically the reorganisation adhered stringently to the principle of division along linguistic lines, since easily identifiable 'national' units created attractive possibilities for recruitment and political propaganda.[30] However, specialised combat, artillery and engineering units, and much of the administrative and support staff at Albacete, remained thoroughly 'international'. There were simply not enough qualified pilots or artillery spotters from a single country or ethnic or linguistic group to justify splitting them up. Moreover, units from different national contingents continued to meet each other in transports, on leave, at the Albacete base, and, of course, on the battlefield.

Often these – sometimes brief – contacts with 'others' who shared the same broad anti-fascist agenda were later remembered as 'real and touching' instances of transnational solidarity, perhaps best symbolised by the communal singing of the *Internationale.* Socialists, communists and other leftists all knew the tune and could sing along in their own language, creating a transnational harmony. Deep bonds were created by wordlessly shared cigarettes, taking an active interest in other cultures by learning their particular swear words and, of course, being together under fire. However, living and fighting together created transnational discord as well as harmony. What the Italian International Brigades' chief inspector Luigi Longo tactfully characterised as 'differences in language, military experience, and customs' produced numerous frictions both within and between units.[31] Another, perhaps even more important, cause for transnational strife was the tension that could exist – and was often exacerbated over time – between the very different anti-fascisms of the volunteers and the political realities of Spain. These were sharpened by the prominent role played by the Communist International in establishing and maintaining the International Brigades.

Before the International Brigades were established the shape of anti-fascism in Spain, and who or what could be included in it, were not clearly defined. This fluidity thrived in the, often chaotic, circumstances that characterised anti-fascist resistance during the first weeks of the Civil War. According to her husband Paul, Clara Thalmann navigated this chaos with ease, quickly establishing contact with both Spaniards and other European volunteers in the new *Grupo Internacional* of the anarcho-syndicalist Durutti Column. She relished the fight and only later realised that she too had been a witness or perhaps even a party to violent excesses. In 1984 she wrote: 'Knowing what I know today I would not have agreed with ... for example, nuns and suspicious persons being shot immediately. This happened in the heat of battle and was the result of an angry discharge of a generation's suppressed feelings of impotence towards their exploiters and the fascists who plotted the coup.' What did change were her feelings about anarchism. Dismayed at the bickering and infighting, and impressed with the Comintern's organisational prowess as evidenced in the creation of the International Brigades, she reported to Albacete to sign up in early 1937. The International Brigades, however, turned her away: women, she was told, had no place in a professional army. In desperation, she returned to the *Grupo Internacional* but here, too, most of the female fighters had been purged from the ranks. 'The women who built barricades and dug trenches ... were now sent to hospitals', she recalled bitterly in 1985.[32] When during the so-called May Days of 1937 infighting between anarchists and communists led to street fights in Barcelona, Clara and Paul remained at the front. There they were detained by agents of Soviet intelligence. Held separately, they took to singing Swiss folk songs with lines subtly changed in order to keep each other informed of the line of questioning. They were released only following an urgent appeal from the Labour and Socialist International, and immediately left the country. Apparently, there was no longer a place in Spain for their brand of anti-fascism, which fell foul of both established political and gender lines.[33]

The Dutchman Jef Last seemed to fit in much better. He was assigned by the Spanish Ministry of Defence to the Sargento Vazquez militia, consisting of communist day labourers from a Madrid slum. Last fitted in remarkably well with them, writing to his lover André Gide how much he enjoyed and admired their 'simplicity, ... good cheer, enthusiasm and courage'.[34] Last's new Spanish comrades came to appreciate him as well, admiring his willingness to learn the language and to throw himself into combat with almost reckless abandon.[35] It seems that Last had finally left behind his doubts and found companionship with 'real' communists, but his renewed commitment to the cause was not to last. Gide published two hyper-critical essays on the Soviet Union, and Last, whose friendship with and admiration for Gide was well known (even if their relationship was not), was forced by the Comintern to publicly denounce his lover at the International Congress of Anti-Fascist Intellectuals, held in Saragossa in July 1937. Moreover, the Comintern made sure he was transferred from his Spanish unit to the International Brigades, where, he was told, Comintern representatives in Spain could 'better keep an eye on you'.[36] Last confessed in private letters that he agreed to this because he did not want to cause a row: the common anti-fascist cause was simply too important. For the Comintern, meanwhile, Last remained a troublesome but important asset. A prolific writer, public speaker and polyglot, he was frequently sent out on European propaganda tours to advocate the cause of the Spanish Republic.

On 1 March 1938, nonetheless, in the middle of one such tour of France, Belgium and Scandinavia, Last suddenly resigned his membership of the Communist Party.[37] At the time, he claimed that disappointment over the Soviet Union's unwillingness to firmly support the military effort of the Republic was at the heart of the decision. Later he would come to understand it as the logical conclusion of his growing disappointment with communism. However, letters to Gide testify that at the time there was another reason for his sudden decision: he found a new outlet, purer than the advocacy for Republican Spain now tainted by the political machinations of the Comintern, for his anti-fascism. In Madrid, he had been approached by the socialist International Transport Workers' Federation (ITWF) to spearhead a mission to Antwerp and Scandinavia in order to re-establish contact between the ITWF and German sailors' organisations. Naturally, the communist press in the Netherlands denounced Last as a traitor to the cause and a Trotskyite, while not so subtly suggesting that his failures of political understanding had their roots in moral and sexual deviancy.[38] Like Thalmann's, Last's brand of anti-fascism was, in the end, not deemed compatible with those espoused by the International Brigades and the Communist Party.

Whereas Last and Thalmann were set on paths away from the Civil War and communism, for Aurelio Santini the war served to confirm his ideological beliefs, and provided him with a career-making opportunity. After arriving in Spain in early October 1936, Santini quickly distinguished himself as a soldier of the Garibaldi Battalion. An engaging speaker, he was given an additional role as radio propagandist. On 28 March 1937, during one of his addresses, he gave his countrymen a message of hope:

> A young Italian is addressing our martyred nation, Italy ... with a message from this great country, from all those young people fighting for its destiny. This message is to let all young Italians know our fight is in Spain.[39]

In private letters to his girlfriend he added that he was immensely proud that his countrymen had heard him all the way back home and that he was fighting for 'the freedom and happiness of all people' in Italy and Spain.[40] Both his military prowess and his successes as a propagandist were seemingly recognised and rewarded when, later in 1937, IB command sent him to the officers' training school at Pozorrubio for specialised military and political instruction and Spanish lessons. He was then moved from his Italian unit to the 52nd Infantry Division of the Spanish People's Army, where he was to instruct and inspire. Again, this move is highly indicative of the trust placed in him not only by the Comintern but by the People's Army general staff as well.[41]

The Yugoslav communist Ljubo Ilić, too, saw his transnational experiences in Spain give his career within the party a significant boost. Even more so than Santini, he quickly developed into a commander of note, thanks partly to the contacts he made with high-ranking Spanish communists in the Quinto Regimiento de Milicias Populares, a communist paramilitary unit formed just after the outbreak of the Civil War. After the establishment of the International Brigades, he became first political commissar and then commander of his unit, which was part of the Dąbrowski Batallion of the XI International Brigade.[42] A further indication of the faith placed in him by both his military and political superiors was that he, like Santini, was dispatched to Pozorrubio. Here the former student of architecture and French-speaking intellectual was discovered to have a talent for what we now would call irregular warfare. He received additional training by high-ranking Soviet officers in sabotage, infiltration and psychological operations. Ilić then went on to join a guerrilla unit operating behind enemy lines in Córdoba and Granada. After being seriously wounded during the August 1937 Saragossa Offensive, Ilić was withdrawn from active duty and appointed commander of the officers' school in Barcelona, which gave him even greater international influence.[43]

Where Santini and Ilić felt at home in the transnational environs of Spain and moved between different units and up the military and political ladder with ease, Galia Sincari had, at least to begin with, considerably more difficulty fitting in.[44] Upon arrival in Spain she was assigned to the Casa Roja hospital in Murcia, but she had no way of communicating with her Spanish-speaking colleagues. At first, she later recalled, she resorted to using a rudimentary sign language. Later, a German-American doctor took her under his wing and taught her some Spanish. Having found a way to communicate, Sincari seems to have been energised by the war both professionally and politically. Only twenty-five years old, she was appointed chief nurse and put in charge of the nurses' training programme. She testified in 1956 that the Spanish wounded referred to her as 'Madre'. 'I was young, and proud, and at some point, I asked them why they would call me that. Did I look so old? They answered that they called me "Madre" as a sign of gratitude, because I took care of them like their own mothers would.' Among those in her care was a fellow Romanian and her future husband, Mihail Burcă, wounded at the Battle of Brunete. It was hardly love at first sight, confessed Sincari later, as Burcă seemed interested in little else than politics. However, she quickly added, the pair did end up getting married in April 1938, whereupon Sincari joined the Spanish Communist Party (Partido Comunista de España, PCE) – perhaps, as we will see, more to please her new husband than out of a new sense of conviction.[45]

The importance of hospitals as sites of transnational interaction and the importance of language skills are underscored by Jona Brodkin's experience in Spain. After a mere twenty days at the front, his battalion was sent to join the Republican effort at the Battle of Jarama. 'We suffered heavy losses and had a plenty of dead and wounded comrades', he recalled, adding that 'our dressing stations soon became overburdened, and our understaffed units now freely intermixed.' In the midst of this transnational chaos, Brodkin was hit in the leg and transported to the IB hospital at Tarragona, where his wound developed gangrene and his leg had to be amputated. From Tarragona, he was transported for continued treatment to the Casa Roja hospital, and then on to the IB hospital at Albacete base. Like the medical staff, the wounded formed quite a transnational group. Brodkin soon became somewhat of a central figure, according to his own autobiography. His life in Palestine and in exile in Austria and France had made him a polyglot. In a Comintern questionnaire, which he completed in March 1938, he claimed to speak Yiddish, Hebrew, Arabic, German and French, which allowed him to act as a translator and, if needed, a mediator.[46] The ability to speak another language was certainly a boon in transnational Spain and often went a long way to increase transnational harmony. But being able to communicate did not in and of itself produce understanding, especially in situations where the hopes and dreams of individual volunteers clashed with an increasingly homogenising and communism-dominated anti-fascism.

Reimagining and reinventing Spain

In mid-1938, in a final effort to localise the war, the British and French governments put forward a plan to withdraw all non-Spanish troops from Spain. At first, the republican government balked at the suggestion, but on 21 September 1938 the Republican prime minister Juan Negrín announced a sudden reversal of policy. Recognising that the Popular Army could not hope to win the war against the rebels, who enjoyed tank and air superiority and were better trained and led, he hoped that if the rebels would have to make do without Italian and German help they might be inclined to agree to a negotiated settlement.[47] By contrast, the Republican Army could easily do without the remaining International Brigades, who were by now largely a spent force. The Non-Intervention Committee facilitated an orderly retreat, at least for those brigades hailing from north-western European countries; the Central and Eastern European dictatorships simply refused to let their countrymen, who had often been stripped of their nationality, return home.[48]

A significant number of International Brigades therefore simply ignored the 21 September 1938 order to retreat and disband. They could not go home and hoped to turn the tide on the battlefield at the eleventh hour. Žanis Folmanis made his way to Palafrugell in Gerona province where other Central and Eastern European International Brigades – Poles, Czechs, Bulgarians, Yugoslavs, Lithuanians, Latvians, and Estonians – had converged. From there, they hoped to march on Barcelona to defend it against the encroaching rebels who had begun an invasion of Catalonia in late December 1938. But rebel forces moved too quickly and Folmanis's group instead moved to Figueres, where the republican government had relocated. They could not join in Republican Catalonia's last stand, as the rebels mercilessly bombed Figueres's communication lines, preventing them from reaching the city. Folmanis, like many others, therefore had no choice but to flee to France, where he arrived on 8 February 1939.[49]

Galia Sincari's hospital, meanwhile, had been evacuated to S'Agaró, two towns away from Palafrugell. In a 1956 interview she recalled longingly watching ships in its harbour, each one offering the tantalising possibility of rescue. When, instead, one such ship opened fire on the town, the hospital staff decided to join Folmanis and countless others and flee to France. So, when all the wounded and the civilians had left, and the dying had been euthanised, the remaining hospital staff huddled together in a single lorry and drove to France over roads crowded with refugees and under fire from rebel planes.[50]

Aureliano Santini and Ljubo Ilić stayed behind. Now that they were officers in the Popular Army rather than in the International Brigades, the order to retreat did not formally apply to them. They served with the Republican forces to the very last, and bore witness to the final defeat of the Republic before making the desperate flight in the only direction open to them: the French border.[51] Last was, as we have seen, denounced as a deserter, and the invalided Brodkin was part of the first wave of evacuees and had been granted a temporary stay in France to recuperate in a Parisian hospital.

After the collapse of the Spanish Republic there was no place for the volunteers who had come from all over Europe to fight for the anti-fascist cause. The outbreak of war in 1939 intensified nationalism and increased intolerance of those who had willingly left their homelands to fight for a now discredited cause. France, though a republic, shut up in internment camps Spanish Republicans and International Brigaders who fled over the Pyrenees. A few volunteers tried to reach the Soviet Union, but in the era of the Great Purges they too were regarded with suspicion. The Soviet Union's Non-Aggression Pact with Nazi Germany shattered what remained of a Popular Front; although most Communist Party members remained loyal and trusted Stalin's tactical genius, it horrified those outside the Party. The defeat and occupation of so many European countries by Nazi Germany and Fascist Italy demoralised the mass of citizens for a long time before, in the wake of the German invasion of the Soviet Union in June 1941, resistance movements began to push up tender shoots.

Our eight volunteers navigated these challenges in very different ways. Some kept the anti-fascist faith, others wavered, and a few lost it. All, however, survived the war – here they are, unfortunately, atypical – and were then faced by new political paradigms. Fascism and Nazism were defeated by the Allied powers. Communism, championed by the Soviet Union, was in the ascendant and came to power in East-Central Europe, keen to purge those who were considered to have betrayed it. In their political choices, and in the paper trail they left, they were obliged to tell their story not necessarily as it was but as it had to be in the Cold War world of post-1945. Reinventing a past as a resistance fighter was a question of political survival.

Alone of our eight characters, Ljubo Ilić needed no lies or omissions to prove his loyalty to the cause. He remained faithful to Comintern directives throughout the war, following the switch of Soviet policy from Popular Frontism to the 1939 Non-Aggression Pact with Germany, and from Allied warfare to the Cold War. He spent the war in France, initially in internment camps, where his experience in Spanish army command caused him to be looked upon for leadership, and then, after he escaped from prison in 1943, as commander of all foreign forces active in occupied France. Although the Comintern initially seemed to question his 'independent-mindedness' and his apparent inability to 'break with petty-bourgeois affections', his status as war hero cemented his political career in Soviet-aligned Yugoslavia.[52] Politically he survived the Tito–Stalin split of 1948 and served his country as military official and ambassador, his service in Spain and France now reinterpreted as a heroic life in exile spent fighting for Yugoslav ideals and Titoism *avant la lettre*.[53]

Aureliano Santini, by contrast, chose to omit certain details of his life story from the public record after the war, when he rose to a position of prominence in the Italian Communist Party (Partito Communista Italiano, PCI). He glossed over the fact that he had petitioned the Fascist government to be allowed to return to Italy from the French internment camps. He was even briefly drafted in the army of Fascist Italy upon his return, but deserted quickly after the Allies invaded Sicily without seeing any combat. He then became a chief organiser for resistance activities in his native Tuscany, where his Civil War-era experience with sabotage and guerrilla warfare proved extremely useful.[54]

After fleeing to France Žanis Folmanis, too, was interned in a camp. In May 1939, like Santini, he begged the Latvian legation in Paris to allow him to return home and similarly managed to bury this embarrassing fact after 1945. His request, unlike Santini's, was quickly turned down, since the right-wing dictatorship of the day had no intention of allowing someone considered a dangerous left-wing radical back into the country.[55] However, the invasion and subsequent forced incorporation of the Baltic States into the Soviet Union in June–August 1940 suddenly changed Folmanis's legal position. He had become a Soviet citizen and was released and repatriated. He remained in contact with fellow Latvian veterans of the Spanish Civil War, and joined them in forming a volunteer battalion when the Germans invaded the Soviet Union in June 1941. Quickly promoted to battalion commander, he led his Latvian volunteers in rearguard actions, participating in the defence of Leningrad. He then joined the Latvian Rifles division of the Red Army as an intelligence officer, making handy use of his Civil War-era knowledge of topography and artillery spotting.[56] After the Second World War, now part of the ruling political elite, Folmanis finally embarked on the literary career of which he had dreamed before going to Spain. He published short stories and novels based on his experiences during the Spanish Civil War, highlighting his own efforts, and those of his Latvian countrymen, in the 3rd Kolarev Battery as paving the way for communism in their own country.

Galia Sincari, too, managed to reach France following the fall of Catalonia, but evaded internment. She found shelter in Saint-Privat, a village in the Hérault department whose socialist mayor sympathised with the plight of Republican Spain. It appears that only here, in exile, Sincari became a dedicated communist, celebrating May Day in 1939 together with her fellow communist refugees. Burcă joined her there in July 1939. He had been identified by Comintern as a future leader of the Romanian communist movement and was therefore allowed admission to the Soviet Union in order to receive additional political instruction and grooming. Sincari followed her husband to Moscow and spent the war years serving as a nurse in Soviet hospitals. In September 1947 Burcă was appointed deputy to the minister of the interior, which no doubt helped her to secure testimony from several former co-workers at the Iași hospital confirming her supposedly deep-rooted communist convictions; any evidence to the contrary might be construed as a threat to their own career. In a meeting organised in 1956 for Romanian ex-International Brigaders, she claimed that her decision to go to Spain was the ultimate, and necessary, result of a life spent in service to the party, pointing to her membership of the PCE as proof.[57] In the Cold War context wartime collaboration with socialists and other non-communist leftists, and with Westerners in general, was interpreted by Stalinist hardliners as 'evidence' of treason.[58]

Jona Brodkin, like Burcă, was also regarded by Comintern as a good investment as a militant. This is made clear by the fact that he was not sent back to Palestine but was, instead, therefore transported from his French hospital to the Soviet Union for continued treatment and, more importantly, continued political instruction. The latter, apparently, he did not take. After the war, Brodkin did not return to Palestine to become a leading revolutionary, but settled in Poland with his wife to live a quiet life. In 1968, however, he fell victim to an anti-Jewish campaign waged, as part of a complicated internal power struggle, by the Polish Communist Party. Despite the fact that Brodkin did not occupy any position of power, political and media pressure forced him to emigrate to Israel.[59] There the Jewish International Brigades gained increasing recognition as Jewish resisters against Nazism and the Holocaust, whose fighting spirit was now embodied in the new state of Israel. Although Brodkin, in his memoirs, expressed absolutely no interest in becoming a figurehead, Israeli memory politics turned him and his fellow Jewish Brigaders into symbols of national rather than anti-fascist resistance, conveniently ignoring the Communist Party politics that made many of them abandon partisan strife in Palestine for the Spanish Civil War in the first place.[60]

Other former volunteers for the Spanish Civil War were even less lucky, falling victim to the national backlash in their home countries. Clara Thalmann was sentenced *in absentia* to a ten-month prison sentence by a Swiss court for attempting to recruit others to fight in Spain. After her release from Spanish prison she moved to France and largely kept her head down during the German occupation. She did not join any of the left-wing resistance cells, probably because of lingering disappointments over her experiences during the Civil War, but she resisted as she had fought in Spain: in her own way, by distributing leaflets and hiding Jewish refugees.[61] After the war, Thalmann found fault with both ideological options on offer during the early Cold War. Instead, she and her husband bought a plot of land near Nice on the French Côte d'Azur and created their own perfect society in miniature, where the permanent social revolution they had fought for in Spain could finally be put into practice.[62]

Others still fell into deep despair when confronted with the misery wrought by the Second World War. After the failure of his attempts to galvanise support for socialism among German sailors, Last bore witness to the German invasion and subsequent occupation of the Netherlands in May 1940. He responded by descending into alcoholism and, albeit briefly, considering suicide. Fascism, he concluded, was unstoppable. 'Everything I have worked twenty years for, everything I fought for, everything was lost, my best friends, my Spanish comrades ... lost or captured, everything was lost', he wrote despondently. Early in 1941 he even toyed with the idea of joining a collaborationist political movement. Germany's invasion of the Soviet Union and the broadening of the Allied coalition gave him hope, and he decided to resist. But his status as a former communist made joining formal resistance movements difficult; distrusted by both mainstream socialists and communists, he only formally joined a resistance cell at the very end of the war.[63]

Conclusion

The International Brigades fought for 'your freedom and ours'. Their rallying call was, ostensibly, directed at all anti-fascists to join a battle *in* Spain but not purely *of* Spain: an essentially transnational battle cry. However, this transnational call to arms did not mean that everyone who heeded it saw the fight to preserve the Spanish Republic in quite the same terms. In fact, it was interpreted, and thus experienced, very differently through the prisms of equally different social, political and personal viewpoints, which were in turn shaped by diverse past experiences and expectations. The Spanish Civil War might be a chance to battle personal demons or fight a 'good fight', to hit back against stand-ins for local dictators, to partake in a revolutionary experiment, to prevent a fascist Spain from being a springboard for Hitler's and Mussolini's planned world domination, or some shifting combination of them. Given all of these meanings ascribed to the Spanish Civil War, it is no wonder that involvement in it could generate disillusionment and disappointment as well as enthusiasm or a renewed commitment to left-wing politics, especially communism.

Crucially, diverse transnational experiences of Spain often began before a would-be volunteer actually arrived there. They were often forged in transnational 'nodes' such as Paris, home of exiles, or the Moscow training institutes for communist cadre members. In other cases, they were shaped on the transnational 'line' from Paris to Spain, during the dangerous night trek across the Pyrenees. After the borders of Spain were closed by international agreement in early 1937 almost no-one made it to Spain without outside help, and the Comintern-organised 'underground railway' from Paris to Spain became even more crucial.

In Spain, the scope for transnational experiences within the International

Brigades were circumscribed by a number of different factors. The first was time. The creation of the International Brigades in October 1936, and their subsequent reorganisation in mid-1937, limited the scope for encountering other nationalities within single units – although not so for members of smaller national or language groups. The second was language ability, especially in mixed-nationality units. Some knowledge of a foreign language could be of vital help in connecting with others. The third was the growing professionalism of the International Brigades and an insistence on political reliability. Anti-fascism, which was never the same thing as communism, became ever more closely circumscribed as the Comintern-appointed International Brigades' leadership limited the ability of some anti-fascists to square their personal or political interpretations with the new realities of the war in Spain.

Finally, the transnational experiences undergone in Spain changed people. Fighters learned new skills, connected to existing networks or built new ones, and gained new appreciations of what it meant to be an anti-fascist. Some came away with their (party-) political convictions deepened, while others saw them shaken and, openly or privately, abandoned them. These effects continued to influence the trajectories of Spanish Civil War veterans during the Second World War they had fought so hard to prevent. After 1945 a carefully edited version of one's work in Spain might be useful to enable one to advance politically. Pressed into national or narrow party-political moulds, the global histories of the Spanish Civil War slowly became – to borrow a phrase from the Spanish Republic's most famous icon Dolores 'passionflower' Ibárruri – 'legend' rather than 'history'. It would take a long time for them to become history again.

2

The 'Spanish matrix': transnational catalyst of Europe's anti-Nazi resistance

Yaacov Falkov and Mercedes Yusta-Rodrigo with Olga Manojlović Pintar, Diego Gaspar Celaya, Cristina Diac and Jason Chandrinos

During the night of 13 November 1941, a group of the Soviet South-Western Front officers gathered at the longwave radio station of the Russian city of Voronezh. The sweeping Nazi advance into the Soviet inland had not yet been stopped, and the Front engineering department's chief General Georgy Nevsky set aside his combat managing tasks in favour of a highly clandestine subversive operation. This was the wireless detonation of sophisticated radio-controlled mines in the Nazi-occupied Ukrainian city of Kharkov, some three hundred kilometres south-west of Voronezh. In the preceding months, a wide net of those mines had been carefully laid in Kharkov's centre and suburbs by a team of miners composed of Red Army soldiers and Spanish republican exiles – Civil War veterans who had been welcomed by Moscow in 1939–40 and authorised to join the Soviet anti-Nazi struggle. The detonation destroyed a series of important buildings and installations and killed dozens of the Nazi officers and soldiers. This was regarded by the Red Army command as a significant operational success. The Soviet commander, Colonel Ilya Starinov, himself a veteran of the Spanish Civil War, wrote in his postwar memoirs of the Spanish republicans, 'I bow low to them now, many years later, both to those who survived and those who died defending freedom and justice.'[1]

The argument of this chapter is that so-called 'Spanish fighters' formed a matrix providing organisation, skills and motivation that catalysed local and national resistance in countries occupied by fascist and Nazi forces in a chain from France to the Soviet Union. They included both Spanish republican fighters and veterans of the International Brigades who had been forced to flee after the collapse of the Spanish Republic and in a position to offer leadership to disparate, emerging resistance

2 The Eastern Front, July 1943

activity. From the Spanish Civil War they had derived rich knowledge and practical experience of command, combat and underground activity. They had also learned strict discipline, a high motivation for anti-fascist and anti-Nazi struggle based on many years of political involvement, and a desire to avenge the lost Spanish war. In addition it may be argued that at best a sense of brotherhood, common destiny and historical mission bound the two constituencies of Spanish republican soldiers and the Interbrigadists.

There was no foregone conclusion about the discipline, effectiveness and unity of these Spanish fighters. During the war itself the Comintern had many doubts about the viability of the International Brigades it was organising. Recently released Comintern files show that in the spring of 1937 senior Comintern operatives in Spain and their superiors in Moscow were anxiously monitoring rumours within the PCF and the leaks in the French non-communist press, such as *L'émancipation nationale* and *L'écho de Paris*, about frictions between different IB national groups. Some of those rumours and leaks, allegedly based on the letters sent by IB French volunteers to their relatives and friends at home, claimed that

> Our leaders do not give a damn about us; in the General Staff, all the highest commanding positions are occupied by Germans and Poles ... This command should be called nothing but dictatorship ... We are being sent to slaughter ... All French comrades wish to return home.[2]

Similarly, a letter written in September 1938 by a Bulgarian volunteer, Vasil Vesov, reveals that there were tensions within IB tactical command between a Swiss communist major, Otto Brunner, and his Serbian comrade Dimitrije Georgijević, who allegedly 'surrounded himself with his fellow Serbian men'.[3]

Other conflicts broke out over the Nazi–Soviet Pact of August 1939 and the outbreak of war the following month. Moscow's line was that the war was declared by British and French 'imperialists' but that many foreign fighters had been pressured to join the French Foreign Legion and the Polish forces that fought in France. A Comintern report, written in German by an unknown source and dated 15 November 1940, argued that the call by the PCF to French communists and Spanish Civil War veterans on the French soil to assist the French war effort was a mistake. It allegedly gave a birth to 'different interpretations of the war's character' between PCF members and the 'Spaniards'. This destructive political division, continued the source, was widened by the phenomenon of *nationale Isoliertheit* or 'national isolationism' among IB veterans in different internment camps and outside:

> The groups ... have not always been successful in overcoming the tendency to national isolationism and taking a right position in favor of the entire party.[4]

Many of the national groups of IB veterans, including the Polish, Czechoslovak, Germano-Austrian, Italian, Romanian and Hungarian, were criticised. The Poles, for example, were presented as slow to abandon their predisposition to discrete, 'family-style', management. The only way to restore the IB cohesion developed during the Spanish Civil War, concluded the report, was the imposition on the former Interbrigadists and their PCF colleagues of the world view dictated by Moscow. 'The unity and the combat skills of International Brigades should be preserved', he insisted, through a 'healthy political assembly of all IB units ... political alignment of all national groups and proper coordination of their cooperation.'[5]

This was all well and good, but after the defeat of the Spanish Republic International Brigaders fled with Spanish republicans over the Pyrenees or across the Mediterranean to North Africa. A quarter of a million Spanish republicans were arrested by French police and interned in makeshift camps along the Pyrenean border or in North Africa.[6] Other former International Brigaders tried to return to their country of origin, but they had often fled from these to escape persecution and these were now generally under Nazi rule. A few 'Spaniards' accepted Moscow's invitation to take refuge in the Soviet Union. They had lost a war to Franco's nationalists and were not in a good position to begin resistance against the Herculean power of fascism and Nazism.

And yet when resistance activity did eventually begin in occupied countries such as France, Poland and Yugoslavia, it was often former International Brigaders or Spanish republicans who were in positions of command. There are three reasons for this. First, despite narratives of national liberation developed after the war, local populations were generally cowed by defeat, occupation and repression at the hands of fascists and Nazis. Resistance, when it came, was sporadic, tentative and undertaken by only a small minority. Second, the International Brigaders and Spanish republicans, although scattered and in shock, had belonged to specific military units which had experience, discipline and an esprit de corps that could be reconstituted. These include the XIII International Brigade, named after a nineteenth-century Polish independence activist and hero of the Paris Commune, Jarosław Dąbrowski, and the XIV Guerrilla Army Corps. Third, the international communist movement was keen, as the report of November 1940 indicated, to support former International Brigaders and communist rank-and-file who were willing to offer resistance. Thus for the French case the Romanian former Interbrigadist Gheorge Adorian (György Adorján) recalled after the war that

> The first French communists who took up arms to fight the Nazis were former volunteers in the International Brigades. There was no need to

> persuade comrades who had fought in Spain, who had been held in internment camps. Their determination was very high, even if their physical condition was seriously affected by the years of war and shortages. They definitely did their duty, as communists, as revolutionaries.[7]

Adorian's claim was echoed by his compatriot and former Romanian comrade-in-arms Charlotte (Sarolta) Gruia, who testified that 'Those who had fought in Spain, in the International Brigades, were the first of us to be involved in the French Resistance.'[8]

A transnational founding trio in France

In France, early resistance activity was either sporadic protest or demonstrations or small groups seeking to release POWs, procure military intelligence or spread propaganda. Armed resistance began in the summer of 1941, shortly after the German invasion of the Soviet Union, and was the work of communists. It was spearheaded by a trio of communists – French, Catalan and Romanian – who were all veterans of the International Brigades. Their task was to set up a military wing or Organisation Spéciale of the Main d'Oeuvre Immigrée (MOI), the foreign workers' organisation of the Communist Party that had been founded in 1926.

The Frenchman was Henri Tanguy, a sailor's son from Brittany, born in 1908, who became a communist aged seventeen in 1925. He served as an army conscript in Algeria in 1929–30 and subsequently as an activist in the French metalworkers' union. In February 1937 he volunteered for the International Brigades. His excellent commanding skills and commitment to Marxist-Leninist doctrine ensured his rapid promotion to political commissar in the Franco-Belgian André Marty Battalion of the XIV International Brigade, and then to political commissar of the entire brigade.[9] These positions in the International Brigades' command hierarchy facilitated his contacts with Spanish and other non-French comrades, developed his knowledge of the Spanish language and enhanced his adaptability to the complicated local realities. 'Speaks French and basic Spanish', read his personal file kept by the Spanish communist authorities in March 1938, a year after his arrival in the country.[10] '[He is] well accustomed to the Spanish difficulties', later wrote Lucien Bigouret, the head of the Communist Party organisation in the XIV Brigade.[11] Severely injured in the Battle of Ebro, Tanguy was sent to hospital and then back to France. Following the outbreak of the World War, he was conscripted into the French army. After Operation Barbarossa and Moscow's subsequent shift to endorse European communists' anti-Nazi struggle he became involved in establishing communist resistance in France and adopted a *nom de guerre* – Colonel Rol – to honour Théo Rol, a close friend who had been killed in Spain.[12]

The Catalan was Conrado Miret i Musté, who had been Tanguy's aide-de-camp in Spain. Born in Barcelona in 1912, he became a militant in the early 1930s of the Socialist Union of Catalonia (USC) and later of the Catalonian Communist Party (PSUC). He joined the Spanish republican military forces and fought against the Francoists until February 1939. Interned in the French camps of Argelès-sur-Mer and Saint-Cyprien, he escaped and after March 1941 – with his brother Josep – took an active part in developing covert anti-Nazi activity in Paris. He adopted a French alias, 'Lucien', both to protect himself in the French operational environment and as a transnationalist gesture expressing solidarity and close partnership with his new comrades-in-arms.[13] Unfortunately his resistance career was short-lived. He fell into the hands of the Vichy police and in February 1942 was tortured to death by the Gestapo.[14]

Fortunately, Tanguy had close ties to another close aide from the Spanish Civil War, the Transylvanian Jew Francisc (Ferenz) Wolf. Born in 1906 in a small town with a mixed Hungaro-Romanian-Jewish population, he became a communist activist in the early 1920s and spent six months in the Timişoara prison, after being accused of 'rebellion'. He embarked on an international path by studying chemical engineering in Prague and joined the Czechoslovakian Communist Party in 1926. Returning to Romania, Wolf became a vigorous communist dissident and acted as a Transylvanian regional leader of International Red Aid, a Comintern-led organisation providing material and moral assistance for imprisoned communists around the globe.[15]

Underground, prison and transnational encounters and experiences seemingly strengthened Wolf's self-confidence and ambition. In the summer of 1937 he decided to get to Spain by walking from his native Romania across Czechoslovakia, Austria, Switzerland and France. Arriving there in January 1938, he hispanicised his Romanian name Francisc to Francisco, a clear sign of his solidarity with the republican cause.[16] Assigned to a battalion of the 45th International Division – a multinational formation established in mid-1937 from different scattered IB units – he fought on the Aragon front and was regarded by his IB superiors as *bon volontaire*.[17] Wolf's Comintern records testify that he remained in Spain after the official withdrawal of International Brigades, and in October 1938 he crossed the French border with the remnants of the republican forces in early February 1939.[18] After a year in the French camp of Argelès-sur-Mer, where he acted as a head of the Romanian group, he escaped during the French deportation of IB veterans to North Africa and joined Organisation Spéciale (OS) resisters in Paris as a rank-and-file fighter and specialist for explosives.[19] He adopted various *noms de guerre* including József Boczor and, more simply, 'Pierre'.

It was largely thanks to the transnational trio of Tanguy, Miret i Musté and Wolf that the MOI was successfully militarised as the OS-MOI and subsequently the Francs-Tireurs et Partisans (Sharp Shooters and Partisans of the Immigrant Labour Organisation, FTP-MOI). Its units were composed firstly of the experienced former Spanish republican soldiers and Interbrigadists and supplemented later by younger foreign fighters without a Spanish background such as young Polish Jews. The FTP-MOI units developed into an anti-Nazi guerrilla force engaged in sabotage actions against German military installations and railway tracks, as well as in occasional attempts on the lives of the high-ranking Nazis and French collaborators. Tanguy himself later asserted that 'just like the International Brigades in Spain, in France the MOI played the role of shock troops'.[20] In July 1941 Wolf commanded the derailing of two German convoys in the eastern Paris suburbs and was later a member of the FTP-MOI's famous Manouchian Group, being executed with them on 21 February 1944.

When the French Resistance spoke Spanish

In the spring of 1942 the biggest and the strongest foreign group linked to the FTP-MOI – up to 500 fighters – was that of the Spanish emigrés. These were the most accustomed to the clandestine guerrilla operations because of their Civil War experience. Some of them had settled in France before 1936, as was the case with Celestino Alfonso, who had emigrated to France in 1930 but returned to Spain as an IB volunteer, was interned at the Saint-Cyprien camp and later also joined the Manouchian Group.[21] The majority, however, belonged to the vast community of the Spanish republican refugees – close to half a million men, women and children – who came to France following the end of the hostilities in the Iberian peninsula in 1939.[22] They provided, in spite of Comintern, more than 20,000 fighters to the French military forces in 1939–40, almost a third of whom perished before the armistice with Germany was signed. Not all of them were communists on the day of their arrival in France, but the PCE had managed to build up its influence among the Spanish refugees, the Spanish inmates of the French internment camps and later on the Spanish forced labourers of the so-called Groupes des Travailleurs Étrangers (Foreign Workers' Teams, GTE).[23] Consequently, the PCE was able to launch guerrilla activity on French soil in the spring of 1941. The first well-known Spanish resistance group was established in April 1942 by veterans of the former Republican XIV Guerrilla Army Corps in the

Pyrenean department of the Aude, at the Majou property of Dr Delteil, a member of the Gaullist resistance movement.[24]

One of the founders of the XIV Guerrilla Army Corps was Vicente López Tovar, known by his two francised aliases 'Colonel Albert' and 'Fernand'. Born in Madrid in 1909, he spent his childhood and youth in Valencia and Barcelona and returned to the Spanish capital two decades later, following military service, attracted by its turbulent political life. In 1936 he joined the PCE and almost immediately took active part in the famous two-day siege of the Montaña Barracks that prevented the rebelling military from occupying Madrid and saved the Spanish Republic. As the rebellion turned into civil war, Tovar enlisted in the Republican Army, assumed command responsibilities, including a senior position in the German-Scandinavian IB Thälmann battalion, took part in all the war's major battles and finally accompanied the last republican prime minister Juan Negrín and his close affiliates in their escape to the French city of Toulouse, in March 1939. Local communist comrades warmly received the exiles and helped them adapt to their new life in every possible way, thus creating the atmosphere of brotherhood and unity of destinies. In Tovar's own words:

> Little by little we began to contact the comrades ... to regroup them and to employ some of them with the assistance of the French Communist Party. We sent them to the aircraft factory Dewoitine and Breguet. The French comrades took care of them and taught them the trade.[25]

Close cooperation between Spanish and French communists continued after the defeat of France in June 1940. Failing to flee to England, via Bordeaux, Tovar returned to Toulouse. A local forestry company, Entreprise Forestière du Sud-Ouest, became a sanctuary, weapons stockpile and training base for the Spanish resisters, including the escapees from French internment camps. At the end of 1941, when the PCE was organising its own armed groups across France, Tovar founded the 3rd Brigade of the XIV Spanish Guerrilla Army Corps. After a setback in April 1943 it linked to the FTP-MOI and became also a transnational enterprise.[26] By the end of the Nazi occupation of France, in the summer of 1944, over 60,000 Spaniards were involved in the so-called French Resistance. Mostly active in the Massif Central, the Alps, and south-western France, they organised their own 'mono-national' fighting formations, led by the communist XIV Spanish Guerrilla Army Corps, which was renamed the Agrupacion de Guerrilleros Españoles in May 1944. However, they also joined the existing units of the French communist underground across the country, where they worked with resisters of other nationalities.[27] In January 1944, Tovar was dispatched by the MOI staff to the south-eastern Dordogne department in order to optimise the military activity of the local MOI 5th Region. In full compliance with the organisation's spirit of internationalism, Tovar's second-in-command there was a Romanian former Interbrigadist, Pavel Cristescu, an escapee from Le Vernet camp.

The liberation of Poland: national, international, transnational

There are two dominant narratives about the liberation of Poland from Nazi occupation and persecution. The first is that it was liberated by the AK of Polish patriots who were loyal to the Polish government in exile in London. The second is that Stalin cynically waited for the uprising of the AK in Warsaw in August 1944 to be crushed by the Germans before sending in a government of Polish communists who had been trained and prepared in Moscow.[28]

The reality is more complicated. A key role in the liberation of Poland was played by International Brigaders of Polish origin. Some, it is true, had found refuge in Moscow from persection by the Polish government in the 1930s and by the Nazis after 1939. Others, however, were Polish migrants who had moved to work in countries like France for reasons as much economic as political. In 1931 there were over half a million Poles working in France, notably in the coalmines of the Nord-Pas-de-Calais region and the steelworks of Lorraine. There were substantial communities of Polish-Jewish clothing workers in Paris.[29] What brought them together in the liberation of Poland, however, was the shared past and common experience gained fighting in Spain. About 14 per cent of the 35,000 IB foreign volunteers were Polish-speakers, Jewish and non-Jewish. Many of them had multilingual skills as well as experience of crossing borders and surviving in alien environments. In Spain they established predominantly 'Polish' units like the XIII International Brigade – the Dąbrowski Brigade, named after the hero of the 1871 Paris Commune Jarosław Dąbrowski – but they also joined other national and multinational units, such as the French-Belgian XIV Brigade 'La Marseillaise' or the German-Austrian Ernst Thälmann Battalion. Poles and the Polish Jews fought on different Spanish fronts, took part in all the principal military operations and suffered heavy losses, up to 40 per cent of their manpower.[30] The Poles' multiple contacts with other fighters from all over the world, alongside with their rich combat and command activity, made them into one of the most multilingual, well-networked and well-experienced Interbrigadists' groups. About three thousand of them came to France in 1938–39, and the French Resistance profited from their unique features on a large scale.[31] Their resistance was thus national in that they were fighting to liberate their Polish homeland, and international in that this was generally orchestrated by the Comintern, but transnational in that they were on the move and resisted fascism in exile in Spain and France before they resisted it at home.

Jan Rutkowski, who was born in 1900 in a small village in mid-eastern Poland, became a leading facilitator of transnational contacts in the French Resistance. He migrated to France at the age of twenty-three to become a miner in the Nord-Pas-de-Calais region and quickly added French to his Polish-Russian vocabulary and became literate for the first time in his life. In 1924, he joined both the PCF and its union, the Confédération Générale du Travail Unifié, and became an agitator and organiser of mass events among his Polish compatriots. He was twice detained by the authorities for organising mass protests and street fights against French fascists and participated in the PCF's eighth National Congress in January 1936. A year later, not least to avoid further prosecution in France, he volunteered to defend the Spanish Republic.[32]

To his French and Spanish comrades Rutkowski was known as 'comrade Simon', a francised version of his earlier political Polish alias 'Szymon' which doubtless expressed his mixed Polish-French identity. He became a rank-and-file soldier of the XIII Dąbrowski Brigade, and was highly appreciated by his commanders and fellow fighters for his bravery and political devotion, becoming a battalion political commissar and then chief intendant of the entire brigade with the rank of captain. In November 1938 'Simon' felt 'Spanish' enough to seek full membership of the PCE, probably in order to be able to stay in Spain after the official dismantling of the International Brigades. Unfortunately, his military and political activity on Spanish soil was cut short by a severe injury and a consequent long medical treatment.[33]

Evacuated to France in early 1939, Rutkowski was interned and spent two years in the camps of Gurs and Le Vernet. He proved highly effective within the camps' communist organisations, being elected a member of the inmates' committees and a secretary of the Polish committee of the Communist Party at Gurs. The party ordered him and a group of twenty comrades to volunteer to work in the factories of the Third Reich as a way of getting back to resist in occupied Poland. However, Captain 'Simon' escaped from the train taking him to Germany in April 1941 and returned to the Nord-Pas-de-Calais. After the German invasion of the Soviet Union in June 1941, and inspired by Moscow's broadcasts, he gathered his comrades together and made a speech linking anti-Nazi resistance on French, Polish and Soviet soil to the French revolutionary tradition:

> We swear to the heroic Red Army, to the Polish brothers who fell while defending the motherland, and to the French Communist Party, in the memory of the Great French Revolution and its Communards ... that we,

> Polish Communists on French soil, will struggle until the last drop of our blood against fascism, Hitler's occupiers, for the mutual liberation of the Polish and the French peoples.[34]

Working with the French communist underground in the Nord-Pas-de-Calais, Rutkowski organised miners' strikes and sabotage attacks on trains travelling to the Third Reich. Then, in late 1941, having become a target of the German security authorities, he moved to Paris and joined the Polish section of the French communist underground. There he organised former comrades in the XIII Dąbrowski Brigade to do what he himself had shunned, to transfer their resistance activities from France to occupied Poland.

One of these comrades was Bolesław Mołojec (*noms de guerre* 'Edward', 'Edo' and 'Długi), who was born in 1909 into a poor peasant's family. Joining the Polish Communist Party at the age of nineteen in 1928, he quickly rose to a senior position in the Young Communist League of Poland.[35] Hunted down and imprisoned for six months by the Polish authorities, he fled to Moscow, where he became a student at the Communist University of the National Minorities of the West (KUNMZ), a hotbed for the future leaders of the 'fraternal' communist parties. He learned Russian, made friendships with foreign comrades, gained a taste for international communist activity and became an ardent Stalinist. That said, it was against the will of his party leadership that he volunteered for the International Brigades in January 1937. He started as a rank-and-file fighter in the Dimitrov Battalion, which was composed of Balkan exiles – Bulgarians, Greeks and Yugoslavs – but rose to subaltern command positions and then major in the XIII Brigade.[36] He amused his subordinates by organising 'solidarity concerts' at which volunteers from different countries performed their national songs and dances.[37] He openly praised his Jewish comrades for 'contributing their blood and lives for our common cause' and condemned anti-Semitism and the persecution of the Jewish population in Poland and in other countries.[38]

In December 1938 Mołojec was given the difficult task of dissolving the XIII Brigade.[39] In his last appeal to its remnants, he promised that 'the fire of the great sentiments that joined us until now will not disappear after our dispersion across the globe'.[40] Following the defeat of the republic, he moved to France, escaped internment by the French authorities, and worked underground in Paris on behalf of Comintern to reorganise Polish communist networks in France and across Europe. In 1940 he was ordered to return to Moscow. Some contemporary Polish historians claim that the Kremlin probably saw him as a potential 'Poland's Stalin' and therefore actively prepared him for future political and combat assignments in his

Nazi-occupied motherland.[41] Ironically, he was a candidate because in 1937–38 Stalin, scared by the alleged threat of foreign spies and Trotskyists, dismantled the Polish Communist Party and either killed the cadres who had earlier been granted asylum in the Soviet Union or sent them to the Gulag. And so in December 1941 – about a year after his return to the Soviet state and six months after the Nazi invasion of the Soviet Union – 'Edward' was parachuted into Nazi-occupied Poland. As a senior member of a so-called 'initiative group' that enjoyed full patronage of the Soviet secret police, Narodnyi Komissariat Vnutrennikh Del (NKVD), he was put in charge of establishing the Polish communist underground and commanding its combat arm, the People's Guard.[42]

In order to build this underground unit Mołojec needed recruits. The most promising were former members of the International Brigades who were still in France. A few managed to make their way back to Poland via Germany by posing as volunteers to work in German factories. One of these was Józef Mrozek, a former Polish infantry non-commissioned officer, journalist and social activist who had gone to Spain in 1937, aged twenty-nine, and there joined the local Communist Party and XIII Dąbrowski Brigade, rising to the rank of captain.[43] Recovering from injuries in the military hospitals of Murcia and Orihuela, Mrozek encountered many Spanish and foreign fighters. After the republic's defeat, he was interned in France and joined the PCF. Possibly using a false identity, he volunteered to work in a German factory; he arrived in Bremen early in 1941 but absconded that autumn and reached Warsaw. There he became a member and propagandist of the People's Guard established and led by Mołojec. Shortly afterwards he went to the Piotrkowskie forests in central Poland, where he took part in nascent communist partisan activity.[44]

Mrozek's resistance career did not last long. In June 1942 he was captured by the Nazis and sent to Auschwitz. This brought home to Mołojec that his recruitment would have to be much more organised, along a 'German channel' from France to Germany and thence to Poland. In August 1942, under a special arrangement between the re-established Polish Communist Party, Comintern and the PCF's Polish section, Mołojec went under cover to occupied Paris and arranged the relocation of a few groups of IB veterans to Poland via Germany.[45] About forty fighters successfully made their way to Poland in the second half of 1942 and early 1943.

One of these was Franciszek Księżarczyk, a Polish-French miner, comrade of Mrozek in Spain and PCF member. In February 1943 he, two Polish comrades and three escaped Soviet POWs were supplied by the PCF Polish section with forged German papers that presented them as naturalised French citizens of Polish descent volunteering for the German factories in occupied Poland. 'The movement of French citizens through the Reich's territory was by that time relatively intensive', explained Księżarczyk in 1965. He added that 'when it was necessary, we spoke French because the Germans respected this language much more than Polish'.[46]

After their return to Poland, Mołojec's 'Spaniards' developed the People's Guard and organised actions in such provinces as Podlasie, Lublin, Kielce, Radom and Cracow. The commander of the 300-man-strong Tadeusz Kościuszko 'operational group' of the People's Guard was a former sergeant of the IB Dąbrowski Brigade, Stefan Kilanowicz (alias 'Grzegorz Korczyński'). He arrived in Spain in May 1937 and served in different subunits of the XIII Brigade, including the Naftali Botwin Company, which was composed mainly of Polish Jews.[47] Interned in Gurs, he later joined the PCF and was active in the Paris region. After his repatriation he became one of the most successful communist guerrilla commanders in eastern Poland, rising to lieutenant colonel in the People's Guard. He organised operations of the Polish Communist guerrillas against both Germans and the Polish national underground, said to be extremely cruel towards the local non-communist populations.[48] At the same time, however, he showed great openness in absorbing different non-Polish elements, including escaped Soviet POWs and the Jewish inmates of the Janiszów labour camp, captured by the group in November 1942.[49] Kilanowicz's positive record of close cooperation with his Jewish compatriots and of saving some Jews from Nazi mass-murder did not, however, spare him from postwar accusations of anti-Semitism. This badly affected his image in the subsequent Polish historiography of the Second World War.[50]

Mołojec himself was not lucky enough to witness the meteoric rising of Kilanowicz and many other former Interbrigadists within the People's Guard. In December 1942 he fell victim to harsh infighting within the leadership of the Polish communist resistance.[51] His former IB comrades nevertheless kept on arriving in their motherland from the Soviet Union. Their Soviet patrons appreciated them greatly for their rich combat experience, political puritanism, discipline, outstanding fighting spirit and multilingual skills. No wonder therefore that many of that group's representatives rose to senior positions in the military and intelligence wings of the Polish communist apparatus after 1945.[52]

Soviet patronage of Spanish fighters

Resistance movements in Central and Eastern Europe were not only organised from the bottom up by former International Brigaders. They were also organised top-down by the Soviet military and security services. Because of Soviet involvement in the Spanish Civil War, Soviet agents had multiple contacts with both International Brigaders and

Spanish republican soldiers who might be drawn on to organise guerrilla warfare in occupied Poland and also to help with the Soviet guerrilla effort itself.

A key player here was Major Ilya G. Starinov (aka 'Rudolf Wolf') of the Soviet military intelligence, a veteran of the Red Army in the Civil War and leading advocate of guerrilla warfare. He was one of the four thousand people, of whom six hundred were military advisors and instructors, who were sent by the Soviet Union to work with the Spanish Republican Army.[53] Among those he worked with were Henryk Toruńczyk, a Polish Jew with no communist background and a graduate of a Belgian university, and a Spanish republican, Domingo Ungría.

How the work of these former Spanish fighters played out depended on the regional political context which held the national, international and transnational in a powerful tension. Comintern and the Soviet authorities behind them were keen to draw on the technical expertise and fighting experience of individuals who had fought in the International Brigades, but the exposure of these fighters to political currents and ideologies far from Moscow and over which it had no control was a cause for concern. What won out in the end depended on the national context, so that what was possible in Poland for Toruńczyk, who enjoyed some autonomy from Soviet control, was not possible for Ungría, who remained under total Soviet control.

Internationalised by his university education in Belgium, Toruńczyk volunteered for Spain in May 1937 and was promoted to deputy commander and then chief of staff of the Palafox Battalion of the XIII Dąbrowski Brigade. He was highly prized for his organising talent by the brigade's commander, Mołojec, and joined the PCE. In January 1939 Toruńczyk led a short-lived unit formed from Italian, Balkan and Polish IB veterans which remained in Spain after demobilisation. Interned in the French camps Gurs, Le Vernet and Djelfa in the Algerian Sahara, he was released by the Allied troops in 1943 and invited to Moscow in July 1943. There he met up again with Starinov, who was now a lecturer at the guerrilla warfare schools training Ukrainian and Polish leaders of the partisan movement.[54] Toruńczyk joined the Moscow-backed 'Berling's army' as a colonel, and in early 1944 – under close NKVD supervision – he was charged with establishing the Polish Independent Special Battalion. This 300-man-strong commando, including Poles, Polish Jews, Soviets and Spanish republicans, was parachuted into occupied Poland to engage in sabotage and intelligence operations. Powerfully transnational, it combined many who could barely communicate but shared a common fighting experience from Spanish days. In May 1945, thanks to his success in that field, Toruńczyk was appointed first commander of the Internal Security Corps, a military formation answerable to Communist Poland's Ministry of Public Security and intended to protect the key public infrastructures, as well as to fight anti-communist guerrillas.[55]

Differently spectacular and less fortunate was the military career of Domingo Ungría. Born in Andalusia in 1902, he joined the PCE and began his struggle against Franco's revolt by forming militias in Valencia, where he met Starinov. Within a year and with the help of Starinov, Ungría found himself the commander of a 3,500-man-strong XIV Guerrilla Corps of the Republican Army.[56] Starinov returned to the Soviet Union in late 1937, and Ungría, having managed to avoid internment by the French authorities after the defeat of Republican Spain, reached the Soviet Union via Oran in Algeria in the spring of 1939. Speaking Russian thanks to his previous contacts with the Soviets, he joined a group of his fellow countrymen working in a tractor factory in Kharkov (Ukraine). Because of their military or guerrilla background, they were sent to different military academies, where they received both political and military training. In the first months of the German invasion, Ungría requested the Kremlin's permission to volunteer in the Red Army and was allowed to join Starinov in his attempt to establish a guerrilla force – the 5th Engineers Brigade – in the Red Army. It was this unit that, prior to Kharkov's occupation by the Nazis, successfully planted the sophisticated mines in its key facilities that exploded on 13 November 1941.

By then, it had already recruited about two hundred Spaniards, many of them veterans of the XIV Guerrilla Corps, who served both as saboteurs and as instructors for their inexperienced Soviet comrades. These fighters participated in a series of major battles in Moscow and elsewhere and were dispatched to various Soviet guerrilla detachments and subversion groups in Nazi-occupied territories, mainly in central Russia and Belarus. 'Their role in the early war stages cannot be overestimated', wrote Starinov in his postwar memoirs.[57] Ungría himself, in a letter to the famous Spanish communist leader Dolores Ibárruri, 'la Pasionaria', now based in Moscow, revealed how much the Soviets appreciated the guerrilla experience of the Spanish veterans:

> Good use has been made of us. Our Soviet comrades wish us to pass on to them our knowledge from the Spanish war, as well as our knowledge of guerrilla tactics, which is what I can best teach them.[58]

That said, there was a tension between the military value of the Spanish fighters to the Soviets and the political risk they were thought to pose. Increasingly, Starinov's and Ungría's 5th Engineers Brigade and other units of Spanish fighters were sent far from Moscow, either to the north Caucasus to participate in some action that never materialised or to the south Russian areas of Kuban and Rostov, where the Wehrmacht was advancing in summer of 1942.

The Spanish communist leadership based in Moscow was also increasingly sceptical about transnational resistance activity. In mid-1943 Dolores Ibárruri asked the Soviet authorities to stop sending Spaniards to the front, mainly in order to spare experienced fighters for the future struggle on the Spanish soil. The Soviets responded positively. This was precisely the time of Comintern's dissolution, and the Kremlin was happy to get rid of overactive foreign communists. The majority of Spanish guerrillas were thus confined to Moscow until their official demobilisation. Only a few of them were sent to local guerrilla schools as instructors or insisted on remaining at the front, as members of the Soviet regular and irregular formations.[59]

Return to Spain: transnationalism marginalised and betrayed

The final act of the Spanish fighters' anti-fascist struggle on European soil began in the autumn of 1944 when, following the liberation of France, a force named Agrupacion Reconquista de España (Guerrilla Groups for the Reconquest of Spain) was formed on the French side of the Franco-Spanish border with the intention of launching a cross-border invasion and occupying the neighbouring Spanish Arán Valley. Vicente López Tovar, the acclaimed veteran of the Spanish Civil War and the French Resistance, was appointed the commander of the invading force of about five thousand men. The 'reconquerors' entered Spanish territory on 19 October 1944, only to discover that the Francoists were well aware of the operation and thus implemented aggressive and skilful anti-guerrilla measures, involving the forced transfer of the borderland's rural population, and soon compelled Tovar's force to retreat. Other no less powerful negative factors were the refusal of London and Washington to allow the opening of an anti-Franco front in southern France and Stalin's consequent decision to promote the struggle against Spanish fascism by compelling the PCE to cooperate with the London-based exiled republican government instead of prolonging communist insurgency on Spanish soil.[60]

This military and diplomatic failure provoked fierce infighting within PCE ranks for control over the French-based Spanish guerrillas and over links with the anti-Franco underground's remnants in the motherland. The winner was the communist leader Santiago Carrillo, who had himself chosen prominent transnational fighters such as Domingo Ungría, and sent them clandestinely to Spain to take charge of the anti-Franco guerrillas.[61] Unfortunately, some of these brave men and women became prey not only to hostile Franco forces, but also to their own superiors, who were seeking to impose Stalin-style strict party discipline on their subordinates, including field commanders in Spain. The most trusted and quickly promoted were the NKVD-grown cadres, while others – Starinov's former aides-de-camp and especially those who fought in France – were suspected as less controllable and thus less politically reliable. Thus Domingo Ungría disappeared in the south of France in mysterious circumstances, possibly eliminated on the orders of the PCE leadership.[62]

Conclusion

The transnational contribution of the Spanish fighters was shaped by a number of factors. Those who came to Spain to fight in the Spanish Civil War were often already 'on the move', as economic migrants or as political exiles, whether in France or the Soviet Union. Fighting in the Civil War was often as divisive as it was unifying, but after the defeat they managed to reinvent themselves as a matrix in different theatres. This was explained by three principal factors: military experience which prepared Spanish fighters for armed resistance in a way that was closed to civilian resisters; shared experience in specific International Brigades and units of the Spanish Republican Army; and the patronage of Comintern and beyond that, the Soviet authorities.

These factors both boosted the Spanish fighters' operational skills and enhanced the group's unprecedented cross-border mobility, which was preserved even after Nazi conquests on the European continent. It was thanks to this unique capability that the Spanish fighters reached the major geographical theatres of resistance – firstly and foremost in France, but also through the camps of French North Africa or the 'German channel' of Third Reich factories – to Poland and the Soviet Union, before in some cases returning to Spain at the end of 1944.

The most important outcome of the Spanish fighters' dissemination across occupied Europe was the catalysis of local resistance processes. They brought not only their outstanding knowledge, experience, discipline and motivation, but in many cases also already existing guerrilla nuclei ready for immediate deployment, capable of networking with other similar formations, local resisters and the populace. Without this 'dowry' brought by figures like Mołojec, Tanguy, López Tovar and Starinov, anti-Nazi resistance in many European lands would have been very different. As Starinov himself said,

> It was thanks to Spain that the partisan movement in Europe reached such a strength. One can say with confidence that modern partisan diversionary warfare was born in Spain and from there spread to other countries.[63]

The practical outcomes of this process – multiple German, collaborationist and anti-communist infrastructures, military and human targets damaged or annihilated, the Wehrmacht's advances and retreats slowed or prevented and significant territories recaptured – had long-lasting strategic effects, both militarily and politically. In Poland the communist regime was able to impose itself on local populations with significant help from Spanish fighters. In France it was thanks to the unity between the local and the foreign Spanish fighters that the FTP-MOI evolved together into a highly effective guerrilla force and allowed Moscow to strengthen its positions within the political system of liberated France.

This analysis nevertheless reveals major limitations on Spanish fighters' ability to influence the European anti-Nazi and anti-fascist struggle. First, there were rivalries within different national communist leaderships, such as those that caused the deaths of the transnational resisters and guerrilla leaders Mołojec in Poland and Ungría in France. Second, there was the reservations of the Allied powers Great Britain and the USA to permit the invasion of Franco's Spain by Spanish republicans after the liberation of France, together with the hostility of de Gaulle himself to the presence of 'foreigners' in the French Resistance. Transnational fighters were as much a threat to the Western Allies as to the Soviets. Third, the Soviets supported transnational Spanish fighters when it suited them militarily but turned on them when they were seen as a political threat. Spanish fighters' involvement in the anti-Nazi struggle in occupied Poland and the Soviet Union was significantly restricted – in terms of manpower, timeline and geography – by the Kremlin's grave suspicion of foreign communist exiles, by its total control over the structure of the local guerrilla forces and their activity and, finally, by the typical attitude of the Soviet field commanders who frequently treated their subordinates as little more than cannon fodder.

3

Camps as crucibles of transnational resistance

Robert Gildea with Jorge Marco, Diego Gaspar Celaya, Milovan Pisarri, Enrico Acciai, Bojan Aleksov and Yaacov Falkov

In 1974 Franz Dahlem, a communist Reichstag deputy and former veteran of the International Brigades, interned in the high-security French camp of Le Vernet in the Pyrenees, reflected that

> The French government made the mistake of concentrating the cadres of the International Brigades and the apparatchiks of central committees of communist parties in countries with fascist regimes or occupied by the Nazis in the Le Vernet camp. They constituted a formidable force that the French could not subdue by hunger or cold or threats or arguments or provocation, neither by the danger of death or by gunfire. They were subdued in 1940 only by a thousand armed police.[1]

This analysis was a sharp insight into the paradox that interning foreign fighters and militants in a confined space and under harsh conditions was not the best way to deal with the spectre of communism that was intensely felt by European powers, reaching a high point after the Nazi-Soviet Pact of August 1939. On the contrary, bringing together those considered to pose military, political and ideological threats was likely to increase at one and the same time their solidarity, their political education and their frustration and promote the very menace of transnational resistance they were designed to snuff out.

In the archipelago of camps that sprang up across Europe in the period leading up to and especially during the Second World War, 'foreigners' considered a danger to national security or required for national survival were the inmates par excellence. Among them were political exiles, often communist; refugees, often Jewish; soldiers who had become POWs; and, later in the war, forced labourers recruited to sustain the Nazi war effort. Political exiles were rounded up because they were on the move to fight or in flight, and then segregated into different categories to prevent them communicating. Any coming together to resist was either sanctioned within the camp or disrupted by deportation of individuals or whole groups to other camps. These were often even more isolated, whether in occupied Poland, remote Mediterranean islands or the sands of the Algerian Sahara, to disrupt any resistance organisation that might develop.

And yet, in spite of and often because of these measures, these camps became crucibles of transnational resistance. They were stopping points in the trajectories of people on the move who were often dramatically changed by their experiences. First, although they were generally segregated in the camps by national origin or political affiliation, and were often divided from each other by national and political conflict and linguistic difference, the very coming together of resisters from very different backgrounds and experiences meant that opportunities were created for the formation of new political, religious or national communities, often drawing on older structures but renewed and reinvented in the context of internment and preparing for the future. Second, just as prisons have been described as universities of crime, so internment camps provided a political education and may be described as universities of resistance. Study groups, work groups and sporting groups were set up. Battles and revolutions were commemorated. Internees learned from each other about their experiences of oppression and struggle. They learned more about communism and anti-fascism and about how resistance was taking place in different parts of Europe, indeed globally. Third, despite or indeed because of the brutality of the camps, some of them found ways to organise transnational resistance. Eugen Kogon, who spent much of the war in Buchenwald, pointed out that the top-down camp organisation might be subverted to provide an element of self-government by inmates in the camps.[2] This might reinforce oppression or increase division but it might also provide a vehicle to articulate dissent within the camp, to organise escapes, and to make contact with resisters outside the camps. In this way camps might become springboards or platforms of transnational resistance.

This chapter will explore a number of case studies drawn from what might be called the French, Italian and German systems of camps. Much has been written about the system of camps in Germany, in German-occupied Europe and in countries both allied with and opposed to it. A hundred facilities designed to imprison some 10,000 political opponents were set up from 1933, including Dachau, Sachsenhausen and Buchenwald camps in 1937. Many camps rapidly evolved into complicated systems of 'parent camps' and numerous *Außenkommandos* or sub-camps, so that the whole gulag system came to include 30,000 forced labour camps, a thousand POW camps and a nearly identical number of concentration and extermination camps.[3] After its victories of 1939–41 the Germans set up about a thousand POW camps. These included *Stalags* or main camps and *Durchgangslager* (*Dulags*) or transit camps. Victory also made possible the recruitment of millions of forced labourers from occupied territories to work for the war economy and the deportation of millions of Jews to the extermination camps. The literature on the main concentration and extermination camps is extensive, so here we will explore transnational resistance in two POW camps, Fallingbostel X1-B in north Germany and Schwanseestrasse in Munich, as case studies.

In Italy the fascist regime introduced regulations in 1926 and 1931 providing for the arrest of those considered a threat to the 'public security and national order' and their internment in isolated locations. Between 1926 and 1943, fifteen thousand individuals (about five thousand of whom were political opponents) were interned in 262 camps.[4] These were located on the Italian peninsula and the annexed territories, particularly in remote places in the south or on Mediterranean islands such as Ponza. After Italy entered the Second World War, these were extended to Ventotene, Ustica, Pantelleria and Lampedusa, forming a veritable gulag archipelago. After Yugoslavia was invaded in 1941 and an uprising broke out, the Ministry of the Interior and the army set up special internment camps for Yugoslav Partisans and civilians in Lovran, Kraljevica, Bakar, Prevlaka, Bar, Mamula and the islands of Molat and most notoriously Rab. The army established its own internment system, with several concentration camps for civilians in Italy and the occupied territories as well as Albania under Italian control.[5] Focus here will be on the island of Ventotene, which was the main centre for political prisoners and International Brigaders, the mainland camp of Renicci, near Arezzo, to which many were transferred, and the island of Rab, which held Yugoslav opponents and later Jews.

Camps in France were established not only by the Vichy regime but also by republican France, which had an 'authoritarian' turn in 1938–39 under its prime minister Daladier. A first string of camps was established along the Pyrenean frontier with Spain and in French North Africa to deal with a mass exodus of Spanish republicans and International Brigaders fleeing Franco's victorious armies. Camps were set up in the coastal region of Algeria but also deep in the Saharan interior. After the Nazi–Soviet Pact and the outbreak of war in 1939 the Republic interned communists who were now regarded as traitors and 'dangerous, suspect and undesirable' foreigners, including German anti-Nazis and Italian anti-fascists. The defeat in 1940 led to thousands of makeshift POW camps being set up by the Germans before the deportation of 1.5 million POWs to Germany. Foreign Jews, including many expelled by Germany in the autumn of 1940, were now interned in camps across France. This chapter will explore the Pyrenean camps of Saint-Cyprien, Gurs and Le Vernet, together with Morand near Algiers and the Saharan camps of Djelfa and Bossuet.

The French camp system: from the Pyrenees to the Sahara

In April 1939 there were about 150,000 Spanish republicans and International Brigaders in Pyrenean camps while between 10,000 and 12,000 Spanish republicans and International Brigaders fled by sea to North Africa.[6] To explore the transnational experiences of some of these veterans we will look into the life of Ramón Via, who had fought in the Spanish Republican Army, and who escaped to North Africa in March 1939 on board *The Stanbrook*, a British coal ship that evacuated more than 3,000 Spanish republicans from Alicante just before it was taken by Francoist troops.[7] Republican evacuees were interned in camps near the cities of Oran and Orléansville, but former Brigadists were taken to isolated internment camps such as Camp Suzzoni and Camp Morand, both in the desert near Bogar and Boghari. Via was sent to Morand, the largest internment camp in French North Africa, holding more than 3,000 Spanish refugees in May 1939, together with a number of Polish and Yugoslav members of the International Brigades.[8]

Within the camps internees were segregated into different categories in order to prevent communication and what would today be called 'radicalisation'. The International Brigaders and their Spanish communist comrades called their huts '7th November', the mythical date of the International Brigades' intervention at the besieged republican capital of Madrid and 'El Foro', 'The Forum', paying ironic homage to their public debate.[9] Via worked with the PCE to ensure that most of the key jobs in the camp were given to communists, thus subverting the camp administration, but also provoking rivalry between the Spanish communists, anarchists and socialists.[10] To overcome these rivalries and to build morale and solidarity among the internees, Via developed a programme of cultural and sporting activities. Several huts were turned into schools where classes were taught in general culture, history, maths and the Spanish, French and English languages. There was a music band, a handicrafts workshop and collective reading of newspapers, which provided material for discussion.[11] Via had been an amateur boxer in the 1920s and set up football, gymnastics, athletics and boxing teams.[12] On 14 July 1939 the internees organised a 'martial' parade with the French and Spanish republican flags to celebrate the 150th anniversary of the French Revolution, which most of the internees considered a founding moment, followed by a gymnastics display and football match against French officials. Finally, the band gave a short recital, playing both the *Marseillaise* and the *Himno de Riego*, dedicated to the Spanish Republic.[13]

All these activities used for political education were supposed to result in political activism, including escaping from the camp to develop resistance activities outside. In September 1939, on the orders of the PCE, Ramón Via escaped from Camp Morand with the help of Lisette Vincent, a schoolteacher from Oran, and a Hungarian refugee by the name of Gustave Erdos.[14] Via began to rebuild the banned Algerian Communist Party (Parti Communiste Algérien, PCA), which again would produce underground publications such as *Lutte Sociale* and provide assistance to political prisoners, POWs and refugees in the camps and prisons of Algeria.[15] The PCA was from the outset composed of various nationalities – French, Spaniards, Italians, Germans and Jews. Cooperation was not always easy to achieve, however, because Via himself only spoke Spanish. Lisette Vincent translated in meetings and prepared propaganda and press material in three languages: French, Spanish and Arabic.[16] In what remained a colonial situation, however, relations with Muslim members, such as Ahmed Smaïli, who joined the PCA in 1931 and fought with the International Brigades in Spain, were not good. When in August 1941 Smaïli complained that the PCA simply passed from French to Spanish tutelage but remained in the hands of European settlers he was expelled.[17]

Across the Mediterranean, in the Pyrenean camps, International Brigaders and communists also tried to promote organisation, political education and solidarity. At Saint-Cyprien, Ljubomir Ilić, major of the XIV Corps, recalled in 1986 that the internees were confused and depressed, until one day comrade Bruno from the Italian Garibaldi Brigade struck up the *Internationale* on his accordion. 'Suddenly the depression lifted', said Ilić, indicating they experienced a transformative moment that again started to make them into a community. The International Brigaders then formed a general staff of former political commissars and heads of national groups. Internees began to educate themselves politically, reading the papers and learning each other's languages. Contact was made outside the camp with French, Belgian and American friends in an attempt to secure treatment as POWs under the 1929 Geneva Convention. Faced by this demand, the colonel in charge of the camp however simply laughed, Ilić recalled bitterly: 'They saw us not as soldiers but as international revolutionaries and the worst criminals in the world.'[18]

In April 1939, to disrupt possible resistance, those regarded by camp authorities as troublesome International Brigaders were moved to Gurs, at the western end of the Pyrenees. Before long a 'people's university' was founded. Because of the many different national backgrounds of the people involved, sixty-two courses with no fewer than 523 students, mainly

Poles, Germans, and Austrians, were organised in various languages.[19] 'We discuss Italian fascism', wrote a German internee, 'geopolitical problems in the Mediterranean, the Jewish question, German farm workers, the history of Czechoslovakia, the Berne Convention, trade unions, agriculture, relationships with the Catholics and youth.'[20] For the 150th anniversary of their common inspiration, the French Revolution, an Italian and a Romanian Brigadist made a huge sculpture from mud from the camp to celebrate liberty, equality and fraternity.

In the event there was little time for celebration. The Nazi–Soviet Pact divided internees between communists and non-communists and the communists against themselves, and enabled the French state to outlaw the Communist Party and to round up its militants. The right-wing Basque deputy Jean Ybarnégary, whose constituency included Gurs, demanded all interned Interbrigadists to be shot in batches of fifty as agents of the Comintern.[21] Despite all this at Gurs, attempts were continued to preserve the international solidarity developed in Spain. The Yugoslav group declared, 'United in Spain. United in the concentration camp. United we will carry on fighting for the freedom and progress of humanity.' In response the Romanian group declared, 'Total unity in the anti-fascist camp', while the Italians of the Garibaldi Brigade echoed hopefully, 'Always united, as in Spain.'[22]

Repression in France intensified after the outbreak of the Second World War, which sharpened concerns about fifth columns and treachery. A new high-security camp was opened at Le Vernet in the centre of the Pyrenees to take in 'dangerous, suspect and undesirable' foreigners.[23] One of those sent there in October 1939 was Franz Dahlem, the communist former Reichstag deputy who had fled to France in 1933 and found a welcome in the 'red belt' Ivry-sur-Seine, whose communist mayor was Georges Marrane. Dahlem had served in Spain as a political commissar, then returned to Ivry as the underground head of the KPD exiled in France. When war broke out he requested asylum from the Daladier government as an anti-Nazi. Instead he was arrested as doubly treacherous: first as a Lorrainer who in 1918 had opted for German citizenship instead of French citizenship when France recovered Lorraine, and second as a 'convinced Muscovite' who defended the Nazi–Soviet Pact.[24] Another 'enemy alien' arrested in Paris and sent to Le Vernet was the Hungarian-Jewish Arthur Koestler, who had gone to Spain as a war correspondent of the *News Chronicle* and was taken prisoner after the fall of Malaga, and who remarked of the Le Vernet International Brigaders in his *Scum of the Earth* (1941) that 'one half of the world adored them as heroes and saints, the other half loathed them as madmen and adventurers'.[25] Among the Brigaders who joined him and Dahlem were Luigi Longo, who had been political commissar of the XII Garibaldi Brigade and then general inspector of the International Brigades, and Alessandro Vaia, from Milan, who was described by the authorities as a 'dangerous communist anarchist'.[26]

Although the French government was hostile to foreigners, many of these foreigners were seasoned anti-fascists who, looking at from a different perspective, could contribute to the French war effort. Internment camps were therefore plundered for fighters; Spanish republicans were sometimes threatened with being sent back to Franco's Spain if they did not join up. Because they were not French citizens they were not welcome in the regular French national army, but they enrolled in the Foreign Legion, the Régiments de Marche de Volontaires Étrangers (Foreign Volunteers' Infantry Regiments, RMVE) or labour battalions, working on defences like the Maginot Line. The 13th Half Brigade of the Foreign Legion, including Spanish republicans and Central European Jews, was sent to Narvik in April 1940.[27] Through their enrolment in such schemes they were made useful to the French state and believed to be a reduced security risk. However, Yugoslav Brigaders in Gurs remained faithful to the ruling of Moscow under the Nazi–Soviet Pact that the war was an imperialist war declared by France and Britain and therefore refused to be drafted into work battalions. Ilić described in 1986 how French soldiers came for them on 2 April 1940:

> So loud was the shouting [of the internees] that the soldiers were forced to withdraw. The shouts became a thunder of protest that was taken up throughout the camp as far as the Spaniards on the other side of the road. Everyone was outside, up against the barbed wire, singing Spanish Civil War songs, the *Marseillaise* and shouting slogans ... One of the Brigadists struck up the *Internationale*, which carried across the camp with the speed of an explosion. The soldiers froze and the officers were silenced. They did not know what to do.[28]

As punishment for this defiance, 270 International Brigaders, including Ilić, were sent from Gurs to high-security Le Vernet just as German armies invaded France in May 1940.

The Vichy regime, created in July 1940, denounced Jews, communists and *métèques* (foreigners) as 'anti-France' – subversives who had undermined 'eternal France' from within and brought about its defeat. They were to be purged in order to make France whole again. This had its impact on the internment camps. At Le Vernet there were now three to four thousand internees under armed guard. They were segregated into three blocks: Block A for those with a criminal record – the Paris underworld or *milieu*, together with refugees (often Jewish) whose papers were not in order; Block B for left-wing activists, above all communists and anarchists; and Block C for International Brigaders and former combatants in Spain. However, as Franz Dahlem later observed, it was a mistake to concentrate former International Brigaders and the leaders of international communism on the same site. As in Morand, communists established themselves in most of key posts of camp administration, and communists developed links outside the camp. Dahlem communicated with the PCF and KPD through his wife of twenty years, Käthe, who had gone with him to work for Comintern in Spain, becoming known as 'the mother of the International Brigades' for the work she had done with young fighters of German origin.[29] Käthe made contact with Georges Marrane, who now headed the PCF's Front National in the Free Zone, and with Otto Niebergall, a German communist, exiled from the Saarland after it voted for reunification with Germany in 1935, who had escaped from Saint-Cyprien in July 1940. With instructions from the Dahlems, Niebergall went to Paris in April 1941 to in order to contact the leaders of the MOI, the PCF's umbrella organisation for foreign workers. [30]

Although Le Vernet was in the Free Zone, under the terms of the Franco-German armistice the Germans retained the right to inspect it. In theory this was to verify good treatment of their own nationals, but in practice it was to track down and deport anti-Nazis from Germany and German-occupied countries. A commission headed by the German Foreign Office official Ernst Kundt made a first visit to Le Vernet on 17–18 August 1940.[31] A second visit, on 24 February 1941, was to deport International Brigaders from the Polish and Slovak areas the Germans controlled. This provoked a riot which began among the International Brigaders of Block C, led by the Yugoslavs Ilić and Guido Nonweiller, an agricultural engineer, and spread to the communists and anarchists in Block B. Prisoners massed behind the barbed wire, shouted, refused to work and went on hunger strike.[32] The trouble was quelled with reinforcements from the nearby town of Foix, and 102 inmates were arrested. The alleged ringleaders were put on trial by Vichy and sentenced to three months in prison. In March 1941, meanwhile, over fifty Italian International Brigaders were 'delivered' by Vichy to the Italian Fascist authorities in Menton, on the Mediterranean coast, while on 23 April 1941 the Kundt commission took seventy-six German International Brigadiers back to Germany.[33]

The German invasion of the Soviet Union in June 1941 and the surge of communist resistance activity behind German lines produced a significant power shift within the camp. The German communists, who were organisationally the most powerful but now also the most at risk of deportation, became less active. The Vichy authorities noted that Dahlem and comrades had 'a huge fear of deportation and had completely withdrawn from any visible activity'.[34] As a result, political initiative shifted to the

Italian communists led by Luigi Longo, who became the 'spiritual guides' of the Spanish communists. These were now leaderless because most of their chiefs had managed to obtain visas to go to the Republic of Mexico.[35] Vichy officials tried to check the Italian resistance by moving Longo to the secure prison of Castres, eighty miles away, in November 1941. In January 1942 he was handed over to the Italian authorities and sent to the island prison of Ventotene, where he arrived in May 1942.[36] The Germans finally seized hold of Dahlem, who was deported from Le Vernet on 4 August 1942 and ended up in Mauthausen.

Vichy now decided that the best way to deal with troublesome inmates in the Pyrenean camps was to transport them to camps in Algeria. In 1941 it established a new generation of camps, including disciplinary camps like those of Bossuet and Djelfa, in the southern part of Algeria that was Saharan desert. Prisoners would be put to work building the Trans-Saharan railway, which was supposed to break all who were sent there physically and mentally. Deportation might nevertheless bring together different constituencies in new forms of transnational resistance.

On 22 March 1941 a convoy of International Brigaders was taken from Le Vernet to the coast at Argelès, to be put on a boat to the Algerian port of Oran. They were held in a special camp at Argelès next to a camp for refugee Spanish republican women. Gendarmes were sent in to manage the embarkation of a first selection of Soviet Russians, Czechs, Poles and Romanians. One of the Russians, Semion Kramskoi, later wrote from Algeria:

> In the morning the gendarmes were joined by two Colonial Infantry companies and, to everyone's surprise, a French Navy escort dropped anchor fifty metres from the beach. At 8 a.m. the prefect arrived and took charge of the embarkation. We were given an ultimatum but cried, 'We want to go home', 'We want our families' ... The gendarmes, who were armed to the teeth, began to beat the comrades and force them into the trucks. At this moment the women and the children [from the neighbouring camp] smashed through the wire fences shouting and attacked the gendarmes. They blinded them with sand and broke the first line. The gendarmes were forced to deploy full force against women and children, and a detachment from the naval vessel came ashore to assist. Comrades were hit in the head and chest by rifle butts and dragged by the legs to the trucks. Around 1 p.m. two more companies of gendarmes arrived and used the utmost force. In spite of this, of the 180 who were supposed to embark, only 78 did so, and 24 hours later than intended.[37]

Across borders and barbed wire, various groups of internees and prisoners seemed to recognise that they were part of the same community and acted on this realisation, thus formenting these bonds. The prisoners who avoided the forced embarkation to Africa were taken back by train from Argelès to Le Vernet.[38] Preparing themselves for escape, they formed pairs: one French-speaker and one who did not speak French. Among them were the Romanian Jews Nicolae Cristea, Mihail Patriciu and Francisc Wolf, but also Poles, Hungarians, Bulgarians and Yugoslavs. The groups had addresses in Toulouse, so that they could contact the underground Communist Party organisation. In total eighty-two internees managed to escape from the train, and many of them, such as Patriciu and Wolf, subsequently contributed to the FTP-MOI resistance effort in France.[39]

Eighteen months later, on 8 November 1942, the landing of the Allies in North Africa transformed the situation, although not at once. The French regime of Admiral Darlan and then, after his assassination on 24 December 1942, General Giraud, was simply Vichy under American protection. That said, the Americans pressurised the French to release Spanish republicans, International Brigaders and communists from the camps. Some former Spanish republican inmates of Djelfa did not join the fight against Italy and Germany but, in accordance with their aim at liberating their own country from Franco, were trained by Ramón Via, who in September 1943 took over the training school in Oujda (French Morocco) set up by the first US Operational Group in North Africa. His aim was to send them to Spain to organise the resistance groups in the interior of the country. In November 1944, with the support of the OSS, Via led ten men into the south of Spain and organised an urban guerrilla group in Malaga, which he called 'Mosqueteros del Llano' ('Musketeers of the Plains') and which was based on the French model of the FTP-MOI. Experiences from the Spanish Civil War impacted the shape of resistance groups in France, and now French experiences again influenced the shape of resistance groups in Spain. A year later, however, one of the members of the group tipped off the Spanish police, and Via was arrested and imprisoned.[40]

Back in France, the camp at Le Vernet was more or less dissolved. Between November 1941 and February 1942, those considered the most dangerous of the remaining internees were sent to the prison of Castres. They included Italians like Vaia, Germans such as Rudolph Leonhard and a group of Yugoslavs headed by Ilić.[41] Castres would become another crucible of resistance bringing together experienced resisters who would become influencial figures in the French Resistance. On 16 September 1943, following the Italian surrender to the Allies, a mass escape from Castres was orchestrated by Ilić and Nonweiller. They were in contact with the FTP-MOI in Lyons, over three hundred miles away. The connection outside the prison was provided by Werner Schwarze, a former International Brigader, and Noémie Bouissière, a local woman with communist sympathies.[42] Thirty-five prisoners managed to escape, among them eighteen French resisters and Allied agents, twelve from the International Brigades (Yugoslavs, Italians, Germans) and German political exiles. In late 1943 and 1944 they became leaders of various networks of resistance in France and Italy. These men now combined their fighting experience in the International Brigades and their activities in a succession of camps and prisons, and thus brought a great deal of military and political experience to the relatively new French resisters, most of whom had taken to the *maquis* to avoid forced labour conscription to Germany. They were particularly suited to leading FTP-MOI units which were composed of resisters of immigrant origin, many of them young Jews fleeing the round-ups, with no previous military experience.[43] The FTP was mainly run by French communists, while the FTP-MOI was led by non-French communists. Ljubomir Ilić became commander of the FTP-MOI in the Southern Zone, based at Lyons, and was then promoted to the national general staff of the FTP, a significant recognition of his expertise. Alessandro Vaia got to Toulouse, where he obtained forged papers from a former Italian Brigadist and was sent to join an FTP group in Marseilles which, unlike most FTP units, was 'composed solely of foreigners, mainly of Jewish origin'.[44] These units would forge their identities as transnational resisters in France, although after the war as a national narrative of resistance was imposed their contribution to the French Resistance was overlooked.

The Italian camp system on sea and land

The Italian camp system brought together a number of disparate groups of different generations. First, there were the domestic political prisoners of fascism, whether communists, socialists, anarchists or the liberal socialists of the Giustizia e Libertà (Justice and Liberty) movement, many of whom had been in prison since the 1920s, and second, the Italian International Brigaders, many of whom were shipped back to Italy from Vichy France in 1941 and 1942. Third, there were those considered political enemies from parts of Yugoslavia (Slovenia, Dalmatia) annexed by the Italians in 1941; lastly there were Jewish internees from among the six thousand Jews who escaped from German-occupied Serbia, Ustaša-occupied Croatia and Bosnia and Italian-occupied territories. This mixture of very different constituencies might provoke rivalry and antagonism, but could also produce fruitful exchanges between Italians and Yugoslavs, Italians and Albanians, and Yugoslavs and Jews from many origins with regard to resistance activities.

The island of Ventotene, off Naples, was one of the prime detention localities for Italian political prisoners. The first contingents deported there in 1930 were mostly communists, socialists and anarchists. Inside the camp they continued their active struggle against the regime by organising political activities and preparing themselves for power after the fall of fascism. In June 1941 Altiero Spinelli, who had broken with the Communist Party, and Ernesto Rossi, of Giustizia e Libertà, wrote a manifesto on cigarette paper, which was smuggled to the Italian resistance on the mainland. It was entitled 'For a Free and United Europe: A Draft Manifesto' and also known as the Ventotene manifesto. This demonstrated the early existence of cross-party resistance structures within the camp and links to resistance outside. It was not published until August 1943, however, just before the Italian armistice with the Allies.[45]

Italian prisoners of Ventotene who had fought in the International Brigades brought wider experience to anti-fascists who had remained in Italy, but also acquired detailed information about how fascism had developed in Italy. A clear exemple of this is the story of Giovanni Pesce, a Piedmontese migrant who had worked as a miner near Alès in the Cévennes, and who joined the Garibadi Brigade in Spain when he was only eighteen. Arrested in Piedmont in 1940 and sent to Ventotene, he later recalled how he learned about anti-fascist resistance in Italy from the Jewish academic Eugenio Curiel, who had been arrested in 1939. In turn he taught Curiel about the Spanish Civil War.

> For me, [the internment at] Ventotene was a highly significant experience that I later drew upon during the War of Liberation … . Ventotene helped open my eyes, awakening me to the reality of my country … . When he found out that I had fought in Spain, Eugenio Curiel wanted to meet me and talk. He obtained all the details from me: the military policy of the IBs, the history of the Garibaldi Brigade, the technique of the battle, the clash between Italians and Italians in Guadalajara, the long, exhausting guerrilla war in Ebro.[46]

As the war in the Balkans developed, Yugoslav and Albanian opponents were also interned on Ventotene, as well as on the islands of Ponza and Ustica. Pesce observed that the internees also included Albanian veterans from Spain, among them Mehmet Shehu, one of the future leaders of the Albanian resistance.[47] This encounter challenged Italian prejudices about Albanians as a peasant people. Altiero Spinelli discovered that the Albanians, far from being mountain herdsmen, as his prejudice had told him, were multilingual intellectuals just like them. There were

> ten or so intellectuals that had studied at the famous universities of Europe and spoke three or four languages … . They quickly forged good relationships with the Italian prisoners, developing politically preferential bonds, some with the Communists, others with the 'giellisti' [members of the Giustizia e Libertà movement].[48]

After the fall of Mussolini in July 1943, many of these prisoners were transferred to the mainland and released. However, the anarchist group there was considered to be too big a threat by the new Italian authorities. While the Badoglio government managed to find a compromise with both communists and socialists by appointing some of them to key positions in the re-established trade unions and promising cooperation in the new democratic order, the anarchists were excluded from the deal. Together with about four hundred Yugoslavs, the anarchists were transferred to the internment camp of Renicci, near to Arezzo. One of the anarchists was Alfonso Failla, who had been repeatedly arrested in the 1920s for his anti-fascist activities before being sent to the *confino* in 1930, first to Ponza island, then to Tremiti and finally to Ventotene. Some 4,500 Yugoslavs (Slovenians and Croats) had been interned in Renicci in 1943, and the camp was divided into different sections for Italian political prisoners, Yugoslav anti-fascists and Croatian and Slovenian civilians. The anarchists immediately started their political work among the other prisoners and managed to build bridges between the different camp sectors. They succeeded in forcing the camp commander to give more food rations to the Yugoslav civilians. As a result, the opinion of the Yugoslav internees was radically changed. Until then they had considered all Italians fascists and racists; now they looked positively on the intervention of the Italian anarchists and began to work with them.[49]

On 8 September 1943, when Italy capitulated to the Allies, the ability of the Italian authorities to control the camp crumbled. On 9 September the inmates organised protests in all the sections of the camp, asking the commander to give them the weapons to fight the Germans. The commander brutally repressed the riots and ordered guards to open fire on detainees who were trying to escape.[50] On 15 September, however, he was unable to prevent a mass escape of Italian and Yugoslav prisoners. Luigi Longo, who had been political commissar of the XII Garibaldi Brigade and a former prisoner of Le Vernet, immediately found the partisans and fought until the end of the war as member of the high command of Garibaldi Brigades, now reincarnated in Italy to finish the anti-fascist struggle begun in Spain.[51] Alfonso Failla fought in Tuscany and Liguria, then in Lombardy, mainly with anarchist units such as the Bruzzi-Malatesta Brigade and the Lucetti Battalion.[52] Others formed new battalions as the 'Dusan battalion' composed mainly of Yugoslavs. Many Yugoslav ex-internees wanted to return home to continue the fight. A clandestine network of anti-fascists, including the anarchists, was set up with the task of collecting money and organising the Yugoslavs to get back across the Adriatic.[53]

From July 1942 the Italians ran their biggest camp on the island of Rab, in the Adriatic off Croatia. This camp was established for the so-called 'precautionary internment' of Slovene and Croatian political enemies and their families. Among over 15,000 interned, there were some 2,000 children. According to existing sources over 3,000 died as result of poor condition and maltreatment; the memorial park built in the 1950s lists 1,490 identified victims.[54] In May 1943, following German and Ustaša pressure to deport the Jews who escaped to Dalmatia, the Italian Army brought over 3,000 Jews from other parts of annexed or occupied Dalmatia into 'protective internment' on the island far up north because it was close to mainland Italy and thus considered safer for eventual evacuation. The Jews were interned alongside a separate camp holding 6,500 Yugoslavs, mainly Slovenes, former Yugoslav army officers, trade unionists and Yugoslav or Slovene nationalists. Corralling them on the same island immediately invited exchange between a Jewish camp communist cell and a Slovene camp committee. Among the Jews, especially the young Sephardi from Sarajevo and Belgrade, there were many members of the leftist Jewish youth group Hashomer Hatzair and sympathisers of the Yugoslav Communist Party like Viktor Hajon, a famous pre-war waterpolo player.[55] Once the joint committee of the two camps was established it liaised with resistance in the town of Rab, outside the camp. With Italian defeat on the horizon, the communists in both camps worked actively on spreading news about the partisans while also grooming more than 150 potential fighters to join the partisans across the sea in Croatia.

Upon the Italian capitulation the members of the Slovene and Jewish camps' committees were the first to react. They disarmed the Italian guards and took possession of all stores including weapons. Hajon acted as liaison.[56] Most Italian guards rejoiced together with their former Slovene and Jewish inmates; only the camp commander was arrested by the Slovenes and committed suicide in custody. Two days later partisans came down from the mountains in Croatia crossing the narrow sea and invited all able-bodied to join them. They formed the so-called Rab brigade of Slovene and Jewish fighters, the latter forming the so-called 5th Jewish Rab Battalion of over 240 men and women, and took control of the camps. Slovenes took some Jewish women as nurses back to Slovenia to join the partisan resistance there. Among the young Jewish men to join the partisan resistance was a refugee from Vienna, Imre Rochlitz, who was previously miraculously released from the Ustaša-run Jasenovac concentration camp in Croatia and fled to the Italian-held Dalmatia. Now barely eighteen, Imre left Rab after its liberation, and became an unlikely member of the Yugoslav Partisans.[57]

Staying on the island was not safe as Germans launched the offensive to take over previous Italian possessions. The Zionist lawyer and writer Hinko (Haim) Gottlieb, the most respected among the refugees, asked the Allied liaison officer with the partisans, British Captain Hunter, for the evacuation but was turned down.[58] In the next couple of months, with the help of the partisans, more than 2,500 of the Jewish internees, at times under German air bombardment, were transported into the mountainous regions of Lika, Kordun and Banija in Croatia. The Hungarian and later Yugoslav writer and revolutionary Ervin Šinko (born Spitzer Franjo), who led the official Jewish camp committee, persuaded the great majority of internees to join the partisans. One of these, the young Croatian Jew Elvira Kohn, who had taken pictures of the liberation of Rab with her Leica camera, was invited to join their propaganda department.[59]

As demonstrated by the historian Emil Kerenji and others, the evacuation of Jews from Rab and the eventual survival of most of them with the partisans cannot be understood in terms of 'rescue' driven by abstract ethical considerations. Rather it was part of a collectivist vision of the struggle against fascism of the Yugoslav Partisans that the Jews now joined.[60] That said, Jews who did not support the cause of the Yugoslav Partisans were not evacuated from Rab. About three hundred Jewish internees paid local fishermen to transport them to the safety of southern Italy, now controlled by the Allies.[61] Meanwhile 200 mostly foreign Jews who had no resources and no affinity with the partisans remained on the island of Rab. They were captured by the Nazis in late March 1944 and deported to Birkenau, where they were all killed.

Once they reached partisan-held territories, the Jewish internees were expected to espouse partisan ideology and join the anti-fascist resistance. The 5th Jewish Rab Battalion was disbanded and lost its Jewish identity. Its members – and many more Jews who volunteered to join the partisans in the meantime but had no military training or experience – were reassigned to the 7th Banija division of the Partisan Army, which consisted mostly of local Serb and Croat fighters. Jewish women and elderly non-combatants were assigned to medical and other auxiliary positions. Those too weak or old were housed in villages of Banija and Kordun, where partisans reluctantly and with little means organised their care for next eighteen months, since the British delayed their evacuation until spring 1945. According to Romano, among those evacuated 1,339 joined or were recruited into partisan groups, of whom 119 died in battle and a further seventeen died before the end of the war. Among the 1,812 non-combatants, 126 were killed in enemy raids and fifteen died from disease before they were finally evacuated to southern Italy.[62]

The continued violence could be a traumatic experience. Yet the overwhelming majority of survivors bore no grudge against the partisans or Serb or Croat villagers who looked after Jewish refugees in miserable circumstances and under constant attacks.[63] There was some suspicion and anti-Semitism among the partisans, but most of the conflict and prejudice was cultural and between rural peasant partisans and urban bourgeois Jews. Some like Hajon climbed the ladder of the partisan communist leadership; Aleksandar Goldštajn (Goldstein Sandor) became head of the legal department of the partisan government in Croatia. Elvira Kohn became the first woman war photo reporter. Imre Rochlitz, with only some fragmentary high school attendance before the war, became assistant to the only veterinarian of the guerrilla army, which only had eight hundred horses and mules as mode of transport.[64]

The German system of POW camps

As in the French and Italian camp system, POWs held in German camps and separated into national categories found ways of overcoming those divisions. They used units where nationalities mixed, such as workshops or hospitals. They set up clandestine organisations which brought together POWs of different origins and also linked to communist workers outside the camps. Unfortunately the German authorities were aware of these organisations, which is how historians know about them, and stepped in to smash them in late 1943 and 1944.

In a first phase, *Spanienkämpfer* or Spanish Civil War veterans provided a good deal of yeast for resistance activity in the camps. Many were brought to the Reich's territory from different French internment camps in the autumn of 1940.[65] One of the best examples is a group of Austrian veterans of the International Brigades who were sent to the Dachau concentration camp and quickly took key positions in the structures of prisoners' self-administration in order to use their skills to defend their own interests.[66]

From the spring of 1943, in the aftermath of Stalingrad, it was Soviet POWs who acquired political and organisational weight in the camps and often became the drivers of transnational resistance activities. They established relations with POWs from other countries who were separated from them in the same camps, and with local German resisters. Points of contact were places where people mixed, like hospitals and factories.

Fallingbostel (XI-B), between Bremen and Hanover, set up in September 1939, became one of the Wehrmacht's biggest POW camps, bringing together many tens of thousands of POWs from the Netherlands, Belgium, France, Britain, Australia, Poland, Yugoslavia, the Soviet Union, Czechoslovakia and the USA. Although the nationalities were separated, resistance activities developed. Max Mintz, a Soviet artillery officer of Jewish origin who was captured by the Germans in November 1941, avoided immediate execution by presenting himself as a Russian called

Mikhail Minakov; the Polish-Jewish POW Adam Sten (aka 'Adam Tzur' and 'Mirko') and the French lawyer and communist Henri Cornil were key in these activities.

Adam Sten developed ties with POWs of different nationalities, particularly with the French whose resistance activity was significant, and with local German workers, using his organisational ability and language skills. He later wrote that he set up 'a printing house for publishing illegal literature in Russian and German and distributing it among the workers and soldiers ... There was a well-established connection to French resisters and the camps of foreign POWs that were getting our instructions and worked alongside with us. During this work, I became a great friend of Max ... I served as a constant intermediary between him and the foreigners since I speak German, French and Polish, and Max is quite fluent in English.'[67] He thus underscored the importance not only of practical skills brought into the resistance networks, like printing, but also of mastering and combining useful languages to bridge borders between national groups.

Max Mintz-Minakov developed links with French POWs engaged in clandestine activity, notably a socialist verging on communism called Marcel. Through the French he established contact with a Serb called Vladek Krestnik who was, as Max said later, 'a medical student, employed at a French-Serbian hospital as a doctor or a doctor's assistant. Krestnik in turn introduced me to some Serbs – Chicha, Chainichek (a Czech but from Serbia), Mirko and others. This introduction helped us to spread our clandestine work.' He continued:

> Thanks to Krestnik, I also met a Belgian, Henri Cornil, a professional lawyer, who operated under a nickname 'Pit'. He had already organised a communist group of French and Belgian citizens. Being a communist party member since 1933 and a Spanish Civil War veteran, he knew our ideas literally by heart ... He has never been in the Soviet Union but loves the Russians very much.[68]

Cornil had access to copies of the French communist underground paper *L'Humanité*, which were passed round. Connections with French, Belgian and Yugoslav POWs also enabled the Soviet POWs to gain access to Red Cross parcels and even parcels sent from the POWs' homes. In these parcels it was possible to smuggle in items including money, food, a radio receiver, a typewriter, forged German documents, maps and compasses that would help those who escaped from the camps.[69]

Although the Nazis were concerned that Soviet soldiers were infected by Bolshevik ideas, military and economic requirements came first. Hitler's *Russeneinsatzbefehl* of 31 October 1941 required that Russian POWs should be 'extensively exploited for the needs of the war economy'. POWs were not enough to supply the German factories, and by the end of 1944 nearly 2.8 million forced workers were recruited from German-occupied Ukraine and Russia to work in the Reich.[70] POWs and *Ostarbeiter* were thus brought into contact with German workers. Mintz-Minakov was sent to work in local Volkswagen factory, where he realised that not all Germans were Nazis: some were working against the regime:

> In my first few weeks as a POW and a forced labourer in Germany I had an impression that all the Germans are the same ... But suddenly my acquaintance with a young turner, Helmut, convinced me that I had been mistaken. One day, when I was passing his machine with a heavy plank on my shoulder, he suddenly stopped me and, after looking around quickly, put a piece of bread in my hand ... When I decided to talk to him, it became clear to me that not all Germans are the same ... My conviction strengthened when he introduced me to his uncle, an old communist working in another workshop, and to other workers I had feared to approach earlier. Thanks to these people, I understood that there are still progressive forces within the German people and that they are preparing themselves for the right moment when they will be able to remove the terrible monster of German fascism from the shoulders of European people.[71]

In May 1943 Mintz-Minakov and Cornil had managed to bring together Soviet, Belgian, French, Serbian and Czechoslovak POWs and set up a Committee for the Struggle against Fascism. It was composed of about twenty POWs, mostly officers.[72] The 'committee' disseminated clandestine orders to 156 underground branches and cells in forty-six German cities and villages where the foreign POWs and forced workers were present.[73] In addition, it maintained very close relationships with another underground organisation which had been active at the Bergen-Belsen camp.[74] The committee's activities at Fallingbostel were smashed in June–August 1944 by the Gestapo in a series of major arrests of its leaders and ordinary activists. Mintz-Minakov himself, accompanied by Adam Sten, had escaped the camp prior to the arrests, hoping to reach Yugoslav Partisans. Mintz-Minakov was captured in Austria and incarcerated in various camps until he was liberated by the Red Army in 1945. Many of his close comrades perished in Sachsenhausen, Buchenwald and Mauthausen.[75]

Another powerful organisation of transnational resistance inspired by Soviet POWs also came into being in the spring of 1943. A few internees of the Russian sector ('Russenlager') of the Schwanseestrasse officers' camp, in Munich's south-east Giesing quarter, decided to resist their Nazi oppressors. They founded a group called Bratskoe Sotrudnichestvo Voennoplennykh (Fraternal Cooperation of Prisoners of War), referred to in the Gestapo files and in other German sources as 'BSW'. Its prime movers were two Russians, Roman Petruschel and Mikhail Kondenko, together with a Latvian. Karl Ozolin, and Josef Feldmann, a Jewish officer in the NKVD who had got into Germany disguised as an *Ostarbeiter* and was working under a false Ukrainian name, Georg Fesenko.[76]

By the end of 1943, the BSW had successfully recruited hundreds of Soviet citizens in order to establish a series of branches at thirteen different POW camps and forced labour factories in Munich and its vicinity and in even more distant places like the cities of Karlsruhe and Baden-Baden. The 'relocation' of Petruschel and forty other Soviet POWs from Munich to the Rastatt POW camp near Strasbourg only served to extend the reach of the organisation. Like Mintz-Minakov, Petruschel and his comrades made contact with French POWs who were held in camps but also obliged to work outside the camps; one of them, a former Russian emigré, served as a translator. Meanwhile, back in Munich, the BSW also built a bridge to the Antinazistische Deutsche Volksfront or Anti-Nazi German People's Front, which was formed of communists and left-wing Catholics. A contact was made between Wasilii Kozlov, a senior BSW member, and Emma Hutzelmann, an accountant at the Fettfabrik Saumweber, where Russian POWs and forced labourers were employed. Emma, her husband Hans and another member of the Antinazistische Deutsche Volksfront, Karl Zimmet, hosted weekly clandestine meetings with the BSW representatives at their Munich flats. Translation during these meetings was provided by Karel Mervart, a Russian-born Czech who lived in Munich. Emma was also able to steal and illegally sell fat from the factory, using the money to buy clothes and weapons for BSW escapees.[77] A Gestapo hunt for the BSW leaders and rank-and-file members began in late 1943 and resulted in the arrest of about 380 men and women, of whom 130 were consequently killed in Dachau and Mauthausen.[78]

In some instances, the POWs and the *Ostarbeiter* provided direct assistance to Allied intelligence agents and paratroopers who infiltrated into the Reich's territory. That was one of the declared purposes of the Cologne-based Committee for the Struggle against Fascism, which was discovered and liquidated by the Germans in May 1944, and of the Hanover-based Fedjajew's communist network, which ceased to exist a month later.[79] The most propitious moment for an uprising in POW or forced labour camps came as Allied forces approached. The transnational character of underground committees and previously established channels of cooperation proved invaluable in securing agreements about the temporary governing of the camps between different groups of inmates, preventing conflicts between different groups and individuals, and defending against retreating SS and Wehrmacht units. On 5 May 1945, for example, the Mauthausen camp was ruled by the committee of former inmates under supervision of the Soviet major Andrei Pirogov. The committee organised the camp's defence from the retreating Nazi forces, using weapons that had previously been obtained by the Spanish comrades employed at military factories. Tensions between the camp's inmates themselves – especially the Soviets and the Poles – were successfully defused at the moment of liberation.[80]

Conclusion

Camps were crucibles of transnational resistance in three ways. First, they were 'universities' which provided a political education for the 'scum of the earth', making them into trained resisters profiting from the knowledge and experience of the communist cadre and seasoned Spanish veterans, and combining these skills with local knowledge about language, useful contacts and local resistance groups. Second, they could provide new bonds of solidarity and identity across diverse origins and pathways, defying attempts by the authorities to segregate them. German anti-Nazis were thrown together with International Brigaders and Spanish republicans at Le Vernet after the Nazi–Soviet Pact and outbreak of war in September 1943. Yugoslav and Albanian POWs were put together with Italian anti-fascists after Italy's invasion of the Balkans in 1941. Russian POWs captured during the German drive east were able to contact POWs from Yugoslavia, France or Belgium, together with forced labourers drafted from many countries and local German anti-Nazis. Third, camps permitted the organisation of transnational resistance, whether through a process of getting activist individuals or groups such as communists or anarchists into commanding positions, through the organisation of escapes or through building connections to underground resistance networks beyond the camps.

The camps were no utopias of peaceful transnational exchange and of fostering of mutual understanding and solidarity. They were places of violence from the outset, often harshy ruled and with sparse food and material conditions. There was rivalry and antagonism between national and political groups, which often fell out with each other. Resistance activities were often momentary and were disrupted by brutal repression and the removal of inmates to other camps, whether in Germany, Italy or French North Africa. Activities constantly needed to be reinvented in new locations with new people. However, many of those who escaped or were released from camps went on to become involved in or even leaders of resistance networks outside. Prisoners released from the North African camps in late 1942 or early 1943 went on to join the Corps Franc d'Afrique (CFA), SOE or OSS, or made their way to the Soviet Union to join commando groups that would be parachuted into occupied Poland or Romania. The multinational prisoners who escaped from Castres in

September 1943 became leading light in FTP-MOI resistance. Italian and Yugoslav internees who escaped from Italian prisons the same month combined in partisan units fighting the Germans whether in Italy or Yugoslavia. It was thus rare to find a leading resister with transnational experiences who had not passed through one or several camps, whether Italian, German or French.

4

From regular armies to irregular resistance (and back)

Zdenko Maršálek and Diego Gaspar Celaya

The Bohemian and avant-garde Czech painter Zdeněk Přibyl had completed a two-year compulsory military service in the Czechoslovak army, where he underwent thorough training in heavy artillery, reached the rank of sergeant, and even passed out from a reserve officers' school.[1] Five years later, in 1928, he went to Paris, where he attended lectures by the famous Czech abstract artist František Kupka and became involved in the Parisian artists' community.[2] As a convinced communist, he left for Spain in October 1936 to join the International Brigades. He might have supported the Spanish Republic as an artist, but in the critical autumn days of 1936 his previous military knowledge was more important. He was therefore commissioned to the French-Belgian artillery battery that fought at Madrid, Jarama, Guadalajara, Brunete and Belchite.[3]

After the withdrawal to France in February 1939, Přibyl was interned in the camps of Saint-Cyprien and Gurs, finding a way out by enlisting in the Czechoslovak army-in-exile. Serving again with the artillery, he further deepened his military knowledge. Under instruction from the PCF, he did not evacuate to Britain with the remnants of Czechoslovak units after the French defeat in June 1940 but remained in France. The Vichy authorities sent him to a labour company where, because of his rank, language skills and experience, he was appointed a warrant-officer. Released in 1943 thanks to his friends' connections, he joined the resistance movement in southern France. He was warmly welcomed because of his sixty months in military uniform, familiarity with the training and weapons of the Czechoslovak, Spanish and French armies and experience of heavy front-line fighting. Living in a multinational community for more than fifteen years, with France becoming his second home, he had no problem in moving around transnational resistance networks. He used his skills and courage during the hard-fought battles on the Vercors Plateau, serving as one of the commanders of the famous Pons company.[4] This was one of the few units which survived the tragic massacre there and went on to liberate the city of Valence. For Přibyl, however, the fight was not yet over. Responding to the appeal of the Spanish *maquisards* who, after the liberation of France, wanted to continue the struggle in their native land and launch a rebellion against Franco, he became operational officer of the Spanish 551st Brigade of *guerrilleros espagnoles* during the unsuccessful raid of the Val d'Aran in October 1944.[5] Demobilised in March 1945, he returned to Paris to join the activities of the Czechoslovak National Committee.[6] Only then, after eight years from the autumn of 1936, did he lay down his gun and uniform and again become a full-time artist.

Přibyl was only one of thousands of individuals whose trajectory moved between irregular resistance activity and regular armies and back again. These included, among others, former Spanish soldiers, political exiles, German and Italian anti-fascists and Jewish refugees. Such transitions reveal very interesting dynamics. On the one hand, these fighters brought military skills and experience to regular armies; on the other, they threatened to undermine conventional discipline by ideological commitment. Regular armies generally neglected their extensive experience, did not recognise the ranks they had obtained as irregular fighters and tried to gag their political ideas. Either they sought to integrate them into a unified mass under the army's own training scheme, or they sidelined them in auxiliary units destined for foreigners. National armies prioritised national war aims – the interests of their own country – while these fighters were generally committed to a much wider anti-fascist struggle that knew no frontiers. Some of them managed to integrate with national armies, embraced new national identities, and even pursued remarkable military careers. Others, however, did not adjust well to strict military hierarchies, national priorities and often a reactionary or anti-Semitic culture. They resorted to low-level resistance within the armed forces or left to take part in other forms of combat, joining resistance movements with transnational profiles in occupied countries.

Although the transition between irregular and regular forces and back was going on permanently through the war, it is possible to trace several main phases. In a first phase (1939–40) many former transnational fighters, predominantly veterans of the International Brigades and held in French internment camps, were recruited into the French army or its auxiliary service and into the Czechoslovak and Polish exile armies fighting on French soil. In a second phase, after the subsequent defeat of many European countries in 1940–41, some fighters abandoned the remnants of national armies and returned to irregular warfare. Other former irregulars joined other national armies, such as the British army, the US army or the Free French forces. In the case of the British and US armies they were generally directed to special forces where their military skills were valued, even if their irregularity was not. In a third phase, from the end of 1942, irregular fighters held in internment camps in French North Africa, along with foreigners assigned to labour battalions or the Foreign Legion, were drafted into an auxiliary unit of the French army, the CFA, before being reassigned to Vichy's Army of Africa or the Free French forces, and some of them ended up being the first units to liberate Paris in August 1944. Finally, many former irregulars joined their own national armies when the Allied units reached their occupied homelands in the final phase of the war.

From internment camps to regular armies

After the fall of Catalonia at the beginning of 1939, an exodus of almost half a million Spanish refugees joined more than 2.5 million foreigners in France. These were economic migrants, seasonal workers, political and Jewish refugees, students and artists of all kinds. Many Spanish fighters and refugees, joined later by German anti-Nazis, were interned in camps as political suspects.[7]

Although under French law only French nationals were entitled to serve in the French regular army, the demographic deficit faced by France made it imperative to draft foreigners into the war effort.[8] Their first option was to join the Foreign Legion with a five-year mercenary contract. For many foreigners vegetating in internment camps this was a chance to get out. Spanish republicans in particular were given protection from being sent back to Franco's Spain, which they had just fled. Of 8,465 new recruits enlisted in 1939, 3,052 (36 per cent) were Spanish, 18 per cent were Germans and Austrians, almost 8 per cent Italians and over 7 per cent Poles.[9] Given the large volume of refugees, this number was in fact rather small, and many foreigners preferred to remain in the camps. The Foreign Legion, with its strong reputation of a rigid, reactionary discipline, the Spanish equivalent of which had provided Franco's shock troops in the Civil War, was not attractive to former anti-fascist fighters. When two recruiting gendarmes offered Antonio Soriano, a Spanish former republican soldier interned at Bram near Carcassonne, the choice between returning to 'Spain or [joining] the Legion', he replied, 'Neither Spain nor the Legion. What we want is to be soldiers, soldiers of the French army just like you are, but as a part of republican units. ... We are not legionnaires, we are an army with an ideology.'

Those Spanish fighters who did join the Legion adapted with difficulty and sometimes organised forms of resistance within it. Many were hostile to the French for their previous internment. One of them, A. D. Printer, a former soldier of 12th Foreign Infantry Regiment who made his way to the United States after the French defeat of 1940, recalled that the only French contacts the Spaniards had had before they joined the Legion were the Gardes Mobiles (gendarmes) or the Senegalese guards in the internment camps. Once in the Legion, he said,

> in order not to be lonely, they formed 'cells', which were against the spirit of the Legion and which isolated them still more. For the officers and the NCOs the Spanish legionnaires were a nuisance. They did not fit in. They had been members of a popular army; now they were subjected to the iron discipline of a mercenary unit. They brought with them a typical Spanish individualism. They also brought a great sense of personal dignity, which was constantly trampled upon in the units where German sergeants and veteran French colonials beat the outlaws of Europe into soldiers. Most of the left-wing extremists preferred to remain in the concentration camps. Those who joined the Legion were loyal young soldiers of the Republic; professionals of the Spanish army, a few intellectuals and tradesmen.[10]

The war that broke out in September 1939 was a turning point in recruiting efforts. Until then, the prospect of serving with the Foreign Legion to defend French imperial interests in the North African deserts could attract only adventurers or willing fighters. France's entry into the war made enlisting in the army an opportunity to begin a new phase of the struggle against fascism. 'For me', said Enrique Ballester, 'this war was the continuation of the Spanish war; that is why, despite having no inclination for war, I would rather face the risks of a soldier in the field than the humiliating condition of a refugee surrounded by wire fences.'[11] The same attitude was expressed by Manuel Fernández, who escaped from a Francoist prison and reached France in May 1940, just as the German offensive was launched:

> I had one thing in my head: in France there was war against the Germans, and this was an occasion to take my revenge ... I crossed the border, and the next day I was in barracks. I did not come to France to hide myself in a field. I came to make war. After eight or ten days I was on my way to the front with the Foreign Legion."[12]

The French authorities created a broad variety of options to incorporate foreigners into the overall military effort.[13] Those who hesitated to join the fighting were liable to be sent to internment camps, if they were not already there. They had to decide between 'the ranks or the camps'. The majority of Spanish exiles chose to join the Compagnies de Travailleurs Étrangers, the Foreign Workers' Companies, with 55,000 men forming 230 such companies by June 1940.[14] From the outbreak of war, foreigners could also sign a military contract 'for duration of hostilities'. Such recruits might serve in the newly created field units of the Foreign Legion, or in the RMVE. These units were a real transnational amalgam of various nationalities, with significant proportions of Spaniards and of Poles of Jewish origin. Of the 3,015 soldiers of the 11th Foreign Infantry Regiment, for example, 30 per cent declared Polish nationality, 22 per cent Spanish and 10 per cent Italian.[15] Independent of their nationality, 40 per cent of the soldiers of that regiment were of Jewish descent.[16] This amalgamation of nationalities was not without its difficulties. The French authorities regarded the Spaniards as excessively politicised, even criminal. Quotas were imposed for Spaniards within particular units, and in training they were separated from the recruits of other nationalities. As Zosa Szajkowski, a Polish volunteer in the 12th Foreign Infantry Regiment, recalled, 'They forbade us [the Poles] from fraternising with the Spaniards, from training with them, even talking to them ... They were [kept] in reserved areas, they were treated as criminals.'[17]

In September 1939 the French government permitted the formation of Czechoslovak and Polish armies-in-exile, which could mobilise all their citizens on French soil. The ideological and military core of each of the armies was provided by the military and political exiles who had fled from their occupied homelands. Nevertheless, about two-thirds of the armies were made up of Jews and national minorities who had already fled to France in the interwar period to escape persecution and anti-Semitism in their home countries. Last but not least there were also hundreds of Polish and Czechoslovak soldiers of the International Brigades, interned in various French camps.

Volunteering for national armies by communists and their sympathisers was made very difficult by the Nazi–Soviet Pact of August 1939. There was a contradiction between the Comintern's instruction not to participate in the 'imperialist war' declared by Britain and France and the PCF's orders to join the national flags. Following guidelines of the PCE, Spanish communist militants declared that they would consider the possibility of joining French ranks only on three conditions: that they were allowed to claim status as exiles, that recruitment was on a voluntary basis, and that they were incorporated into the regular French army on the same terms as French citizens. The leadership of Yugoslav Interbrigadists, which espoused a strict pro-Stalinist line, fully complied with the Comintern's directive and preferred to remain interned. Czechoslovak internees split into two groups: some refused to join the 'bourgeois' army, but a majority, instructed indirectly by the PCF, opted to enlist. When a Czechoslovak colonel visited Gurs in October 1939 he found no fewer than 539 Czechoslovaks interned there. He was impressed by their military experience and concluded that 'a healthy army should be able to absorb a certain disruptive risk that the presence of the Gurs group might cause'.[18] The Czechoslovak military authorities assigned one Interbrigadist to each squad 'in order for the whole army to be reinforced by people with the latest war experience' but also to isolate individuals with 'certain experiences, ideologies and opinions, entrenched customs and ill will'.[19]

The tension between Interbrigadists and the military authorities was further deepened by the problem of military ranks. Officers' ranks from the Spanish army were not recognised in the French, Czechoslovak or Polish armies. These volunteers were enlisted either as privates or with their previous rank in their respective national armies. Such a strategy was defensible in respect of service and combat uniformity but was seen as ignominious by the individuals concerned. Alois Samec, one of the most experienced of the Czechoslovak Interbrigadists, who had participated in the famous amphibious raid on the Francoist prison in Carchuna near Granada in May 1938 and been promoted to captain, was demoted to private in the Czechoslovak army-in-exile in France.[20] Anticipating that the coming war would be a conventional military conflict of front-line battles, his superiors were not interested in his experiences of guerrilla warfare but in his former civilian occupation of electrician, and sent him to join the ground personnel of the air force.[21] The denial of officers' ranks won in Spain was considered a hostile act by former Interbrigadists and Spanish republicans. These feelings were strengthened by occasional cases of the arrest of soldiers accused of communist propaganda within the army.[22] Once in the army, the communist leadership created clandestine networks to agitate and spread their ideas. According to their postwar memoirs they considered their 'bourgeois' officers to be enemies, often no different from fascists and German Nazis.[23]

On the military hierarchy side, initial suspicious attenuated over time. Even during the training period in the first months of 1940, Colonel Robert, commander of the 1st Regiment of the Foreign Legion, expressed a general satisfaction with the behaviour of the Spanish legionaries, and began a rehabilitation process of Spanish fighters originally stigmatised by the French military authorities. He reported that

> in general, the impression given by those enlisted from Spain is satisfactory. The arrival in the ranks of the Legion of such a mass of recruits, accustomed to a command and discipline system completely opposed to ours, might be cause for concern. It is good to know that these concerns are not justified. ... From a psychological point of view, they are docile, easy to control and full of good will.[24]

The fighting skills and morale of former soldiers from Spain were most reliably rated by those officers who observed them directly in combat. As a part of the Allied reply to the German attack on Norway in April 1940, the 13th Half Brigade of the Foreign Legion was sent to the Battle of Narvik. The highly transnational Half Brigade, which included Spaniards, Italians, Hungarians and Poles, demonstrated excellent fighting skills there.[25] General Antoine Béthouart, commander of the French Expeditionary Force and the 13th Half Brigade, wrote in his memoirs:

> Disciplined, firm, accepting the hard discipline of Bel Abbes [the training camp for Legion's recruits], the Spaniards demonstrated an exceptional solidarity, making clear to some non-commissioned officers anchored in the traditions of the Old Regime that the times of intimidation and fear had passed. Many officers did not trust them, called them 'communists' and even regretted that they gone to Norway. But, as heirs of the military virtues of their race, the reds or ex-reds fought like lions in the snowy mountains of Norway.[26]

Similarly, Czechoslovak Interbrigadists, despite persisting political distrust, were also recognised by their superiors as worthy soldiers. Clear evidence was provided by the fact that most of them were promoted once, twice, or more in the couple of months before June 1940.[27]

The challenges faced in the Czechoslovak and Polish national armies were not only those posed by communism. There was also the challenge of national minorities and those of Jewish origin, who were nevertheless Polish or Czechoslovak citizens. Poland faced issues from Ukrainians and Jews from Galicia, the former Austro-Hungarian province incorporated into Poland after 1918. Many of these left their homelands because they experienced national hostility or anti-Semitism and could not find employment. In 1931 Polish Jews accounted for over a third of overall Jewish immigration to France.[28] Meanwhile the Czechoslovak army-in-exile had issues with Germans, even though they were mainly Jewish and anti-fascist. In an environment of growing nationalism, all 'others' were seen 'dubious' or 'suspicious'.

Generally speaking, the environment in the Czechoslovak army was more tolerant of Jews than the Polish one was. Clear evidence for this was the large number of Polish Jews who preferred to enlist in the Foreign Legion or in the French regiments of foreign volunteers, rather than in the Polish army, whereas the Czechoslovak army included a good proportion of Jews. That said, conditions in the Czechoslovak army were far from ideal. Because of the Nazi occupation, strong anti-German tendencies became intense. Most Czechoslovaks did not distinguish between German Nazis and German anti-Nazis, even though most of the latter were Jews. Speaking German in the Czechoslovak army was regarded as a provocation. 'Anyone who still speaks German today', said one Czech company commander in June 1940, 'is bound to be a Gestapo agent.'[29]

As a Czech-German communist from a Jewish family, Fritz Beer had a complex, multinational identity. Faced by the Nazification of Germany and Austria, he decided in 1938 to abandon his cosmopolitan German-Jewish identity and to fully assimilate into the Czech nation. He spoke and wrote in Czech and even changed his first name from the German Fritz to the Czech form Bedřich. He voluntarily enlisted in the Czechoslovak army in France in 1940. When he witnessed anti-German antipathy there, Beer declared a German nationality to the military authorities, if only to prove that there were also democratic Germans fighting side by side with Czechs. The reply of the army captain was, 'German and without a confession? The Gestapo bastard! Show him what you think of him!' The other soldiers duly beat him up.[30]

Later, when he was based in Britain, Beer's direct superior was Sergeant Josef Gabčík, one of two future assassins of Reinhard Heydrich, German *SS-Obergruppenführer* and Deputy Reich Protector of the Protectorate of Bohemia and Moravia. Beer spent a lot of time talking with Gabčík, whose opinions illustrate the attitude of the average Czech or Slovak soldier and clearly demonstrated the problem of accepting transnational volunteers. Fifty years later Beer remembered that

> his views of good and evil were clear, firm and simple: the Germans had occupied the country, and it was the obvious duty of every Czechoslovak to expel them. In his model of the world he could not find a place for a German-speaking Jewish intellectual, and he was puzzled that I had joined the army as a volunteer.[31]

Despite these problems, Beer remained in the ranks of the Czechoslovak army throughout the war. He overcame his youthful fervour of communism and, sceptical about postwar developments in Czechoslovakia, remained in Britain after 1945. He was not fully incorporated into the national body during army service, retaining his multiple Czech-German-Jewish identity, to which he added the British citizenship after the war. As a writer, he returned to German and became the chairman of the German-language section of the International PEN, dedicated to freedom of expression. As a British citizen, however, he was for his achievements made Officer of the Order of the British Empire in 1976.[32]

From regular armies to irregular fighters

The national armies mentioned above – French, Polish and Czechoslovak – were overwhelmed and shattered by the six-week German Blitzkrieg of May–June 1940. Soldiers found themselves encircled and trapped by German armoured columns. Others were in headlong retreat, desperately trying to escape capture. Deprived of collective discipline and chains of command, different groups and individuals made different decisions.

In the chaos, Czechoslovak Interbrigadists and communists were unable to obtain instructions from their ideological centre. Nobody knew the attitude of the Soviet Union and communist leadership to those critical events and what political lines should be followed in the new international situation. There was heated discussion about whether to evacuate to Britain, continue the fight on French soil or rather return to the motherland. In the end, they decided that one half, including those most at risk, particularly Jews, should evacuate to Britain with the remnants of the army, while the other half should stay in France. Some would slip back to the occupied homeland, while those who had some connections or background in France later tried to join the French Resistance.

Spanish volunteers and German, Italian and Jewish exiles serving with the Foreign Legion, volunteer regiments or labour companies were also caught up in the turmoil of events. Those who had signed a contract 'for duration of hostilities' were demobilised, but now found themselves as unwanted foreigners in Vichy France. Unless they escaped from France they faced the same dilemma as a year earlier: 'ranks or camps'. In these critical circumstances, only a narrow range of options remained. The fear of renewed internment and the even greater danger of being deported to Germany led many to sign a contract with the Foreign Legion, now under the control of the Vichy regime.[33] Thus many who in 1939 had considered conditions in the Legion humilitating now decided to enlist, even though conditions were far worse and Vichy France was collaborating with Germany. Spaniards thus represented about 40 per cent of new recruits between the autumn of 1940 and 1942.[34] They were sent to French North Africa, as were as many of their former comrades-in-arms who were again interned and forcibly incorporated into the GTE, the labour companies of the Vichy authorities. Either way, the conditions in the Saharan desert were harsh, but at least they were beyond the reach of the Gestapo, which was deporting Spanish POWs to Mauthausen. The majority of them considered the Legion their best hope until another option, such as desertion or defecting to the Allies, became possible.

Among those who remained in France was the Czechoslovak Interbrigadist Osvald Závodský. Born in the Czechoslovakian part of multinational Silesia in 1910 to a very poor family, he soon found his way into communist circles. Between 1932 and 1934 he did compulsory military service, being promoted to corporal and appointed an instructor of recruits' training. Shortly after the outbreak of the Spanish Civil War, the Communist Party sent him to Spain, where his military experiences and political firmness were put to use. Fighting with the International Brigades, he rose to political commissar of the battalion, and was promoted to lieutenant. After the retreat to France, Závodský shared the common Interbrigadist experience of internment in Saint-Cyprien and Gurs. From there, in December 1939, he enlisted in the Czechoslovak army-in-exile. His Spanish officer rank was not recognised there, and he was given his pre-war rank of corporal. However, despite being known as a communist activist, he was soon promoted sergeant and appointed commander of a machine-gun squad, which he led during the French campaign in June 1940. Obeying his communist seniors, Závodský did not follow the remnants of the Czechoslovak army to England but stayed in France. Under the alias 'Joseph Bart', he was later involved in the creation of the FTP-MOI resistance network and became commissar of its Paris guerrilla unit. He took part in direct actions against the Germans until he was caught by Gestapo in December 1942. Thanks to his fluent French, he tried to outwit Germans by declaring himself a Frenchman, and as such was sent to the Fresnes prison. He was nevertheless transferred to Mauthausen in September 1943.[35]

Among the foreign fighters who returned to their homeland were many Czechoslovak and Yugoslav Interbrigadists. The latter were called home by the Yugoslav Communist Party after the defeat of France in the summer of 1940, even though Yugoslavia was not yet in the war. In interwar Yugoslavia communists were harshly persecuted and did not have the opportunity to gain wider military education or experience. As battle-hardened cadres the Yugoslav Interbrigadists thus became significant after the Axis invasion of Yugoslavia in April 1941 and during the subsequent creation of the communist resistance network. They rose to the most important functions within the partisan movement which later became Tito's Yugoslavian National Liberation Army. Four of them even became commanders of individual field armies. The price, however, was high: of 250 Interbrigadists who returned to Yugoslavia, 130 died during the war.[36] Their role was clearly defined by Slovenian historians:

> They were good organisers of the National Liberation Army, prominent among the commanders, commissaires and chiefs of staffs. ... Their knowledge brought confidence to inexperienced partisans, because a large element of the national liberation fighters were young people who had not yet served the army. Spanish experience, both technical and in the military-political field, was therefore valuable, especially at the start of the national liberation struggle, since the Yugoslav Communist Party did not have other personnel with military experience, and even fewer with combat experience.[37]

One of those who returned home, juggling different identities as a means of survival, was Ivo Vejvoda. Born to a Czech father in the Croatian town of Karlovac in 1911 and a Yugoslav citizen, he used his dual national identity to his own benefit. Already a member of the Yugoslav Communist Party, he studied architecture in Prague, from where he went with other Yugoslav students to Paris and thence to Spain. In December 1939, as an internee in Gurs, he persuaded his Yugoslav communist seniors to allow him to enlist in the Czechoslovak army-in-exile. There, declaring himself a volunteer from compatriot community, he won the trust of the officers. Soon he was promoted to lance-corporal and then even sent to a French officer school.[38] Trying to escape home after the French defeat, he asked the Yugoslav consulate for a Yugoslav passport. Dressed in a French cadet uniform, he declared himself a former volunteer in the French army, concealing his participation in both the Spanish and Czechoslovak armies, which was already posing problems. He obtained the passport without difficulty and sailed back from Marseilles to Yugoslavia. While all his comrades were arrested on landing as Interbrigadists, he drove freely home because the valid passport proved him a 'decent' citizen.[39]

Many decades later Vejvoda returned to the reasons why he reported to the Czechoslovak army and subsequently to the French officers' school: in Spain he discovered how important military knowledge was and how far idealistic volunteers lacked it. Thus, to be better prepared for future battles for social justice, he decided to obtain as much military experience as possible elsewhere, even with a 'bourgeois' or even 'imperialist' army:

> I didn't know what awaited me in Yugoslavia, but I thought that there would be times when war experience would be necessary and I saw how much the anti-fascists in Spain lacked military expertise. For this reason I voluntarily applied to the French artillery cadet school.[40]

After the Axis attack on Yugoslavia in April 1941, thanks to his military experiences in the Spanish, Czechoslovak and French armies as well as his ideological firmness, Vejvoda was steadily promoted to high positions in Tito's army propaganda apparatus. After the war he became one of the most influential Yugoslav diplomats, serving in Brazil, Czechoslovakia, Britain, Italy and France.

Czechoslovak Interbrigadists, on the other hand, were less fortunate with their attempt to transfer their guerrilla warfare knowledge to the home resistance networks. Alois Samec, one of the most experienced *guerrilleros* from Spain, was summoned home from occupied France with other Interbrigadists in 1941 to help with organising resistance networks there. He immediately became involved in the underground activities, but serious forms of guerrilla struggle in Bohemia did not develop until the end of 1944. By then most of the Interbrigadists were in prison or concentration camps or had been executed. Alois Samec was caught by the Gestapo in 1942 and, spending the rest of the war in German prisons, was not able to deploy his exceptional skills.[41]

Many foreign soldiers were evacuated or fled on their own to Britain after the French defeat. Among them, after their famous battles in Narvik and France, were soldiers of the 13th Foreign Legion Half Brigade. They were now confronted by another choice: whether to be repatriated to France, which had sued for an armistice, or to continue the fight under the flag of the just emerging Free French movement of General de Gaulle. Some Spaniards, exhausted by war or disgusted by the iron drill of the Legion, but simultaneously scared to be delivered to Franco or the Germans, rejected both options and mutinied.[42] Similarly, 160 Interbrigadists from the former Czechoslovak army evacuated from France, followed the instructions of the Comintern to disrupt the 'bourgeois' Czechoslovak army and, despite the critical stage of war, triggered a mutiny as well.[43] Beside communists and their sympathisers, Jews and German- or Hungarian-speaking soldiers were most numerous. They objected to the drill and rigid discipline and were fired by the clash of tense nationalisms escalating with the onset of national catastrophes. They felt excluded from the Czechoslovak national community because of their 'otherness', whether racial, national, linguistic or political.[44]

That said, the majority of mutineers and other dissatisfied soldiers were still willing to fight fascism and, shortly afterwards, joined the British army or Free French. According to their contemporary letters and reports they found a greater degree of tolerance and a more hospitable environment in the British army. While Polish, German and Czechoslovak Jews as well as national minorities were received as 'our suspicious co-citizens' in their motherlands, the British (and French) considered them 'just' foreign volunteers. This allowed many to 'turn the page' and start their lives in an environment free from earlier antipathies and prejudices. Some of them even managed to achieve remarkable military careers.

One of these was Ferdinand Otto Miksche, a fighter with a transnational trajectory and multiple identities. He was born in Troppau in Silesia in 1905 into the multilingual environment of a German-Hungarian military family, which was accustomed to moving around the Austro-Hungarian Empire for the demands of service. After the breakup of the empire in 1918, Troppau was incorporated into Czechoslovakia and thus Miksche became one of its citizens. Despite this and following the family tradition, he went to study at the well-known Ludovica Military Academy in Budapest. He did not finish his studies, because he was accused of spying for Czechoslovakia and arrested. Exchanged for a Hungarian spy, he returned to Czechoslovakia, where he joined the artillery branch of the army. He was disappointed not to be given an officer's rank and left the Czechoslovak army after three years in 1936 to go to Spain. For this he was demoted and accused of desertion. In Spain he joined the International Brigades, falsely declaring himself a lieutenant. Appointed an instructor and commander of an artillery battalion, he achieved considerable successes and was steadily promoted to major. However, having punished two officers, who happened to be communists, for drunkenness and insubordination, he came into conflict with the communist apparatus, and was discharged from his command and sent on another mission. Escaping to France in February 1939, he reconnected with the Czechoslovak military authorities in exile. Since only Czechoslovak military ranks were recognised by the exile army, and not his Spanish rank of major, he embroidered the facts again, declaring that he was a former Czechoslovak lieutenant. Once again he was let down: an artillery battalion commander in Spain, he was now charged with an ordinary function several ranks lower.

Doubts about his officer rank also emerged after evacuation to Britain in June 1940. He now left the Czechoslovak army for a second time and joined the Free French, a force that was only just being formed and that suffered from a lack of officers. There he was warmly accepted, and he gradually worked his way up to an important function within the Operational Department of the Free French general staff. Such an illustrious career was largely explained by his growing reputation as a military writer and theorist. His first book, *Blitzkrieg*, published in 1941, caused a real sensation, while his second book, *Paratroops* (1943), was similarly remarkable. The latter became the subject of a scandal and an investigation for possible espionage. At the beginning of 1944 intelligence officers were astonished to find out that Miksche's theoretical plan of a combined assault on the continent was in detail identical to the Overlord plan which was just being prepared, especially in the area of the Cotentin peninsula. Whether the architects of the largest amphibious landing operation in the history were inspired by Miksche, and if so to what extent, remains a valid question to this day.[45]

Following a transnational life-path from birth, Miksche found that his several attempts to incorporate himself into a particular national body met only limited success, mainly because of his excessive self-confidence and desire for recognition. Most of time he oscillated between several personal identities, according to the situation. Similarly, his ideological statements changed from left to right several times. His publishing success was explained undoubtedly by his talent but also by his transnational experience and ability to exaggerate his previous military career.

Irregulars in regular armies: Churchill's aliens and Donovan's communists

It is true that within the rigid, centralised and unified mainstream of the regular armies, preparing masses of soldiers for conventional front-line battles, there was little interest in examining and utilising the unconventional experience of transnational fighters. A different situation nevertheless obtained in the various special services, branches of the army that oscillated on the border between conventional and unconventional, irregular warfare. In these branches, those skills neglected by conventional army officers, such as experience of foreign environments, an understanding of working with international networks and language skills, were warmly welcomed.

Some units composed of transnational volunteers were deliberately set up by Allied armies. Among them were the British commandos formed after 1940 at the express request of Winston Churchill. In the summer of 1942 they were reinforced by a new unit which would amalgamate volunteers of the occupied nations, the 10th (Inter-Allied) Commando, in which French, Dutch, Belgian, Norwegian, Polish and Yugoslavian troops were included. One of the first groups, the 3rd 'Miscellaneous' Troop, was set up in July 1942 mainly from German, Austrian and Jewish anti-fascists.[46] The entire troop spoke German, with the purpose of accompanying shock troops, assisting with interrogation, searching for secret documents and facilitating penetration into the enemy lines. They were present in many actions such as Overlord, Market Garden or the amphibious attack of Walcheren Island (Operation Infatuate). The latter was a truly transnational action with Norwegian, Belgian, Dutch, two French and the 3rd 'Miscellaneous' Troop combined with British commandos under overall British command.[47]

The advance party of the new transnational commando was very modest to begin with. Only seven or eight privates came on the first day to the training centre. Most of them were bilingual Sudeten-German Czechoslovaks of a multinational German-Jewish-Czechoslovak identity. One of these was Jan Theilinger, a Czechoslovak citizen and former Interbrigadist in Spain who was released from Gurs internment camp in January 1940 to join the Czechoslovak army. After evacuation to Britain in June 1940 he joined the mutiny in which more than five hundred soldiers refused to obey the orders of 'bourgeois' officers and were interned by the British.[48] Since, however, the majority of mutineers were keen to fight the Nazis, he responded to the British offer to enlist in the British army. He served in the Pioneer Corps and volunteered for the commando in 1942. Like most other soldiers from the occupied countries, he invented a false

British identity, using the alias 'John Robert Taylor' for security reasons in case of captivity. He decided to stay in Britain after the war, keeping his alias and receiving British citizenship in 1946.[49] Sudeten-German by origin, Czechoslovak by his citizenship, leftist and Interbrigadist, he became British by choice and by all accounts found a home.

The US army also found a place for fighters with a transnational background. When the USA entered the war, it looked for individuals who would be able to operate behind enemy lines in Europe. The American OSS, the younger sibling of the British SOE, set up by 'Wild Bill' Donovan in June 1942, looked to those of recent immigrant origin from Central and Eastern Europe. These were often Jewish and were sometimes former Interbrigadists who had served with the Abraham Lincoln Brigade in Spain. How well they integrated in the postwar USA is more difficult to say.[50]

Irving Goff was born in Brooklyn in 1911 to a Jewish family from Odessa which had recently migrated to the USA. He was a professional acrobat when he met Milton Wolff, another working-class Brooklyn youth whose Jewish family had come from Lithuania and Hungary. Wolff had joined the Young Communists and persuaded Goff to volunteer with him for the Lincoln Brigade, arriving in Spain early in 1937. Wolff was promoted captain of the George Washington machine-gun company, which he commanded at the Battle of the Ebro. Instructed by Soviets and guided by Spaniards, Goff was involved in sabotage behind enemy lines. 'I'm a kid from Brooklyn. I was hardly ever in a mountain', he later told the journalist and oral historian Studs Terkel, 'what do I know about guerrilla warfare? I learned everything in Spain.'[51]

The Lincoln Brigade was repatriated in 1938, and its fighters were under suspicion as communists. After Germany invaded the Soviet Union in 1941 they were keen to fight again and were sought out by the nascent OSS. Their communism was still an issue, and they were not made officers. Goff later complained, 'Everyone who graduated from the OSS school came out full lieutenants, captains, majors. All the Lincoln guys came out enlisted men. They considered us all communists. Because of Spain, we knew ten times more than any of the other guys', he proudly boasted.[52]

OSS agents were landed in North Africa after Operation Torch. Their first task was to train former Spanish fighters released from Vichy's camps, with a view to a guerrilla intervention from Morocco in Franco's Spain that went badly wrong.[53] Goff's main contribution, however, came after the Allied landings in Italy, when OSS set up its base in Naples. Goff was authorised to use his former connections in the International Brigades as a lead to the PCI in the city with a view to recruiting agents who would provide military and political intelligence from behind German lines. 'In

Naples', recalled Goff, 'the Communist Party had 150,000 members. Every sector of the front was commanded by a guy who fought with the Garibaldi [Brigade] in Spain. The guy who captured Mussolini and strung him up by the feet was Muscatelli. He fought in Spain.'[54]

As the Soviet Union advanced, however, the US authorities became concerned that the PCI would use the intelligence it received to facilitate a seizure of power. Donovan told Goff to 'make sure the Communist Party doesn't come out ahead'. 'I said, "That's valid. They're out to win the war, we're out to win the war. I'll do the best I can to win the war". He said "fine", and left.'[55] Donovan was nevertheless hauled before the US Congress in March 1945 to meet accusations that his agents were communists. As soon as Germany surrendered, he was obliged to recall Goff, Wolff and the other the Lincoln veterans who were serving with OSS, rather than sending them to China to fight the Japanese.[56] As so often, the ideological and political threat posed by fighters with transnational experiences worked against the military benefits they might offer.

From irregular to regular forces: the CFA and 'La Nueve'

Just as the French, Czechoslovak and Polish armies had drawn on international fighters interned in French camps in 1939–40, so in 1942–43 the Allied armies based in North Africa after Operation Torch drew on the international fighters interned in Vichy's camps in the Algerian Sahara. They progressed from irregular to regular combat, although they were not welcome in the French Army of Africa, the jewel in Vichy's crown, but incorporated into a special auxiliary force.

The Allied landings and the defeat of Vichy forces in North Africa did not give rise straight away to the liberation of these camps.[57] General Giraud, who exercised military and political power in French North Africa in 1943, kept intact Vichy's repressive and exclusionary system, including the removal of citizenship from Algeria's Jews, who made up a fifth of the European population. Early in 1943 Western journalists visited the camps and were horrified by the sight of thousands of Spaniards, Poles, Jews and other internees living in terrible conditions. A few weeks later, in response to the reports they published in the press and to US government pressure, the French authorities began a programme of releasing prisoners.[58]

These internees were not eligible for the French Army of Africa, which was restricted to French nationals and to soldiers drawn from the indigenous Muslim population of Algeria, who were subjects but not citizens.[59] Instead, they were incorporated in the CFA, officially set up on 25 November 1942 and commanded by the Breton General Montsabert.[60] The CFA was based on six light battalions in which, as far as possible, combined volunteers into homogeneous units according to their origin. Subsequently, the CFA was restructured into a light brigade composed of two infantry regiments of three battalions each. The first battalion was composed of a large number of former French internees and local French settlers in Algeria. The second, fourth and sixth battalions drew on indigenous Muslims, especially North African youths, training in Taza (Morocco). The two remaining battalions were made up of foreigners – Spaniards in the third and Yugoslavs from French North African camps or Italian POW camps – based at Ain Karma (Morocco).[61]

Recruitment campaigns for the CFA began in February 1943. These were headed by Lieutenant Zalif Tahar, an indigenous Muslim soldier born in Constantine, Second Lieutenant Drago Knežević and Joseph Putz, a Belgian-born French infantryman who had been gassed in the Great War and volunteered for the International Brigades, becoming a lieutenant colonel in the Spanish army.[62] Putz was assisted by Miguel Buiza, a Spanish naval navy officer, best known for being the commander of the Spanish republican navy during the Spanish Civil War, and by Miguel Campos, a Spanish escapee from the Francoist 180th Workers' Battalion deployed in Spanish Morocco who joined the CFA in Oran at the end of 1942.[63] Recruitment campaigns drew not only on the camps but also on the Foreign Legion, which included many Spaniards, and on the labour battalions that Vichy had used to build the Trans-Saharan Railway.

One of these recruits was Harry Bober, a Dutch-Jewish journalist born in Frankfurt in 1912.[64] Fleeing Nazism, he arrived in France in 1939 and joined the Foreign Legion, but after the armistice he was sent to Morocco and incorporated into one of the labour companies. After the Allied landing, he fled the labour camp and reached Casablanca, where he enlisted with the CFA.[65] Another recruit was a German, Arrue, who deserted from the Legion and spoke warmly of the way in which former Spanish fighters were now treated by their own commanders:

> When the war [in Tunisia] ended, many of the survivors deserted the Legion and joined the CFA ... That's when I met Campos, a brave man from the Canaries, a very good person, who took the greatest care of all the Spaniards in the corps. He looked out for them and convinced them to desert, taking with him whole trucks of men to enlist them in de Gaulle's Free French forces.[66]

In the Allied offensive on Tunis the CFA was deployed not with the French army but first with the 1st British Army, then with the 9th US Infantry Division. In early July 1943 this extraordinary international corps was dissolved. Its soldiers were given the choice of joining the French Army of Africa under Giraud, especially the 3rd Algerian Infantry Division, or the Free French of de Gaulle, who had arrived in Algiers on 30 May

1943 to become co-president with Giraud of the French Committee of National Liberation. Those who choose to join de Gaulle followed Putz to the Régiment de Marche du Tchad (Chad Infantry Regiment), where he was appointed commander of the 3rd Battalion.[67] Of its companies, the 9th had the largest proportion of Spaniards, with 90 per cent. One of the fighters, Antonio Van Baumberghen, a Spanish republican officer who had been interned in Saint-Cyprien in 1939, reached Oran in 1940 and served in the 3rd Battalion in Bouïra district of Algeria, recalled how little enthusiasm was elicited by the visit of one of Giraud's representatives:

> The visiting colonel ... spared no words to praise the combativeness of the Spaniards and to flatter them, lamenting how poorly dressed we were and the scarcity of modern material in our unit ..., promising us the earth. In the afternoon, our comrades were taken to a field near the Bouïra women's prison where a vote was taken. ... The result could not have been more catastrophic for Giraud ... 5 per cent went with the American-friendly general, most of them French officers. Ninety-five per cent remained in the CFA with Putz and merged with Leclerc' s forces, setting up the 2nd Armoured Division.[68]

There were many reasons why the Spanish fighters preferred to join de Gaulle rather than Giraud. These included anti-fascist ideology, a desire to seek revenge against the Germans, opposition to Vichy, which had kept them in brutal camps and labour battalions, and a repressive regime that was continued for far too long by Giraud, but also the affinity with de Gaulle and the Free France cause which, they hoped, would ultimately lead to the liberation of Spain.[69] As the former combatant in Spain, refugee in France and former soldier in the French Foreign Legion and the CFA Manuel Fernández pointed out:

> I heard about the Leclerc Column and the Free French troops coming from Libya after the Tunis campaign. Immediately I deserted [from CFA] and joined them. At that time, it was not Colonel Leclerc who encouraged me to enlist because I did not really know him. It was General de Gaulle. For me de Gaulle was the man who had not surrendered to the Germans and represented freedom.[70]

Irregular soldiers who had fought in Spain and suffered in camps under the burning sun now joined the 2nd Armoured Division of General Leclerc, which was part of a modern regular army funded and equipped by the Americans. Manuel Fernández recalled that 'In Spain and Tunisia we had no weapons, we fought with old rifles, but now, with American supplies, I knew that we could face [the Germans] without fear. Moreover, we all thought that with that material, we could cross the Pyrenees to carry on the fight against Franco once the war was over in Europe.'[71]

Paradoxically, the recruitment of Spanish republicans into the 2nd Armoured Division entailed the exclusion of black African troops who had fought their way with Leclerc from Cameroon and Chad. This process, clumsily known as *blanchiment,* was justified by a number of reasons. One was the mechanisation of the division with the use of tanks which African soldiers were claimed not to be able to operate. Another was a fear that, as the war moved into Europe, colonial hierarchies might be overtuned by armed black troops. A third was that the division that was going to spearhead the liberation of France should look as 'national' or 'European' as possible. On 2 August 1943 General Leclerc asked de Gaulle for 'white reinforcements to replace black soldiers who are unsuited to war in Europe'.[72] This process was supported and indeed reinforced by the intervention of the American military authorities. In January 1944 Eisenhower's chief of staff, Major General Walter Bedell Smith, wrote in a confidential memorandum that 'the Second Armoured Division, with only one fourth native personnel, is the only French division operationally available that could be made one hundred percent white'. Given the fact that the British army did not segregate its forces, a strong objection was expected from the British military chiefs. However, against all odds, the British general Frederick Morgan expressed a similar view to the Allied Supreme Command on *blanchiment*: 'It is unfortunate that the only French formation that is 100% white is an armoured division in Morocco. ... Every other French division is only about 40% white.'[73] This process was commented upon by Spanish republicans who were incorporated in the place of the African troops. According to Daniel Hernandez, '[When the 2nd Armoured Division was formed] the new forces that joined the Free French replaced the black soldiers of the Régiment de Marche du Tchad. The indigenous soldiers were left aside – on orders from above – having fought for three years with General Leclerc.'[74] Thus Spaniards who had previously been in the CFA and the French Foreign Legion, and before that in Vichy's African camps, were a majority in the famous 'La Nueve', the 9th Company of the Régiment de Marche du Tchad, a key unit of the 2nd Armoured Division, who were the first regular soldiers to enter Paris on 24 August 1944.

Conclusion

Volunteers with transnational trajectories and international ideas, whether they were former Spanish soldiers, German and Italian anti-fascist political exiles or Jews fleeing persecution and worse, spent longer or shorter times serving in various regular armies. For many, pulling on a foreign uniform was the only chance to escape the misery of the internment camps.

Thus a former Interbrigadist who had fought for anti-fascist ideals on the fronts of Spanish Civil War could find himself in the strict, militaristic, imperialist and mercenary formation such as the French Foreign Legion. Others joined special volunteer regiments, auxiliary labour companies or first-line field units of this or that army.

These volunteers brought to regular armies their remarkable previous battle experiences and knowledge of such fighting techniques as guerrilla warfare. However, they were often seen as 'suspicious' for political or ideological reasons, and their military expertise was left undervalued and neglected by the regular professional officers. This was often symbolised by the fact that their rank in irregular armies was not recognised in regular units. Exceptions were rare and usually confined to the various special services which actually sought those skills and experiences, but even then prejudices such as anti-communism and anti-Semitism were not absent.

Some former transnational fighters were able to integrate in these national units, embracing new national identities. Others, demotivated by the heightened nationalism, frequent anti-Semitism and harsh military drill, often left the regular armies to find more attractive options in the continuation of their fight against fascism. They joined resistance movements in their homelands or elsewhere in occupied Europe. The skills and training learned in regular armies significantly broadened their previous knowledge. This might be of paramount importance in resistance movements that often lacked any military experiences at all.

During the course of the war, some transnational fighters moved several times from the regular armies to the irregular forms of fighting in the resistance and back. They became the bearers and intermediaries of a transfer of fighting techniques between national armies as well as between those armies and the resistance movements. This gradually improved and developed their individual and collective battle knowledge and a transnational experience. Unfortunately, the national remobilisation that prevailed in almost every country after the war and the creation of a national 'image of the resistance' led to the marginalisation both in practice and in memory of the contribution of foreigners and transnational volunteers in regular national armies.

5

Inherently transnational: escape lines

Megan Koreman, Diego Gaspar Celaya and Lennert Savenije

Every time Hitler and his subordinates made a move towards implementing the Nazi New Order, whether it was branding an entire group of people as undesirable or conquering another country, some individuals slipped into the clandestine world of fugitives living underground. The occupation closed off political migration, meaning that anyone who wanted to escape Nazi persecution during the war had to either hide or steal out of occupied territory. Such fugitives needed to cross borders illegally, obtain false documents and purchase food, lodging and local currency on the black market. Some made it to safety on their own, but many more relied on the assistance offered by resisters belonging to escape lines, resistance networks created to rescue men, women and children from the Nazis.

No matter where or when they operated, escape lines always had both a destination and a goal. Lines with the same destination, for example Spain, might have had very different goals, ranging from taking Jews and other civilians out of the Nazis' reach, to returning Allied service men to their bases so they could defeat the Third Reich and end the war, or even to fomenting insurrection in Spain. Escape lines ran in all directions across or out of Nazi-occupied Europe, but the specific destination of each one depended on the people who asked for help and those who offered it. It would make sense to take a Jewish family to Switzerland where they could live as refugees. It made less sense to take an Allied aviator there, because he would be landlocked and unable to return to his base.

Some escape lines grew from grassroots initiatives to help particular refugees. Others were organised through the Allied forces or embassies in order to get particular people – most often military personnel – out of occupied territory. Some helpers organised their escape lines in service to a larger ambition such as a Jewish homeland or democracy in Spain.

Others had no agenda beyond helping the persecuted, whoever they were. In the context of the time, of course, that in itself was a highly political, anti-Nazi agenda. Such differences meant little to the German authorities. They punished the men and women of all ages whom they caught helping others to escape as they treated all other political prisoners, with torture, deportation to the concentration camps and in some cases execution.

The experience of helping strangers to escape from the Nazis had a transformative effect on the men and women involved. The nature of escape lines meant that people from different socio-economic levels within the same community worked together as well as with men and women from other nations. It also meant that those same people came into contact with fugitives who came from other nations and other classes.

An escape line was a complicated, illegal organisation with many needs. One such need was hiding places, which usually required a property owner. Another was false documents, which required civil servants to provide information and forms and people with the skills and willingness to become forgers. Escape lines also needed a great deal of money, some of which was stolen and some of which was exchanged and transferred in dubiously creative ways. Such special financial arrangements required bankers, business owners and other affluent people. Escape lines needed couriers to make arrangements, a task often given to young women by resistance groups according to the hopeful theory that the Germans were not as suspicious of women as of men. Finally, escape lines needed guides who were willing to leave their homes and travel sometimes long distances to escort dangerous fugitives to their destinations. Crossing from the Netherlands to Belgium could mean a twenty-minute stroll around the back of a customs post, but crossing from France to Spain could easily mean trekking over mountains in the dark and snow for two or more nights. The job of guide was best done by people without regular jobs or with jobs that required travel, such as students or salesmen.

Some of the helpers were themselves on the run, such as Spanish republicans guiding fugitives across the Pyrenees or Jews hiding in plain sight by smuggling other Jews into Switzerland. But the majority of men and women in escape lines remained in their pre-war homes and social circles. After all, a clerk at city hall lost access to necessary information and the forms and stamps needed to forge documents if they left their job. Most helpers were respectable members of their communities who became law-breakers as soon as they offered a meal to a fugitive stranger. They adjusted to breaking the law, lying, hiding things, living with anxiety and bluffing their way past armed guards for the sake of rescuing others. Resisters of all sorts experienced this identity shift from upstanding, or at least law-abiding, citizen to outlaw resister. The men and women who resisted by rescuing others in escape lines also experienced a transnational shift in their identities.

The everyday work of an escape line demanded constant transnational exchange. Taking fugitives across borders, in some cases several borders, required dealing in multiple languages, currencies and occupation regulations. It also brought people of many nations into contact in intense situations, including fugitives who may have come from across Europe or even, in the case of military evaders, from across the globe.

On a more individual level, the transnational experience of involvement with escape lines gave men and women a certain disregard for the prerogatives of the nation-state. They crossed borders illegally, exchanged and transferred money in direct contravention of the law, falsified their identities, regularly lied to the authorities and broke any number of lesser rules on a regular basis. Escape lines also encouraged men and women to re-imagine the map of Europe from a collection of sovereign states into a dichotomy of occupied/unoccupied territory. More profoundly, the category of 'other' broke down in the escape lines as the common task and its inherent danger levelled helpers and fugitives into a common status as human beings, without any national distinction between one and another. In the process of rescuing men, women and children from the power of a political system that glorified the nation in the particularly vicious way of the Nazis, escape lines not only flaunted the power of nation-states but broke down the nation's power to categorise and control individuals' imaginations and thoughts.

Escape lines all shared the common goal of getting people to safety, but the details of where, how, who and why differed from one network to the next. Escape lines responded to the particular circumstances of a particular place at a particular time in the war. In Western Europe, for example, there were few Allied airmen to rescue early in the war and, unfortunately, many fewer Jews to rescue late in the war. An escape line that responded to the needs of forced labourers would not exist until there were forced labourers who needed to escape.

Some escape lines had a patriotic aspect. For example, resistance groups in Czechoslovakia – initially mainly the central military group Obrana Národa (Defence of the Nation) – created a number of lines which took willing patriots out of the occupied homeland so that they could serve with the government or army-in-exile. These Czechoslovak lines operated from 1939 to 1941, relying on the interconnection of domestic resistance networks, military intelligence officers abroad and, where possible, diplomats in Czechoslovakian consulates and embassies.[1]

Even before the outbreak of the war, such lines operated to Poland with the help of smugglers and railway workers. Thus Ludvík Svoboda, then a lieutenant colonel and later a general and a Czechoslovak president, escaped from his occupied homeland hidden in a brakeman's cab.[2] After the defeat of Poland, which closed off the Baltic, the so-called Balkan Route was used until April 1941 (and sporadically thereafter), leading from occupied Bohemia via Slovakia and Hungary to Yugoslavia, and from there further by sea to France, either directly or through the French Mandate of Syria-Lebanon. From 9 September 1939 to 24 June 1940, a total of seventy-seven transports with 2,058 persons were dispatched from Belgrade to Beirut and on to France, with several dozen others making their way directly to France. After the defeat of France, another five hundred volunteers used this line to join the Czechoslovak unit in the Middle East.[3]

These lines helped approximately five thousand professional officers, highly trained airmen and other patriots keen to continue the fight, including some Jews, to escape from the German occupation of their homelands. They formed the nucleus of all Czechoslovak military units wherever they were organised, in Poland, France, Great Britain, the Middle East or the Soviet Union.[4]

Lines that specialised in helping volunteers or POWs were joined over time by lines that helped downed Allied aviators to evade capture. Some of these lines, such as the Burgundy and Shelbourne lines, were run by American or British secret agents who parachuted into Shelburn occupied territory to organise local men and women into a network. In other cases, civilians gathered these men up when they crashed and escorted them to safety despite the German threat to execute all men and deport all women in any family found to be aiding downed Allied airmen.[5]

The members of some other escape lines shared a common political vision. For example, Polish communists created a 'German channel' line that, unusually, went from France to Poland to take Poles who had fought in the International Brigades and posed as volunteers to work in German factories from Paris to Warsaw so that they could organise the communist resistance in Poland. Between August 1942 and April 1943 this unnamed line took some forty-five people into Poland.[6]

There were also escape lines run by Jews from many nations, who worked together to rescue other Jews and contribute to the clandestine immigration to Palestine known as Aliyah Bet. For instance, the Danube line got 33,000 Jews out of Central and East-Central Europe between 1938 and 1944. In France, about 150 Jews from across Europe worked together under the leadership of Abraham Polonski, born in Białystock in 1903, in the Armée Juive and with funding from the American Joint Distribution Committee from the winter of 1941 to get hundreds of young Jews out of occupied France towards Spain and North Africa.[7]

There were also a few massive rescue operations across international borders that served as temporary escape lines. The famous Danish campaign to evacuate almost the entire Jewish population of Denmark to Sweden in 1943 is not the only example of such a massive illegal rescue mission.[8] A much less famous mass rescue took place on the Swiss border in September and October 1944. This one relied on the pre-war connections on both sides of the border in the Ticino region of Switzerland and northern Italy. Swiss and Italian socialists relied on those long-established sympathies and relationships to organise the illegal transfer of over a thousand wounded partisans and two thousand malnourished children from the Partisan Republic of Ossola in northern Italy to Switzerland, where they would be safe from Nazi retribution.[9]

In addition to the escape lines that took fugitives between occupied and unoccupied lands, there were other smaller, more local escape lines that operated over national borders within occupied Europe. These tended to be the work of local people who lived on both sides of a border and specialised in helping people over that particular border. To give just one example, the Smit–van der Heijden, group led by a Marechausee (member of the Dutch military police) and a schoolteacher, began helping Allied soldiers from the Netherlands into Belgium in the spring of 1940. As time went on the group helped other sorts of fugitives, including Dutch Jews, until arrests stopped them in late 1943.[10]

Such local escape lines often made unlikely new alliances within the local community and a reinvention of roles. José Gistau, known as Barranco, a Spaniard who moved to France in 1927, was a *paquetero* or smuggler of cattle and consumer goods between France and Spain. During the Spanish Civil War, he first smuggled supplies from France into Spain and then helped Spanish refugees get to France. As he later recalled, 'a lot of leftists, especially teachers, worked together; all the material that arrived here came across on mule back. One night we went through the border village of Bielsa with a hundred mules. We had everything, weapons, ammunition, food, blankets.'[11] During the Second World War Barranco used these same skills and knowledge of the mountains as a *passeur* or guide for fugitives. He worked with communists and property owners in a resistance network that used the passes of Bielsa, Puerto Viejo and Barrosa. When the Germans found their base, they massacred most of his colleagues. Barranco, however, continued his activities, first helping *maquisards* across the border and then, after the war, resuming his trade as a smuggler.[12] He was now, however, also a resister, and thus among the local community's elite.

Barranco's experience in the Pyrenees illustrates how transnational experience of escape lines had a transformative effect on borderland communities as well as on individuals. Not only did individuals from both nations on either side of the border work together in a common illegal goal of smuggling strangers to safety, but they worked with people across social, economic and political lines. Catholic university students like Simone Calmels, who worked with Dutch-Paris in Toulouse, were unlikely to have associated with people like Barranco before the war. Their wartime association would have continued after the war, albeit in different ways.

Barranco, however, was one man in one place. Escape lines ran across and through Europe in every direction, acting as vectors of transnational experience and transformation. This chapter will explore in more depth how the examples of the Pyrenees borderlands, the Pat O'Leary line, the Dutch-Paris line and the Außenministerium line illustrate ways in which escape lines transcended the nation-state in the actions and the thoughts of their participants.

The Pyrenean borderlands

The Pyrenean mountains that divide France from Spain provided one of the busiest 'theatres of escape' in Western Europe between 1936 and 1948. During the Spanish Civil War more than a half a million Spanish civilian and military refugees crossed the mountains to seek asylum in France.[13] During the Second World War some 80,000 men and women from all nations who were fleeing the political, racial and sexual persecution launched by the Nazi regime and its collaborators crossed into Spain using 200 or so crossing points hidden in the mountains.[14] At that time the Spanish army controlled movement on the south side of the mountain range while the Vichy police and German special border forces and Sicherheitspolizei (security police) monitored the north face. At the same time that an active collaboration among German, Spanish and Vichy security forces developed, some members of these same security forces chose to work together in resistance by helping refugees escape to Spain.[15] Sometimes they did so by simply turning a blind eye or giving directions. For example, a young Polish Jew reached the French–Spanish border in the mountains thanks to a French guide who accompanied him from Gavás to the border under the Midi d'Osseau peak and was then helped by a Spanish guard named Salvador Garcia.[16]

The International Railway Station at Canfranc served as one of the most important spaces in which German, French and Spanish forces coexisted with those who were trying to run away from them, to fight against them or to help others to reach the Allies in England or North Africa or a safe haven in South America.[17] Antonio Galtier was a Spanish officer working at the Spanish border post in the mountain village of Canfranc who witnessed hundreds of escapees who tried to get to Spain through the International Railway Station there. Fifty years later, in an interview about his activities during the Second World War, Galtier remembered how the Germans operated in the passenger lounge on the French side, reviewing 'passports, ages, professions, origins and individual and family destinations. It was impressive to see people who had crossed half of Europe, and saw themselves almost free in Spain ... Many were arrested; others just jumped off the train and ran down the tracks, fleeing from the Germans.'[18] According to the personal records of the French resister Honoré Baradat, about 1,400 people escaped via the Portalet pass and Canfranc between 1942 and August 1944.[19]

The pivotal man for escapes through Canfranc was the French customs chief Albert Le Lay. After fighting in the French army as a very young man during the First World War, Le Lay joined the customs service. He was posted in Hendaye, Brest and Paris before being sent to Canfranc when the international station reopened in 1940. Although the Free French combat unit for which he volunteered rejected him, Le Lay made contact with André Manuel, alias Pallas, leader of the Information Section of the Free French Intelligence Service (later the Bureau Central de Renseignements et d'Action). Manuel ordered Le Lay to remain in Canfranc in order to facilitate escapes through the central Pyrenees.[20]

Like other French officials who held key posts along the borders, Le Lay ended up working for several resistance networks that needed an agent with access to information in a pivotal place. In early 1941 he joined PIC, an information network based in Pau and run by a French dentist named Roche. He joined another network, Mithridate, in December 1941. Mithridate was founded in June 1940 by Pierre Herbinger at the request of MI-6 (the British Secret Service) and then assigned to the French Bureau Central de Renseignements et d'Action in January 1942. It numbered more than 1,600 Allied transnational agents distributed throughout Belgium, Italy and France. Although Le Lay's most important service was to help hundreds of Allied secret agents, pilots and fugitives cross out of occupied Europe, he also smuggled supplies.[21] For example, the first radio set that allowed the local resistance to communicate with London travelled north from Canfranc, Spain, towards Oloron-Sainte-Marie, France, in a suitcase supervised by Le Lay.[22]

One fugitive to successfully cross through Canfranc was the Polish-born Jewish resister Henri Dorfsman, who migrated to Paris with his family in the mid-1930s. Naturalised French in 1938, he enlisted in the French army the same year and was captured at Dunkirk in June 1940. He escaped from a POW camp in France, reached the Free Zone and joined the Armistice Army being deployed in Morocco. He left that post because Vichy's anti-Semitic laws stopped Jews being officers or non-commissioned officers in the Armistice Army. Returning to France, he then crossed into Spain via Canfranc in July 1941. After almost two years in the Spanish internment camp at Miranda de Ebro, he reached London and enlisted in de Gaulle's Free French forces in June 1943.[23]

As Dorfsman's case illustrates, the transnational journeys of many fugitives did not end when they escaped occupied territory. Many crossed the Pyrenees only to be immediately detained in Spanish prisons and camps until their diplomatic representatives could arrange their release. Between February 1943 and December 1944 the French Red Cross organised at least thirty-five convoys of transnational resisters who left the Iberian peninsula from Lisbon, Algeciras and Malaga. Vichy's ecclesiastical attaché, who had excellent connections in the Francoist establishment, coordinated one such expedition in late December 1943. It took 1,200 transnational escapees who had been interned in Spanish prisons and camps and most of whom were French, to French North Africa.[24]

Although escape lines in France stopped operating with the Liberation in the summer of 1944, it took some time for the Pyrenees to return to a peaceful footing.[25] Certainly the clandestine movement of people across the mountains did not end with the Second World War. In particular, Spanish republicans who had fought with the French Resistance during the war did not demobilise. Counting on the complicity of new, Liberation-era local authorities who had been their comrades in battle, guerrillas belonging to the Union Nacional Española (Spanish National Union) managed to gather a significant number of troops in the Pyrenees and invaded Spain on 19 October 1944. Led by the PCE, this operation, known as the Reconquista de España, intended to liberate a zone from Francoist control and use it as a base for national insurrection. More than 3,000 guerrillas crossed the Pyrenees and disbursed in Spain, especially in the Aran Valley. They failed as a result of poor communication, a rapid reaction by Franco's forces and a lack of enthusiasm for the operation on the part of the local population.[26]

Defeated, the Spanish guerrillas withdrew from the valley to reorganise their opposition to Franco. As part of this, they set up clandestine routes into and out of Spain. One of the guides on this postwar line was the Spanish anarchist and resister Martin Arnal Mur. As a Spanish republican refugee in France in 1939, Arnal Mur worked in a Compagnie de Travailleurs Étrangers unit until July 1940. Making his way to Toulouse, he found a job and joined the 11th Group of the 7th Brigade of Spanish Guerrillas attached to the Forces Françaises de l'Interieur (FFIs, French Forces of the Interior). After the Liberation of France, Arnal Mur joined the 186th Union Nacional Española Battalion, which operated on the

Spanish border, serving as a guide between October 1944 and March 1945. He worked in the Gistain and Bielsa valleys, between Saint Lary (Hautes-Pyrenées) and Bielsa (Aragon), a little village located twelve kilometres inside Spain.

As Arnal Mur remembered, the journey into Spain took about a week. They climbed on foot up the river from Saint Lary and camped one night on the French side of the border. The next day they reached Spain in about six hours. It took another three days to descend the Spanish slope to Ainsa. They never went down from Ainsa, where the Cinca River broadens. The guerrillas 'were the owners of the Cinca River going down, the Francoists going up'.[27] The politics might have changed, but the Pyrenees borderlands continued to be a stage of transnational activity and experience.

The Pat O'Leary line

As the gateway to Spain and therefore to all of the world outside occupied Europe, the Pyrenees attracted the attention of many long-distance escape lines, especially those helping Allied soldiers and aviators. One of the most important of these was the Pat O'Leary line. Specialising in the recovery, protection and escape of Allied soldiers and pilots in Western Europe, it organised about six hundred evasions through the Pyrenees, as well as various rescue and escape operations from a number of French camps and prisons. The line had several routes that ran through Holland, Belgium, Luxemburg and France to Spain and then onward to Portugal and Gibraltar, from where the men could leave for Britain and French North Africa.

An escaped British POW, Ian Garrow, began organising the line in Marseilles. After Garrow's arrest in June 1941, a Belgian resister named Albert Guérisse, whose codename was Pat O'Leary, assumed command of the line until his own arrest in March 1942. Leadership of the line then passed to a French woman, Françoise Dissard, who renamed the line Françoise.[28] The transnational character of the leadership accurately reflected the membership and experience of the line. Of the 475 agents and contributors of the line officially recognised by the French government, more than 89 per cent were French. But the rest came from more than ten other countries including Great Britain, Spain, Belgium, Italy, Switzerland, Poland, Greece, Australia, Germany and the Soviet Union. A group of Spaniards led by Francisco Ponzán, who were mostly anarchist refugees from the Spanish Civil War, played a key role as guides over the Pyrenees.[29]

A schoolteacher in civilian life, Ponzán specialised in information and sabotage missions during the Spanish Civil War. Like many Spanish republicans, he fled to France in 1939. There, Spanish immigrants who had lived in France since the 1920s helped him to get out of a French internment camp and find a job. But Ponzán had not given up the fight, nor had the other Spanish republicans whom he recruited into his group of resisters and guides.[30] As the Vichy intelligence agent Robert Terres, aka Lieutenant Tessier, said in his memoirs, they came 'within the most irreducible and most idealistic notions of anti-fascist refugees determined to continue the fight against Franco and ready to accept any help ... in the form of protection and money'.[31]

Terres himself worked for Vichy's counterespionage organisation, which maintained a certain distance from German and Italian control, at least until November 1942, and claimed to be playing a 'double game'.[32] According to Ponzán's personal activities log, his group of Spaniards worked with Vichy through Terres. This allowed them some room for manoeuvre, including several missions launched from a base in Toulouse to liberate anarchist militants from Francoist prisons in Spain in 1940 and 1941.[33] Having heard about these rescues, Ian Garrow recruited Ponzán and his compatriots for Pat O'Leary in the summer of 1941 through two French resisters as intermediaries. The Spaniards also worked with the Belgian Sabot line.

These many connections hint at the very complicated clandestine alliances and transnational experiences happening in the Pyrenees during the war. They also suggest how small the world of escape lines really was. Not many people knew the Pyrenees, or any border, well enough to guide fugitives across them and were willing to run the hazard and extreme risk of doing so. This scarcity of qualified people for key roles, such as *passeurs*, meant that people like Albert Le Lay in Canfranc often worked for more than one escape line, and often for Allied intelligence lines as well as escape lines.

Dutch-Paris

Like Pat O'Leary, the Dutch-Paris escape line also took Allied soldiers and aviators over the Pyrenees to Spain, but these military men represented only a small fraction of the fugitives helped by the line. Dutch-Paris began as a constellation of individual reactions to the deportation of Jews from the Netherlands in early 1942.[34] During that year, hundreds of Dutch Jews chose to attempt the illegal journey to Switzerland rather than report for removal to the east as ordered. Some of these fugitives made it to safety on their own, but many more ran into trouble along the way and asked for help.[35] Some of the people they asked for help in Brussels, Paris and Lyons responded by committing themselves to rescuing the refugees either by hiding them or getting them to Switzerland.

The escape line relied on a pre-existing network of Dutch business-people, diplomats and Reformed Church pastors. In Brussels the pastor of the Dutch Protestant church in the city, A. G. B. ten Kate, and two Dutch-Jewish businessmen, Maurice Bolle and Benno Nijkerk, organised an illegal welfare operation called the Comité that both hid Jews in and around the city and sent Jews and Dutch resisters to Switzerland and Spain.[36] In Paris the diplomat Herman Laatsman gathered together other Dutch expatriates such as the student Suzanna Hiltermann, the railway official Jean-Michael Caubo and Brother Rufus Tourné. Others such as the secretaries Catherine Okhuysen and Gabrielle Weidner, both the daughters of Dutch expatriates; the engineer Albert Starink, and the student Anna Neyssel also helped fugitives in Paris before joining Dutch-Paris. In Lyons, the future leader of Dutch-Paris, Jean Weidner, responded to a letter that a Dutch-Jewish business acquaintance wrote to him from a Vichy prison by smuggling the man and his wife into Switzerland.[37] Most of these expatriates had lived in their adopted country for years. They owned property or businesses there, sent their children to school there and had personal friends and acquaintances within the community.

All of these resisters recruited helpers from among their acquaintance. Jean Weidner, for example, built his original escape line between Lyons and Geneva with his French wife, Elisabeth Cartier, his young French secretary Raymonde Pillot, a Belgian Jew who had been arrested by Vichy police while carrying false Dutch papers named Edmond Chait, the French shopkeeper Marie Meunier and friends from his home village on the Franco-Swiss border who were French and Swiss. As the leader of Dutch-Paris he recruited people he thought were trustworthy and courageous enough for the job, whether that was a Dutch priest serving in a parish in Toulouse, Belgian or Dutch refugees who were willing to leave the safety of Geneva, a Swiss bookseller in Paris or a young French man hiding from the forced labour draft in his mother's cousin's restaurant near the Swiss border.[38]

In order to either hide the persecuted or smuggle them out of occupied territory, the men and women of Dutch-Paris had to find hiding places, obtain false documents, bargain for food and sometimes medical care on the black market and find safe routes over heavily guarded borders. They also had to find the money to pay for all of it. Many of the businessmen among them used their own money until it ran out. Then they found ways to raise money, exchange it and transfer it across strictly controlled borders without the authorities' knowledge. Even so, by late 1943 Weidner and his colleagues in southern France were low enough on funds to ask the Dutch government-in-exile for money. The ambassador in Bern offered to finance the rescue work if Weidner would expand his network all the way to the Netherlands and Spain. He agreed as long as he retained complete control over the line in occupied territory. He then offered a share of the money and a complete route to Switzerland and Spain to like-minded Dutch resisters such as ten Kate in Brussels and Laatsman in Paris if they linked their local groups to the expanding line.

By this time, autumn 1943, most Jews had been arrested or gone into hiding. New categories of fugitives had replaced them. The imposition of forced labour drafts in Western Europe in 1943 inspired young Dutchmen, Belgians and Frenchmen to go underground or even to get out of occupied Europe in order to volunteer with the Allies. Similarly, resisters whose identities had been disclosed in their home towns also asked for help. The increasing number of bombing raids over Germany also created an increasing number of downed Allied aviators who needed help to evade capture.

The complete Dutch-Paris escape line, running from the Netherlands to Switzerland and Spain, began operating in November 1943. Bowing to pressure from among his colleagues and requests from other resisters, Weidner authorised his colleagues to start taking downed Allied airmen to Spain in January 1944. By the end of February German counter-espionage agents had arrested most of the men and women of Dutch-Paris who were involved with helping aviators in Paris, Brussels and Lyons.

The rather public rumour that the men and women of Dutch-Paris had routes to Switzerland and Spain and were willing to help just about anyone had an unexpected consequence: Dutch-Paris became a courier service to the resistance in Western Europe. For a clandestine organisation the line had a surprising number of contacts and alliances with other resistance groups and individuals in three countries. Some of these contacts were made because one party or the other needed false documents or materials to make them. Some contacts were made because local resistance groups were hiding Allied aviators whom they wanted to get to Spain. Some were made because families or colleagues were looking for ways to communicate despite the censorship imposed by occupation. Geneva served as a hub. The line's couriers carried cash from churches in Geneva to pastors in occupied France and from Jewish aid agencies in Geneva to Jewish resisters in Brussels. They carried reports of atrocities written by Quaker observers in Toulouse to Geneva as well as lists of the names and hiding places of Jewish children from Brussels to Geneva. They also carried military and other information gathered by resisters to Geneva or Spain so that it could be handed over to the governments in exile or the Allies. The young Raymonde Pillot once carried an envelope clearly addressed to General de Gaulle. More officially, they carried microfilms from the Dutch resistance to the Dutch government-in-exile.[39]

The experience of working with resisters from so many other countries to rescue strangers, with whom they sometimes did not even share a common language, encouraged a new, transnational perspective in the men and women of Dutch-Paris. In the first place, the experience of routinely subverting the prerogatives of the nation-state by forging identity documents and smuggling people and cash across borders meant that Dutch-Paris's guides, couriers and leaders stopped thinking of the countries they travelled across as individual states. To them, the map of Europe simplified itself into 'occupied' and 'unoccupied' areas. Their clandestine courier service contributed to this sense of a new landscape by tying together resisters within occupied Western Europe despite the national borders that the German army itself was trying to enforce. As couriers, they created a transnational community of resisters.

In the second place, they resisted Nazism by rejecting the Nazi hierarchy of human value based on race. They helped people who needed help, no questions asked, unless they had reason to fear an agent provocateur. After the war a Polish Jew who had been fleeing with his family for many months before meeting Weidner in southern France remembered that when he told Weidner that he and his family were not Dutch, Weidner replied that it made no difference. He did not see Dutchmen; he saw human beings.[40] The entire line, including its financial backers, operated on this policy, whether it was in deciding to whom to offer help or in funding that help.

The intense experience of their illegal work in the thoroughly transnational milieu of Dutch-Paris had an unsettling or uprooting effect on some of the most active members of the line. After the war most of the Dutch-Paris men and women who had been arrested, tortured and deported to concentration camps chose to be repatriated to the site of their resistance work, France, rather than to their home countries. Indeed, Weidner continued to serve as Dutch-Paris's *chef de réseau* for many decades by writing letters on behalf of his colleagues' applications for recognition as resisters from the French, Belgian, Dutch, American, British and eventually West German governments. The men and women of Dutch-Paris had rescued people across borders and therefore considered themselves resisters in many nations. The status of 'transnational resister', which would have more accurately described them, was not available to them. Nevertheless, in recognition of their transnational illegal work, Weidner and many of his colleagues received medals and honours from several nations, including the Netherlands, Belgium, France, Great Britain and the USA.

The Außenministerium

Escape lines continued to appear in occupied Europe in response to changes in the military situation and occupation policies. Wherever people needed to escape from the Nazis, other people offered them help. This was as true for civilians as for military men and for prisoners in the Third Reich as individuals in occupied territories. Allied POWs started escaping from their German captors as soon as they were caught in 1940. When the Germans started transporting civilians into the Third Reich as forced labour, they also started trying to get back home.

German authorities put almost six and a half million foreign civilian forced labourers to work as *Zwangsarbeiter* in Germany and the occupied territories in Europe. These men and women worked and lived together in barracks and camps. Most of them were Eastern European prisoners called *Ostarbeiter* by the National Socialist regime, but some two million came from Western European countries, especially France.[41]

Although forced labour had a transnational dimension, the German authorities normally divided and controlled forced labourers according to their nationalities. The Western European civilian forced labourers were placed under a different regime from their counterparts from the East. They resided under better circumstances, in boarding houses and better furnished camps or sheds, had more relative freedom and could stay in better contact with their relatives back home. Almost from the start, aid was given to them by their home front, through the Red Cross and other international organisations.

Aid actions, more or less clandestine, also evolved from within the context of pre-war civil society, which at the time was under National Socialist pressure. Lay Catholic organisations such as the Belgian Jeunesse Ouvrière Chrétienne (JOC, Young Christian Workers) or Katholieke Arbeidersjeugd (Young Catholic Workers, KAJ) gave assistance to Belgian workers drafted to work in Germany. Another example is the Nederlandse Informatiedienst Arbeiders Duitsland (Dutch Information Service for Labourers in Germany, NIAD), an aid network founded by the Dutch clergyman O. Schellekens. The organisation made lists of workers in Germany and helped them by sending goods, food and letters to raise their morale. Relatives back home were at the same time informed about the whereabouts and conditions of the workers.[42]

In general, the aid for civilian forced labourers was based on helping them in their labour camp and work surroundings rather than helping them get out. Some of them nevertheless tried to escape on their own initiative, just as some POWs did. They hid in freight trains, left unattended work camps or failed to return from leave.[43] Others, however, were assisted by supervisors and medical examiners, who provided falsified passes and declarations so that they could repatriate.

In the spring of 1943 the German occupying authorities called up Dutch university students for forced labour in addition to young men of other social classes. In response, a growing number of students went into hiding in the Netherlands. However, because of the risk of retribution against their families and of German reprisals, some 2,900 Dutch students reported to go to Germany. The student I. A. M. Schmutzer was one of them, but he was keen to return to the Netherlands illegally as soon as possible. With help from the Swedish embassy in Berlin, he succeeded in leaving his assigned work place to travel to the Dutch border, where local friends helped him cross back home and into hiding.[44]

Between August and September 1943 Schmutzer left for Spain via another escape line. Before leaving, he passed the idea of an escape line for Dutch students who were forced to work in Germany to W. Zeeman, a student from the Delft Institute of Technology, who had also escaped back to the Netherlands. Zeeman gathered a group of students around him with the intention of helping and repatriating greater numbers of Dutch students. They called their initiative – with a wink – the Außenministerium (foreign ministry). It was a tongue-in-cheek name, probably chosen because the students regarded themselves to be something of a Foreign Affairs division of the Dutch resistance.[45]

Zeeman returned to Germany in November 1943 and again in February 1944 to visit the Berlin-Hanover region. He expanded his network and recruited co-workers on the ground. These students did not themselves escape, but stayed in Berlin to organise the escape line. They were helped by locals like I. M. Schröder, a German-born associate of the Reichsarbeitsdienst in Berlin-Teltow, who lived in the same building as D. Latzko and A. Schouten, two important associates of Zeeman in the German capital. A similar base for the network in Duisburg, in the Ruhr, was planned but eventually postponed.[46]

At the same time colleagues in the Netherlands were instructed in how to help the students cross the Dutch–German border. Afterwards the repatriated students went into hiding with help from the Landelijke Organisatie voor Hulp aan Onderduikers (National Organisation for the Help of People in Hiding, LO), the most extensive Dutch resistance organisation at the time. In many ways, the Außenministerium indeed acted as a transnational branch or 'foreign ministry' of the 'national organisation'.

Between late 1943 and the summer of 1944, more than two hundred Dutch students and other forced workers were helped across the border by co-workers from the Außenministerium network. Most of them could reach and pass the border controls with falsified papers. Others were smuggled in, on occasion in tool boxes from the international D-trains. Members of the network travelled between Germany and the Netherlands frequently to distribute false papers and to check the contacts and lines. The repatriated students were asked in their turn to write reports so that the network could learn from their experiences and the problems they encountered when they returned home.[47]

One of the most important local hubs within the Außenministerium was based in the town of Nijmegen near the Dutch–German border. Border crossing and smuggling were not unusual in the German-Dutch border region around Nijmegen, a gentle farmland area with small border crossing points. Just like in the Pyrenees and elsewhere in Europe, pre-war experiences of smuggling and helping evolved during the war into escape line help. Students were smuggled into the Netherlands near Nijmegen by P. J. Weijs, a garage owner and resident of the Dutch border village of Siebengewald. Weijs maintained good relationships with the German border authorities. He was able to purchase customs and document stamps and therefore served as one of the most important border crossers for the Außenministerium. He normally hid the student escapees, who were picked up at the train station in the small German border town of Goch, in the boot of his car, drove back across the border at Siebengewald and then continued on to Nijmegen.

The local LO, which functioned as an organisational bridge between the north and south of the Netherlands, was helpful in providing the first needs of the repatriated Dutch students. The Nijmegen-based LO-Falsificatiecentrale (Falsification Service), a division that specialised in forging papers, stamps and the like, was also a helpful partner. J. G. M. Moormann, a headmaster and Dutch-language teacher of German heritage, belonged to the LO as a logical extension of his pre-war social engagement in the local Catholic community. He and his family represented the Außenministerium in Nijmegen. His son, F. R. Moormann, was especially closely associated to the Außenministerium, but eventually the entire family was involved. Zeeman was introduced to them by the university teacher and priest G. M. van Ogtrop, who figured as a local contact for the Dutch national student resistance. In a predominantly Catholic town like Nijmegen, the church organisation played an important role in organising resistance.[48]

Until the spring of 1944 the repatriation in the Nijmegen area proceeded without problems, but after members of the Moormann family were arrested on Easter Monday 1944, escape work in the region had to be postponed. The Allied military operation Market Garden and the liberation of the Nijmegen area in September of that year brought a definitive end to the activities in the southern part of the Netherlands.

The Außenministerium as a whole stayed more or less active in helping students until the end of the war.[49]

On the surface the Außenministerium looks like most other escape lines, with inventive helpers and refugees following transnational paths. On further reflection, however, it also stands apart from other escape lines. The Außenministerium went from Germany to an occupied territory, and not from an occupied country to one of the neutral countries. In addition, the Außenministerium network was aimed at helping civilian forced labourers rather than Jews or Allied airmen. It was created by Dutch students to help other students to escape their enforced labour conditions and to go into hiding in their home country, although the network eventually also helped a few Dutch POWs to escape.[50]

As with some other escape lines, but in contrast to Dutch-Paris and Pat O'Leary, helpers and escapees generally shared the same nationality. It was more or less a foreign mission of a 'national' resistance organisation. The involvement of I. M. Schröder, however, shows that the Außenministerium also received help from German locals, and operated in a transnational sphere of action. In contrast to Dutch students who went into hiding before they could be forced to work, the repatriated students underwent the transnational experience of working in and escaping from Germany. Nevertheless, many students who did go into hiding and did participate in the Dutch resistance movement thought that their repatriated fellows had made a wrong choice in the first place. In their opinion, the forced labourers should have gone underground in the Netherlands rather than taking the risk of getting back only after they experienced the effects of forced labour. For many resisters, this transnational experience should actually have been prevented.

Conclusion

Between 1936 and 1948 fascist persecution and the rigours of war and occupation put millions of people into dangerous situations from which they tried to escape. These included soldiers of defeated armies who wanted to return home or get out of occupied Europe in order to continue the war alongside the Allies, as well as downed Allied airmen hoping to return to their bases. They also included Jews and other groups targeted for destruction by the Nazi regime. As the war went on, they came to include civilians who were not reviled by Nazi racial ideology but who were nevertheless endangered by Nazi occupation, such as resisters, young men who wanted to volunteer with the Allies and forced labourers.

Few fugitives in occupied Europe could on their own obtain the false documents, black-market food and illegal border crossings they needed to reach a safe haven. The men and women who offered to help them resisted the Nazis by sheltering people who the Nazis considered to be their enemies. The complexity of the task of rescue meant that in all but a few cases of rescue by hiding someone, the helpers organised themselves into networks known as escape lines.

Escape lines varied tremendously in their details. Some of them, like the French customs officials at the International Railway Station at Canfranc, helped fugitives to cross a border at a particular place without creating a wider network to bring those fugitives from far away to the border. Some, like the Außenministerium, operated over one border, in this case the German–Dutch border, and helped civilians. Others, such as Pat O'Leary, operated across many countries from the Netherlands to Spain, Portugal and French North Africa and specialised in helping military men. Some escape lines restricted their help to particular types of people, while others helped whomever needed help.

Escape lines had to rely on local people for many things: knowledge of a border, of course, but also the provision of false documents for that zone and information about local laws, law enforcement and hiding places. But by their very nature, escape lines took fugitives across borders and sometimes across several borders. This meant that an escape line could not be a merely local or national resistance network. It involved people from more than one nation in the task of smuggling people of different nations across national borders and against national laws. Indeed, escape lines united individuals against the nation-state in a common mission to subvert the nation-state's prerogatives of policing borders and citizens.

The postwar continuation of the phenomenon also suggests the transnational nature of escape lines in the sense that they rejected the structures and privileges of the nation-state. Spanish *guerrilleros* wanted to continue the fight against fascism in their homeland. The Armée Juive, renamed the Organisation Juive de Combat (Jewish Combat Organisation, OJC), linked up in May 1945 with the Jewish Agency for Palestine and spirited Jewish youth from displaced persons camps to ferry them to Palestine in 1946–47 in the teeth of opposition from the British Mandate authority. [51]

But it was not only the disregard for borders and laws that gave escape lines an inherently transnational dimension. Rescuing individuals, especially if it involved taking them across the continent, was far too expensive for even wealthy individuals to finance on their own. The lines that specialised in military evaders such as Pat O'Leary, for example, often received money from the Allied army personnel. Jewish escape lines relied on money from international Jewish organisations with offices in Geneva, such as the American Joint Distribution Committee. Dutch-Paris had a complicated financial structure involving loans from people living in

Belgium and France, at least one church in the Netherlands, the World Council of Churches in Geneva and the Dutch government-in-exile. It also used funds from the American and British military attachés in Geneva to pay for help to aviators.

The experience of working in escape lines created even more subtle and personal transformations. Many of the men and women involved in them had to break all ties to their pre-war lives in addition to turning their sense of themselves as respectable citizens upside down in order to live uncertain and dangerous lives underground. Others stayed in their everyday lives to provide shelter, false documents or information but now lived in constant fear of capture and reprisal against their families.[52] As happened with most resisters, their identities shifted from law-abiding citizens to law-breaking outlaws.

But in escape lines their identities also shifted from citizens of a particular nation to transnational rescuers. Their routine disregard for the solidity of borders meant that the map of Europe shifted in the perspectives of members of escape lines from a collection of sovereign states to a dichotomy of occupied versus unoccupied or safe versus unsafe areas. Furthermore, the resisters in escape lines often rejected the categorisation of individuals into parts of this or that nation in favour of seeing all men and women as, simply, human beings.

The almost 'private' nature of hiding individuals – as opposed to publishing illegal newspapers or sabotaging trains – has given escape lines a lesser role in the story of resistance and even in the organisation of national archives. Women's contributions of hiding fugitives in their homes or escorting children and elderly people has often been considered too normal and unheroic to count as resistance, even though they suffered the same penalties of torture and concentration camps as their colleagues involved in other types of resistance. Escape lines have not fitted neatly into the postwar narrative of national resistances against the Nazis. But they do brightly illuminate the history of transnational resistance to nationalist governments between 1936 and 1948.

6

Transnational perspectives on Jews in the resistance

Renée Poznanski, Bojan Aleksov and Robert Gildea

A study of the role of Jews in rescue and resistance is one of the most powerful lenses through which to study transnational resistance. Many Jews fought in the Civil War in Spain, joined illegal groups resisting the German or Italian occupiers of their countries, were at the core of resistance activity in the camps, organised rescue actions or were saved thanks to escape lines. In the opening lines of his introduction to *The New Transnational Activism*, to demonstrate his thesis, Sidney Tarrow draws on the example of his father, Moishke Tarabeur, who, caught in the 1920 war between Poland and the new Soviet state, left Kletzk, his *Shtetl* in Poland, for New York. Eight years later he returned to Poland to find a wife and provided his native village with a health clinic. Back in the US, he became active in his labour union and in organisations that worked to get Jews out of Europe. In the immediate postwar period he worked with international aid agencies to locate survivors of his *Shtetl*, then to collect money to help resettle refugees in Palestine.[1]

During the Second World War, which Tarabeur avoided directly, millions of Jews in Europe were faced by the terrible dilemma of flight or fight. This was not new to them. To some extent, for historic reasons, they were prepared for the challenge. In other ways, however, the scale of the threat was so unprecedented that they were obliged to improvise and develop new means of rescue and resistance.

As a diasporic population, Jews had been migrating from one country to another for centuries, escaping persecution and looking for safer havens. European countries saw the successive development of prosperous Jewish centres, which were then dislocated and rebuilt in other places. With the development of modern nation-states in the nineteenth century and the first half of the twentieth century, along with a nascent and rapidly growing anti-Semitism, the myth of the wandering Jew, inherited from the Christian tradition, was transformed into the image of the cosmopolitan Jew, incapable of any loyalty towards the nations in which they resided. The emigration of Jews from ethnically mixed Central and Eastern Europe intensified, but the paths they took were not random. For support in the countries they passed through or where they settled they relied on local or international Jewish organisations, set up by Jewish communities which had lived there for generations or had migrated earlier, as well as by Jews coming from other places. This created a Jewish transnational milieu, with each Jewish community having its own diaspora in other European countries and a history of emigration which included several temporary locations. It was based, according to Tarrow, not on some cognitive cosmopolitanism which looked in an idealised sense to the world community but on a 'rooted' cosmopolitanism based on Jews' relational links to their own societies, social networks and international institutions.[2] In this way historic pathways and networks were laid down that could be activated for later transnational activism in rescue and resistance.

These were required only too soon. In 1939–45 the world war between the global superpowers was accompanied by a singular war waged against the Jews. In different countries – those occupied by the Nazis or under regimes collaborating with them – and following diverse rhythms and rules, Jews were persecuted, transformed into second-class citizens, deprived of their rights and despoiled, before being hunted down, interned in camps, deported and exterminated. This specific attack called for specific patterns of response, whether based on rescue or resistance. Jews were not alone in this endeavour but for the most part they were the instigators, organisers and financers of rescue operations. For the success of those enterprises relations with the local population were crucial, but the level of popular anti-Semitism undermined this relationship. Rescue and resistance efforts by Jews in the Second World War, using old and new pathways and networks, could therefore only be transnational. Transnational perspectives on the Jews' involvement in resistance in Europe thus sheds new light on resistance as a whole.

The legacy of the pre-war years: emigration and political involvement

Anti-Semitism reached a climax in Eastern and Central European countries in the interwar period. Battered by the global economic crisis, these countries installed fascist or conservative nationalist regimes that resorted to political persecution and anti-Semitic legislation. In this atmosphere many Jews, like Moishke Tarabeur, sought to migrate to the New World, but immigration quotas prevented many from doing so. Closer refuges were to hand in European countries which had not (or not yet) fallen prey to these political and social upheavals. Throughout the 1920s, thousands of Jews fleeing Russia after the Bolshevik Revolution, or Poland or Romania and Hungary following the 1919 Béla Kun revolution, made their way to France, Italy and Yugoslavia. After 1933 they were joined by thousands of Jews fleeing from Germany and by Jews from the Austrian and Czechoslovakian territories after these were annexed or occupied. A vast majority made their own private arrangements but from 1939 to 1941 there were a few transports organised by Zionist organisations as part of Aliyah Bet or covert migration to Palestine in the face of British restrictions. Many of these remained tragically stuck in Yugoslavia when the war broke out.[3]

Prominent among Jewish refugees to Yugoslavia were those who had been politically active in their homelands before their emigration, usually as communists or social democrats. Jews were active in intellectual and usually left-wing political movements which led naturally to forms of international and transnational resistance. Among these refugees were Jakob Altmaier and Alfred Becker. Altmaier was born in Flörsheim am Main in 1889 to a family of bakers. He became an activist in the Sozialdemokratische Partei Deutschlands (German Social Democratic Party, SPD) in 1913 and after the First World War, in which he was severely wounded, took part in the 1918–19 German revolution. He became a well-known left-wing journalist in the Weimar republic, writing for Kurt Tucholsky's *Weltbühne*, and a Berlin correspondent for *the Manchester Guardian*.[4] Forced into exile, he continued to write from Paris, Belgrade and Spain during the Civil War for the Sozialdemokratischer Pressedienst and *Vorwärts*. Alfred Becker, on the other hand, came from a family of a rich Prussian landowner and SPD politician, Arthur Becker, a rather rare combination and a prominent figure described as 'Red Jew' by his conservative enemies.[5] Alfred inherited a landed estate near Schwerin and became an expert in agriculture economics but like his father chose a political career instead, working towards land reform for the SPD and in the League for Human Rights. The latter got him into trouble with Nationalist Socialists and he fled to the Netherlands and France. In 1936, however, we find him with his family in Yugoslavia, employed in the Ministry of Agriculture.

By 1939 both Altmaier and Becker were engaged in a British-organised anti-Nazi network in Yugoslavia. Yugoslavia was then part of a tug of war between Great Britain and the Axis powers, both sides hoping to draw it into their respective system of alliances or, if that was not possible, preventing it from moving into the opposing camp. The British spymaster in Yugoslavia was Julius Hanau, a South African Jew born in 1885 who fought on the Salonika front in the First World War with the Serbian army and remained in Belgrade after the war. There he became a representative of several British companies and was one of the founders in 1927 of Radio Belgrade, set up with capital from Marconi Wireless Co., which he was representing. Hanau was fluent in Serbian, among many other languages, and maintained ties with many Anglophile members of Belgrade political and military elites. Under the codename Caesar, Hanau led the British Secret Intelligence Service (SIS, MI6) D Section in Belgrade, whose agents were mostly British engineers in the Yugoslav mining industry, together with German-Jewish exiles such as Altmaier and Becker.

Altmaier and Becker produced anti-Nazi pamphlets, fliers and magazines, mostly directed at the German ethnic minority in Yugoslavia.[6] They also smuggled German-language propaganda into Austria and Germany. Becker was also directly involved in acts of sabotage organised by the British, infecting cattle bound to Germany with foot-and-mouth and mad cow disease, and he established links with anti-fascist and national liberal Slovenian underground in both Yugoslavia and Fascist Italy. This subversion campaign was nevertheless busted in 1940 by Gestapo who subsequently put pressure on Yugoslav authorities. Altmaier fled from Belgrade to Athens, where he continued working as a propagandist, and eventually to Cairo, where he spent the wartime in the British headquarters as a Balkan expert. Becker fled to Istanbul, where he recruited other fellow Jews for subversive British warfare and then proceeded to join SOE operations in Palestine and Kenya.

Leading Austrian communists frequently hid or met in Yugoslavia and in 1939 made Zagreb their headquarters in exile. This was headed by a prominent Viennese-Jewish communist architect Julius Kornweitz.[7] Many exiles were not political at all – or not when they started out – but were artists, writers and performers. Belgrade became a hub for Viennese Jewish artists or 'Das vierte Tor', named after the so-called Fourth Gate Jewish section of the Viennese central cemetery.[8] Stella Kadmon, who set up a Vienna cabaret 'Der liebe Augustin' with the writer and performer Peter Hammerschlag, fled in July 1938 to Belgrade, where, like many other refugees, she entered a marriage of convenience and continued performing with Hammerschlag.[9] They were joined there by Peter Hammerschlag's friend Piero Rismondo, who was born into a wealthy Trieste family, owned the 'Dalmatia' shipping company and lived in Vienna as a journalist and dramatist, becoming famous for his 1936 anti-fascist play about the Romantic Austrian playwright Grillparzer.

From the same circle in the Viennese theatre came the Austrian-born Jewish authors Franz Theodor Csokor and Alexander (von) Sacher-Masoch. Theodor Csokor, born in 1885, was a dramaturge at the Raimundtheater and Deutsches Volkstheater in Vienna and was among the initiators of the famous anti-Nazi petition at the PEN congress in Dubrovnik in 1933, which had his works banned in the Third Reich. Sacher-Masoch, born in 1901, was an author and leftist political activist in Weimar Germany who moved to Vienna after 1933 and thence in 1938 to Belgrade, where he was correspondent of the Swiss newspaper *Der Bund.* With his co-émigré Piero Rismondo he wrote a drama about exiles, *Das unsichtbare Volk* ('Invisible people'), in 1938–39. The following year Sacher-Masoch published a book of poems, *Die Zeit der Dämonen* ('The time of demons'), with a Belgrade Jewish publisher, Paul Bruck, which circulated among Belgrade Jewish and other émigré intellectuals. It painted dramatic images of National Socialist violence under Hitler's totalitarian rule and remains one of the most poignant reminders of the farsightedness and engagement of anti-fascist resisters before the eruption of war and Holocaust.

On the heels of established Viennese artistic figures came younger German-Jewish exiles fleeing to Yugoslavia after *Kristallnacht* on 9 November 1938. By September 1939 about two-thirds of the Jewish community had left Germany. Fritz Cahn was born in Munich in 1922 to a large Jewish family. He lost his apprenticeship to a Jewish locksmith when the latter was sent to a concentration camp in 1938.[10] After his father was imprisoned twice in Germany, the family decided to leave. His father went to Italy and eventually to Hungary, where he was later killed. Fritz followed and stayed in Trieste for seven months with a number of German and Austrian Jewish refugees, housed by the Jewish community there. After anti-Semitic laws were introduced in Italy in 1939, many decided to go to Yugoslavia, and the Jewish community of Trieste paid for a fishing boat to take the group to their destination. At this time, however, the Yugoslav authorities were arresting or expelling Jewish communist and anarchist activists who had come from Germany, Poland, Romania and Hungary.[11] Eventually the Jewish community in Zagreb intervened, and Fritz and his fellow travellers were housed in hotels in Samobor near Zagreb, from where he was transferred to Mostar at the beginning of the war and acquired new friends who helped him to join the communist-led partisans.

While Jewish solidarity generally transcended borders this was not universal. Some Yugoslav Jews objected to helping bourgeois German Jews who were fully integrated in the German society. The precarious position of refugees was described by Ernst Pawel, born in 1920 in Breslau, who came with his family from Berlin to Belgrade in 1933. One way for young German Jews to integrate in the new environment was to join the youth branch of the Boy Scouts or Young Men's Christian Association (YMCA). These were often infiltrated by the illegal communist movement. Pawel was himself approached by the local organisation of Ha-shomer ha-Za'ir (Hazair) Hashomer Hatzair, whose main goal was to educate and prepare Jewish youth for the pioneering work of building a Jewish state in Palestine. Yugoslav police registered it as a 'communist-suspected Zionist organisation'.[12] Pawel managed to emigrate to the US with his family but soon returned to fight the Germans as an American GI.[13]

Yugoslavia thus became a significant place of refuge for German and Austrian – especially Viennese – Jews fleeing persecution after 1933 and especially after 1938. Even larger cohorts of Jewish refugees from Central Europe, however, streamed into Belgium and France. From 1933 on, the majority of them were German, Austrian and Polish Jews, together with a large minority of Romanian and Hungarian Jews. Discriminated against, frustrated in their professional ambitions as Jews and often tracked as political activists, they had little choice but to emigrate. They tried to make their way into Western European societies at a time when restrictive immigration laws blocked the shores of the USA.

One case of a refugee who fled to Belgium was Joseph Schwarzberg. Born in Leipzig in 1926 to a family of tailors of Polish-Jewish origin, he wavered initially between his German and his Jewish identities. He went to a German school, where he was surrounded by non-Jewish pupils, while his parents sewed clothes for non-Jewish Germans. Joseph's closest friends, however, were Jewish, and he joined a Zionist youth group, following with enthusiasm the achievements of the nascent Jewish community (the Yishuv) in Palestine. Ambitions to integrate as Germans were brutally checked by the anti-Jewish pogrom of *Kristallnacht.* The Schwarzbergs, like many German families, had to split up in order to leave Germany. They chose Belgium as their destination. Joseph's father went first and was held in a camp for illegal immigrants on his arrival. His mother paid smugglers to take Joseph and his six-year-old sister over the border, and followed them a week later. In Brussels they received help from local Jewish organisations, and mingled in a new community of Jews who had fled from many countries. 'A colourful mix of people gathered there, making for a practical education in diversity', Joseph later wrote, 'and I learned the customs and dialects of people from all over Europe, including Austria, Southern Europe, Czechoslovakia, Hungary, Romania and the Balkans.'[14]

France was a particular place of attraction for fleeing Jews. In the 1930s Paris became the European capital of political exile, and therefore of Jewish political exile. This owed a great deal to the French Constituent Assembly's law of 27 September 1791, which gave Jews French citizenship. It also owed a great deal to the French Republic, secure after 1870, and Pierre Birnbaum has shown that the fate of the Jews in France was structurally linked to the republican regime.[15]

One of those who enjoyed these benefits was Lew Goldenberg, whose Jewish parents left Russia for Paris to escape oppressive Tsarist policy after the failed 1905 revolution, and whose father became a doctor. Lew, born in Paris in 1908, received a classical French education attending the Sorbonne and Paris Law Faculty, changed his name to Leo Hamon, became a barrister at the French Constitutional Council in 1930. His parents subsequently returned to the Soviet Union, and Leo joined the PCF after the fascist riots of 6 February 1934, because he saw the party as 'the heirs of 1793, devoted to liberty and full of salutary hatred of what they called fascism'.[16]

The participation of Jews in resistance activity during the Second World War was to a large extent shaped by their participation in revolutionary and resistance movements before the war. Much of this pre-war activity was undertaken in international organisations, and many of the leaders followed transnational activist trajectories. It is significant that key leaders had been born in Jewish communities in the Pale of Settlement from the Baltic to the Black Sea, which fell within the former Russian and Austro-Hungarian empires, had fled anti-communist and anti-Semitic persecution in highly nationalist successor states such as Poland, Hungary and Romania, and in some cases had volunteered for the International Brigades in Spain. Often they changed political loyalties as a result of their encounters, switching from Bundism or Zionism to communism, or espousing the patriotism of the country in which they were resisting. They also changed their names, which suggested a change of identity, for instance becoming less Central or Eastern European and more Spanish, more French or more Yugoslav. That said, conflicts and tensions sometimes occurred when identity questions came to the fore.

Michał Feintuch, born in Galicia in 1906, was one of these figures. His father, an itinerant tradesman, had served in the Habsburg army in the First World War, but Galicia was twice occupied by the Russians. 'By the force of circumstances', he remembered, 'having begun my schooling under the Austro-Hungarian monarchy, I had learned German; then, during the year of the Ukrainian Revolution, I started Ukrainian. After which, all of my professional schooling took place in Polish. At home, we spoke Yiddish and my father had forced me to learn Hebrew.'[17] When Poland was formed he joined the Polish Communist Party, but this was anything but Polish. Of the first illegal meeting he attended in February 1923, he wrote, 'I appreciated above all the sense of internationalism evident in the presentation. I felt myself instantly transported into a large family without borders, in which Russians, French and Germans, along with the rest of us, were united in the same struggle.'[18] He was told that 1917 was a revenge for the bourgeoisie's crushing of the Paris Commune in 1871.

Expelled from Poland for communist activity in 1927, he went via Berlin to Liège, where he became a steelworker. Expelled from Belgium in 1929 for communist activism, he went to France, which he saw as 'the country of the Great Revolution of '89 and of the rights of man'.[19] He joined the PCF, agitated among Polish miners in the north of France in 1932 and became involved in sending aid to Spain during the Civil War. Going underground with the communist FTP in 1942, he adopted the classically French name of Jean Jérôme.

Another revolutionary product of the Austro-Hungarian Empire was Mendel Langer. Born in 1903 to a Jewish family in Galicia, Mendel was exposed to its mixed Polish-Russian-Jewish-German population and culture and learned four languages. In 1914 Mendel's father Alter, an activist in the Jewish socialist Bund, rescued his family from growing anti-Semitism by taking them to Prague and six years later to Palestine. There Mendel became a railway fitter, learned Hebrew and Arabic, joined the Palestinian Communist Party in 1923 and became a member of its regional committee in Haifa. 'He thought the Zionist movement useless and even backward', recalled one of his comrades. 'For him the solution of the Jewish problem was a huge combat that would end all oppression: the liberation of all oppressed peoples.'[20] The British Mandate authorities imprisoned him twice, in 1924 and 1925, he was expelled from the Railway, Postal and Telegraph Workers' Union and altogether from Palestine in 1930.[21] With the help of international communist organisations he settled in the French city of Toulouse, found work in a gas factory and joined the large community of Polish-speaking workers, many of whom were in the PCF and the MOI. [22] Further to integrate, however, Mendel changed his name to the Gallic Marcel, and when he was sent across the Franco-Spanish border by the PCF superiors in October 1936 he maintained a studied ambiguity. 'He has declared his French nationality to our service', complained the Polish section of the IB Personal Service in January 1938, 'while he told he French section that he was a Pole … his statements are not completely clear.'[23]

In Spain, Langer worked in the repair workshops at the International Brigades section of the Albacete arsenal and, in the summer or autumn of 1937, was sent to the southern front as a gunsmith in the multinational XI International Brigade, part of the 35th 'International' Division of the Republican Army, where he was promoted lieutenant. Langer learned Spanish, read the PCE newspapers, joined the PCE branch in Albacete, married a local girl, Cecilia Molina Sevilla, and even applied for Spanish citizenship. In late 1938, after the dissolution of the International Brigades, Langer remained in Spain and became an officer of the Spanish army. By this time, he obviously had no affinity with his Austrian-Polish-Jewish past and compatriots – to the extent that in the summer of 1940 senior Polish veterans of the Spanish Civil War regarded him as untrustworthy and proposed a thorough investigation of his past.[24]

While substantial numbers of Jewish immigrants from Central and Eastern Europe were affiliated to the socialist Bund or to communist parties, a minority were part of the Zionist movement dedicated to promoting the transfer of persecuted Jews to a Jewish homeland in what was now the British Mandate of Palestine. One of these was Abraham Polonski, who was born in Białystock in 1903. His family fled a Russian pogrom to Palestine in 1910 and then fled Turkish occupation of Palestine in 1915 to Egypt. He returned to post-revolutionary Russia, where he joined the Komsomol, and then escaped Polish persecution when the Poles retook Bialystock, going to France. He qualified as engineer and found employment with the National Industrial Nitrogen Office in Toulouse. He made contact with David Knout (also known as Fixman), a poet from Bessarabia who had lost eight of his twelve siblings in a pogrom of 1905 and fled the Russian Revolution. Polonski and Knout attended the twenty-first World Zionist congress in Switzerland in August 1939, where the question of legal versus illegal immigration to Palestine was passionately debated.[25]

Thus, at the outbreak of war in 1939, Belgium and France had become refuges of choice for Jews of Russian, Polish, Austro-Hungarian and Yugoslav origin. Some were simply refugees who kept their heads down; others were politicised, espousing communism or Zionism. Some tried to maintain a high life, criticising Nazism through their art, while others indulged in spying on behalf of Germany's enemies or even went to fight in Spain with the International Brigades. Whether they chose flight or fight, however, they were far from being safe. They would now be faced by the consequences of Belgian and French defeat, German occupation and Vichy collaboration.

A singular war within the world war

Alongside the world war there was fought a war within the war. In Nazi-occupied Europe all European Jews became a direct target for the occupying powers and for their allies in the local population. They were stripped of their rights and eliminated from the public, economic, cultural and social life of the country. Jews living abroad were transformed into stateless refugees. This was to facilitate the enactment of the upcoming deportation policy by creating categories of groups to be sent to the east, according to a meticulously planned extermination project.

Because of this project of persecution and extermination, collaboration with the occupiers and their allies was not an option for Jews. Some were recruited to bodies set up by the Nazis to 'handle' Jewish affairs. Different types of *Judenraten* in Eastern Europe or in Western Europe Unions such as the Union Générale des Juifs de France (UGIF) were set up, whose leaders tried to alleviate the plight of the Jews by acting from the inside but often, unfortunately, found themselves cogs in the Nazi machine.

Going underground and becoming involved in resistance was another option. Given their different political backgrounds and experiences, there was not a single form of Jewish resistance. Jews who were highly integrated into the culture and politics of their adopted country tended to espouse the national resistance movement in that country. Those who were integrated into communist movements which organised foreign Jews naturally continued with communist resistance movements. Zionists, likewise, became involved in Zionist rescue and resistance. Many Jews nevertheless reinvented themselves as a result of persecution, displacement and new encounters. Some Jews who felt perfectly integrated into their adopted nation turned to Zionism when they were excluded from it. Some Zionists became communist partisans because the communists were the avant-garde of active armed resistance. Meanwhile communists came to espouse projects of national liberation because they imagined that a reconstituted and reformed nation might lead to a communist utopia.

Much depended on the geographical context in which Jews found themselves. This section will concentrate on two theatres where Jews were heavily involved in rescue and resistance: France and Yugoslavia. Both were occupied relatively late by Germans and Italians, and had become destinations for Jewish flight. Conditions in the two areas, however, were very different. France had a government, based at Vichy, that was nominally sovereign throughout the whole country and in full control of the Free Zone in the south until that too was occupied in November 1942. Many of the measures against Jews were passed by the Vichy government, and on German orders the round-up of Jews began in Paris in August 1941. Some work of associational self-help, rescue and resistance could go on legally, especially in the so-called Free Zone, during the first two years of the occupation.[26] By contrast Yugoslavia was invaded on 6 April 1941 and fully partitioned between Germany and Italy, with some areas given to Hungary and Bulgaria. King Peter II and his government were driven into exile, and the Nazis installed a puppet government in Croatia run by the fascist Ustaša. There was thus no government to offer protection to the population, and the Axis powers indulged in far more brutal repression than in France. Moreover, the massacre of Jews began almost at once.

For a while, before the invasion, Belgrade remained a hub of information gathering, resistance and a refuge for many on the run because of their Jewishness or anti-fascism. It was in its bars, night clubs and hotels that Jewish refugees turned spies and saboteurs met with American and British journalists, who also doubled as agents in months leading up to the invasion. Among the most flamboyant was the American heiress and photographer Ruth Mitchell, who had been stationed in the Balkans since 1938 and was active in helping Jewish refugees.[27] In February 1941 the Belgrade PEN association hosted a welcome party for Theodor Csokor, who had arrived from Vienna via Romania. He described the atmosphere in Belgrade as a mixture of the Balkans and Paris, one of the last truly neutral countries on the continent: 'When Hitler appears on the screen in a news-reel', he wrote, 'everybody whistles and becomes agitated.'[28] According to David Walker of *The Daily Mirror* the only thing alluding to impending war was that in the night clubs people would sing 'It's a long way to Tipperary', recalling Serbia's fight alongside Britain in the First World War.[29]

Some refugees in Belgrade left early. The cabaret owner Stella Kadmon fled in 1940 via Greece to Tel Aviv, where she opened the Hebrew-language Papillion Cabaret, but Hammerschlag returned to Vienna and was later murdered in Auschwitz. During the invasion of April 1941, the journalists and many Jewish refugees and other foreigners in Belgrade helped each other in a chaotic escape towards the Yugoslav coast, which was to be occupied (and partially annexed) by the Italian army, because they all expected a better treatment by the Italians. Franjo Spitzer and his wife fled to Italian-held Dalmatia and would later organise the evacuation of over three thousand Jews with whom he was interned in the Italian camp on the island of Rab to the partisan-controlled Croatian mountains.[30] Sacher-Masoch and Csokor fled via Sarajevo to Dubrovnik and Split respectively and eventually landed on the Italian-occupied island of Korčula. There they stayed until November 1943, producing the most detailed albeit novelistic accounts of anti-fascist resistance and exile of European Jews and others in Yugoslavia.[31] Despite these sympathies Csokor and Sacher-Masoch disapproved of and clashed with partisans when the latter briefly took control of the island, executed Italians and other innocent victims and destroyed many Venetian monuments. Both eventually evacuated to Bari in southern Italy, where they joined the Allies' Radio Bari German broadcasting services contributing to the Allies' propaganda and war effort.[32]

The majority of Belgrade Jews and foreign Jews who had fled there nevertheless remained, and by the summer all the escape routes were closed. The mass execution of Jews began very shortly afterwards, and after only a year of German occupation Serbia was the first country in Europe to be declared *judenfrei*.[33] In Croatia the Ustaša acted on their own initiative to eliminate the Jews.[34] Even in the Hungarian zone, Hungarian forces undertook a raid on Novi Sad in January 1942 in alleged reprisal for resistance activities which murdered 1,200 Jews and almost three thousand Serbs. One of them was Ilse (Elisabeth) Lev(w)inger, who had escaped from Vienna to Novi Sad and soon became a leader of the Savez Komunističke Omladine Jugoslavije (Young Communist League of Yugoslavia, SKOJ) and then secretary of its regional party committee, one of the biggest in the country.[35]

The destruction of Jewish communities removed the protection provided by Yugloslav Jews to those Jews fleeing from Central and Eastern Europe. Jewish youth groups organised by Hashomer and another smaller group, Tehelet Lavan, all crossed over into the Yugoslav communist youth movement because the Jewish networks were destroyed, while the underground communist networks survived largely by fleeing into the mountains. For many Jews in flight thus resistance became the only option. This was of course dangerous, but at least resistance networks offered protection against arrest and deportation, and a chance to fight back. The young German-Jewish refugee Fritz Cahn, who was interned in Mostar in summer 1941, joined the communist-led partisan resistance, not for any ideological reason but because it offered to protect him. He could barely speak Serbo-Croatian, having spent previous two years with other German refugees, but was an accomplished pianist, had brought his accordion with him and soon became very popular among the partisans. He embraced their cause, survived the heaviest fighting and eventually joined the Communist Party in 1944. Having lost his family in Germany in the Holocaust, Cahn decided to stay in his new homeland, changing his name to Fric Kan, the Serbo-Croatian phonetic version of his German name. He was sent to finish his music schooling and eventually joined the newly formed orchestra of the Belgrade garrison of the Yugoslav army and had a long career as both a player and a conductor.[36]

Few Jews sought protection from the Četnik (monarchist) resistance too, but they later vacillated between resistance and collaboration and displayed a chequered record on anti-Semitism, so the communist guerrilla became the only option. In truth, the Yugoslav Partisans did not have a well-articulated ideological position on anti-Semitism. While the movement accepted Jews as equals in its ranks, it did not perceive the organised persecution of Jews separately from the general situation in the country. For practical reasons the rescue of the Jews could never be a priority for a guerrilla movement constantly pursued by German, Italian, Hungarian and Bulgarian armies, as well as by local collaborationists. While some instances of partisan anti-Semitism were recorded, the fighters actually embraced thousands of Yugoslav and foreign Jews. If escape to Italian protection could not be achieved, survival with the communist partisans was an alternative.

This protection for Jews offered by communist partisans was not supported by the British government, which had SOE missions in Yugoslavia and backed Tito's resistance movement from the beginning of 1944. The communists repeatedly pleaded with the British military to evacuate over 3,000 Jews who had been rescued by Yugoslav Partisans but were dying of hunger and from German and Ustaša attacks in the remote mountains of Croatia. In his Army Post Office 394 report on 25 September 1944 Sir Clifford Heathcote-Smith of the Intergovernmental Committee on Refugees, at the Headquarters of the Allied Control Commission, warned that no political – especially anti-Semitic – movement should be caused by this evacuation, insisting that Palestine had not yet replied to the request that the Jews in Yugoslavia be added to the list of emigrants. In truth, the British government wanted to keep the doors of Palestine closed to new Jewish refugees.[37]

While young German-Jewish refugees could only be the footsoldiers of the Yugoslav Partisan resistance, its leadership was highly dependent on former members of the International Brigades for their political and guerrilla military experience. Among the first partisans in Serbia and among the first to fall victim was Boro Baruh, a painter and communist who recruited Yugoslav volunteers for the International Brigades, along with his four siblings (Jakov, Isidor, Simha and Berta), turning their Belgrade Baruh Sephardi family into martyrs of partisan resistance.[38] Boro Baruh was part of the generation of Yugoslav Jewish intellectuals and artists who studied in Paris and, faced by the threat of destruction, joined communist and anti-fascist transnational networks.[39] Many former Spanish fighters of Jewish origin, together with other Jewish communists, were among the instigators of anti-fascist uprisings in Yugoslavia. Moše Pijade, one of the Yugoslav communist leader Tito's closest associates, was among the organisers of the uprising in Montenegro. The uprising in Croatia was launched by Robert Domani (Domany), commander of the Liebknecht battery in Spain, who was killed in 1942, and by his fellow International Brigadists Pavle Pap (born Papp), Drago (Adolf) Štajnberger and Ilija (Elias) Engel, killed as partisans respectively in 1941, 1942 and 1944. Vojo Todorović (born Samuel Lerer) escaped internment in France to arrive to Yugoslavia in July 1941 and become the first commander of the partisan battalion Gavrilo Princip (named after the assassin of Franz Ferdinand in 1914) in Bosnia. Other uprising organisers in Bosnia included Slaviša Vajner Čiča (born Weiner), killed in 1942, and Pavle Goranin (born Eliahu Steiner), who died fighting in 1944 along with his brother and father.

Almost all the Jewish Brigadists mentioned here slavicised their names, which was common among Yugoslav Jews and one of the indicators of their assimilation. Many of the Balkan Jews, especially the Sephardi whose ancestors settled there in the sixteenth century, embraced armed struggle and displayed the same temperament as their fellow South Slav fighters. They came to actively promote the communist project of a new Yugoslavia based on brotherhood and the equality of its peoples. Eventually, all the above Jewish communists and transnational activists were declared Yugoslav national heroes for courage demonstrated in the armed struggle against Nazism and its collaborators, the highest recognition possible. Out of 4,466 Jews who participated in partisan resistance there were 2,897 fighters and 1,569 in other capacities, with 720 (29 per cent) killed among the former and 599 (38 per cent) among the latter. By the end of the war fourteen Jews were awarded the rank of a general in new communist-led Yugoslav army.[40]

In France, the southern half of which was not occupied until November 1942 and where some low-ranking officials of the Vichy regime were prepared to help, the possibilities of rescue were more extensive than in Yugoslavia. In 1939–40 Jewish organisations were already in place, dealing with refugees. Most important was the Oeuvre de Secours aux Enfants (OSE), which had been founded in 1912 to deal with child victims of the pogroms in Russian Empire and had moved its headquarters to Berlin in 1923 and thence to Paris. The French-Jewish Scout movement, the Éclaireurs Israélites de France (EIF), founded in 1923 and authorised by the Vichy regime until January 1943, provided youthful help with the practicalities of ferrying refugees to safe places.[41]

Many of the leading rescuers came from Alsace and the Moselle, while others were Jewish refugees from Poland and Russia. Alsace-Moselle was a borderland, part of Germany between 1870 and 1918 and again between 1940 and 1944. Because the 1905 French law of separation between the state and religion was not implemented there, Jews from that region were fully able to develop their Jewish identity. They were also sensitised very early to the crisis suffered by Jews after 1933 in Germany and Austria, to the arrival of Jewish refugees and to the need after 1939 to evacuate French people from Alsace and the Moselle who did not want to fall under the Nazi regime.

One of these was Georges Loinger. Born in 1910 in an observant family of Polish origin, he stated in the beginning of his memoir: 'I am a son of Alsace, I feel deeply French – did I not grow up in the shadow of the Strasbourg Cathedral?'[42] Paradoxically, Strasbourg was in Germanised Alsace at that time. His father fought in the Austrian army during the First World War, while he himself fought for France in 1940. 'I am a man of borders, a smuggler [*passeur*]', he added.[43] As a young boy, he joined a Zionist youth movement (Hatikva – Hope) which had been created in 1870 by young German Jews in Strasbourg. During the 1930s, when anti-Semitic groups began flourishing in the region and German Jews began fleeing Nazi Germany, Jewish self-defence began to develop in the city. Attracted by physical activities and keen to train young Jews, Georges Loinger abandoned his engineering studies and moved to Paris to train as a youth sports instructor. He worked in Jewish schools to develop physical activities there. In this way he became involved in the EIF and attended all its summer camps. The social network constituted before the war by the OSE and the EIF played a central role in the rescue of Jews both before and during the war. French Jews from Alsace and the Moselle, which were once again annexed by Germany, were driven by a strong French patriotism and a clear Jewish identity and helped young Jewish refugees to find their way to France. In this they could rely on the help of French social workers, whether attached to religious associations or the state, both under the Republic and in the early phase of the Vichy regime.

Quite different was the trajectory of Abbé Alexandre Glasberg, curate of Notre-Dame de Saint-Alban in Lyons and a leading figure in Jewish rescue there. Born a Jew in the Ukraine in 1902, he migrated to France in 1931, converted to Catholicism and was ordained as a priest in 1938. He worked closely with Nina Gourfinkel, a native of Odessa who came to France in 1925, was well established in the Jewish literary milieu in Paris and was active in an international bureau collecting information on Nazism. They joined forces with the Strasbourg medical doctor Joseph Weill, a central figure in the OSE. Early in 1941 they founded the Direction des Centres d'Accueil in order to house foreign Jews whom they managed to have released from the camps. Glasberg headed an ecumenical organisation, Amitié Chrétienne, which included Catholics and Protestants as well as Jews, and tried to save Jews during the 1942 round-ups. In July 1942, at a triage centre at Vénissieux, a suburb of Lyons, he was instrumental in using inconsistencies in Vichy orders to take possession over a hundred Jewish children bound for deportation.[44] One of the shelters used was the Château du Bégué in Cazaubon (Gers), created in August 1942 and run by Abbé Glasberg's brother, Vila Glasberg, who went under the name of Victor Vermont. It sheltered both young Jews who had escaped the round-ups in the occupied zone to come south and young men who refused to be sent to work in Germany under Vichy's Service du Travail Obligatoire (Forced Labour Service, STO) scheme of February 1943. One of those sheltered was Joseph Schwarzberg, who had fled to France from Belgium in 1940.

Increasingly the Vichy and German authorities closed these loopholes and stepped up repression. The escape lines now had to go underground, aligning rescue and resistance. From the end of 1942 Loinger was an active member of a resistance network, Bourgogne, which helped Allied pilots shot down over France to escape. Through Bourgogne he heard of Jean Deffaught, the mayor of Annemasse on the Franco-Swiss border. Deffaught did not hesitate to help him, although other members of this network argued that putting an end to German occupation was the highest priority and that all resistance activity should aim at this goal. To help, Loinger used his Alsatian background to contact another Alsatian, Eugène Balthazar, who was a director of Vichy's main charitable organisation, the Secours National.[45] Between February 1943 and June 1944, thanks to this cooperation between a Jewish activist, a French mayor and an Alsatian social worker, nearly a thousand Jewish children, mainly refugees from Central or Eastern Europe who until then had been sheltered in one of the OSE or EIF homes, were smuggled over the Swiss border.[46]

The line between rescue and resistance was fine: one activity could easily lead to another, and rescue in itself might be seen as resistance to the Nazi project. Other forms of resistance were much more obvious. They included resistance by those who left occupied countries to take part in resistance organised by the Allies or governments in exile, and resistance within the occupied countries themselves. Jews were involved in all these activities, and more so than many categories of the population. Even in these resistance movements, however, issues arose between Jews and non-Jews because popular anti-Semitism was also found in resistance movements.[47]

The French government-in-exile, unlike the Yugoslav, was a motor of resistance activity. Among the first to reach de Gaulle and the Free French in London were leading French Jews such as Raymond Aron, André Weill-Curiel, René Cassin, Georges Boris, Jacques Bingen and Jean-Louis Crémieux-Brilhac. As members of the French intellectual and political establishment, they identified completely with the French national Resistance, although the compliment was not always returned. Georges Boris, who had run the private office of Léon Blum in his second Popular Front ministry in 1938, which was attacked by the right-wing press as a 'Jewish' cabinet, joined the Free French with the hope that 'the participation of well-known Jews and socialists would not undermine the work of General de Gaulle, alienating conservatives and military people of whom he had need'.[48]

Jean-Louis Crémieux-Brilhac, a POW who escaped from Germany and reached Britain via the Soviet Union and was responsible for Free French propaganda broadcast to France from London, accepted that they should not draw too much attention to the persecution of Jews for fear of being denounced by Vichy as 'Judeo-Gaullists' or 'Jewish deserters'. 'We knew but we did nothing', he admitted in 2010. On 23 January 1944 he sent to France a full report on the extermination of over three million Jews in

Europe. It was not picked up in any underground resistance paper. When in March 1944 Albert Cohen of the Jewish World Congress asked the Free French to help a thousand Jewish children to escape from France, he was told by Georges Boris that escape lines were available only to downed Allied airmen. Crémieux-Brilhac agreed with Boris that 'the logic of war came first'.[49]

After the liberation of France, Georges Zérapha, an industrialist, prime mover of the Ligue Internationale contre l'Antisémitisme (International League against Anti-Semitism, LICA) and one of the main leaders of Libération, concluded that from June 1940 to December 1941 Jews led the way from bottom to top in the majority of subgroups of the resistance.[50] His point was well made. We find them among the founders of the Musée de l'Homme network in 1940, publishing the first issue of the magazine *Résistance* on 15 December 1940. Of the six founders of Libération in July 1941, three were Jews. Jean-Pierre Lévy, a Jewish industrialist from German-annexed Alsace, created and ran Franc-Tireur. Robert Salmon, a student at the Sorbonne, was one of the two founders of *Défense de la France*; he chose the name of this new journal, the first number of which appeared in July 1941. These examples give only a partial idea of the early and massive Jewish presence at high positions in all the various French movements.[51]

For French Jews, there could be no ambiguity concerning the question of resistance. They could not accept the basic values of the National Revolution, which aimed to purge 'anti-France', including Jews. This was far from being the case in those resistance movements which supported the Vichy regime – or part of it – until May 1942, while organising in the underground to fight the occupiers. Some of the disagreements on that question between Jews and non-Jews who were otherwise close friends and activists in the same movement revolved around this question: Georges Zérapha versus the Catholic democrat Emmanuel Mounier of *L'Esprit* would be an example, Robert Salmon versus his fellow Sorbonne student Philippe Viannay, who for a long time supported Pétain, would be another.[52] It is no surprise that Jean-Pierre Lévy founded one of the few resistance movements which opposed the Vichy regime from the outset. The commitment of Jews to the republican values explained their very strong patriotism.

Léo Hamon was fully part of the French republican establishment but had espoused his parents' communism until he broke with the Party over the Nazi–Soviet Pact. After the defeat of the French armies and the armistice he escaped to Toulouse, in the non-occupied zone, where most of his intellectual friends became rapidly involved in French Resistance. When the Vichy government began implementing an anti-Jewish legislation, he decided to ignore it as if it were irrelevant, in order not – in his words – to be 'ghettoised'.[53] That said, he could not ignore the threat to the Jewish community. In Toulouse he met Mordko (Marc) Jarblum, a socialist Zionist activist born in Warsaw in 1887, who headed the Fédération des Sociétés Juives de France, the most important organisation of immigrant Jews in France at the time. At Jarblum's request, Hamon went to Paris in April 1941, met all the Jewish leaders there and wrote a full report on the situation of the Jews in the French capital ten months after the beginning of the occupation.[54] Many years later, recalling the circumstances of this trip and this investigation, he referred to the Jewish community in Paris as a big village. He added that he could gather a great deal of information because, as a Jew himself, he was trusted. This report circulated widely between Jewish organisations, including the American Joint Distribution Committee (known as the Joint), a Jewish-American institution which was set up in 1914 to legally help financing persecuted Jews in Europe and continued financing their rescue illegally when this became necessary.

What is interesting here is that both Hamon and Jarblum were committed to rescue and resistance, but they took very different paths in order to achieve it. Hamon committed himself to French Resistance organisations, including Action Ouvrière and the Action Committee against Deportation, which was aimed at STO dodgers and not at Jews in hiding. He later stated that 'participation in the resistance was a deliberate decision to choose France, the French nation with all its ills, greatness and combats'.[55] Jarblum, on the other hand, was committed to financing escape lines for Jews who were seeking to avoid deportation – if not for themselves, then for their children. He financed elements of the Armée Juive set up by Abraham Polonski in Toulouse, which was less to fight than to get persecuted Jews out of France to Switzerland or Spain and eventually to Palestine. Based in Geneva, Jarblum was visited several times across the French border by Kania Geiger, born in Poland in 1920 and known in France as Anne-Marie Bonnard. With her fiancé, Ernest Lambert, born in Thionville (Lorraine) in 1918, she ran the Lyons branch of the Armée Juive under the cover of a stationers' and newsagents' shop at 149 Grande Rue de la Guillotière. They set up a Service d'Évacuation et de Regroupement des Enfants which between April and August 1944 ferried up to 130 children to Spain. The children were escorted as far as Toulouse by Andrée Salomon. Of these, seventy-nine were found passage in October on the *Guinée*, which sailed to Palestine.[56] This began to fulfil the Zionist project of saving Jews and especially Jewish children from the jaws of Nazism in order to continue building a Jewish homeland in Palestine.

Hamon and Jarblum represented the mainstream non-communist and Zionist strands of resistance in France. A third and very powerful strand was firmly communist. It was centred on the MOI of the PCF, which, as we have seen, had a powerful Jewish component. Under the German occupation three Jews headed the central apparatus of the MOI's language units: Louis Gronowski (codename Brunot) and Jacques Kaminski (Hervé), leaders of the pre-war Jewish group, had arrived in France from Poland, while Artur London (Gérard) was born to a German-speaking Czech family. They managed three different elements of MOI activity: Travail Allemand (German Work), the intelligence service and liaison activities.

Travail Allemand was in charge of the distribution of a clandestine publication, *Der Soldat im Westen*, among German soldiers, of infiltration into the occupiers' premises for intelligence purposes and of the recruitment of anti-Nazi German soldiers. These extremely dangerous activities required a native knowledge of German and were therefore undertaken by German and Austrian activists. Many of these, however, were suspected by the communist leadership of being more interested in the political regime of their native countries than in the liberation of France. For that reason, Jews, considered more reliable, could be found at different levels of the organisation. Jewish women played a significant role in approaching German soldiers. One of them, Irma Mico, born Irma Rosenberg in Czernowitz, Bukovina, belonged to a family which was attached to its Jewish cultural origins while feeling completely integrated into the Austrian nation. Arrested as a result of her communist activities, she had to move to Bucharest in order to enter university. Interestingly enough, the clandestine Romanian Communist Party was encouraging its Jewish members, who made up 80 per cent of the membership, to leave the country, in order to proletarianise the Party by strengthening its native Romanian component.[57] This is how Irma Mico ended up in Paris in 1937 and there became a permanent activist of the MOI. Until August 1942 she headed MOI's central technical services before joining, and a few months later heading, the Travail Allemand women in the Parisian area. This group consisted of fifteen women, all but one Jewish, from Austria, Germany, Romania and Poland. They befriended German soldiers whenever possible in order to extract intelligence or even persuade them to desert their own armies. Their action was not very successful but had a huge symbolic meaning.

The intelligence service of the MOI also included several Jewish women and was headed by Cristina Boïco, a Jewish biology student from Romania. It located military targets by studying the itinerary of German army units, verifying exactly when and where they would pass, and provided the fighters with bombs.[58] A woman could more easily stroll through the streets of Paris than a man to carry out reconnaissance operations without attracting attention. Jewish women were also prominent in the liaison service of the FTP-MOI. They carried compromising documents, delivered weapons to fighters for an attack and then secreted them, and were sent on rescue missions when an underground leader feared that his cover had been blown.[59] The service was headed by Olga Bancic, a young Romanian-Jewish communist born in Bessarabia in 1912 who had fled to France in 1936. Arrested by the Gestapo in November 1943, she was sentenced to death with the FTP-MOI Manouchian Group on 21 February 1944 and deported to Stuttgart, where she was beheaded.[60]

The Manouchian Group, over half of whose members were Polish, Hungarian or Romanian Jews, was only the most famous of the FTP-MOI groups that engaged in urban guerrilla warfare with the German military in France. Another was led by Mendel (Marcel) Langer, who, after the fall of the Spanish Republic, in 1939, was forced to return to France leaving his wife and daughter in Franco's Spain. Considered a political threat like all former members of the International Brigades, he was interned in the camps of Argelès and Gurs. He escaped, returned to Toulouse and rejoined his former MOI comrades, who were now acting illegally against the German occupying forces. They also helped former International Brigaders to escape from Gurs and Le Vernet and provided them with false papers. In late 1942, after the German invasion of southern France, Langer announced the formation of the FTP-MOI 35th Brigade, named after the 35th International Division, in which he had served in Spain. This new unit proved a transnational melting pot for its Polish, Spanish, Italian and Yugoslavian members. Former International Brigaders provided the leadership for younger people, who were often young Jews who had escaped the round-ups in Paris, fled to Toulouse and calculated that to resist was the best way to survive. Within six months the 35th Brigade had become a strong combat organisation, carrying out armed attacks on Wehrmacht soldiers and collaborators. Unfortunately, Langer himself did not witness this development. He was arrested by the Gestapo in the Toulouse outskirts early in early 1943 with a briefcase full of explosives, and guillotined in the Toulouse Saint-Michel prison on 23 July 1943. After his death, his group was renamed the 35th Brigade Marcel Langer and taken over by his close aide Jan Gerhard, a former Polish soldier of Jewish descent and a brilliant guerrilla commander. Gerhard organised the revenge attack on the public prosecutor who had demanded the death penalty for Langer as he walked to church in Toulouse on 10 October 1943.[61]

The classic structure of the FTP-MOI units was command exercised by former International Brigaders, while the rank and file was provided by young Jews, Spanish republicans or Italian anti-fascists. Claude Lévy, a French Jew, was fifteen at the beginning of the occupation. Confronted with the anti-Semitic laws, he had no idea of what being a Jew meant and went to the municipal library in Lyons in order to find out. His first readings on Jews were books by anti-Semitic authors. He joined the EIF in order to add some content to an identity he felt had been imposed on him.[62] For a time, he inclined to Zionism, but he later wanted to join a more energetic group undertaking military actions and ended up – by chance – in the 35th Brigade Marcel Langer in Toulouse. Among his young comrades were Catherine Varlin, born Judith Heytin to a Jewish doctor from Odessa, banned from practising by Vichy, who had joined the EIF and helped to relieve the suffering of inmates in Gurs and Le Vernet.[63] Also in the group was Damira Titonel, from an Italian family which had fled Mussolini's Fascism to settle in the Garonne valley, only to have to resume the struggle in France.[64]

Other young Jews were organised by the MOI into the Union de la Jeunesse Juive, a front organisation designed to recruit young Jews who were eager to resist occupation, whatever their ideological beliefs. The idea of a front organisation was not new. But the Communist Party leadership had made a somewhat astonishing decision. Young Jewish activists of immigrant origin but born in France, educated in French schools and not Yiddish-speaking would normally join a French group and not a 'language' group. However, in 1942 the Communist Party decided to put them in the Jewish groups. One of those was Joseph Schwarzberg, who had fled from Belgium to France in 1940 as he 'erroneously considered Pétain's Vichy France to be free'. He joined the MOI, although he was not himself a communist, and was then moved to the Union de la Jeunesse Juive. Organisations linked to the Communist Party had an obligation to transfer 10 per cent of their members to fighting units, so Schwarzberg found himself in one of those as the only Jew and the only refugee. Towards the end of the occupation, during one of the local battles, his unit made German prisoners and Joseph became the official translator, holding quite a high position in the group. Yet, having encountered anti-Semitism among his fellows-in-arms, he decided that after the war, he would 'emigrate to British Mandate Palestine', which is what he did.[65]

In the spring of 1944 things became too hot in Toulouse for the Armée Juive, and a Jewish *maquis* was organised far out of the way, at Espinassier in the Tarn, by Pierre Loeb, a French Jew from Lorraine who had fought in the French air force in 1940. Just before D-Day, the Jewish group was ordered to join a larger *maquis* on the Montagne Noire under Raymond Levy-Seckel, a former reserve officer and textile engineer from Mulhouse who was a local commander of the Armée Secrète. Of three platoons, one was composed of Frenchmen and the second of Spanish republicans and former Russian POWs who had been drafted into the Wehrmacht but deserted, and the third was a Jewish platoon which highlighted its identity by wearing blue and white shoulder flashes. It was called the Trumpeldor platoon in honour of a Zionist hero killed in Palestine in 1920. Although the Jewish platoon was a model from the military point of view, its distinctiveness upset one French commander, Captain Kervanoël, who announced, 'Your Jewish problem gets up our noses. Change your names, marry some Christian girls, and in a generation there will be no Jewish problem.'[66]

Meanwhile, in the capital, there was a stand-off in the Comité Parisien de Libération (Paris Liberation Committee, CPL), set up in October 1943, between communists who were planning insurrection and non-communists who preferred to await the arrival of Allied and French forces. Léo Hamon was the effective leader of the non-communists on the CPL, and in August 1944 feared that Paris would suffer a tragic insurrection like Warsaw. He was opposed on the CPL by André Carrel. Ironically, both were sons of revolutionary Russian-Jewish parents, born and brought up in France. Carrel's real name was Hoschiller; his father had fled the Bolsheviks and as a journalist defended the Comité des Forges steel cartel. André never recovered from being called the son of an arms dealer and became a hardline communist, accepting – unlike Hamon – the Nazi–Soviet Pact.[67] On 18 August 1944 the communists on the CPL won a majority for an insurrection the next day, headed by the FFIs' leader Henri Rol-Tanguy. Hamon was responsible for liberating the Hôtel de Ville on 20 August but then met the Swedish ambassador to organise a truce with the German authorities to give more time to the approaching armies, which arrived on 24 August.[68]

Conclusion

A transnational study of Jews in rescue and resistance sheds light not only on specific questions facing Jews but on the workings of transnational resistance as a whole. The repertoire of Jews in rescue and resistance may be traced back to the interwar period. The development of Jewish self-help activity across the diaspora, whether at the local level or through international organisations – Bundist, communist or Zionist – suggests that the roots of transnational resistance have to be traced to 1918 and even earlier. For Jews, the Second World War was a singular war of persecution and extermination within the world war. It made collaboration almost impossible and increased the urgency of organising rescue and resistance. It points the way to investigating other marginalised and excluded groups as most likely to be found at the heart of resistance activity.

There was no one Jewish resistance. Because of their backgrounds and trajectories, Jews took many pathways to resistance, some national, some communist, some Zionist. The geographical context made a huge difference to what they did. Rescue was easier to organise in France, which retained its own government and half of which was not occupied for two and a half years, than in Yugoslavia, which was invaded and partitioned between four powers and suffered the depredations of a fascist puppet state. Only in the Italian zone was it possible for Jews to survive until Italy capitulated and these areas were occupied by Germany. Resistance became the only alternative, and resistance also became a form of survival for embattled and often starving Jews.

The impact of persecution, displacement and new encounters caused many Jews to reinvent their identities. They changed their loyalties over time, as a result of encounters or experiences. Many felt fully integrated into their adopted country and did not assume a Jewish identity until they found themselves excluded from the national community and indeed threatened in livelihood and life. Some embraced a Zionist identity and dedicated themselves to helping fellow Jews to escape, with Palestine as a distant goal. Others, once of a Zionist disposition, came to realise that only communism and communist resistance could save them. A number of Tito's closest associates, such as Moše Pinjade, were of Jewish origin. Communists themselves, however, also found themselves fighting for national liberation as a prelude to hoping to found socialist societies. That said, Jews were not always accepted by the resistance organisations they joined, whether these were national or communist. Anti-Semitism persisted even in resistance movements, and would reappear after the war, not least in purges undertaken by communist regimes at the onset of the Cold War.

7

SOE and transnational resistance

Roderick Bailey

During the early summer of 1944, Peter Lake, a twenty-nine-year-old British officer who had parachuted into the Dordogne to assist the French Resistance, walked into a forest south of Villefranche-du-Périgord and found 'quite a large number of men who were obviously living in the open air. They all looked very fit. And the first thing that I noticed was that they were not young men, as I had rather expected to find. In fact most of them were refugees from Spain and particularly from Catalonia.' The majority, he soon discovered, consisted of 'seasoned veterans' who had been 'heavily engaged' in the Spanish Civil War: 'They weren't afraid of anything or anybody.' Over several days he taught them to use sub-machineguns, explosives, fuses, detonators and time delays, a task he accomplished 'largely in Spanish, assisted by a few words of Catalan': Lake had been brought up in Majorca and studied Spanish at university. He also remembered that 'a lot of them had already been extensively trained in subversive methods and were fully equipped for moving around the countryside without being seen'.[1]

In 1944 Peter Lake was a member of SOE, a clandestine British organisation set up early in the Second World War to encourage resistance and carry out sabotage inside enemy territory. The principal means by which it sought to achieve those aims was dispatching trained agents to carry out particular tasks, from derailing trains and arming guerrillas to establishing a means of productive communication between resistance fighters and the outside world. Britain was not alone in attempting this type of work. With similar aims, the USA established the OSS in 1942, while the Soviet Union had its NKVD. Of these, SOE had the greatest reach and the widest range of commitments and contacts. In Europe, OSS, by agreement, was the junior partner to SOE, while the NKVD's interests rarely extended further than the Eastern Front.

Using SOE as a case study and concentrating on flows, contacts and activities that lie mostly beyond national narratives, what follows seeks to illuminate and illustrate transnational features of clandestine Allied support to resistance fighters in occupied Europe. It seeks in particular to demonstrate the spread and diversity of those exchanges while providing a sense of their wider implications and consequences. Sources range from declassified SOE files to the recollections of former agents. Evidence has been selected with an eye to encounters that have hitherto attracted little attention from historians.

The chapter begins with a brief introduction to SOE and the cross-border nature of its tasks, before highlighting pertinent characteristics of its own personnel – international and hybrid backgrounds that made them useful in countries different to those of their birth, for example – and how it assisted other Allied agencies in deploying agents of a similar type. It then explores, through three case studies, SOE's rich and varied interactions with foreign fighters in the field. The first considers Albania, where SOE was able to both support fighters like those, including former enemies, and harness their services to aid its own work. The second looks at SOE's transformative impact on exiled Spanish republicans in southern France, which enabled them to become a highly effective fighting force. The third throws light on SOE's dealings with foreign fighters within the highly political setting of occupied Greece, which included opportunities for SOE to see how foreign fighters interacted with homegrown resistance movements as well as occasions when the presence of its agents – foreign fighters themselves – could both influence and aggravate those relationships.

SOE and resistance

SOE was created in the dark days of 1940, when Britain was on the back foot against the Axis and its leaders were anxious to find cheap and original ways of hitting back. A few plans and personnel were inherited from three short-lived predecessors: Section D, an offshoot of Britain's Secret Intelligence Service (SIS), set up in 1938 to counter the intentions of enemies and potential enemies; Military Intelligence (Research), a War Office department that had evolved from an earlier section, GS(R), established in 1938 to research matters of military significance from modern conflicts like those in Ireland, China and Spain; and Electra House, another two-year-old organisation, which had been concerned with developing subversive propaganda. These were under-resourced and unpromising beginnings, and SOE, suspect as young and unproven, struggled for some time to convince senior commanders and government ministers that it justified much support. Gradually, however, it established itself. It also expanded. By the end of the war, when SOE was dismantled and closed down, it was operating on a global scale.

Distorted by the priorities of popular histories and postwar journalism, SOE's historiography has been dominated for decades by the exploits of British agents in Nazi-occupied France.[2] The reality is that, while France was an important area of operations where a thousand agents were deployed, SOE came to work in every enemy-occupied country in Europe, as far away as Mexico, Madagascar and Japanese-occupied Malaya, and with groups as varied as communist partisans in the Balkans and head-hunting tribes in Borneo. Today, buoyed by an improvement in the quality and seriousness of research being undertaken, understanding is growing not only of SOE's multilayered involvement with occupied populations worldwide but also of the full range of irregular activity in which it was engaged, from the handling of peace-feelers to the manipulation of black markets.[3] As the Cabinet Office minister responsible for SOE remarked to Churchill in 1944: 'Bombs, sabotage, parachutes, etc., are of course only the shop window.'[4]

When considering this spread and range of activity, it is important to acknowledge, too, that no Allied secret service engaged in such work operated in a vacuum. SOE might assess guerrillas' needs and arrange for them to be armed, but the weapons it channelled into their hands were widely sourced: a significant proportion of the munitions dropped and shipped to partisan bands in the Balkans, for instance, were of German and Italian manufacture and came from stocks captured by Allied forces in North Africa and Sicily.[5] The direct assistance of conventional armed forces, like the Royal Air Force (RAF) and Royal Navy, was similarly essential not only to the cross-border infiltration of agents, funds, propaganda, arms, equipment and the like, but also to the safe extraction under SOE auspices of myriad resources of importance to the Allied war effort, ranging from thousands of evaders and escaped prisoners anxious to rejoin Allied armies, to supplies of Swedish ball bearings valuable to Allied industry, V2 rocket parts of interest to Allied researchers and the expertise of Niels Bohr, the Danish atomic physicist, whom SOE helped in 1943 to smuggle to neutral Sweden, facilitating his participation in the Manhattan Project.[6]

Indeed, so much of SOE's activity was necessarily hidden from sight that air and naval support for its operations could be the only evidence visible to occupied populations that outsiders were trying to help. In some countries this impression not only gave encouragement at the time but also endures today. 'Everybody knew the aircraft had crashed', remembered Frank Griffiths, pilot and sole survivor of an RAF Halifax that went down over Annecy in August 1943 when poised to drop stores to an SOE mission in Haute-Savoie.

> They even knew my name because they'd got my [flying] helmet, and they knew what was in the [aircraft's] load, and suddenly the Resistance, everybody in the area, was pro-Ally. Indeed afterwards I said to the mayor of Annecy how sorry I was [that] I'd made such a hash of it (this was some years later) and he said, 'No, no. You were the *chiquenaude*.'
>
> And I had to find a dictionary.
>
> '*Chiquenaude*: The fillip. The match that lights the fire.'[7]

Today, Griffiths and the fate of his crew feature centrally in an SOE display in Haute-Savoie's principal *Résistance* museum.[8]

For all of SOE's dabbling in piracy and currency speculation, the promotion of local resistance in enemy territory was generally its principal aim. To achieve it, SOE knew that the right kind of human resource was required. This meant committed and trustworthy volunteers capable of performing key technical roles: some were required to be leaders; others would need to be sabotage experts, couriers or weapons instructors, or able to operate the radio sets essential for sending out reports and calling in deliveries of reinforcements and supplies. It could also mean people with languages and local knowledge. Some agents were British-born, but, generally, SOE's experience was that the right combination of linguistic and technical skills necessary to blend seamlessly and immediately with local populations in most European countries was not readily found among British nationals. It was no coincidence that most of SOE's British agents – Peter Lake was one of the exceptions – were recruited for liaison- and commando-type work in relatively remote locations, like the Balkans, where they lived like guerrillas, wore uniforms and used interpreters and essentially shared the outlaw life of the local fighters with whom they worked, having comparatively little need to maintain a secure cover. For SOE's work in most parts of Europe, the go-to candidates were either nationals of the countries concerned or other non-Britons who could convincingly pass as them.

Foreign fighters as SOE agents

When it reached peak strength in mid-1944, SOE employed an estimated thirteen thousand personnel. Of these, about five thousand were training to be agents or already deployed in the field. One of them was Stanisław Makowski, a Pole whom SOE sent that year into France. Makowski's enlistment by SOE illustrates well its interest in non-British backgrounds and its need for skills and knowledge particular to certain countries. It also demonstrates how his own peripatetic past had shaped some of the attractive qualities that he had to offer, including his availability.

Born in 1914 in what is now Moldova and was then the Russian province of Bessarabia, Makowski was the son of a wealthy Polish winemaker. After school and a year's army service he had studied agriculture at the University of Poznań, then continued his studies in Antwerp, Grenoble and Montpellier, as preparation for taking over his father's estates. When Germany invaded Poland, however, he joined General Sikorski's forces in France. In June 1940 he was evacuated to Britain, where he was seconded to the British army, serving subsequently in Gambia as an officer in the Royal West African Frontier Force, before returning to Britain and, in November 1943, volunteering for SOE. 'Possesses the necessary linguistic and geographical qualifications', SOE recorded of his suitability for France as his application was formally approved.[9] For one SOE officer assigned to watching him as he trained, Makowski impressed as 'a pleasant, neat, careful man', and not 'the dashing romantic Pole of legend':

> If I had met him without knowing his nationality I should have thought him an Austrian. He has many of the characteristics[:] gallantry without flamboyancy, a certain sentimentality, weakness of character, the '*gemütlichkeit*' and easygoing quality which are agreeable, a mild pre-occupation with being a gentleman without snobbishness ... [He is a] typical example of a sociable European. To say I would place implicit faith in him would be an exaggeration, but if I wished to spend a pleasant evening, if [an] unexciting [one], which would afford gastronomic rather than intellectual delights, with him I should be in good company. The evening would not end in roistering but a quiet drink about 2300 hours, a click of the heels and so to bed.[10]

Makowski possessed 'the great advantage of being a European with continental mind and manners', the officer went on, and greater awareness than other trainees 'of what the work is likely to be like, and of its difficulties, and is not, I think, quite sure about it'.[11] Makowski was worried, too, about Poland, and had been deeply affected by the recent death of his first child. 'He is a very gentle [and] affectionate person', continued the report, 'in love with his [English] wife whom he misses. He is an extremely nice, pleasant man, and I sometimes wonder if he wonders what this has to do with him.'[12]

Makowski completed his training and was dropped by parachute into France in April 1944 as an agent of SOE's French Section. For his first month he worked in the Indre, in central France, training local fighters. Later he organised several *maquis* in pockets of the Sologne. After D-Day he led his main group at Souesmes, near Salbris, in a series of effective attacks on enemy communications and supplies. Well liked by resistance leaders across the region, he was observed by another SOE agent to have charmed even the FTP, France's communist-led resistance movement. In August, Makowski was wounded and captured while trying to evade German checkpoints, then handed to German military police, who tortured and killed him.[13]

Although they benefited from SOE's resources and facilities, the allegiances of many non-British agents were to their governments- or armies-in-exile. Most Poles and Free French, for example, came under the orders of their own authorities. Some agents, though, were able and content to be independent of their countries' forces and use SOE's offices to work exclusively as 'British' agents. Stanisław Makowski was one of these. Another was Wladimir Petro-Pavlovsky, whose prior allegiances had been to France and White Russia before that. Born in Kharkov to a Russian father and French mother in June 1897, he had served during the First World War in the Russian Imperial Army before fleeing the Revolution for France, where he secured French citizenship, a transfer to the French army and postings to Morocco and Siberia, the latter with French forces sent to fight the Bolsheviks. Between the wars he had spent nearly twenty years in China as a civil engineer. He was still in China when France fell in 1940, whereupon he offered his services to the British in Hong Kong. Assigned to local intelligence work before transferring to SOE in late 1941, he was wounded in the leg when the Japanese attacked but escaped via Macao to China, then was assigned to what was called the China Commando Group, a unit composed mostly of Danes, with which SOE planned to assist Chiang Kai-Shek's Chinese forces in their war against Japan. After that project was abandoned, Petro-Pavlovsky worked in Washington, DC, from October 1942 until April 1943, as an SOE liaison officer to OSS. In September 1943 his itinerant career continued when, after special training at schools in Britain, he was dropped by parachute into eastern Serbia with orders to penetrate Bulgaria. That task proved impossible, so he concentrated instead on gathering intelligence. Withdrawn the following April, he saw out the war working in the Ceylon headquarters of SOE's Far East arm.[14] Evidently Petro-Pavlovsky's skills and past experiences made him suitable, in SOE's estimation, to the varied tasks that it gave him, but its records also contain a clue as to why, despite having French nationality, he spent the war nowhere near French territory: 'It must be remembered', SOE noted in 1943, 'that as a technical deserter from [the] French Army it may cause difficulties if he goes to any area where [the] civil administration is predominantly ex-Vichy.'[15]

Men and women whom SOE recruited in the field formed another category of volunteer. These included service personnel from conventional British and Commonwealth armed forces whom the war had stranded as fugitives in enemy territory, such as shot-down airmen or escaped prisoners. Among the latter was an Arab Christian from Palestine, Mikhail Khalil Shibli Khouri, who had been captured in Greece in April 1941 while serving as a private in a Palestinian company of the British army's Auxiliary Military Pioneer Corps. According to officers of the first SOE mission sent to Nazi-occupied Greece, to which Khouri presented himself after its arrival in the autumn of 1942, he had escaped from a train of prisoners being taken out of the country and, since then, survived on the generosity of Greek villagers, which he repaid with his peacetime skills as a carpenter and by joining a band of Greek guerrillas in the hills.[16] When he met the mission he was already armed and wore the insignia of a British army lieutenant. 'I asked him what his proper Army rank was', recalled the mission's senior officer, who immediately made him revert to it. 'He said he was really only a private, but that he found it easier to obtain food when dressed as a British officer. I soon discovered that the grandeur of his self-obtained commission had [also] facilitated the successful wooing of a Greek girl.'[17] Officially absorbed into the mission, Khouri would be the only man to participate in both of SOE's most iconic sabotage operations in Greece: the demolition of the Gorgopotamos viaduct in November 1942 and the destruction of the Asopos viaduct in June 1943. By the time he was withdrawn from Greece in 1944 to return to his home in Haifa, SOE had promoted him to sergeant and awarded him two gallantry medals.[18]

Not all local recruits were Allied service personnel like Khouri whose credentials could be assessed in the field with relative ease. More were civilians who were less easy to vet, so it helped if there were existing links to Britain via employment, families or friendships. Sylvia Apostolidou, whose mother was English, was nineteen years old and living in Athens when, in 1943, she was recruited there by an SOE officer, a New Zealander, who had previously known her siblings. 'I could not stand the idea of the Germans in my country', she recalled in 2017 of why she wanted to help; 'I did not want them here so I felt I had to do something.'[19] In time, she assisted SOE's missions in Greece with gathering intelligence, moving and hiding explosives and other stores and the escape of British and Commonwealth soldiers on the run. 'At first she was given charge of the administration of a group of [local Greek] agents who were employed in collecting information from the German controlled aerodromes', SOE recorded of some of her activities.

> She paid the agents their weekly salaries, [and] received all their reports which she translated and collated before they were forwarded to this HQ. The bulk of this work was carried out in her father's [dental] surgery which was used as an HQ thus endangering not only herself but also the whole of her family.

> In addition to these intelligence and administrative duties she received and stored consignments of ammunition ... to be employed by the members of the group operating in Athens. She invariably transported this ammunition through the city in a taxi and on several occasions had extremely narrow escapes from capture by the Germans. Once she was fired upon by a German road block guard and twice was arrested by the Greek police.[20]

Local helpers like her are mostly absent from lists of 'official' SOE agents, but their work could be just as important as that of the latter, and the dangers they faced might be worse. Betrayed and arrested in 1944, Apostolidou was brutally handled by German *Feldpolizei*, then condemned to death, and was at one point brought out before a firing squad.[21] On SOE's recommendation she was later awarded Britain's George Medal, second only to the George Cross for gallantry not directly in the face of the enemy.[22]

Secret services can live or die by the personal loyalties of those who wish to work for them. SOE was no different, but duty to Britain and blind allegiance to the Crown were not hard-and-fast conditions when it was looking for recruits, especially when candidates were few. Recalling his recruitment of Noor Inayat Khan, a candidate for SOE's French Section, whose father, a Sufi teacher, came from an Indian Muslim family, her interviewer in London recalled that her 'first loyalty' was to India: 'If I had to choose between Britain and India', he remembered her saying, 'I would choose India.'[23] Khan was selected, then trained as a radio operator, and went on to work and be captured in France. She died in Dachau and was awarded a posthumous George Cross. She has become a staple subject for books and articles about SOE's activities in France and its women, and the question of her 'first loyalty' is often included in these, sometimes coupled with her interviewer's additional remark that 'that was the only time I met a loyalty that was not directly British'.[24] The significance of that story can be overplayed, however. For hundreds of agents who were not British, hopes and fears about homes and families under enemy occupation could matter rather more than any 'loyalty' to Britain.

SOE assistance to Allied agencies

In addition to recruiting foreign volunteers to work as agents in enemy territory, SOE assisted Britain's allies in sending out their own. The American OSS, for example, depended heavily on SOE's experience in its first two years, with the result that early OSS agents who went into France, for instance, were effectively seconded to SOE: they received SOE training, were clothed and equipped by SOE and were dispatched on SOE-devised and -directed missions.[25] SOE even helped the NKVD dispatch a few of its own agents into Europe by providing training and equipment and arranging, with the Royal Navy and RAF, the submarines and the aircraft needed to send them.[26] Another organisation with which SOE collaborated closely was the Polish government-in-exile's Sixth Bureau, responsible for communicating with Poles engaged in intelligence and resistance activities in occupied territories. Among its officers was Józef Maciąg, the first Pole to be dispatched to the Balkans on a mission agreed with SOE.

As well as exemplifying these forms of cooperation, Maciąg's case, like that of Sylvia Apostolidou, demonstrates the perceived value to secret services of individuals with 'hybrid' backgrounds. When he was recruited for his mission, Maciąg was a twenty-eight-year-old professional soldier serving with Polish forces in the Middle East, and what was wanted was a Pole capable of carrying out two tasks in Serbia. First, he was to explore and establish ways of facilitating the clandestine movement of information and personnel from Poland to Cairo and Istanbul; second, he was to look after any Poles whom he might find locally.[27] According to SOE records, Maciąg was 'the only suitable candidate' for that job.[28] Those documents do not elaborate on why that was the case, but it is likely, to judge from details recently obtained from his relatives, that he was assessed as having a combination of attractive qualities, including country knowledge and language skills. His father, Michał, was an ethnic Pole from Kolbuszowa, a small town in the Rzeszów region of what, until 1918, was Austrian Galicia; but his mother, Rozalia, was from Dalmatia: Michał had met her in Bosnia while he was serving as an artillery officer in the Austro-Hungarian army. Though always a Pole, Józef, their first child, was born and spent his earliest years in Viŝegrad, in eastern Bosnia, where Rozalia had grown up. Later, after Michał returned from the First World War among the Poles of the *Błękitna Armia*, General Haller's Blue Army, the family had resettled in Biała Podlaska, a town north-east of Lublin in the new Polish state. But they retained their links to Yugoslavia, and Józef had last visited in 1939, recuperating from a broken leg suffered while skiing.[29]

Maciąg's subsequent career also provides another illustration of the twisting paths taken by many agents towards dangerous missions in countries of which they were not citizens themselves. By 1943, in addition to his Yugoslav heritage, he was able to offer military skills, battlefield experience and a proven record of loyal service to Poland's cause, as well as prior experience of underground work. Following his father's path, he had been commissioned as an officer in the Polish army in 1934. According to a note sent by the Sixth Bureau to SOE, he had fought the invading Germans in September 1939 and then worked for a year underground for the Polish resistance before leaving for the Middle East as a clandestine courier.[30]

On arrival he joined the Samodzielna Brygada Strzelców Karpackich, the Independent Carpathian Brigade. Formed in Syria in April 1940 under Colonel (later General) Stanisław Kopański, this was a Polish military unit comprising exiles and escapees and had been part of France's Armée du Levant until the French defeat, whereupon it had marched to Palestine and joined the British. In 1941 the brigade fought in North Africa, alongside British troops, at Tobruk and on the Gazala Line. In 1942 it was withdrawn to Palestine and joined General Władysław Anders's Polish army, which had arrived recently from the Soviet Union.

Maciąg was at the British staff college at Haifa when, in February 1943, the call came for him to be attached to SOE. From then on, so far as preparation and support for his mission were concerned, he came largely under SOE's wing and effectively became, in many regards, one of its own. It arranged for him to attend training courses in parachuting, weapons-handling and other specialist skills. It issued him with clothing and equipment and provided him with funds. In June, when he parachuted from an RAF Halifax into the Homolje mountain range in eastern Serbia, he was still an officer in the Polish army, answerable to his Polish superiors, and tasked with the mission given him by the Polish Sixth Bureau. But in the hope that he might benefit from the established presence of SOE's missions there, he wore British uniform, carried the insignia and identity documents of a British army captain and would live and work among British missions on the ground, as well as use their wireless sets to communicate with the outside world and be known to everyone – Briton, Yugoslav or Pole – by the pseudonym John Nash.[31]

Jasper Rootham, the British officer in command of the SOE mission in Serbia, thought that Maciąg was 'haunted by the tragedy of Poland. I recall his stony face when I had to tell him, some weeks later, that I had just heard on the wireless of [the Polish chief of staff and prime minister-in-exile] General Sikorski's death in an aeroplane crash at Gibraltar; and his reply: "The only man," he said, "who could prevent my country from committing suicide."'[32] Maciąg formed a small unit of Poles, requested supply drops to clothe, arm and equip them and was hoping to use them in action. He was also sending out intelligence that SOE considered valuable enough to pass to SIS.[33] Postwar Polish accounts claim that Maciąg did indeed raise a local force of Poles, mainly escaped labourers from the Bor copper mines, and that it carried out a series of sabotage operations.[34] SOE records do not confirm those operations, but they do make clear that little resistance activity could be expected by then from anyone else in that part of Serbia: it was an area where local sympathies lay with General 'Draža' Mihailović's royalist 'Četnik' guerrilla movement, which, though it had fought the Axis for a time, was becoming increasingly preoccupied with confronting Tito's communist partisans. In December, Maciąg and a party of Poles and British were living precariously in the mountains when German soldiers suddenly surrounded the isolated farmhouse in which they were hiding. 'Captain Maciag [sic] fought bravely', reads a Sixth Bureau report, 'making it possible for the [British] wireless operator to escape through the window.' But the fighting was fierce, and Maciąg was killed by a German hand-grenade.[35]

Jewish SOE agents

For some non-British volunteers who lacked national bodies to represent them, SOE seemed to offer the only opportunity for action. These included dozens of Jewish refugees who had reached Britain seeking sanctuary from Nazi persecution, and whose recruitment and careers underline SOE's focus on skills and knowledge suitable for operations in particular countries, and especially in this case Germany, Austria and Italy. Their reasons for volunteering also provide grounds for further reflection on what could be important, in terms of motivation, to those with international and transnational pasts.

One Jewish refugee was Heinz Günther Spanglet. German-born, he had arrived in Britain in spring 1939 shortly after his twenty-second birthday. Although a sister would follow on the *Kindertransport*, most of his relatives, including his parents and a brother, would die in concentration camps, and he had himself spent time in Sachsenhausen after being arrested on *Kristallnacht*. When Britain went to war with Germany, he was rounded up and interned as an enemy alien: the standard treatment for refugees on British soil when their countries entered the war as Britain's enemies. Months later, he was one of two thousand internees, mostly Jewish refugees from Germany and Austria, put aboard the *Dunera*, a British passenger ship bound for Australia, to be held in camps there.[36] In 1941, reclassified as a 'friendly' alien, Spanglet returned to Britain and was permitted to join the British army's Pioneer Corps, which was where SOE found him in early 1943.

Specialist training followed. So did a new name, which Spanglet kept for the rest of his life. The choice of name was his, but the change was made on SOE's recommendation that it might afford its Austrian and German volunteers greater protection if they were captured. Erich Ignaz Schwarz, a Jewish refugee from Austria who also joined SOE from the Pioneer Corps, recalled the day when he and other Germans and Austrians were visited in their SOE training school by 'a man from the War Office' who sat them in a room and gave each man a form, an hour in which to choose and record a new 'English-sounding' name, the explanation 'that if we were caught in enemy territory we had a very good chance of being treated as spies' and advice 'to stick to the same initials'. He said, 'Sometimes, under pressure, you start writing your old name and you sometimes have a chance of remembering in time; it's a small thing but it helps. So when all but two minutes of the hour had elapsed, I couldn't think of anything else and I wrote "Eric Ian Sanders".'[37] Spanglet ignored the advice about initials. 'I changed my name to Stephen Patrick Dale', he recalled fifty years later. 'I chose Dale because it was unobtrusive and insignificant.'[38] Assigned to work with partisans in northern Italy, Dale parachuted into the eastern Dolomites in October 1944. Three Austrians accompanied him: one was Jewish and had trained with him; the other two were ex-Wehrmacht soldiers who had switched sides after capture. Dropped in the wrong place, he was quickly captured, narrowly escaping execution, but survived the war.[39]

Another Jewish volunteer was Gabor Adler, a young Hungarian. His own path to SOE was rather different from Dale's, although pre-war persecution played its part. Born in September 1919 in Satu Mare, a city today in north-west Romania but then in eastern Hungary, he had moved with his family from Hungary to Italy in the 1920s and then, after schooling in Germany, settled in Milan, where he worked in an advertising office, then for a Russian engineer and finally for a Russian fur merchant. In 1939 Italy's introduction of laws discriminating against Jews compelled him to leave for Morocco, where, in Tangier, he worked as a waiter, cook and house-painter before asking the British consulate, for which he had done some decorating, if he could join the British army. In late 1941 and with the consul's help he was duly put aboard a boat for Gibraltar, from where, in January 1942, he reached Britain. While in Gibraltar he had volunteered to join de Gaulle's forces but in London, when his Italian background became known, SOE persuaded the Free French to release their claim on him: SOE was under pressure to prosecute its war against Italy more effectively, but suffered from a paucity of Italian-speaking recruits. He began his SOE training in February 1942.

At first glance, it might be tempting to assume that Adler, as a Jew, had cause enough to volunteer to kill Germans. But a different picture emerges from assessments made by SOE observers who came to know him while he trained. 'This man is very intelligent and quick-witted and keeps abreast of the course of study without much effort', one report reads:

> He is an all-round man and displays an equal aptitude for both the mental and physical side of the course.
> He is inclined at times to display a rather superior and critical attitude ... In the last few days he has settled down much better and reacts with docility

> to the various regulations of the school. He has a very redeeming sense of humour even if it is at times markedly cynical, is an agreeable companion and, once you have got to know him, very easy to get on with.

With regard to Adler's motivation, however, the same observer recorded, perhaps not without prejudice:

> He does not appear to have any marked anti-fascist or anti-German feelings, and I would say he is in the game to get as much as he can out of it ... I think his main object in volunteering for the British forces is to enable himself to get a British Passport after the war (he is a Jew of the International type, without any particular national root) ... and he is continually asking me how much one gets paid for this and that ... He has no personal quarrel with Germans or Italians; he and his family have suffered no active persecution from them, they have never invaded his own country, and he has only a vague sympathy for his fellow Jews in the sufferings they have undergone.[40]

To SOE, the fact that Adler's motives seemed rather mercenary was of minor account. SOE saw hostility to the enemy as a desirable quality, but it was not essential, and plenty of successful operatives demonstrated other motives for volunteering, from a desire for financial gain to a simple wish for adventure. Even when Adler expressed doubts about being able to kill in cold blood, SOE remained unfazed. It may have helped that he had expressed those doubts himself. 'Adler was quite frank with me on the point of being unable to say whether he could take a life', the head of SOE's Italian section recorded, 'and in fact asked to be put under fire for a time to test his reactions.'[41] In the end, Adler never secured a British passport or saw conventional action against the enemy. In January 1943, in civilian clothes and with a Sardinian-born agent to assist him, he was put ashore by submarine on the coast of Italian-occupied Sardinia with instructions to assist local anti-fascists. He and his colleague were captured within twenty-four hours. Removed eventually to prison in Rome, Adler was still there in June 1944 when, hours before the city fell to Allied forces, German soldiers shot him.[42]

Jasper Rootham, to whose SOE mission Józef Maciąg had been attached in the mountains of eastern Serbia, reflected in 1946 that, while his mission and its local helpers had comprised men of many nations, they had been united in ways 'that newspapers and statesmen sometimes seem to forget'. 'We were only a collection of ordinary individuals thrown together by a world upheaval', he wrote of the 'motley' band – 'Serbs, Vlasi [Vlachs], Poles, Greeks, Italians and Soviet Russians' – with whom he lived and worked for months, 'and the lesson we learned from it was that the most important word in the sentence I am writing is "individuals".'

> We appreciated or disliked one another not because we came from this or that country but for the possession or lack of qualities which are common to all men; and the two qualities which I believe all of us prized most highly and were perhaps surprised to find were humour and, for want of a better word, charity. Of course, it may be that we were simply held together by nothing more than a common purpose of hate and self-preservation, but I like to think that it was a little more than that.[43]

The motives of Gabor Adler may underline Rootham's point. Adler was Jewish, a fact that undoubtedly helped shape the journey that led him to SOE, the shores of Sardinia and an early grave in Italy. But given SOE's assessment that he wished to secure British citizenship by accepting the opportunities offered him and seemed not to be burning with hatred for Nazi Germany, it may not have been the defining characteristic that led him to volunteer.

SOE and foreign fighters in Albania, 1943–44: a study in cooperation

During the course of the war, SOE trained, equipped and dispatched to the Balkans and south-east Europe several hundred Allied personnel. Scattered about the region in individual missions, from the northernmost tip of Yugoslavia to the easternmost islands of the Aegean, many encountered other foreigners whom the war had thrust into these places and saw at first hand how they, too, cooperated and interacted with local populations and resistance fighters. Albania, occupied by Axis forces in 1939, provides a useful snapshot of how, within the borders of one of Europe's smallest countries, SOE could find itself able to not only witness and record the activities of fighters of multiple nationalities, including former enemies, but also support and benefit from them.

Between May 1943 and the end of 1944, SOE sent into Albania over a hundred officers and non-commissioned officers – almost all of them British – to seek out local fighters and wage guerrilla war. Characteristic of SOE operations throughout the Balkans, this uniformed force was dispersed around the country in individual teams who lived like guerrillas and sought to channel weapons, funds and equipment to any belligerent locals prepared to fight the Axis. In practice, this meant Albanians of various political hues and social, racial, ethnic and religious backgrounds. The partisans of Albania's communist-led national liberation movement, with which SOE chiefly dealt, numbered eventually in the tens of thousands and, from its earliest days, comprised Tosks from southern Albania, Ghegs from the north, Vlachs, ethnic Greeks and Slavs, Greek Orthodox Christians, Roman Catholics and Muslims. Among the movement's founders was Baba Faja, a hard-drinking Bektashi priest. Over time, fighters from beyond Albania's borders also bolstered the partisan ranks.

A few were Wehrmacht deserters of Soviet origin – some of them Kazakhs and Tajiks – who had entered German service after being captured originally on the Eastern Front while serving with the Red Army.[44] Many more were Italians. SOE estimated that about 20,000 Italian soldiers took to the Albanian mountains after Italy surrendered in September 1943 and Germany took over the occupation, and several hundred of them joined the partisans. Living among them in the mountains, SOE personnel saw the Italians at close range and recorded numerous ways in which they contributed to the partisan war effort. The fighting quality of the all-Italian Antonio Gramsci Battalion, attached to the partisan 1st Brigade, was assessed as especially significant. Important, too, was the added Italian firepower of the 75-millimetre mountain guns of a 160-man battery of mule-carried pack artillery.[45] In the summer of 1944 SOE arranged for 400 extra artillery shells to be sourced from Italy and dropped by parachute to replenish its diminishing stocks.[46] Also praised in SOE reports were the efforts of Italian medical personnel in treating partisan sick and wounded.[47]

In addition to arming Italians attached to the partisans, SOE missions in Albania employed others to assist with their own work. Most were used in non-combatant roles to ease the day-to-day burdens that missions endured in the mountains. Some who spoke Albanian acted as interpreters, for example. Others became cooks and sanitary orderlies or cared for the mules that missions needed for carrying their kit. One mission employed an Italian military veterinarian to look after its animals, two Italian mechanics to keep the mission's radio sets working and an armed platoon of Italian soldiers to carry out guard duty.[48] Italian medical officers and orderlies also treated British casualties.[49]

A handful of Italians were employed by SOE in more active roles. One was Giuseppe Manzitti, a lawyer in Genoa before the war. Previously an intelligence officer in Albania with the Italian army's Parma Division, after the armistice he offered his services to the British and contributed to their work in a variety of valuable ways: wearing civilian clothes, he gathered intelligence in German-occupied towns; he helped out as an interpreter; and once, when hostile Albanians threatened to kill an SOE officer with whom he was working, he intervened and saved the man's life.[50] Manzitti was recommended for a British decoration and forged lifelong bonds with SOE officers with whom he worked.[51]

SOE and foreign fighters in France, 1944: a study in efficacy

The smooth collaboration between SOE agents and Spanish fighters in Nazi-occupied southern France provides a vivid and detailed example of how effective, militarily, transnational exchanges could become. Peter Lake reflected in late 1944 that the 'tough, experienced veterans' whom he had trained in the Dordogne had carried out 'some of the best work' that summer, blowing bridges and harassing convoys 'particularly at Castelnaud and Groléjac'.[52] It is unclear whether Lake actually saw those fighters in action, but at least one SOE agent in France fought beside Spanish guerrillas in addition to arming them. Bill Probert, who parachuted into the Ariège, a département in the Midi-Pyrénées sharing a border with northern Spain, in early August 1944, was an experienced British officer who had seen prior service in Madagascar and North Africa. Within days he was able to appreciate at first hand the commitment of Spanish fighters to resistance activity in that part of France, as well as provide support essential for them to perform a major role. Documented in a report written a few weeks afterwards, Probert's experiences also suggest that such interactions could be particularly successful, in terms of results against the enemy, when everyone's interest in local politics was minimal.

With his mission commander, a French army officer named Marcel Bigeard, Probert had worked closely with the local brigade of the Agrupación de Guerrilleros Españoles, the all-Spanish component of France's communist-led FTP.[53] The brigade's commander was twenty-eight-year-old Pascual Gimeno, known locally by his *nom de guerre*, Royo, who had fought in Spain as a republican officer and crossed into France in February 1939. Probert reported later that Royo's brigade was about 225-strong and 'formed the nucleus of resistance to the enemy in the Ariège, and [its members] were all and without exception veterans of the Spanish Civil War who had taken refuge in France after the Republican defeat. They were extremely well organized and disciplined and were certainly neither mercenaries nor bandits.' When Probert first met them, they were also badly armed: 'Apart from a small number of rifles and revolvers, they possessed three (3) [sic] French *fusil-mitrailleurs* [a magazine-fed light machine gun] and 400 rounds of ammo.' This was a weakness that he was in a position to remedy. Transmitted to SOE headquarters by wireless set, immediate appeals for suitable weapons, and especially more and better light machine guns, led to the mission receiving, between 8 and 16 August, a series of supply drops from Allied aircraft flying from bases in North Africa.[54]

These stores reached them just as German activity in the area was increasing, 'with the result that it became literally a question [of] taking the arms from the containers, giving a ten-minute course of instruction to the maquisards and then sending them off immediately to ambush Jerry convoys'. This tactic 'bore immediate fruit' when, armed with grenades, one small group of Spaniards killed or wounded thirty passing Germans. On 19 August, Probert watched more of them in action during a major attack on the Ariège's principal town of Foix. The German garrison was well entrenched, well armed and more numerous than originally believed: 150 soldiers rather than 80 to 100. 'Moreover, our attack was expected.' Nevertheless, the assault went in, spearheaded by Probert and a small but well-armed Spanish band, and after fierce street fighting the Germans surrendered: twenty-five officers and over a hundred men.[55]

The transformative impact of SOE's intervention continued in subsequent days. As detailed by Probert, fresh actions included the interception on 20 August of an eighteen-truck convoy at Prayols, south of Foix, where, after a two-and-a-half-hour battle, fifty Germans were killed, forty wounded and another forty captured, for the loss of one Spanish officer killed. 'There were no other casualties [on our side]', Probert reported. 'Amazing but absolutely true. The tactic of organising ambushes [of] three to five LMGs [light machine guns] was giving marvellous results.' Next day, a sixty-strong party 'composed mainly of Spaniards' halted another German force on the road between Foix and Saint-Girons. Probert and others arrived in support, and together they resisted strong enemy attacks, which included barrages of heavy mortars and a bayonet charge, before withdrawing to a fresh barricade up the road. The German force advanced until it reached this, whereupon fresh fighting broke out, beginning a stop-start pattern of costly progress along the road that continued for thirty six hours, at the end of which the surviving Germans gave themselves up. The latter's losses, Probert recorded, were 220 men killed, 120 wounded, 1,250 taken prisoner and dozens of trucks, three anti-tank guns and large quantities of arms and ammunition captured, against fifteen killed and forty wounded on the French-Spanish-British side. 'Never at any time did the maquis forces exceed 240', noted Probert, who had been in the thick of the fighting, 'and at the blackest periods was not more than 50.'[56]

One final form of assistance that Probert's mission gave the Spanish was to distribute gold coins, sent originally to finance his mission's work, as compensation for the families and dependents in Spain of those killed fighting in the Ariège. It is unclear whether SOE authorised this expenditure, but it is certainly evident from Probert's account that he both admired and liked Royo and his men, although he suspected that they could be ruthless, too. The alleged killing, apparently at the end of SOE-delivered sub-machine guns and grenades, of the twenty-five German officers captured at Foix may provide an illustration of that. Probert heard 'unofficially' a few days after that attack that at two o'clock one morning, while these prisoners were being held together in a stable, their Spanish guards 'had tossed a dozen or so Mills grenades among the sleeping officers, and had then completed their work with Stens and revolvers. Among the 'deceased' was one Frenchwoman who had refused to leave her German lover.' In general, though, Probert found these Spanish fighters impressive and, having no political axes to grind locally, certainly more effective, determined and reliable than many Frenchmen. The FTP, he felt, wanted Allied weapons 'not with the intention of using them against the enemy but in order to be able to present a force to take over power, administration, etc., after the departure of the Germans'. Indeed, if the 'initiative' had been left to them, it was probable, so it seemed to him, that 'the whole of the enemy forces in the department would have been allowed to wend their tranquil way to Toulouse and thence back to Germany. This, however, was not good enough for the mission, nor, let it be said to their credit, was it good enough for the Spaniards.'[57]

SOE and foreign fighters in Greece, 1943–44: a study in disharmony

By the end of September 1944, when Probert filed his report, the fighting in the Ariège had been over for nearly a month, but he believed that 'more will be heard' of his Spanish friends 'as they are now filtering over the Spanish frontier [into Spain] in large numbers. The mission wishes them good hunting.'[58] Whether Royo and his men took their weapons with them is not recorded, but Probert's remarks raise the question of whether one reason for their readiness to fight hard in France was a desire to secure arms and ammunition for subsequent use at home. It is certainly clear that SOE agents' interactions could be more productive, in terms of action against the enemy, in areas where resistance fighters were less invested politically. Its experiences in Greece, to which SOE sent over 200 British and Commonwealth personnel as well as several Sixth Bureau Poles, underline how local politics and tensions between indigenous guerrillas could complicate activities considerably. This included occasions when cross-border flows of men and materiel, and sometimes merely the promise of them, increased local friction and reshaped homegrown fighters' perception and treatment of outsiders, including SOE's own agents.

The contemporary reports of Adam Kula, a Polish army officer dropped by parachute into central Greece in September 1943, are particularly illuminating in this regard. Another Sixth Bureau officer attached to SOE, Kula had been tasked with looking for Poles and exploring the possibilities of subverting those whom he found in German service. In all, in three months, he met about a hundred. Among the first was a Jewish soldier, Aleksander Queller, who, like Mikhail Khouri, had been captured in Greece in 1941 after being sent with a Palestinian unit to fight beside British forces. After escaping from German captivity, he had eked out an existence working on the railways and in the fields, learning Greek in the process, and finally joined an SOE mission in the mountains as a runner and interpreter. But most Poles whom Kula encountered were deserters from military service or escapees from labour units, plus a few sailors who had deserted from ships in Piraeus. The majority, he reported, came from Poznan and Pomerania, and around 20 per cent from Warsaw. Their average age seemed to be about twenty-three, and all of them impressed him as 'genuine [Polish] patriots'. Some had grasped willingly at opportunities to fight for Ellinikos Laikos Apeleftherotikos Stratos (ELAS), Greece's communist-led resistance movement, serving mostly in what was known as the Battalion of Death, where they 'were used in the front line and were reckoned to be the best soldiers in the partisan ranks'. Moreover, 'at every opportunity [they] beg to be allowed a chance to fight against the Germans. One of the reasons for this is that they consist primarily of people whose relatives have been shot by the Germans or put into concentration camps.' Kula added, however, that relations between the Poles and ELAS were deteriorating. This was a time when ELAS was becoming increasingly hostile to Allied efforts to arm other Greek guerrillas whom it considered rivals for postwar power, and he felt that his own arrival had something to do with the downturn.[59]

Until then, so Kula noted, ELAS had been able to blast its Poles with 'violent communist propaganda ... reiterating amongst other things that a Polish Government and a Polish army existed only in Russia'. Some of the Poles had believed this, 'as they had absolutely no sources of objective news from the time of their capture by the Germans', but, once they met Kula, this changed:

> Every time I came into contact with the Poles I was subjected to a host of questions on the subject of the Polish Army and the Polish Government, the Allied Armies, the Katyn tragedy, about which they had heard only German propaganda, the death of General Sikorski, etc. I may add that after contacting the group of Poles in the so-called Battalion of Death for which I obtained permission from the ELAS authorities, and speaking with them for a whole day, I was forbidden further contact with them on the next day on the grounds that I was spreading propaganda contrary to ELAS ideology by mentioning the existence of a Polish Army in the Middle East and Great Britain and of the Polish Government in London.

'I found individual Poles lying in hospital with no covering and no material comforts and dependent on the favours of the people', Kula recorded of the worsening state of affairs. 'I met one Pole in particular from the Battalion of Death, who had been badly wounded in a recent battle, was abandoned by the partisans and without any assistance dragged himself along on crutches, starving, in ragged underclothes and without boots. I could not help him and take him with me, since ELAS would have treated him as a deserter, and shot him.

It was equally apparent to Kula that ELAS, suspicious that the British wished to prevent it from seizing postwar power, was 'utterly opposed' to any attempt by SOE to separate the Poles and help, equip, and command them. 'They openly declared that they could not agree to the presence within the [SOE] Missions of armed Polish units which might, when the time was ripe, be used against ELAS ... They also wanted to make certain that the Missions had no protection and were thus dependent on ELAS.'[60]

A report from inside the Battalion of Death, addressed to 'the Polish Ministry of War' and brought out from Greece when Adam Kula left in December 1943, seems to corroborate his impressions. It was written by Władysław Malanowski, a self-described sergeant-cadet in the Polish army who had commanded the battalion's all-Polish platoon of twenty-eight men after escaping from German captivity. His report explains that relations in ELAS between Greeks and Poles had been satisfactory for a time, then worsened as tensions grew between ELAS and the British, and collapsed entirely when Kula arrived and it became clear to the Greeks that the Poles were not communists.

> Immediately there was a change, the [Greek] officers treating us coolly, and the men treating us irritatingly, and jeering at us for being capitalists and the slaves of capitalists. However, when bread or soup was distributed they gave us smaller helpings and sometimes nothing at all, and their attitude towards us became one of hatred and contempt. A few days later, i.e. October 6th, while these conditions prevailed, a minor battle took place with the Germans. A few minutes before the German attack a state of defence was declared. The Polish platoon, whose members were the first to take up their arms, was placed at an extremely dangerous point, while the Greeks took up positions behind us in the hills ... After the battle the Greeks shamelessly taunted us with the statement that 'five Poles had deserted during the battle' – without mentioning that those in question were the wounded.

Later, when the Poles refused to fight Ethnikos Dimokratikos Ellinikos Syndesmos (EDES), the republican resistance movement that ELAS considered its major rival, the platoon was broken up and Malanowski disarmed, whereupon, so he wrote, he had sought permission from ELAS to join a party of Poles being assembled by the British. '"You have three choices: to be evacuated to Serbia, to go into a concentration camp in Greece, or to return to the Battalion of Death and fight against EDES"'

Malanowski recalled of the ELAS response. 'I replied: "I escaped from the Germans in order to fight together with the Greeks against them, but I will never take part in a civil war in Greece while our common enemy is to be found in Athens."' Eventually Malanowski succeeded in attaching himself to the British base, from where he wrote his report. 'Col. Chris is looking after us very well and protecting us in every way against ELAS, who are demanding that we leave.'[61]

'Col. Chris' was Colonel 'Monty' Woodhouse, SOE's senior British officer in Greece at that time, who recorded in his own reports not only the poor relations between ELAS and the Poles but also similar frictions at that time between ELAS and many fugitive Russians. 'When the first Russians escaped [from German units in 1943], they were rapturously received by ELAS, who armed and equipped them at once', Woodhouse recalled in a long report written in 1945. 'They then told them that they were going off to fight the enemy: which was well received by the Russians until it became clear that the "enemy" was Zervas [the EDES leader].' Soon, Russians, like the Poles, had started turning up at Woodhouse's camp, complaining that 'none of them could understand these Greeks, who kept giving them lectures on Karl Marx and arguing that it was their duty to kill other Greeks'. By the winter of 1943–44, 150 Russians had joined him, all of whom he fed and clothed. At this point, ELAS 'protested indignantly'. 'I replied that I would exercise no coercion on the Russians, and that those who wished to return to serve in ELAS could do so.' A meeting was arranged at ELAS's main headquarters at which General Stefanos Sarafis, head of its general staff, and Kostas Despotopoulos, its political and legal adviser, were present, together with Woodhouse and the senior officer among the Russians. 'The Russian thumped the table, and said that nothing would ever induce any of them to serve in ELAS again.' Then ELAS summoned from its own ranks a more senior Russian to talk the others round, only for this one to decide on arrival 'that he too would like to remain with us, and [he] never returned to ELAS GHQ.' But in the end, so Woodhouse concluded of the episode, ELAS 'won the game': they left 'unmolested' the Russian soldiers who had joined his camp 'but they sent us more and more and more, wherever they could find them, hoping to punish our generosity with an *embarras de russes*. Indeed ... they put us at the expense of keeping the Russians for several months.'[62]

When considering the actions and reactions of men like Kula, Malanowski and Woodhouse, care must be taken to keep in mind the strains and frustrations of their work, their limited ability to see all sides and, in the case of the Poles at least, the possibility of entrenched antipathy to both communism and the Soviet Union, which had invaded and annexed vast swathes of Polish territory in 1939. Yet Sarafis, ELAS's senior military commander, conceded in his memoirs that Poles and Russians had indeed sought to leave ELAS, 'saying that they didn't want to become involved in our internal affairs', as he put it.[63]

Sarafis's proffered explanation for that was that 'British propaganda' had been responsible. 'We tried to persuade them to stay in ELAS and let themselves be concentrated in districts where they would be fighting only Germans', he wrote. 'They would not agree to this and even began complaining about their food and clothing.' He acknowledged that ELAS had consistently refused to permit British missions to arm and employ Poles as an independent force under British orders, but, for him, this again was the fault of the British, whose aim, he claimed, had been to create 'yet more anti-ELAS forces'.[64] British records do not support the allegation that SOE wished to create an anti-ELAS body of Poles. There is little doubt, however, that uncertainty among ELAS fighters about Britain's intentions in Greece contributed significantly to growing tension. Verbal clashes between SOE and ELAS became commonplace, and sometimes the outcome was worse. In September 1943, for example, Bill Jordan, a New Zealander, was on hand to witness and record the killing by ELAS of a fellow SOE officer. He and another New Zealander, Arthur Hubbard, had been sharing a house in Epirus when it came under attack from ELAS guerrillas apparently incensed by Britain's parallel support for Zervas, the EDES leader. Hubbard went out to remonstrate and was shot in the stomach and chest. Jordan and his radio operator exited with their hands up, whereupon, so he recorded in an emotional report written afterwards, 'about thirty frenzied guerillas [sic] swept on us and immediately commenced to knock us about':

> About the only intelligible remarks I could gather were the repetition of the words 'Zervas' and 'Traitor' ... [S]uddenly one of them placed the end of the barrel of his rifle hard against my temple and both Abbots and I were dragged, pushed and buffeted down the slope a little way from the house ... [T]hey stood us against a bank and three guerillas [sic] lifted their rifles and came up on aim to shoot us ... Then a voice from the top of the hill demanded [to know] what was going on. The rifles were lowered.

An ELAS doctor was summoned to examine Hubbard but found his injuries so severe that nothing could be done. Jordan's report concludes:

> Hubbard was conscious but in great pain ... I asked [him] who fired first. He said 'They did and they got me'. I said it was alleged [by ELAS] that he fired first. He said it was a lie and repeated 'they fired first'. I then told him he was going to die. He took hold of my hand, smiled and said 'I can take it, Bill, I am a soldier'. I might add I had known Hubbard and his family since we were children. Our families live in the same town in New Zealand. He had

> volunteered to [join me in Greece] ... Later he said 'Why should they want to kill me?' and his last words were, 'Just tell mother you were with me, Bill'.[65]

ELAS insisted that Hubbard's death had been a tragic accident, but there is little doubt that an anti-British attitude, fuelled partly by suspicions about why British missions were backing its rivals, was embedded by then in its outlook. As for the incident's impact on SOE personnel, reactions ranged from powerful feelings of fury and disgust to disillusionment and despair, and relations with ELAS never fully recovered.

Conclusion

When considering the transnational features of Allied secret services and resistance fighters in Europe, care must be taken when interpreting their significance. The motives of men and women who engaged in resistance were nuanced and varied, and should warn against assuming that all cross-border features of activities that might be described now as 'transnational' were perceived, then, to be meaningful, just as the term 'resistance' risks recasting some wartime behaviours into forms that, at the time, meant little or nothing.

It remains clear that the lens of transnational history is an effective tool for deepening understanding of why SOE was created and where and how it operated, and for advancing knowledge of its intimate involvement with a diverse range of movements of resistance and national liberation. By drawing attention to its nature as a state-backed, multinational, multiracial mechanism for exploiting past experiences and the human capital of other countries, it underlines SOE's significant role in the clandestine circulation of men, women, materiel and ideas, and how these movements and connections affected lives across Europe, including those of its own agents. This includes shedding light on how and why its interventions could shape local action against Axis forces, including that by foreign fighters, as in Albania and the Ariège, as well as complicate relationships, as in Greece.

8

Transnational guerrillas in the 'shatter zones' of the Balkans and Eastern Front

Franziska Zaugg and Yaacov Falkov with Enrico Acciai, Jason Chandrinos, Olga Manojlović Pintar, Srdjan Milošević and Milovan Pisarri

Having been a vast battlefield during the First World War and suffering smouldering conflicts in the postwar era, the Balkans' newly built countries sought to abstain from further international conflicts. They also built regional alliances to guard both against the return of the German, Austro-Hungarian or Russian empires, whose collapse had allowed them to establish themselves as states and to mitigate their own internecine rivalries. Thus a Little Entente was signed in 1920/1 between Yugoslavia, Romania and Czechoslovakia, and a Balkan Pact was agreed in 1934 by Yugoslavia, Romania, Greece and Turkey.

Mussolini, however, had different plans. He wanted to recreate a Roman Empire around a *mare nostrum* including the Adriatic coast.[1] At the crack of dawn on 7 April 1939 Italian troops commanded by General Alfredo Guzzoni invaded Albania. This was only the beginning of Italy's expansion in the Balkans: on 28 October 1940 Mussolini ordered an attack on Greece during the winter months. The campaign failed. In fact, Greek troops were even able to counterattack and to gain territory. Hitler, who was not amused, was forced to send troops to support his Axis partner.[2]

Desperate to ward off attack, the Yugoslav government signed the Tripartite Pact, which locked Hungary, Romania and Bulgaria into the Axis bloc on 25 March 1941. This was anathema to the Yugoslav opposition. Two days later, on 27 March, while Hitler and his Oberkommando der Wehrmacht, or High Command of the Armed Forces (OKW), were coordinating the last steps for Operation Barbarossa, anti-German officers of the Yugoslavian army launched a coup. They overthrew the cabinet of Dragiša Cvetković, forced Prince Paul Karađorđević to abdicate and crowned king the seventeen-year-old Peter II. Hitler, who counted on vassal states in south-east Europe to protect his flank for the upcoming invasion of the Soviet Union now had to change plans. Since Yugoslavia was no longer a friendly regime he decided to attack.[3] The Balkan campaign of 6–23 April 1941 was conducted by German and Italian troops and supported by Hungary. After its capitulation on 17 April, Yugoslavia was partitioned. Serbia, Banat, the northern part of Kosovo, and the larger part of the Sandžak came under German military control, while the rest of Kosovo and bordering territories of Montenegro and Macedonia became part of 'Greater Albania' under Italian control. The eastern part of Kosovo and Macedonia was now assigned to Bulgaria. Although Bulgaria did not participate in the invasion, it claimed parts of Yugoslavia and Greece. Montenegro became part of the Italian Adriatic empire, as did the coastal zone of Croatia. The major part of Croatia, however, became a German vassal state under a fascist regime. Ante Pavelić, leader of the Ustaša Croat Revolutionary Organisation, was appointed head of a state called Nezavisna Država Hrvatska (NDH) or the Independent State of Croatia, which included the major part of Croatia, Bosnia and Herzegovina and the Srem region of the present-day Serbia.[4] Ustaša massacres of Serbs, Roma, Jews and Muslims began from the very first days of the NDH's existence. Slovenia was divided between Germany and Italy, while Hungary occupied a small part of Slovenia and the northern regions of Yugoslavia. Greece surrendered on 23 April and was divided into a German, an Italian and a Bulgarian occupation zone. Finally, Crete fell on 1 June after ten days of fierce fighting against British and Commonwealth forces.[5]

Because of the priority of the Eastern Campaign against the Soviet Union, Hitler transferred thirty-three of his Wehrmacht divisions from the Balkans to the East and left the Balkan pacification to four infantry divisions.[6] It soon became apparent that he entirely underestimated the situation in the Balkans. Retrospectively, in January 1945, the Commander-in-Chief South-East, Field Marshal General Maximilian von Weichs, remarked that

> after the Balkan campaign ended, the Southeast became a sideshow. … German dominance had to be sustained with insufficient means against growing enemy pressure … Although there was no external attack against the extensive coast and although there were only bands one had to fight in the Balkans, it was not a running battle' – no – it was an all-encompassing turmoil.[7]

There were spontaneous insurrections of the local population, especially Serbs, against the Axis occupation and Ustaša massacres. At the same time the Communist Party of Yugoslavia called its members to resist the new regimes. Only three weeks after the occupation Osvobodilna Fronta – The Liberation Front – was formed in Ljubljana. This umbrella

3 Italy and the Balkans

organisation brought together representatives of fifteen political parties and civil organisations on an anti-fascist platform, whatever their political and ideological orientation. In May 1941 the first guerrilla units were composed in Serbia under the command of the Yugoslav government-in-exile in London. The so-called Yugoslav Army in the Fatherland, better known as the Četnik movement, was established under a former Serbian officer, Dragoljub Draža Mihailović, while communists formed the first partisan units in Croatia on 22 June. The Communist Party of Yugoslavia called for an armed uprising against Italian forces in all Yugoslav territories on 4 July 1941, a rising which later extended to the German-occupied territories.[8]

Guerrilla warfare in the Balkans

In the Balkans during those crazy weeks in the spring of 1941 there was a shattering of the new European state system that had been painstakingly constructed after 1918. The lightning defeat of the regular armies of Albania, Yugoslavia and Greece by the Axis powers, followed by occupation and partition, with Hungary, Bulgaria and Croat fascists taking some of the spoils and joining in brutal repression, meant that the only possible response was irregular, guerrilla warfare.

Guerrilla warfare, meaning 'small warfare', was undertaken by the populations of those occupied territories. This was led by nationals, such as Yugoslavs or Greeks, but it was also multinational, international and transnational. It was multinational because the breakdown of the state system led to the transfer of some nationals to join the resistance of others. It was international in that much of it was coordinated by the Communist International or Comintern or by the secret services of the Allied powers. And it was transnational at the level of individual or group participation by 'foreigners' who were on the move because of persecution and who had military experience outside the country with which they were now fighting.

German and Italian authorities in the Balkans lacked a clear plan, but rather reacted with brutality to initial resistance. Extremely high ratios of 'measures of atonement' were prescribed, with the execution of fifty hostages for one wounded and a hundred for one dead German soldier.[9] People were displaced,[10] concentration camps were built,[11] and local men were drafted – often by force – to fight in the Wehrmacht and Waffen-SS.[12] Soldiers of the former Yugoslavian army became POWs and were faced with the option to stay in a miserable camp, to declare loyalty to the NDH (Serbs excluded) or to join German units.

Meanwhile, refugees and exiles from all over Europe were crossing the Balkans hoping to find an escape route over the sea. SS-Standartenführer August Schmidhuber, who was deployed in south-east Europe from 1942, reported an intense 'entry and transit traffic' of 'communist and anti-Nazi immigrants' into the central Balkans, especially the Kosovo region. He gave orders to check every suspicious person and to arrest those who could not adequately explain the purpose of their journey.[13] Jews from Sarajevo tried to cross Kosovo to reach 'Old Albania' – the territory of the Albanian state before April 1941, including Kosovo – while the newly settled Serbs in the Kosovo region sought to return to Serbia to escape destruction and extermination.[14]

In response to occupation and repression, the period between 1941 and 1943 saw the growth of a multitude of different resistance movements.

Some were purely national in conception, such as Balli Kombëtar and Legaliteti in Albania, the EDES in Greece or the Četniks in Serbia, Montenegro and border territories. The project of an umbrella organisation in Albania failed because of the question of a 'Greater Albania' or a 'Smaller Albania', with Yugoslav communists threatening to cancel their support of Albanian comrades if the Kosovo were integrated into postwar Albania. Other movements, inspired by communists and socialists, proposed a pan-Balkan movement with the slogan 'The Balkans to the Balkan peoples'. The most significant difference between nationalist and communist groups was not the national, international or transnational constitution of their forces, but their conception of postwar states. Among communists and socialists the concept of a Balkan Confederation was one of the most important ideas conceived to solve the complicated 'national issue' in this part of Europe.[15] But even national groups hosted combatants from other countries inside and outside the Balkans, profiting from their experience and exchanging cultural understanding. National antagonisms could be challenged and subverted by transnational connections. Moreover, for many individuals in flight the political or national profile of the group they joined was of little consequence. As an Italian report of the political-military situation in Albania in October 1943 observed, foreigners crept 'into the undergrowth with one of the various parties' in the hope of shelter and protection.[16]

One example of a combatant with a transnational trajectory and seeking protection was Pál Markovits, a young Hungarian Jew, who first joined the Serbian Četniks, then switched to the Yugoslav communists. Born in 1917, he studied veterinary medicine in Budapest and opened a veterinary practice in Dunaszerdahely (Dunajská Streda) on the Hungarian–Slovakian border. In 1943, however, he was drafted as a forced labourer to Bor in north Serbia, and because a Četnik unit helped him to escape from the camp he decided to join them. He served there for eight months, recording thirteen other Hungarian Jews in the unit in the summer 1944.[17] His experiences as a foreigner were double-edged; his Četnik comrades both admired and mistrusted him. Personally, he was distressed by the meaningless violence of his voivode chief, who ordered the execution of a communist prisoner and his young girlfriend. To communicate and survive he learned the Serbian language: he procured a Hungarian–Serbo-Croat and later a French-Serbo-Croatian dictionary. Despite his efforts, Markovits remained a stranger among the Četnici. In the summer of 1944, in order to save his life, he shaved off the beard that was a characteristic feature of Četnik fighters and joined the advancing communist partisans.[18] They agreed to make him a veterinary surgeon in Tito's army, where numerous Jews had found shelter and fought since 1941.[19]

The communist umbrella often facilitated international connections, as it did between Yugoslav and Albanian communist groups. After the Italian invasion of Albania, Albanian communists fled to Yugoslavia. Then, after the German attack on the Soviet Union and Stalin's appeal for an anti-fascist war, the dispersed Albanian communist groups began to organise themselves and finally created a party.[20] Shortly after their return to Albania and 'following instructions from Comintern [they] began their organisational and terrorist activities'.[21] In the process, contacts were established with Yugoslav communists and in the summer of 1941, the Yugoslav Communist Party sent two leading members – Dušan Mugoša and Miladin Popović – to Albania to support the formation of the Albanian Communist Party.[22]

Transnational or international connections were nevertheless sometimes unable to overcome national divisions. Even within the 'internationally' oriented communist movement collaboration proved complex. The Bulgarian and Yugoslav communist parties were bitterly opposed on the question of Macedonia and the takeover of the Macedonian Communist Party after the Bulgarian annexation of Macedonia. The case came before the Executive Committee of the Communist International.[23] Individual efforts might on occasion overcome this division. One came from Asem Balkanski, a Bulgarian communist from the region close to the Yugoslav–Bulgarian border. This 'transnational transfer' was very much welcomed by the Yugoslavs, and Balkanski was appointed commander of a partisan unit in the Yugoslav communist-led liberation movement. Balkanski became an effective military leader and was wanted by Serbian police authorities and by the Četniks as well. When preparing for an action on 8 August 1943, a group of partisans led by Balkanski descended from the woods to the nearby village of Topli Dol (near the town of Pirot) and ran into an ambush. Balkanski, just twenty-three years old, was killed on the spot.[24] According to official data reported by Bulgarian military authorities, desertions from Bulgarian units deployed in Bulgaria and the occupied territories in former Yugoslavia and Greece remained fairly rare: by September 1944 only about three thousand soldiers had risked the transnational leap and joined Tito's partisans.[25]

Examples of transnational transfers were more significant in northern Greece, where contacts between Greek guerrillas and Macedonian, Albanian or Bulgarian partisans across the borders were neither circumstantial nor a mere response to the unification of space by the occupying forces. A shared Ottoman past as well as the existence of an 80,000-strong minority of Slav-speaking people commonly known as Slav-Macedonians, found in the north-western Greek regions of Kastoria and Florina, favoured transnational connections. The Kommounistikó Kómma Elládas

(Greek Communist Party, KKE) appealed to the minority as soon as 1941, following up on its 1930s active support of its rights within the Greek state. The Bulgarian occupation had made the borderline redundant, and by the beginning of 1943 the Macedonian Partisan groups had already made their way into Greek territory, an effort facilitated by the existence of the Slav-speaking population. In April 1943 the Damyan Gruev Detachment, composed of thirty men and women – Macedonians, Vlachs and Jews from Bitola – and named after a Macedonian national hero, entered the Greek village of Mpoufi (Buf), where they found shelter, food and, most importantly, their native tongue, probably without even noticing that they were on Greek territory.[26]

There was a possibility that Macedonians and Greeks would unite in a Balkan brotherhood-in-arms. This, however, began to crumble with the rise of conflicting nationalisms. In July 1943, the Greek Ethnikó Apeleftherotikó Métopo (National Liberation Front, EAM) and ELAS rejected the proposal of Svetozar Vukmanović, alias Tempo, Tito's envoy for Macedonia, for the formation of a joint Balkan General Headquarters, and to allow Slav-Macedonians to form independent bands.[27] The Slav-Macedonian Liberation Front, formed by EAM at the end of 1943, was less an internationalist manifesto than a measure to steer the minority away from Bulgarian influence. It attracted less than 5 per cent of its target population.[28] In May 1944 about seventy Slav-Macedonian KKE members accused the Party of being too nationalistic and abruptly fled to Macedonia to join the Communist Party of Macedonia. The Slav-speaking population of Greece gradually shook off EAM–ELAS control, as Yugoslav Macedonia seemed a more and more appealing choice of statehood after the war.

Transnational desertions from the Wehrmacht

A whole new phase in transnational and multinational resistance opened up after the German and Italian armies ceased to advance and began to be driven back. From the end of 1942 the Axis powers were on the retreat. After November 1942 they were dislodged from North Africa by Allied armies, which invaded southern Italy in September 1943. In the same month Italian forces capitulated to the Allies. The Germans were beaten back from the Soviet Union after their surrender at Stalingrad in February 1943. This resulted in two powerful additions to guerrilla efforts. The first was the escape of large numbers of POWs from camps organised by the Axis, including thousands of Soviet POWs held by the Germans and Yugoslav POWs held by the Italians. The second was the desertion from the Axis armies of large numbers of troops from what were in any case multinational armies.[29] There were even desertions from the Wehrmacht of German nationals who were anti-Nazi, often because of their communism, and saw the opportunity to defect to communist guerrillas.

They had always been multinational armies, the Wehrmacht drafting men from subjected peoples as far as Central Asia and recycling POWs into their own forces, while the Italians like the French and British armies used colonial forces from their African possessions. Setbacks suffered by the Axis armies resulted in revolts in POW camps that could no longer be properly controlled and mass desertions not only by non-nationals but even by some nationals, often communist in sympathy, who decided to join those fighting the Nazis. In the German armies, these desertions were limited. When the Italian armies capitulated in September 1943, and the Germans tried to make Italian soldiers POWs, desertions were of a much higher order of magnitude and transformed guerrilla warfare in the Balkans and Greece.

In Greece, probably more than in any other resistance theatre, the Germans faced a distinctive, highly motivated group of foreign resisters. After the collapse of the African Front in May 1943, the 999 African Division, a 'parole' unit of the Wehrmacht into which former political detainees – communists, socialists and trade unionists – were drafted as the price of their freedom, was broken down into *Festungsbataillone* ('Fortress Battalions'), almost all of which were sent to Greece for garrison duties. Most of the units were shipped to the islands where these 'dangerous elements' could be constantly supervised.[30]

From day one, the clandestine networks within the battalions urged comrades with the right personal and ideological qualities to contact the Greek resistance. One of them was the twenty-seven-year-old Gerhard Reinhardt, a Saxon-born former member of the Kommunistischer Jugendverband Deutschlands, or German Communist Youth Organisation (KJVD), who, after three years' imprisonment and forced draft, was eager to follow the footsteps of his brother Bruno, who had been killed in Spain in 1937 as a tank commander of the International Brigades.[31] On 3 August 1943 Reinhardt deserted in downtown Athens and went underground with the help of the EAM. Twenty years later, as a citizen of the Deutsche Demokratische Republik (German Democratic Republic, DDR), he explained his reasons for abandoning the Wehrmacht and joining the Greek resistance:

> My thoughts dwell on the Greek people, my new friends and comrades. I had hardly ever seen young and old women struggling all day long for a piece of bread. I had seen poor kids, their hands reaching out in despair for food. I had seen how the gallant Greek people was being mowed down by the machine gun fire of the fascists day by day. I could even hear the bullets

> hitting and the chilling laughter of Hitler's mercenaries. What a difficult but also very noble and beautiful task had I to fulfil.[32]

Reinhardt was a valuable asset for the Athenian underground. He provided the Eniaia Panelladiki Organosi Neon – United Panhellenic Organisation of Youth (EPON) – with propaganda material in German and participated in 'night actions against Greek, Italian and German fascists' as a member of the Organisation for the Protection of the People's Struggle (OPLA), the urban guerrilla-hit squads of EAM, which surely benefited from the camouflage potentials of a German in a Wehrmacht uniform.[33] In March 1944 he was dispatched to the XIII ELAS Division in Karpenisi, Evrytania, where he met thirty-one-year-old Falk von Harnack, another forced draftee in a 999 unit who had deserted to avenge the fate of his brother, Arvid von Harnack, the leader of the Rote Kapelle group who had been executed in August 1942, along with his wife Mildred.[34] The two men marched thousands of kilometres across mountainous terrain in order to develop a movement that could win over more Germans for the resistance. They followed the guidelines of the 'Free Germany' Committee in the Soviet Union, which encouraged anti-war propaganda and systematic schooling of POWs.[35] On 22 August 1944 Reinhardt co-founded the Antifaschistisches Komitee 'Freies Deutschland', the 'Free Germany' Anti-Fascist Committee of German Soldiers (AKFD), which was attached to the ELAS General Headquarters. By mid-September the AKFD, which claimed a total of 600 members, was already building small groups of German fighters attached to ELAS regiments in the mainland, and it intensified its appeals to mass desertion, even during military operations:

> In trenches along the guerrilla lines ... we became agitators, appealing through loudspeakers to the patriotism of the men in the German fascist positions. In this struggle for a free, democratic Germany, we lost dear comrades, like Otto Stueck, a buddy from Ruhr, who was gunned down by a Nazi lieutenant on 29 August 1944, in the outskirts of Amfissa. [In the midst of battle], he had stood up and walked toward the advancing German soldiers, unarmed, urging them to spare their lives for a future Germany without Hitler.[36]

The retreat of the German armies favoured not only desertions, as in the case of Gerhard Reinhardt, but also the escape of POWs, the most numerous of whom were Russian. A well-documented case is Ivan Barsukov, a lieutenant of the Engineers of the Red Army, who had been taken prisoner in the summer of 1942 near Rzhev, north-west of Moscow. On 1 July 1943, after a year of forced labour and internment, Barsukov broke out of a POW camp in Thessaloniki with another comrade. He recalled in 1962 that

> I will remember [this day] for as long as I live. I was lying on the grass with Aleksandr Ganin and gazed at the beautiful, clear blue sky of Greece. Our minds were drifting on what we had just been through and wondering what was more to endure ... Never before had I sensed such a boiling hatred pouring out of me for our enemies, the German fascists.[37]

As breakouts of POWs soared in late October 1943, an independent unit was formed within the 13th ELAS Regiment of the Xth Division, composed of about ninety Soviets and a few Greeks, Italians and Bulgarians. Barsukov, commonly known as Yannis – the equivalent of Ivan in Greek – was appointed commander. 'It was commonly known as the Ruski company', he said, 'because we were the majority, because the Greeks respected us and because we felt we had to play a special role.'[38]

Barsukov remained company commander until he assumed the command of the 1st Rokossovsky Battalion of the 5th Macedonian Shock Brigade of the 49th Division of Tito's People's Liberation Army. He felt at home among the Slav-Macedonians of northern Greece. He and his fighters had just entered Yugoslav territory when preparations for the coordinated attacks on the retreating German army Group E began.[39] About six thousand 'Russian' troops in thirty-one battalions fought on Yugoslavia. They consisted of the Red Army soldiers who had been brought to the Balkans as POWs, of Soviet civilians engaged as manpower by the Todt Organisation and of those who managed to escape from the various Russian military formations created by the Wehrmacht. Following the liberation of Macedonia in November 1944, Barsukov and other Soviet Partisans were repatriated into the Soviet Union.[40] Their participation in the partisan movement had a great psychological effect on the local population. The bravery of the 'Russian units' strengthened the combat morale and encouraged mobilisation within the partisan movement in the final stage of the war.[41]

'Useful' foreigners in the Soviet Partisan resistance

While Soviets fought with the Greek and Yugoslav resistance, so foreigners also played a key role on the Soviet Partisan resistance behind German lines. The German Wehrmacht had crossed the Soviet border at 4 a.m. on 22 June 1941 and seized vast tracts of Belarussian, Ukrainian, Russian and Baltic territories. It annihilated massive Red Army formations, and by the end of the year was attempting to encircle and occupy Moscow.[42] Reacting to the sudden rapid loss of the extensive western territories, Stalin called on the Soviet people 'to foment guerrilla warfare everywhere, blow up bridges and roads, damage telephone and telegraph lines, set fire to forests, stores and transports'.[43]

For almost a year the Soviet communist regime struggled for survival and actually did very little to promote irregular fighting in the German rear. The emerging guerrilla resistance that came into being suffered from inadequate command and control and from severe lack of funding, material resources and armament, and was staffed mostly by random and unsuitable people – Communist Party bureaucrats, or old or under-age workers and peasants. Military and security personnel were encircled by German forces, frequently demoralised and scarcely prepared for the difficult guerrilla assignments. They were hunted down by the Nazi security apparatus and its local collaborators, and suffered from malnutrition and extreme weather conditions from late 1941 to early 1942, and only a minority of them managed to survive the first year of occupation.[44]

In these tough circumstances, various Communist Party, intelligence and military authorities sought to reinforce partisan groups by recruiting foreigners who were experienced in irregular warfare and underground struggle outside the Soviet Union. These recruits were expected both to communicate their invaluable knowledge to their local comrades and to perform various combat, sabotage and intelligence tasks. The group of Spanish Civil War veterans, who took a refuge in the Soviet Union after the republic's defeat in 1939, proved the most suitable for these two tasks in terms of numbers, competence and fighting morale. During the first year of Nazi occupation of large parts of the western Soviet Union, the Spaniards worked behind enemy lines and as guerrilla instructors saved the Soviets from painful defeats and taught them the basics of the irregular warfare. A former Second World War veteran and partisan claimed in 1991 that the Spaniards

> had the richest experience of the anti-fascist struggle ... delivered that experience to their young [Soviet] comrades, [and thus] their contribution to the enemy defeat in the Battle of Moscow cannot be reduced to the number of mines planted by them for the fascists and their tanks.[45]

Apart from the Spanish Civil War veterans, the guerrilla force of the NKVD – the so-called Otdel'naya Motostrel'kovaya Brigada Osobogo Naznacheniya (Independent Motorised Brigade for Special Assignment, OMSBON), created in October 1941 – recruited many more foreign fighters. About a hundred Bulgarians, as well as Germans, Austrians, Americans, Poles, Czechs, Romanians, Chinese and Vietnamese, mostly communists who had escaped to the Soviet Union before the war, comprised OMSBON's two-thousand-strong 'international regiment'.[46] Among its organisers and most prominent members were Christo Boev Patashev and

Ivan Tsolov Vinarov, two experienced activists of the Bulgarian communist underground born in 1896, who had escaped to the Soviet Union in 1920, joined the Glavnoye Razvedyvatelnoye Upravlenie (Soviet Military Strategic Intelligence, GRU) and served as its senior officers in the Balkan countries, Turkey, Austria, Czechoslovakia, Germany, France and China. In 1936–39 one of their principal tasks was the revelation to the NKVD and internationally of the arms-purchasing channels of General Franco's army. In 1938, during Stalin's purges in the Soviet security system, Boev and Vinarov were expelled from the GRU, but in July 1941, a month after Barbarossa, they were recruited by the NKVD to assist in establishing OMSBON. For some time, Vinarov acted as the 'international regiment's' political commissar. One of his Soviet comrades recalled in 1987 that

> Vinarov exemplified all the best features of the Bulgarian revolutionary people. His selfless service for the common cause provided an inspiring example for many generations to come. His contribution to the strengthening of the Soviet-Bulgarian friendship will not fade.[47]

In 1942–44, Boev's and Vinarov's rich experience in intelligence and guerrilla was utilised by the Comintern and the Bulgarian Communist Party to develop an underground and partisan movement on Bulgarian soil. After the Second World War, the both comrades – now promoted to the rank of general-lieutenant – were warmly 'embraced' by the new communist rulers of their homeland Bulgaria. The former was appointed the head of the Foreign Intelligence Department of the Bulgarian Committee for State Security, while the latter joined the Yugoslavian Partisans in 1944, repatriated to Bulgaria and successively headed the Military Department of the Central Committee of the Bulgarian Communist Party and the Ministry of Railways and Construction.[48]

The next important phase in the growing transnational profile of the Soviet guerrillas came after the establishment of the centralised partisan command, the so-called Central Headquarters of the Partisan Movement (CHPM), in late May 1942. This step, which aimed at improving the Soviet guerrillas' organisational skills, their physical presence and their influence in the enemy's rear, as well as their combat, sabotage and intelligence capabilities, did not immediately bear the desired fruits. This was because of the severe shortage of experienced guerrilla specialists who could carry out operations and train new recruits, as well as the often hostile attitude of the local population in the occupied western Soviet borderlands and effective counter-guerrilla measures of the Germans and their allies.[49] The partisans' answer to these challenges included the recruitment of 'useful' foreigners to provide their hosts with greater military expertise, together with links to local populations in the occupied territories and to the occupying non-German forces. These 'useful' foreigners originated mainly from four groups: first, foreign communists whose transnational trajectory took them to the Soviet Union prior to the German invasion and now volunteered their services to Soviet authorities, like the CHPM; second, evacuees from the Baltic states, eastern Poland, Bessarabia and Bukovina, who had become Soviet citizens only shortly beforehand but in terms of their language, life experience and attitudes were still foreigners; third, inhabitants of those same territories who remained there under the Nazi rule but joined the communist guerrilla either freely or under duress; and fourth, soldiers and even officers of the Wehrmacht, which was a multinational machine, who deserted to the partisans as the army retreated or were captured by them: in the first place Slavs like the Slovaks but also Germans, Austrians and Hungarians.

Unfortunately, the currently available Soviet archival sources do not contain exact numbers of these four groups' representatives absorbed by the Soviet guerrillas. Nonetheless, the common impression is that there were a few thousand foreigners at least who contributed to the Soviet irregular struggle against the Nazis. For instance, Lithuanian historians have counted about 1,800 Lithuanians who made up 36 per cent of the nearly 5,000-man-strong Soviet Lithuanian guerrilla infrastructure that was active inside and along the borders of Lithuania in 1941–45.[50]

Among the foreign communists living in the Soviet Union who volunteered to assist the Soviet partisan movement was Karl Kleinjung. Born in 1912 in German North Rhine-Westphalia, he was already an experienced communist activist in the early 1930s. He fled to the Netherlands and Belgium from the Nazi persecution and in 1936 went to Spain. There he initially joined the Edgar André Battalion – the first formation of the International Brigades – and later graduated from the special sabotage and reconnaissance school managed by the Soviet NKVD advisor of Lithuanian origin Stanislav Vaupshasov (Stanislavas Vaupšas). Following the republic's defeat, Kleinjung moved to the Soviet Union and worked in a local factory. There he improved his Russian, married a Latvian girl and, in 1941, was recruited by NKVD and given additional training for performing covert assignments in the Wehrmacht's rear. This new role took him to the Belarussian forests in 1943. Sent by the local Soviet Partisans into the occupied city of Minsk and disguised as a German officer named Otto Schultz, he performed 'special' tasks, including the execution of traitors and senior Germans. The Soviet regime, grateful for his work, awarded him prestigious decorations for military bravery and after the war made him a high-ranking officer of the East German security apparatus, responsible for internal security and the political loyalty of the armed forces and border guards of the DDR.[51]

The group of Baltic foreigners-turned-citizens contributed prominent partisans, among them a young Latvian communist Imants Sudmalis (aka Anderson). Imprisoned for his underground activity in the late 1930s, prior to the Soviet annexation of Latvia, he became by June 1941 the leader of Komsomol (the communist youth organisation) in the Latvian port city of Liepaja. Following his active participation in the failed attempt to prevent the German conquest of the city, he went underground and spent six months moving between the occupied countryside and the capital Rīga. He then joined Soviet guerrillas in neighbouring Belarus and reached Moscow in early July 1942.[52] On the basis of his first-hand experiences, Sudmalis provided a detailed report on the situation in enemy-occupied Latvia, including an unprecedented description of the genocidal character of the anti-Jewish atrocities.[53] At the beginning of 1943 he returned to the north-western Belarusian forests, joined a nucleus of the Latvian communist guerrilla infrastructure and contributed to its strengthening by sharing his experience in covert underground activity and performing brief cross-border missions on its behalf. In July 1943 Sudmalis relocated to Rīga and started to build a tiny communist underground. Its cells were international in character, merging Latvian, Russian, German and Jewish resisters. They were active also outside the Latvian capital, trying to centralise the local communist resistance, gathering intelligence, disseminating propaganda and organising sporadic terror acts against German and collaborators' installations.[54] Yet, eight months later, in February 1943, Anderson and his close aides, betrayed by their radio operator, fell prey to the Nazi security apparatus.[55]

Czesław Klim, an example of the third group of the Soviet guerrilla's foreigners – those who stayed in the German-occupied territories and joined the Moscow-led partisans later – was luckier than Sudmalis and his comrades. Born in 1899, he became an officer in the Polish army and a member of the Polish Socialist Party. He fought the Red Army twice – first during the Polish–Soviet war of 1919–21 and then in September 1939, when the Soviets joined the Germans in their attack on the sovereign Polish state. Living in eastern Poland and despite his anti-communism, he was forced by escalating hostilities between local Polish and Ukrainian communities to seek the assistance of the Red guerrillas. In the summer of 1943 Klim merged his Polish self-defence unit with the Soviet partisan Pinsk Brigade under the command of Ivan Shubitidze. From the very beginning it was a highly international enterprise bringing together resisters of multiple national and cultural backgrounds: Russians, Belarusians, Ukrainians, Poles and Jews. There were limits, however, to shared transnational experiences in what was essentially a multinational brigade. Within it, Klim's sixty Polish fighters and ten Polish-speaking Ukrainians formed their own partisan group. This grew by the spring of 1944 into a separate Polish 250-man-strong brigade named after a Polish national hero, Tadeusz Kościuszko, and was shortly afterwards absorbed by the newly established headquarters of the Polish Partisan Movement. Czesław Klim, promoted to the rank of major, fought with his men in the occupied territory of eastern Poland and after the war served in the new communist Polish army.[56]

The fourth group of enemy officers and soldiers who chose to join the Soviet Partisans is exemplified by the few hundred Slovaks allied to the Germans in 1941 who became anti-Nazi irregulars on Belarusian and Ukrainian soil in 1942–44. The first contacts between the Slovak Reserve Division based in the Ukrainian-Belarusian area of the Polesian marshes and the local Soviet Partisans were established in the summer of 1942. This led to the first desertions of Slovaks to the forests the following December. The growing number of defecting Slovaks allowed the partisan commander Aleksandr Saburov to create a first Czechoslovak detachment among the Soviet Partisans led by a Slovak captain, Ján Nálepka. Born into a peasant family in eastern Slovakia, he served during the pre-war period as a lieutenant in the Slovakian army and, following the Slovak participation in the attack on the Soviet Union in June 1941, was stationed with his regiment in the Belarusian city of Yel'sk. He was, however, a reluctant ally of the Reich and became involved in passive resistance activities, first disseminating true information about the war events among the local population or misdirecting leading of the German bombers, later searching for contacts with the Red guerrillas. Reaching the forests in June 1943, he joined the Soviet Communist Party, conducted propaganda operations among his compatriots who remained in the Slovakian army and commanded a series of anti-German assaults until his death in November 1943 in a skirmish with the Germans during the attempt to liberate the Ukrainian city of Ovruch. His defection and death were widely used by the Soviet propaganda effort on the Eastern Front to promote the anti-German sentiment and a sense of 'Slavic brotherhood' among Czech and Slovak units serving with the Axis.[57]

Italian desertions to the Albanian, Yugoslav and Greek resistance

The guerrilla situation was transformed even more profoundly by the collapse of the Italian armies and the breakup of the Germany–Italy Axis. On 10 July 1943 Allied forces launched the invasion of Sicily. Two weeks later, on 25 July, Mussolini was removed from office by the Fascist Grand Council and, just hours later, was arrested and interned on the Gran Sasso in the Apennines mountains. King Victor Emmanuel III appointed

Marshal Pietro Badoglio the new prime minister. Fighting continued for some weeks but on 3 September an armistice was signed between the Italian Kingdom and the Allies.

At 6 p.m. on 8 September, the armistice was made public by the Allies. A few hours later, Italian military and political leaders abandoned Rome and took refuge in the city of Brindisi.[58] Although the new government was safe from German reprisals, this was not the case for the overwhelming majority of the Italian armed forces. According to the historian Mario De Prospo, 'Millions of men were now scattered throughout Italy, southern France, the Balkans, Greece and in many parts of the Mediterranean Sea. They were left without any precise orders; either they disbanded, or they were captured and deported by the Wehrmacht.'[59] Over the course of several days, most parts of Italy not occupied by the Allies came under Nazi occupation, Mussolini was freed by a German commando, and a new puppet regime was established in the northern part of the peninsula, known as the Repubblica Sociale Italiana.

The surrender left Italian forces in the Balkans in a difficult predicament. Until now they had been harassed by Balkan partisan movements, but they were now considered traitors by their erstwhile German allies, which tried to execute their officers and round up the rest as POWs. Many decided to join the anti-fascist resistance, although how far they underwent an anti-fascist transformation and how far they just sought protection until they could be repatriated to Italy was an open question.

Italian forces in Albania were not told about the Italian surrender. Many, like Second Lieutenant Nazzareno Garat Crema, heard the news on radio.[60] Even the supreme commanders of the 6th and the 9th Italian army in Albania, General Ezio Rosi and General Lorenzo Dalmazzo, received no orders.[61] Chaos ensued. Over 100,000 Italians were stranded in Albania, crowding into the streets and squares or waiting in vain in the harbour towns to be shipped back to Italy.[62] The Germans pounced and captured four of the six Italian divisions: the 11th Brennero Infantry Division, the 38th Puglie Infantry Division, the 49th Parma Infantry Division and the 53rd Arezzo Infantry Division. Meanwhile, parts of the 41st Firenze Infantry Division and the 151st Perugia Infantry Division defected to the partisans.[63]

Officers – and common soldiers, too – were concentrated near Vlorë and shot by soldiers of the Wehrmacht and Waffen-SS. Surviving Italians reported that 'in Valona [Vlorë] many Italian officers were butchered by the Germans. Every Italian officer – even if unarmed – was immediately shot by the Germans when found.'[64] Second Lieutenant Aldo Carta, who joined with the partisans, said that in Vlorë, '[German] armoured cars prevented the men escaping from the town. We were besieged and stuck.'

His men surrendered their weapons, and the Germans herded them 'like a flock of sheep' into a nearby concentration camp, guarded by German sentinels. Carta and his fellow officers, however, were taken to a special camp at Vlorë. Some surrendered their pistols, while others like Carta hid theirs in their coat pockets.[65] On 14 September the Italian officers were moved to Drashovicë, 12 kilometres from Vlorë. During the night of 15 to 16 October 1943 partisans attacked Drashovicë. The Germans withdrew a significant part of the camp guard in order to boost the town defences; Carta and many captives took the opportunity to escape. They crossed the river Shushicë and reached the partisans in the mountains.[66]

The partisan formations saw Italian soldiers as a useful boost for their troops. Although they had very recently been the enemy, they had equipment, ammunition and knowhow, and they were being killed by the Germans. An Italian soldier remarked that 'The rebels very kindly welcomed the Italians' cooperation.'[67] The various partisan formations actively helped their former enemies to escape the Germans. As the soldier Guido Tecchi said, 'All parties helped the Italian soldiers who escaped from the German concentration camps in whatever way they could.'[68]

The transfer of the Italians to the partisans was generally more pragmatic than ideological, although former membership of the International Brigades created relationships of trust and SOE often played a key mediating role. General Gino Piccini, for thirty-five years a loyal soldier in Italian service, took the unauthorised decision to defect with his men to the Albanian communists on the advice of the SOE representative in eastern Albania, Squadron Leader Arthur George (Andy) Hands.[69] He commanded the rebuilt remnants of Italian units fighting with the partisans, the Comando Italiano Truppe alla Montagna, and organised the repatriation to Italy of thousands of Italian soldiers and civilians.[70] Although he spent much time in Albania, exposed to Albanian culture, he did not undergo much of a transformation. Nonetheless, between 12 June 1944 and 23 August 1945 Piccini commanded the Italian troops in Albania and was appointed official representative of the Italian government's supreme command of the Italian troops there.[71] He remained in Albania after the war, still organising repatriations.

Piccini had dealings with Mehmet Shehu, the right-hand man of Enver Hoxha. Shehu was a former International Brigader who had commanded the fourth battalion of the XII Garibaldi Brigade.[72] Back in Albania in 1942, he immediately began to coordinate the Lëvizja Nacional-Çlirimtare, the communist National Liberation Front. He commanded a group of around a hundred men in the Mallakastër area which grew to a formation of around two thousand.[73] Shehu used his shared experience with Italians in the International Brigades as a way to bring over stranded Italian forces. On 9 October 1943, accompanied by three Italian Partisans, he visited remnants of the Florence Division at the foot of Mount Dajti. Bruno Brunetti recalled that it was Shehu, as a veteran from Spain, who persuaded them to join the resistance: 'he spoke about the Albanian anti-fascists' participation in the war in Spain and the large number of Italian comrades he had met in the International Brigades. He mentioned many names and specified that the Albanian anti-fascists had formed a special solidarity with the Italian comrades.'[74] The day after this appeal, around a hundred Italians presented themselves to the general staff of the division. Shehu suggested that the new battalion, which he described as Garibaldian, be named in memory of the Italian communist of Albanian origins Antonio Gramsci. Sergeant Terzilio Cardinali was duly placed in command.[75]

In Greece, too, former Italian soldiers became the largest foreign national group in guerrilla ranks. German units disarmed 146,000 of the 190,000 Italians stationed in Greece, and killed 14,000 who actively opposed them. The most notable case was the 33rd Acqui Infantry Division, which was massacred after engaging superior Wehrmacht forces in Cephalonia. In April 1944 about 10,000 Italians were scattered across guerrilla-held territory. The majority of them were detained in provisional camps, since the Greeks were more interested in their ability to operate the equipment (mortars and machine guns) than in their mass recruitment.[76] Fewer than 2,000 Italians joined the Greek guerrilla units as individual fighters. The only hint of independent formations were four detachments of Italian POWs, each a hundred strong, who joined the IX ELAS Division in August 1944.[77] A few cases of defection may be attributed to ideological motivation. In October 1943, the official mouthpiece of the KKE published an interview with an Italian Partisan in central Greece, identified as the son of Giacomo Matteotti – the assassinated leader of the Unitary Socialist Party – and a former *Interbrigadista*.[78] There is some doubt as to whether this man really was the son of Matteotti, but the Greek resistance decided to make capital out of it to build a bridge to the Italian resistance. One well-documented case of voluntary enrolment in the Greek liberation forces is that of Mario Ferrari. Ferrari was born in Pontremoli, northern Tuscany, in 1918, and served in Greece as a lieutenant of the 7th Lancieri di Milano Cavalry Regiment. On 18 March 1943 he was captured by the guerrillas near the Jagova Bridge, on the Kozani–Grevena road, and held prisoner. On 4 October 1943, after the new Italian government declared war on Germany, he immediately volunteered and was appointed commander of the II Platoon, Machine Gun Company of the II Battalion, 53rd ELAS Regiment in western Greek Macedonia.[79]

During the winter of 1943–44 the Germans undertook major operations against the partisans in the regions of Montenegro, Dalmatia, Sandžak and eastern Bosnia. The operations were known as 'Herbstgewitter', 'Kugelblitz' or 'Schneesturm' and were followed between May and early July 1944 by operations 'Gemsbock' and 'Steinadler' in south Albania and north-western Greece.[80] The final significant operation – 'Draufgänger' – was carried out in the second half of July 1944 and involved many Wehrmacht and Waffen-SS formations, notably two of the Balkan divisions of the Waffen-SS, the ethnic German Prinz Eugen and the Albanian Skanderbeg. These operations entailed many massacres of partisans and civilians.[81] The partisans nevertheless emerged victorious, and the days of Nazi occupation in south-east Europe were numbered.

From 1942 to 1944 SOE stayed in contact and negotiated with nearly all south-east European resistance groups, providing weapons and military training to sustain the fight against fascist occupation armies.[82] In 1944 it decided to support communist partisans in the Bosnian-Montenegrin-Serbian zone and in 'Greater Albania' only, because all other parties hesitated to launch an open attack on the Germans. This British decision brought about the final breakthrough of communist partisans. It stiffened the transnational troops, and now even their deadly foes considered them as a regular and worthy army:

> The enemies in the operation 'Draufgaenger' were no longer bandits in the previous sense, but homogenous, well-armed, well-trained units in British uniforms remarkably well led. With machine guns the enemy was far superior to our troops. The training level and the combat value of these bandits proved to be surprisingly good. Troops and command have to be put on an equal footing with a fully-fledged regular European army.[83]

In the autumn of 1944 about forty thousand Italians joined the Yugoslav or Albanian partisans who, alongside many other foreigners, were driving the Wehrmacht and Waffen-SS north from Greece through Albania and Kosovo, Bosnia, Serbia and Croatia. One of the most notable events on this route was the liberation of Belgrade between September and November 1944. Two Italian battalions – the Matteotti Battalion, which was part of the 3rd Krajina Brigade, and the Garibaldi Battalion, part of the Yugoslav Liberation Army's elite unit, the First Proletarian Assault Brigade – participated in a seven-day-long battle in October 1944. After the National Theatre building, situated in a strategic position for the control of the city's main square, had changed hands several times, the First Proletarian Assault Brigade command sent in the Italians who managed to hold the building and push back all subsequent German assaults. Eventually, the two battalions merged in the Italia Brigade, reinforced by many liberated Italian POWs.[84] Thus Italians, who had invaded the

Balkans as regular forces of the Axis in 1941, liberated them as part of a transnational coalition in 1944.

'A very mixed bunch' in the Italian resistance

The surrender of the Italian forces in September 1943 was followed by the invasion and occupation of north and central Italy by German forces. The Italian peninsula now became a 'shatter zone' in its own right, fought between the German and Allied armies. The Germans established a series of defences across the country south of Rome, which they held during the winter of 1943–44 and from which the Allies tried with enormous effort to dislodge them. The Battle of Monte Cassino, which held the key to Rome, lasted from 17 January to 18 May 1944. Italian resistance was developed behind German lines, but it was far from being simply a national movement. The PCI commanded a transnational struggle which involved both veterans of the International Brigades and Yugoslav POWs who were able to escape from their camps and prisons to join the fight.

Italian members of the International Brigades had for some time been fighting alongside the French Resistance, but now started to move back illegally to Italy, often on the orders of the PCI. On 8 September 1943 the communist leader Antonio Roasio instructed Francesco Scotti, a veteran of the International Brigades and partisan in southern France at that time, to return to Italy and to organise guerrilla units in the northern part of the country.[85] In the summer of 1943 many other Spanish veterans interned on prison islands were freed after the collapse of the fascist regime or managed to escape to take part in the Italian resistance across the country. Emilio Canzi, an anarchist and among the very early international volunteers to join the Spanish militias in summer 1936, created the first resistance group near Piacenza in the autumn of 1943. In 1944, despite his anarchism and because of his military expertise, he was chosen by the Comitato di Liberazione Nazionale Alta Italiana (Committtee of National Liberation for Northern Italy, CLNAI) to be commander of all the partisan units in the area.[86] As Claudio Pavone underlined, 'The prestige enjoyed by the veterans from Spain, some of whom arrived via the French Resistance, was great – from Luigi Longo to those partisans who sang: We are young Garibaldini, we are the veterans of Spain, we fight the fascist assassins, who torment all of humanity.'[87]

The PCI also employed many Spanish veterans in the organisation of urban guerrilla units, known as Gruppi di Azione Patriottica (GAP). The GAP were an Italian version of the FTP, and many of them had learned their skills in the FTP.[88] Among the first of these urban fighters was Ilio Barontini, an Italian communist who trained in Moscow in the 1930s, briefly commanded the Garibaldi Battalion in Spain and fought within the French Resistance in the Paris area before moving to the Marseilles region, where he trained French, Spanish, Italian, Armenian and Polish resisters in home-made bomb-making.[89] Back in Italy, Barontini spent months travelling between different cities – Bologna, Turin, Genoa, Milan and Florence – training younger resisters and teaching them urban guerrilla tactics.[90]

The majority of foreign fighters in the Italian resistance were Allied or Balkan POWs who managed to escape from fascist internment camps after 8 September 1943. Nearly 50,000 POWs under Italian control left their camps after the collapse of the Italian state, and a number of them joined the first guerrilla units.[91] Already in the spring of 1942, following intensified sabotage activities from the resistance movement, the Italian government had decided to transfer the most dangerous Albanian political prisoners, namely the communists, from Albanian to Italian prison camps.[92] The IB veteran Petro Marko was part of the group that was transferred to the Sicilian island of Ustica in March 1942.[93] There, he wrote, 'the first thing to be done was to get in contact with the [Italian] comrades from there, and that is what we did'.[94] As soon as news spread on the island about his experiences in Spain, Marko was approached by members of the underground communist cell, and he became a bridge between the different national groups interned on the island, including Croatians, Slovenians and Montenegrins. 'We set up a committee with two representatives for each nation', said Marko. 'Elections were held. I was elected military commander, while our comrade Alois, from Slovenia, was nominated commissar.'[95] Marko remained on the island until May 1943, when the Italian authorities decided to move the Croatian, Montenegrin and Albanian prisoners internees from Ustica to a camp in Alatri, near Frosinone, not far from Rome.[96] After 8 September 1943 Petro Marko used the contacts he had developed in Ustica to join one of the first bands of partisans formed in the Terni area of central Italy, composed both of Italian workers from the local steel mills and of Yugoslavs from Montenegro and Dalmatia who had been held in Italian prisons. They had their first clash with German and fascist units on 14 October 1943.

In January 1944 the Tito Company, an official Balkan unit, was formed, consisting of a hundred Yugoslav fighters. In February it was transformed into a battalion, and in March it became one of the seven battalions of the Gramsci Brigade. During this period, the Yugoslav unit suffered heavy losses, but played an important role thanks to its fighters' experience in both the political and armed struggle against fascism. Its commander, Svetozar Laković Tozo, originally from Berane in Montenegro, had a long odyssey. Arrested in Montenego in 1942 by the Italian army for his partisan activities, he was sentenced to twenty years in prison and transferred to the Spoleto prison in Italy, where about four hundred Yugoslavs were already detained. On 13 October 1943 he led a rebellion and organised a mass breakout. With about fifty men he immediately joined the Italian Partisans in the mountains and became the leader of the guerrilla fighters in that region. He and his unit were transferred to the Yugoslav theatre in summer 1944, continuing the fighting against the Nazis until the end of the war.[97]

Another example of a transnational guerrilla unit in Italy was the Banda Mario, so called after its leader Mario Depangher, an Istrian communist fisherman who had been interned in the area before September 1943 by the Italian Fascist authorities. During the early 1930s, Depangher moved to Moscow and was arrested a few years later during an undercover mission in Italy. His unit, as one of its members, the former British POW John Cowtan, wrote in his memoirs, was 'a very mixed bunch', consisting of former POWs from Yugoslavia, France, the Soviet Union and the United Kingdom, a group of young Italians, a small group of Italian Jews and Africans.[98] The latter were about seventy colonial subjects from Somalia, Eritrea and Ethiopia, and had been in Italy since early 1940 to participate in the 'Mostra delle Terre Italiane d'Oltremare', an exhibition about Italy's overseas colonies, held in Naples.[99] In late October 1940 the exhibition was closed but repatriation became impossible because of Italian intervention in the war. The Somalian, Eritrean and Ethiopian civilians, soldiers and members of the Polizia dell'Africa Italiana (Italian African Police, PAI), remained in Naples until the spring of 1943, when, as a consequence of the intensification of Allied bombing in the area, they were moved to Treia in central Italy. In late October 1943 three Ethiopians joined a local group of partisans, and a few days later the same three escapees helped the partisans to free other members of the group. At least twenty-five African internees joined the Italian resistance. Depangher and the political commissar of the unit, Guido Latini, another IB veteran who had been interned in France and Ventotene, politicised the African and Yugoslav fighters, who expressed their new-found communist identity by saluting with a clenched fist.[100] On 25 November the Ethiopian Carlo Abbamagal died in action, and in March 1944 two other African partisans – the Ethiopian Thur Nur and the Somali PAI agent Mohamed Raghé – were also killed.[101]

Multinational partisans and the liberation of Eastern Europe

On the Eastern Front too, the Germans came under huge pressure from the Red Army and partisan units behind their lines. In July 1944 Soviet forces made breakthroughs, capturing the Narva bridgehead to open up the Baltics and arriving at the outskirts of Warsaw. In the late spring and summer of 1944, on the eve of the German retreat from Soviet territory, the Ukrainian Headquarters of the Partisan Movement – once a CHPM branch and later an independent guerrilla staff under the direct control of the Ukrainian communist boss and future Soviet leader Nikita Khrushchev – launched its 'relocation operation' into Eastern Europe, to support 'fraternal' anti-Nazi and anti-fascist resistance movements beyond the Soviet border, notably in Poland and Slovakia, to facilitate the Red Army's advance.[102] Foreigners in the Red Army's guerrillas' ranks proved to be an even more valuable asset than before. Most of the Soviet guerrillas, including experienced guerrilla commanders, had never left their homeland, and thus knew no alien landscapes, spoke no foreign languages and were completely culturally and mentally unprepared for survival in an unfamiliar environment. The foreigners who joined them acted as mediators in their contacts with local populations. They guided Soviet guerrilla units through unknown operational areas, gathered information about the local population's mood and provisions and about the enemy's assets, intentions and deeds, interrogated POWs and disseminated Soviet propaganda both orally and by writing or translating leaflets.[103]

There were broadly two ways in which foreigners were integrated into Soviet guerrilla units. The first were national detachments under only formal Soviet command which had strong national sentiments, spoke no Russian and preferred to fight within their 'own' guerrilla formations, under the command of their fellow compatriots. One such formation was the Hungarian Partisan group that was established by Ukrainian Partisans in Slovakia in the early autumn of 1944, hoping that it would infiltrate neighbouring Hungary, which had been occupied by the Germans in March, and develop pro-Soviet resistance there. Although the group was formally led by a Russian major, Vasilii Kozlov, its de facto commanders were two Hungarian officers, Zoltán Grubicz and Karol Adler. In spite of this national profile, the local Hungarian population nevertheless saw it as basically Soviet, and the Hungarian authorities took effective counter-insurgency measures. The group was forced to withdraw, and Grubicz and Adler later took part in the Slovak National Uprising, which they did not survive.[104]

The second model were genuinely multinational units, of which the Soviet leadership was sometimes drawn from the Jewish minority of the Soviet empire. It is exemplified by the partisan squadron commanded by a young Ukrainian-born Jewish Soviet officer, Leonid Berenshtein, which fought in south-eastern Poland after May 1944 and later crossed the border into Slovakia. Its organisational nucleus was formed in the Ukraine and included experienced guerrilla fighters such as the former

Romanian-Jewish citizen Mikhail Imas, born in the Bessarabian city of Bender, who had served in Romanian and Soviet armies and spoke Romanian, Russian and German. His language skills and knowledge of foreign habits were actively used by Berenshtein to conduct intelligence and sabotage missions in the enemy's rear, as well as to contact the local Polish population. It was important that the Poles saw them not as occupiers but as liberators. Berenshtein later stressed Imas's essential contribution to the group's first steps on Polish soil. In addition, shortly after landing near the Polish village of Dydnia, Berenshtein and his men recruited a local inhabitant and Moscow sympathiser, Władysław Ryniak, as interpreter, negotiator and propaganda distributor and as a link between the partisans and their local informers. Subsequently the squadron recruited many Poles, Slovaks, Hungarians and even a few German deserters who acted as saboteurs and spies. It was mainly thanks to these people that the squadron managed to avoid annihilation and successfully performed its combat, sabotage and intelligence duties in Poland and Slovakia. Imas and Ryniak did not survive the war but Berenshtein proved luckier. He ended the war as a Red Army lieutenant, wrote his memoirs, lectured widely on his anti-Nazi struggle and the guerrilla warfare and ended up living in Israel after the downfall of the Soviet Union. In a 2006 interview Berenshtein still emphasised the importance of incorporating those 'Sovietised' foreigners into his unit and their vital contribution to the group's successes, glossing over any sign of possible discomfort caused by the group's multinational and transnational character.[105]

Conclusion

Despite narratives of Yugoslav, Albanian, Greek, Italian and Soviet partisan resistance, the guerrilla units that took part in the long struggle against German and Italian and to a lesser extent Hungarian and Bulgarian occupation were far from being purely 'national'. The defeat and effective destruction of the fragile states of Eastern Europe and the Balkans, the flight of Jewish refugees to the relative safe havens provided by partisans and then, later in the war, as the Axis powers collapsed, mass desertions from their ranks and the escape of the POWs they held ensured that many of these guerrilla units had a transnational profile. Italians fought in the Yugoslav resistance, Yugoslavs fought in the Italian resistance, and Soviets and Germans fought in the Greek resistance.

This transnationalism was facilitated by the esprit de corps of former International Brigaders who moved from one resistance movement to another, often via prisons and camps in which they had been held. The legacy of the International Brigades was a rallying cry and triggered the imagination and fascination of people who at a certain point might be mobilised against fascism. For many veterans of the Spanish Civil War, their experiences served as a template for their later partisan activities. Transnationalism was also promoted by international communism so that, for example, Albanian, Yugoslav and Bulgarian partisans overcame their national differences because of shared loyalty to the international communist movement.

There were, of course, limits to how far these resistances were transnational. Bulgarian and Yugoslav partisans fell out over the control of Macedonia. The ethnic Slav Macedonians of northern Greece fell out with the Greeks of the Greek communist resistance movement. After the armistice of September 1943 Italian soldiers and officers saw their participation in the Albanian or Yugoslav guerrilla war above all as a way to survive. The Italian general who deserted to the Albanian resistance did so for pragmatic reasons, to avoid capture by the Wehrmacht, but in no way espoused Albanian nationalism or communism.

Exact numbers of foreign fighters given in the records are to be taken with a grain of salt because of two factors. On the one hand German and Italian occupying forces often exaggerated the numbers of partisans and partisan casualties to obtain more support for their next operation, or to legitimate their drastic measures. Often, German and Italian forces counted civilians, mostly women, elderly people and children, as so-called partisan casualties to swell numbers. On the other hand, partisans reported their actions often as more successful than they were in order to underline their contribution to the course of the war, while the documentation of foreigners joining partisan units remained incomplete. After the war, without any critical review, socialist countries confined their national historiography to stories of communist partisans. The history of partisan warfare during the Second World War was used to establish national postwar narratives of national liberation in both Eastern and Western countries. The rediscovery of its transnational, international and multinational dimensions, however, offers a very different interpretation.

9

Transnational uprisings: Warsaw, Paris, Slovakia

Laurent Douzou, Yaacov Falkov and Vít Smetana

Steadily, but unevenly, German armies were forced back. On 4 July 1944 Soviet forces crossed the 1939 border between the Soviet Union and Poland and approached Warsaw, the German-occupied key to Eastern Europe. The Allies made slow progress in Normandy after D-Day on 6 June 1944, but on 15 August 1944 the Allied and French landings in Provence broke the German grip on southern France. With their backs to the wall, however, the German armies were still capable of fighting back. In March 1944 they occupied the territory of their former ally Hungary and at the end of August they occupied Slovakia, which since March 1939 had effectively been a German puppet state.

Resistance activity increasingly moved from the countryside to towns and cities, although German offensives might also drive them back to the rural areas. This chapter will explore three major uprisings: those in the capital cities of Warsaw and Paris and that in Slovakia, around the town of Banská Bystrica. For a long time these risings were written about and commemorated as movements of national resistance and liberation: the triumph of the French Resistance and the Free French, the Polish national uprising and the Slovak national uprising. These narratives were required to overcome national traumas of defeat, occupation, partition and collaboration. By rising up the nations redeemed themselves and threw off the shame and guilt of their recent pasts.

These national myths, defensible though they were in political terms, conceal the fact that the uprisings were far from purely national: they were international, multinational and indeed transnational. There are three reasons for this. First, the capital cities in which the uprisings took place were cosmopolitan: they had large populations of immigrant workers and students, some of whom were now organised by underground resistance networks, whether (to take the French case) communist, like the FTP-MOI, or non-communist, such as the Armée Secrète. Second, the Allies played a key role in these uprisings through SOE, the OSS, which preceded the Central Intelligence Agency, and the NKVD.[1] As with many British who worked for SOE, the Americans with OSS were often national hybrids, from European families that had recently migrated to the USA. Third, the German retreat undermined the system of POW camps, labour camps, prisons and concentration camps that kept their enemies under control. A large number of those who fought in the uprisings were escaped POWs, escaped forced labourers, escaped prisoners and even Jews liberated from concentration camps. To these were added deserters from the Wehrmacht, which had always been a multinational army including non-Germans reluctantly drafted into its ranks.

These factors ensured that the uprisings were extremely diverse in nature. Among those involved were resisters with very long transnational trajectories. Transnational encounters took place between people of very different backgrounds in resistance organisations and fighting units. Transnational experiences were gained working with resisters of different origins, whether they were former POWs of another nationality or local inhabitants committed to a cause. This does not mean, however, that we should now think about these uprisings in purely transnational terms. There were many limits to the transnational experience. To begin with, fighting units were often organised along national lines, making the combat multinational rather than transnational. The role of the Allied agents and of communist parties should be seen in international terms, because interactions were determined by international organisations, not by individuals, and between them the beginnings of Cold War rivalry could be detected. Lastly, although there were a few cases of non-white fighters involved in these uprisings, the policy in most armies was to segregate or remove non-white forces as the struggle against Germany intensified. The main reason for this was a fear that liberation by forces of colonial origin would upset racial hierarchies in Europe.

Eventually, after years of harsh and uncertain struggles, as the Nazis were defeated, cities, towns and countries were liberated throughout Europe. These liberations took place in deep turmoil. Each had a unique character. Fighting took place at very different dates depending on the progress of the Allied armies. Unsurprisingly, liberations were often carried out by a large number of locals who had built strong movements or networks in order to recover their freedom. This aspect of the battles leading to liberation is quite well known. Often few foreigners are mentioned among the resisters, whose patriotism was universally acclaimed. For many at the time, however, combat was in part a transnational experience. This chapter shows how a transnational approach can make us aware of the multilayered nature of these experiences.

Moments of liberation moments were in many ways unexpected as the underground world that had been built year after year eventually broke out in full daylight. Nobody, even those who were in charge of this underground world, really knew what the scattered forces, gathered in the shadows, might turn out to be once freed from the multiple rules that applied in clandestine times. It was certainly a huge surprise to discover to what extent the transnational factor was a key element of the big picture, first, because everybody could see with their own eyes how numerous foreign fighters were and secondly, because these resisters did not come from nowhere. They had long experience, starting as early as the 1920s for the Italians and the 1930s for the Spanish. The numbers and the strength of these transnational forces were first-rank assets.

The Warsaw, the Paris and the Slovak national uprisings will be scrutinised as laboratories of transnational coming together and transfiguration but also of misunderstanding and conflict. Though these three cases are quite different from one another, a close examination makes it clear that their transnational dimension was genuinely important. Yet it was subsequently forgotten or erased for the benefit of narratives written and told in honour of national liberation.

'For our freedom and yours': the transnational dimension of the Warsaw uprising

In the third week of August 1944, at about the time the insurrection in Paris was beginning, an unexpected dispatch in Morse Code reached the London headquarters of SOE. Sent in English through a previously unknown Warsaw underground wireless transmitter, it described the heavy fighting and horror that reigned over the Polish capital. SOE very quickly realised that the man behind the dispatch was none other than John Ward, an RAF sergeant and former POW who had successfully escaped German captivity in 1941 and had been acting ever since as a member of the Polish resistance. By the end of the month, Ward's reports were being widely distributed in the British and the Western press, and the Western public became aware of Warsaw's terrible fate.

The Warsaw uprising against the German occupation lasted for sixty-three days, from 1 August to 2 October 1944. It ended in failure: the complete defeat of the resisters and the deaths of 200,000 civilians. The uprising was not celebrated in Soviet historiography because it was led not by communists but by the rival, non-communist AK. A breakthrough came in 1974 when the Polish resister Jan Ciechanowski, who became a

The transnational origins of International Brigaders

1 The Swiss Brigader Clara Thalmann (sitting on the wall) with a mixed international Anarchist unit, Pina (de Ebro), 1937.

2 The Romanian fighters Galia Sincari (front row, left) and Mihail Burcă (back row, third from left) in Barcelona, 1938.

3 Soviet aviators in Spain. Ilya Finkel, Soviet Jewish aviator, killed near Barcelona on 26 October 1937, is fifth from the right.

4 Spanish guerrillas in Moscow during the German offensive against the city, late 1941 or early 1942. The image of Domingo Ungria (centre) was subsequently disfigured, probably by a Spanish communist leadership opposed to his stance.

5 Sculpture of the French Republic built from mud at Gurs to commemorate the 150th anniversary of the French Revolution by an Italian and a Romanian International Brigadist, July 1939.

6 Ramón Via at Camp Morand, Algeria, 1939, just before his escape. On the left with beret.

A sample of transnational fighters

7 The Dutch International Brigader Jef Last. Self-portrait from the front, 25 May 1937.

8 Gerhard Reinhardt, a German anti-Nazi who deserted to the Greek resistance.

9 Otto Miksche, who moved between the Czechoslovak army, International Brigades and Free French.

10 August Agbola O'Brown, a Nigerian jazz musician who took part in the 1944 Warsaw uprising.

11 Dutch *Engelandvaarders* helped across the Pyrenees by Dutch-Paris on the Spanish side of the border, February 1944.

Guerrilla fighters in the Balkans

12 Giuseppe Manzitti (left), formerly an intelligence officer with the Italian army's Parma Division, photographed in British battledress while serving in Albania with an SOE mission in 1944.

13 Albanian guerrilla Mehmet Shehu with Italian soldiers won over in Albania, October 1943.

The nationalisation of transnational resistance

14 Captain Georges Barazer de Lannurien, commander of the French guerrilla unit in Slovakia in the company of a Slovak woman in national costume, Banska Bystrica, 29 August 1945

Commemoration of Yugoslav International Brigaders

15 Veljko Vlahović, former fighter of the International Brigades, unveiling the monument to the International Brigades in Belgrade, 27 October 1956.

historian at University College London, published *The Warsaw Rising of 1944*.[2] This argued that the Soviet forces outside Warsaw had deliberately held back and allowed the AK to be crushed by the Germans, in order to later orchestrate a communist takeover. It was not until the end of the Cold War that Polish, German and English-language histories put the story of the Warsaw uprising squarely on the map, with studies by Włodzimierz Borodziej (2001), Norman Davies (2003), Halik Kochanski, and Philip Cooke and Ben Shepherd.[3] What, however, remains an almost complete enigma, not only in Poland but in other historiographies, is the uprising's transnational dimension. The active participation of hundreds of foreigners, who desperately attempted to liberate the Polish capital from the Nazis, has never been the subject of an academic monograph.[4] Only since 2010 has foreign participation been acknowledged and very briefly described by the permanent exhibition and the official website of the state Warsaw Rising Museum, and this dimension has not been taught in schools.[5] The only international aspect to be explored in these recent histories is SOE's assistance to the Polish national underground after 1941 and during the Warsaw Uurising in particular.[6]

The exact number of the foreigners – *obcokrajowcy* in Polish – who fought in the uprising is difficult to determine, given the chaotic character of the uprising itself and its aftermath. The Warsaw Rising Museum estimated that they numbered several hundred and represented at least fifteen countries – Slovakia, Hungary, Romania, Great Britain, Australia, France, Belgium, the Netherlands, Greece, Italy, the USA, the Soviet Union, South Africa and even Germany and Nigeria.[7] An analysis of these individuals suggests that foreigners who joined the Warsaw uprising came from five different origins. First, there were economic migrants or political refugees who were living in Poland and its capital before the outbreak of war. These included Slovaks, Hungarians, Georgians and a Nigerian. Second, there were paratroopers sent by SOE from Britain, including Poles who had escaped their homeland in the autumn of 1939. Third, there were French and Soviet POWs, who had sometimes been captured in distant theatres of war, such as the Mediterranean, and had escaped or been released prior to the uprising. Fourth, there were deserters from the German auxiliary forces, especially former Soviet POWs and Hungarians who had been drafted in. Fifth, there were inmates of the Warsaw concentration camp, who were mostly foreign Jews.

These people were absorbed into different fighting and support formations of the Polish underground: the AK. They wore the underground's red-white armband (the colours of the Polish national flag) and adopted the Polish traditional independence fighters' slogan *Za naszą i waszą wolność* ('For our freedom and yours'). This dated back to the 1831 anti-Russian uprising and was widely used by the International Brigades in Spain. It was continued in the anti-Russian uprising of 1863, which attracted up to a thousand foreign volunteers.[8] In 1944 some of the *obcokrajowcy* showed outstanding bravery in fighting the enemy and were awarded the highest decorations of the AK and the Polish government-in-exile.

Current Polish historiography of the uprising claims that its most numerous foreign participants came from two neighbouring Eastern European countries, Slovakia and Hungary. The Slovakian residents of Warsaw, mostly political refugees from the nationalist oppression of the Magyar ruling class in the Austro-Hungarian Habsburg Empire, made their first contacts with the AK at the very beginning of the German occupation. In late 1942 they established the underground Slovakian National Committee (Slovenská Národná Rada) and its military arm, the 'Slovakian platoon no. 535', which was placed under Warsaw's AK command. The commander of the Slovakian National Committee and the Slovakian platoon was Lieutenant Mirosław Iringh ('Stanko'). The son of a Slovakian father who had fled Hungary and a Polish mother, he was a journalist before the war and participated actively in the defence of Warsaw in September 1939. Later he acted as a distributor of the Polish and Slovak underground press. During the uprising, Iringh and his men took part in the fiercest street battles. The young lieutenant also photographed combat scenes and the everyday life of the resisters and civilian population.

In fact, of the Slovakian platoon's fifty-seven fighters only twenty-eight were Slovaks. The rest consisted of other Slavic nationalities (Czechs, Poles and Ukrainians), as well as of Caucasians (Georgians, Armenians and Azerbaijanis). The most numerous were the Georgians, who had either come to Warsaw after the Bolshevik Revolution or had escaped the German camps after being captured as Red Army soldiers. Eventually, a separate Georgian sub-unit was established under the command of a Soviet POW nicknamed 'Russjanschvili' – 'the son of Russia' in Georgian.[9]

Despite Lieutenant Iringh's contribution to the uprising, or perhaps because of it, the new communist authorities in Poland after 1945 did not value his contribution as a brave combatant and reporter. Because of his rank in the AK hierarchy, he was constantly denied a significant post and was reduced to working as unofficial street photographer, dying in 1985. It was only after the downfall of communism in Eastern Europe that Mirosław Iringh became an official hero in Poland and Slovakia and had one of Warsaw's squares named after him.[10]

The Hungarians who joined the Polish resistance, and whose exact number is still unknown, were deserters from Hungarian military units which had participated in German repression in Poland. Their comrades who did not desert were mostly sympathetic to the Polish cause and thus tried to preserve neutrality. They deliberately avoided combat with the AK units and frequently helped the insurgents by supplying ordnance and supplies.[11]

Perhaps the most remarkable story of a migrant resister in the Warsaw uprising is that of a Nigerian jazz player, August Agbola O'Brown, sometimes referred to as Browne. Born in Lagos in 1895, he went to Britain and in 1922 stowed away on a ship sailing to the Free City of Danzig. A short period of hard work in the Polish docks came to an end when he started to perform as a jazz drummer in the leading Warsaw night clubs and became a celebrity of the local musical scene. His first album, recorded in 1928, made history, for he was the first West African jazzman to achieve this. He integrated into Polish society by marrying a Polish woman, and they had two sons. His friends and neighbours at the time remembered him as a very intelligent, courteous person and a polyglot, speaking six languages.

O'Brown's life changed dramatically in the autumn of 1939. In the face of the Wehrmacht's rapid advance towards Warsaw, most of the tiny local African community – largely musicians from different Western countries – fled abroad, but the Nigerian jazzman decided to stay with his new Polish family and friends. In the weeks that followed he participated in the defence of the Polish capital, and after its surrender went underground adopting the alias 'Ali'. Despite the danger of being caught, because of his obviously 'non-Aryan' appearance, he was sometimes seen around Warsaw, distributing the AK news-sheet.

Amazingly, O'Brown succeeded in surviving the next five years of German occupation and actively participated in the Warsaw uprising, as an ordinary fighter of the AK battalion 'Iwo'. He was not injured and successfully escaped German capture. After the communist takeover of Poland 'the African comrade' was rewarded for his struggle against the Nazis, allowed to play jazz at Warsaw restaurants and even employed as a 'cultural officer' for a governmental institution. However, by the end of the 1950s, already aged over sixty, he became completely frustrated with the 'Communist heaven' and got special permission from the authorities to take his family to England. There he lived anonymously until his death in 1976.[12]

The Warsaw uprising struggled to obtain external assistance, but it was not entirely absent. British SOE provided support for the fighting in Warsaw indirectly via a group of about a hundred Polish soldiers who came to the country from France after its defeat in June 1940, and were eventually recruited and trained by SOE as special operations paratroopers. Officially they had been part of a larger military formation called *Cichociemni* ('Silent and unseen'). This was established in 1941, supervised by the Polish general staff-in-exile, and performed guerrilla, sabotage and reconnaissance missions in Nazi-occupied Poland. During the Warsaw uprising the *Cichociemni* fighters served either as field commanders or as rank-and-file fighters, making successful use of the knowledge and operational skills they gained from SOE and could teach to their fellow combatants. They paid a heavy personal price for being the vanguard of the resistance: at least eighteen of them were killed, and many more were wounded, reported missing in action or captured by the Germans, imprisoned and executed.[13]

The survivors suffered from communist persecution, and only a handful of them managed to return to Britain. Their role was obscured for many years in Poland and Britain alike until around the 1990s it was 'discovered' and publicised in a few Polish and English books and documentary films. That said, their story has not yet been adopted by the SOE 'mainstream narrative'. The most recent biography of the organisation's chief, Major-General Colin Gubbins, does not mention the Warsaw uprising and claims only that the AK was quite effective, although the British had no real possibility of supporting it.[14]

Alongside the Poles, who willingly returned from Britain in order to restore their motherland's independence, there were other Britons – mostly escapees from German POW camps – who found themselves more or less intentionally in the eye of the uprising's storm. The most significant is probably John Ward, a young RAF sergeant from Birmingham. In May 1940, aged twenty-one, he was shot down and captured by the Germans in France and sent first to a POW camp, then to a labour camp in Poland. He almost immediately escaped, was recaptured, escaped again and finally found his way to the AK underground. By the outbreak of the uprising, in August 1944, he had already spent about two years in the Polish capital, training Polish radio operators, transcribing BBC broadcasts for the underground press, producing his own illegal newspaper and serving simultaneously as a liaison between the AK and the British authorities and a field reporter for *The Times*.

During the sixty-three days of the uprising, Ward transmitted numerous reports on the combat and humanitarian situation in the Polish capital to SOE and the British press. At the same time he acted as an English-speaking announcer for the underground radio station Błyskawica ('Lightning'), making the Western public and policymakers aware of the uprising and its terrible outcome. When the resistance was over, he was captured while posing as a Pole but escaped to join the Polish Partisans. He was then arrested as a 'spy' by the Soviet secret service NKVD, which suggested that Cold War tensions were already developing. Rescued by an American representative, he finally left the Soviet Union for England. In the early 1990s the AK English radio announcer was still alive to witness the downfall of communism in his beloved Poland. The new Polish government awarded him two high military decorations in recognition of his contribution to the struggle against the Nazis.[15]

Another transnational trajectory was that of Walter E. Smith, a signalman of the Australian Expeditionary Force. Taken prisoner on Crete in May 1941, he was sent like John Ward to a POW camp in Poland. Escaping at his seventh attempt using false documents supplied by the local underground, he contributed to the AK propaganda effort by broadcasting its interview with him, which was reported by the Australian press and distributed worldwide. Smith too was able to return to his homeland following the German retreat from Poland.[16]

Several testimonies of the uprising's veterans confirm the presence of at least five French comrades among the resisters. Only one of them, Jean Gasparoux, is known by name. In his mid-twenties, he allegedly spent all the occupation years in Warsaw and, following the uprising's breakout, joined the AK Bałtyk platoon as a sniper. He was subsequently captured by the Germans and recognised by his comrades at a POW prison, but his later fate is unknown.[17]

Much less has been written about the contribution of the Soviet POWs. Although their exact number has yet to be established, different estimations speak of up to sixty individuals. Among them were twenty Soviet officers, allegedly from the NKVD border guard, released by the AK from one of the German prisons. They volunteered to join the resisters and died in heavy street fighting. No names are known, except that of Lieutenant Viktor Bashmakov ('Engineer'), aged twenty-eight, who served as a commander of the separate Russian AK platoon and was killed along with his soldiers on 30 September 1944.[18]

There were in addition a few Russian escapees from the Warsaw concentration camp, as well as former Soviet POWs – both Russians and Caucasians – who had been drafted into the Wehrmacht's collaborationist forces and assigned to anti-partisan missions in the Polish capital. These now deserted and people randomly joined different AK units, and most of them died in battles in complete anonymity.

Among the inmates of the Warsaw concentration camp were deported Jews. On 5 August 1944, during the initial phase of the Warsaw uprising, a battalion of the AK Radosław group attacked the Gęsiówka concentration camp in the city centre. This had a crematorium and was populated by slave labourers, mostly Jews from the liquidated Warsaw Ghetto and various European countries. At least fifty of the 348 released Jewish prisoners, men and women, including citizens of Germany, the Netherlands, Greece and Hungary, joined their liberators, mostly as supportive manpower transporting injured fighters, carrying arms and munition and fighting fires. Most of them died during the heavy fighting on Warsaw streets or were captured and executed by the Nazis.[19]

Although several hundred foreign fighters made up barely 1 per cent of the total number of Warsaw resisters, their presence demonstrated that, like other rebellions in 1831, 1848 and 1863, the uprising of 1944 had a clear transnational dimension. It is relatively easy to track transnational trajectories and encounters, but it is much more difficult to analyse transnational exprience from the viewpoint of the participants. There was certainly a transfer of martial and technical knowledge and skills from the trained and experienced strangers to their hosts. This is partly because of the destruction of the uprising, which carried away so many potential witnesses. It is also because of the limited nature of many of the sources.

The Paris uprising: a highly transnational event

The Paris uprising (19–25 August 1944) was a highly transnational event. Even as the Warsaw uprising was on many people's minds, and while the Allies were still fighting in Normandy, a decision was made in Paris by Colonel Rol-Tanguy, head of FFIs, to begin the uprising on 19 August. Until then the liberation of Paris was not a priority for the Allies but it became so once the uprising began. General von Choltitz, military governor of Paris, received an order from Berlin to quell the insurrection in the same way as the Germans had done in Warsaw. In these circumstances General de Gaulle insisted that Allied military forces be immediately sent to Paris. He wanted both to avoid a bloodbath and to show how efficient, under his leadership, the French metropolitan resistance could be. The 2nd Armoured Division of General Leclerc was therefore directed towards Paris with the support of the 4th Infantry Division of General Barton.

The liberation of Paris by conventional armed forces was international in that it was undertaken by both American and French forces, and because of the international organisation of the communist movement. It was multinational in that those 'French' forces were formed of many nationalities. It was also transnational in that it involved multiple transnational trajectories, encounters and experiences. There were, however, limits to this transnationalism. These were imposed by the Americans' hostility to black African forces and de Gaulle's imperative to shape a narrative of national liberation.

The 2nd Armoured Division that entered Paris on 24 August 1944 was composed of twenty-two nationalities. Most famous was the 9th Company of the Régiment de Marche du Tchad – 'La Nueve' – with 160 Spaniards, most of them anarchists. It left a vivid trace in the collective memory. Whenever the commitment of foreigners in the Paris liberation is remembered, the feat of 'La Nueve' is evoked and overshadows other very important actors. Their halftracks were named after famous battles of the Spanish Civil War: 'Teruel', 'Guadalajara' and 'Ebro'. The first officer to walk into the Hôtel de Ville in Paris was Amado Granell Mesado, a forty-four-year-old Spaniard who had fought during the Spanish Civil War in the Republican Army and joined the Free French forces in 1942. That said, 'La Nueve' distracts us from the bigger picture that needs to be underlined, that there were many Spanish fighters in the Forces Françaises Libres.[20]

In spite of this international mingling, there was a degree of segregation as far as colonial troops were concerned. Overall, the Armoured Division equipped by the Americans included 3,600 soldiers from the French Empire: Algerians, Moroccans, Syrians and Lebanese. Among their non-commissioned officers was Corporal Alcide Berti. Born in Italy in 1905, a former member of the International Brigades, he had joined the Free French forces in December 1942. He was wounded and died on 27 August in Paris's Necker Hospital.[21] But while the Americans had no problem with troops from North Africa or the Levant, they requested that the division's black African troops be left behind because they still applied a segregationist policy in their own armed forces.[22] Black soldiers of the 2nd Armoured Division thus had had to choose between joining an infantry division and demobilisation. When it reached Paris, the 2nd Armoured Division had no black soldiers in its ranks with the exception of Claude Mademba Sy, aged twenty-one, a Senegalese rifleman and ward of the nation, who had the status of French citizen. He was a law student in Tunis in 1943 when he joined the Régiment de Marche du Tchad and became part of the 2nd Armoured Division as a non-commissioned officer.

General de Gaulle, who led a victory parade down the Champs-Élysées on 26 August, was keen to stage a moment of French national liberation. On the margins of the big picture usually drawn – with 'La Nueve', the MOI fighters at the forefront – unknown foreigners took a significant part in the liberation without any special preparation or political affiliation. They were mostly invisible and destined to remain so. Had not a film by the Comité de Libération du Cinéma Français captured the black face of Georges Dukson not far behind General de Gaulle on the Champs-Élysées, nobody would have noticed or remembered his presence. This twenty-two-year-old French soldier, born in Gabon, escaped from a POW camp in 1943 and was living in a cheap hotel in the Batignolles in the 17th arrondissement. On 19 August, on an impulse, he joined a group of FFIs and fought with them in the rue de Rome and on the boulevard des Batignolles. Wounded in the arm, he kept fighting and attracted the admiration of his fellow combatants, who nicknamed him 'the Black Lion of the XVIIème' or 'the hero of the XVIIème'.[23] On 26 August he squeezed into the front ranks of the victory parade on the Champs-Élysées and was promptly kicked out by those surrounding the general. In the following days, he descended into the black-market business, was arrested and was wounded trying to escape. He died in the nearby Marmottan hospital. The transnational liberation of Paris is also the 'magnificent and pitiful' story of Georges Dukson.[24]

Dukson's actions with the FFIs in the 17th arrondissement exemplified what was happening all over Paris where, for five days between 19 and 24 August, until the arrival of the conventional forces, the FFIs were at the forefront of the Paris uprising. The FFIs were formed by a merger in February 1944 of the Gaullist Armée Secrète, the Giraudist Organisation de Résistance de l'Armée, the communist FTP and the MOI. They had many foreigners in their ranks: Poles, Italians, Spaniards, Slovaks, Yugoslavs, Armenians, Hungarians, Greeks, Russians, Germans, Austrians, Romanians and Bulgarians. This amazing patchwork of nationalities reflected the fact that Paris was simultaneously a national and an international capital. For years, it had attracted women and men from all over Europe. Suffering hardship and oppression in their country, they saw Paris as a haven of the rights of man. In search of work or seeking asylum, many foreigners had migrated to France and especially to Paris. How many there were in August 1944 is impossible to say, but they were certainly several thousand.[25] Because most of them had lived and worked in France for a long time, they were fluent enough in French to communicate with everyone.

Fighters from all over Europe were seen everywhere in Paris acting together in national groups. They organised ambush attacks. They built barricades at Port-Royal. Italians of the Garibaldi formation fought near the École Militaire and in the suburbs; other Italians took German prisoners near the Bastille and the Place de la République in the 11th *arrondissement*. Poles, who had a long tradition of migration to France since the suppression of their own national insurrections of 1831, 1848 and 1863, were especially active at Saint-Paul, Saint-Denis, Argenteuil and Ivry. Spaniards fought near the Opéra or Place de la Concorde. Many Jewish people were active around the Hôtel de Ville and Place de la République. The heavily Jewish FTP-MOI groups were reported to have fought spectacularly in several *arrondissements*. The Rayman group defended the town hall of the 10th *arrondissement* and saw action at the Pont de Flandre. This group was named after Marcel Rayman, who was born in Warsaw in 1923; he was arrested by the Parisian police in November 1943, handed over to the Germans, tortured by them and shot on 21 February 1944. This was a strong sign that foreign heroes of the resistance were already becoming legends who inspired the fighters.

The uprising was certainly multinational, and it was also international in so far as it was directed by the Communist Party. How transnational it was in the sense of encounters and subjective experiences needs to be assessed. Interesting clues suggest that each nationality seems to have followed its own agenda during the uprising: being part of a powerful multinational movement did not keep the nationalities from remembering where they originally belonged. The Russians, for example, some of whom had just been released from the prison of Fresnes, organised a Union des Patriotes Russes et des Prisonniers Soviétiques and took possession of the Soviet embassy in the rue de Grenelle. A group of Czechoslovaks occupied the building of the Czechoslovak colony on 19 August and, the next day, the consulate and the embassy. On 22 August Romanians liberated the general consulate of Romania at 17 rue Bremontier in the 17th *arrondissement*.

Rather than listing the great variety of places where specific nationalities were dramatically involved, it may be useful to examine how the fighting foreigners present in Paris were able to join the uprising. The key point is that they were fighting for freedom in a city which represented the values they cherished and that were the reasons why they had come to Paris in the first place.[26] Liberating Paris was intimately associated with the perspective of a liberated Europe where, in their own native country, they would be able to think, act and live freely.

Many of them had been organised for a long time and were preparing for fighting to come when the final battle would occur. Often they were members of the Gaullist Armée Secrète. Others were involved in the communist movement, which, despite the official dissolution of the Comintern in May 1943, was still internationalist and refused to give up control. The MOI, which was organised by language groups, provided forces for the communist *milices patriotiques*, created in August 1943, working with their French comrades. These fighters had been a true 'avant-garde' in armed combat against the Germans and the French police in Paris and other towns such as Lyons, Toulouse or Grenoble. They had been hunted down and put out of action. In Lyons, for example, in February 1944, several members of an FTP-MOI group were arrested by Vichy's brutal, counterinsurgent Milice. Some of them were tortured; others, like Etienne Toro, alias Léon, born in 1906 in Kanyad (Hungary), were killed. On 19 February ten of these arrested men were sentenced to death and shot. In Paris, the group led by the Armenian Missak Manouchian had been arrested in November 1943. Its twenty-two members, including Marcel Rayman, were shot on 21 February 1944.[27]

Given the toll taken by this repression, the strategy was rethought by those who had devised it, that is to say the PCF leaders. The MOI, closely linked to the *milices patriotiques*, was ordered during the uprising on the one hand to control the entrances to the capital and on the other to occupy the embassies and public buildings of the members' countries of origin. That change of strategy was crucial, as psychologically it meant that foreigners were no longer considered as comrades who fought in France and for France but as partners who fought with France and, consequently, were France. The PCF apparatus wanted all its fighters, whether French or foreigners, to be regarded as a single patriotic and French entity which had worked towards the liberation.

By the end of the war foreigners were integrated in large numbers in groups belonging to the PCF or in resistance movements. How they arrived there, however, was not always straightforward. It is necessary to study and describe individual itineraries to try to grasp how the transnational dimension played a part.

Among those who played a major role was the Hungarian Georges Szekeres.[28] His trajectory was decidedly transnational. Born on 14 July 1914 in Für, a village located in the north-west of Hungary, then part of the Austro-Hungarian Empire and today Rúbaň in Slovakia, Szekeres began medical studies in Prague in 1932. He spoke Hungarian, Slovak, German and French. He attended the meetings of leftist students in the Prague cafés of Wenceslas Square. In August 1933 he settled in Paris to fulfil his intellectual ambitions. He studied philosophy and literature at the Sorbonne and joined a communist group led by Pierre Hervé. In the spring of 1936 he went to Czechoslovakia, where he wrote some two hundred articles on international matters in Magyar Nap, a daily Hungarian-language newspaper that supported the Popular Front elected there in 1935. In the process he learned Czech. In September 1936 he arrived in Budapest but was immediately expelled back to Czechoslovakia. In the summer of 1938 he was once again in Paris. He wrote for Parisian Hungarian-language newspapers and socialised with Paul Nizan, Jacques Kayser and Jean-Paul Sartre. Deeply committed to the anti-fascist crusade, he saw the Spanish Civil War as its dress rehearsal. At the outbreak of the Second World War he volunteered to fight and, as a Czech citizen, was incorporated into the Czech Army Corps, fighting alongside the French. He was seriously injured at the front in March 1940, and in May his unit disbanded near Troyes. After the defeat, he lived in Marseilles and in Lyons. There he became part of the 'Libération' resistance movement, in which he reconnected with his friend Pierre Hervé. In 1943, as a leading personality of the Mouvements Unis de la Résistance in the southern zone, Hervé suggested that Szekeres undertake organised action among the foreign resisters. His fellow Hungarian Peter Mod, national head of the communist cadres inside the MOI, asked Szekeres to lead the Comité d'Action et Défense des Immigrés (Immigrant Defence and Action Group, CADI). When, in

July 1943, the decision centres of the resistance moved to Paris, the CADI became the Comité d'Action et de Résistance des Étrangers (Foreigners' Action and Resistance Committee, CARE). Szekeres was the head of this organisation, which represented sixteen countries and was linked to the Conseil National de la Résistance (National Resistance Council, CNR), which coordinated the metropolitan resistance.

Szekeres was a commanding officer of the FFIs when the Paris uprising broke out and the CADI called on immigrants to take up arms. The order ran:

> Centre d'action et de défense des immigrés (CADI)
>
> Call to immigrants!
>
> Immigrants!
>
> The great days have arrived! The enemy defeated on the Eastern and Western Fronts by the valiant armies of our Allies is withdrawing in disorder on all fronts. The liberation of the French territory continues in leaps and bounds. In a few hours, Paris, the heart of France and the capital of Liberty, will forever be delivered from the Nazi yoke. Free Paris, the symbol of the freedom of all oppressed peoples, means the victory of liberty, fraternity and equality over fascist barbarism.
>
> Immigrants!
>
> You too will do your duty, you will be at the forefront of the fight for liberty, you will help drive the enemy from the land where you live and work.[29]

In its calls to join the uprising the CADI made it clear that the fate of immigrants was closely tied to that of 'the great French people'. It underlined the common fight and fraternal bonds forged with the French. The immigrants were invited to go on strike, to join the FFIs and the *milices patriotiques* and to attack German soldiers: 'In this unforgettable and solemn hour, you who suffered and fought with the people of France them in these tragic times, will share with them the joy of deliverance.'[30]

Politically, immigrants were regarded by the CNR as fighters who had to be integrated into the French Resistance model. In July 1944 the CNR asserted that the only legitimate authorities were the provisional government of the French Republic and the CNR itself; organisations of foreigners had to acknowledge this fact.[31] In other words, even if the movement that took shape during the uprising was international or transnational it was placed under the supervision of a national authority.

The itinerary of Szekeres shows how some foreigners could rise during the underground period to resistance responsibilities at the highest level. It also reflects that each itinerary deserves to be scrutinised. Indeed, Szekeres was a friend of Pierre Hervé and a few other communists who, having lost contact with the PCF, were active in non-communist movements. He was part of a communist underground world in the underground world of the resistance.

In the context of the uprising the transnational dimension did not eclipse either the national dimension or the international dimension. These three dimensions were highly interrelated. Though the multinational aspect of the uprising was clear for everybody at the time, the different and complex layers of the involvement of migrants, refugees, exiles and foreign fighters may explain why, after the uprising, nobody, and especially not the PCF, wished to underline the eminently transnational nature of the Parisian events.

The Slovak uprising through a transnational prism

The Slovak uprising that broke out on 29 August 1944 and lasted for two months was a remarkable chapter in Second World War resistance. In reaction to the growing activity of partisans, who were assisted and directed by paratroops dispatched from the Soviet Union, German military units started occupying Slovak territory in the last week of August. The central underground military organisation Vojenské ústredie (the Military Headquarters) headed by Lieutenant-Colonel Ján Golian ordered the Slovak units to oppose the Germans even though preparations for the uprising were not completed, nor was coordination with the approaching Red Army achieved. The swift disarmament of the two crucial Slovak divisions in eastern Slovakia by the Germans made impossible the 'opening' of the Carpathian passes for the Soviets, who thus had to deal with the full force of the Wehrmacht, fortified in the mountains.

The uprising thus remained limited to the territory of central Slovakia with its headquarters in Banská Bystrica. Politically, it was led by the Slovak National Council, which respected the authority of the Czechoslovak government-in-exile in London and proclaimed the reconstitution of Czechoslovakia. General Viest was dispatched to Slovakia by the government-in-exile, and by October 1944 the 1st Czechoslovak Army numbered 60,000 soldiers and volunteers on Slovak territory. These regular military units, composed primarily of Slovaks, were assisted by approximately 18,000 partisans who were organised in brigades, usually led by Soviet commanders and political commissars and including numerous units of a multinational character. Apart from the Slovaks, over 8,400 people of thirty-two other nationalities from four continents took part in the uprising.[32] These included both those who were already on Slovak territory and those who arrived from the neighbouring countries after the outbreak of

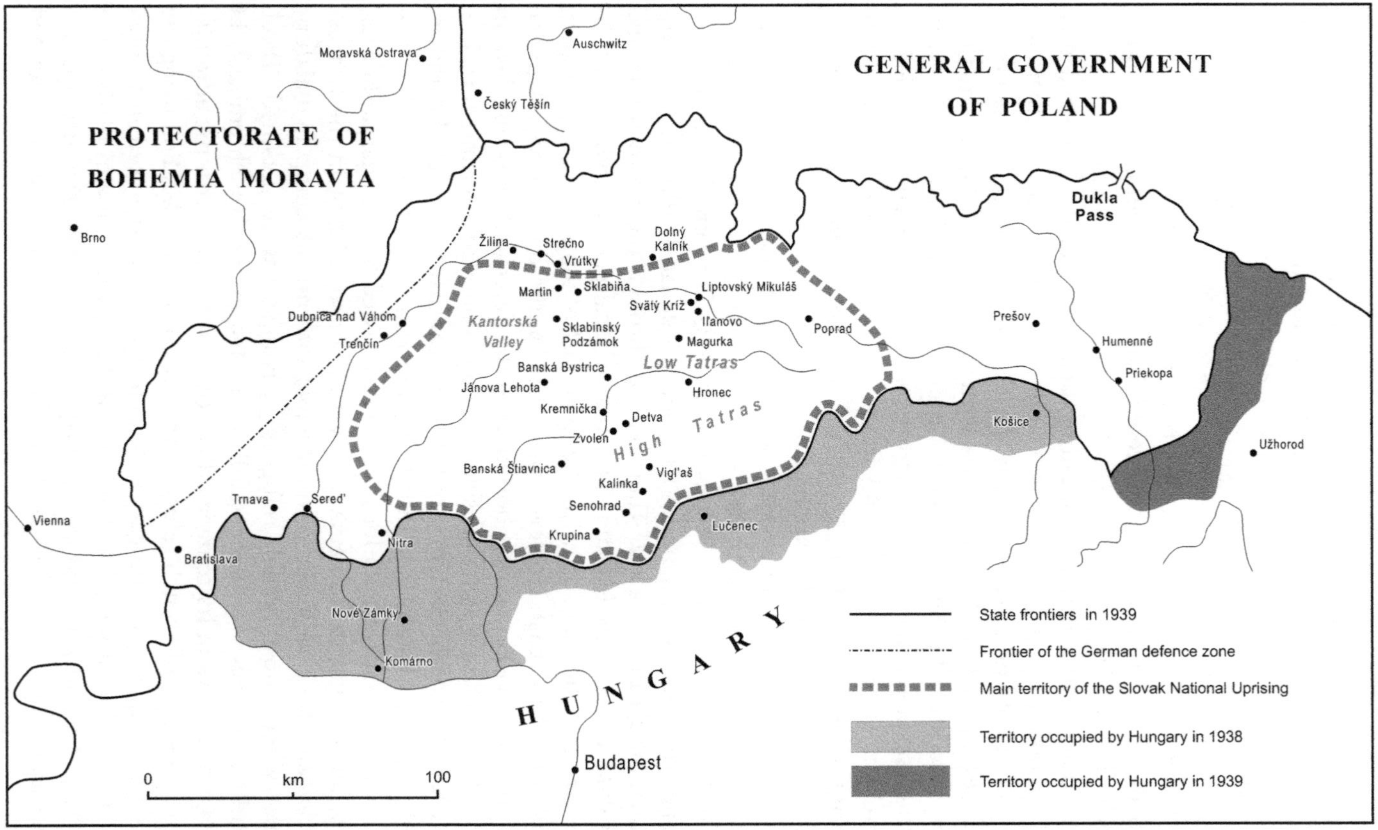

4 Slovakia and the uprising of 1944

the uprising. The partisan struggle in particular, which continued even after the Germans managed to suppress the uprising and Generals Viest and Golian ordered the remaining units to retreat to the mountains on 27 October, bore many traces of transnational cooperation.

In this section we will explore two case studies. One concerns the involvement in the uprising of escaped French POWs under their flamboyant captain. The other is the intervention of the British SOE and American OSS and the hostility they encountered from their Soviet opposite numbers in the NKVD.

A French Partisan unit, amounting to more than two hundred men and operating in central Slovakia, stands as one of the most remarkable cases of foreign involvement in the uprising. First contacts of the French escapees from German POW camps with the Slovak resistance structures were already established in 1942 in Trnava.[33] In early August 1944, when further escapees came to Slovakia from Hungary, a partisan unit called the Détachement Français des Combattants en Tchécoslovaquie was set up in Kantorská Valley in Greater Tatra. It was headed by Captain Georges Marie Charles Barazer de Lannurien.

A son of a French general and graduate of the military academy in Saint Cyr, de Lannurien was captured during the fall of France in June 1940. Together with Lieutenant Michel Bourel de la Roncière, he managed to escape from the POW camp VIII D in Weidenau (Vidnava) in northeastern Silesia in July 1942. They headed through the Protectorate and Slovakia, occasionally fed and sheltered by local people, trying to get to Hungary and the Balkans, with the final goal of joining the Free French units in the Near East. However, they were captured by the Slovak police near the Slovak–Hungarian border close to Sereď. After seven days in prison they obtained political asylum, though under an internment regime in Trnava. Four months later, under the threat that they might be imprisoned in a newly established POW camp in Humenné, they left the town and, with the assistance of local resisters, crossed the Hungarian border. They failed to get to Romania and were imprisoned first in the fortress Siklosz and then in a fairly comfortable internment camp in Balaton-Boglár where most French refugees in Hungary were detained. Three months later, they were successfully extracted by the French embassy in Budapest to work in its refugee office. There they dealt with the administrative concerns of French refugees, mainly escaped POWs. Following the German occupation of Hungary in March 1944, they organised and joined a group of nine other French soldiers in June, with the aim of reaching the Yugoslav Partisans and then perhaps Italy. However, this attempt also failed and they returned to Budapest, where they once again obtained asylum at the French embassy.

Through contacts with the Slovak legation, de Lannurien and de la Roncière learned that an uprising was being prepared in Slovakia. This represented the only opportunity for nearly one thousand French soldiers detained in Hungary to take part in the anti-Nazi struggle. De la Roncière travelled to Bratislava with a French passport and visa secretly issued by the Slovak embassy and informed members of the underground movement, both civilian (the doctor of law Ivan Pietor) and military (Major Jozef Marek), about the possibility of bringing a few hundred French soldiers to Slovakia. He then embarked on organising their crossing of the Hungarian–Slovak frontier, assisted by people-smugglers and other underground workers. The first group, which included de Lannurien, crossed the border on 2 August. Several groups of five to ten French soldiers followed until the end of the month. Most of them had undergone similar experiences: a German POW camp since 1940, multiple attempts to escape, clandestine crossing of borders to Hungary, arrest and a relatively mild internment in Hungary until the German occupation of that country in March 1944, then failed attempts to escape to Yugoslavia or Romania, contacts with the French embassy in Budapest and eventually attempts to get to Slovakia. A few dozen of the French were captured during that venture while the local Slovak baker Vojtěch Stoklasa and his wife, who provided accommodation for most of the French on the escape line in Sereď, were later arrested and perished in Sachsenhausen.[34] Those who succeeded then proceeded to the north to Kantorská Valley, where partisan units assembled for their involvement in the upcoming uprising.

Initially, the swelling French unit cooperated with another partisan group commanded by Viliam Žingor, composed of Slovaks as well as escaped Soviet POWs.[35] On 17 August de Lannurien met First Lieutenant Pyotr Alexeyevich Velichko, who had been dispatched with a team by the Ukrainian Partisan Movement Staff (UPMS) at the end of July from Kiev to Slovakia. The two officers agreed that the French unit would become part of the 1st Czechoslovak Partisan Brigade of M. R. Štefánik, along with another Slovak unit and the Russian Suvorov unit. On 1 September the whole brigade had 368 combatants, but within a month it grew to 1,434. The other six partisan brigades in Slovakia swelled with similar speed. This trend disturbed the supreme Slovak military command as volunteers were desperately needed in the regular military forces, while the partisans were not always disciplined and attempts to coordinate military actions with them often failed. However, neither the UPMS nor the Slovak Communist Party was willing to agree to being subordinated to conventional military command.[36] This was true also for the French unit, despite Golian's repeated efforts.

On 21 August the French unit took part in the brigade's occupation of Sklabiňa and Sklabinský Podzámok, where the restoration of the Czechoslovak Republic was proclaimed. A week later the French unit, now composed of ninety-nine men, received its first orders: to occupy the important railway crossroads at Vrútky. The mission was accomplished, and a dozen German soldiers were captured. On 29 August 1944, the day the Slovak uprising broke out, the French unit joined Slovak soldiers from the Martin barracks in an attack on a German convoy in the valley of the Stráňanský creek and took an advanced position in the Strečno narrows. In heavy fighting against four thousand advancing Germans between 31 August and 2 September, the battling French gained the respect of the Slovak and Soviet military as well as of the local populace. However, the insurgents were disadvantaged by a lack of anti-tank and anti-aircraft weapons and insufficient coordination of the activity of the partisan units. When their defence was broken and the Germans occupied the whole valley including Vrútky, the French unit, now numbering 145 men, retreated to Dolný Kálnik. With the loss of four men killed in action and several wounded, its morale declined, and eight men even deserted from the unit.[37]

Further heavy casualties were suffered in a failed counterattack in the area of Priekopa-Vrútky and in the defence of the Turčianská basin and around Janova Lehota and Svätý Kríž. The arrival of another fifty-eight French escapees from a forced labour camp in Dubnica nad Váhom called for restructuring and training. This took place in Detva, where the unit was visited not only by Golian (who again complained that the leadership of the partisan movement had not allowed the French unit to be subordinated to his military command) but also by the Soviet writer Boris Polevoy. The unit was strengthened by a number of Yugoslav soldiers and, on Velichko's orders, by fifty-four Slovak volunteers who created a Slovak platoon. It now became Marshal Foch Battalion of 287 men, commanded by Captain de Lannurien. This included the French company (four platoons), named after General Leclerc, which comprised 192 French, five Belgians and thirty-six Slovaks and Yugoslavs.[38] Language differences might have been an obstacle to the functioning of the battalion, but interpretation was provided by Vladimír Joanovič Jeršov, a professor of music who spoke French and had belonged to the organisers of partisan struggle in the Turiec region since the early months of 1944.

This unit co-defended the south-western frontier of the insurgent territory in the area of Krupina, where, between 13 and 18 October, it controlled crucial communications and crossroads and destroyed several German trucks and motorcycles.[39] On 16 October, on Velichko's orders, the Foch Battalion was strengthened by another fifty-eight Russians and Slovaks. While the bulk of the unit was engaged in tough defensive fighting near Senohrad, on 19–20 October one platoon, commanded by Lieutenant Jean Geyssely, remained in the enemy rear, south of Banská Štiavnica. There it made contact with the Soviet reconnaissance party Mironov, composed of four men and one woman, which was in wireless connection with the UPMS. Since none of them spoke any French, they had to communicate in German until they were joined by Count Ladomer Zichy, a local landowner whose spouse Martha Himmler spoke German, English, French, Russian and Hungarian. This transnational group embarked on various sabotage activities in the enemy rear, focusing primarily on bridges and railways, including the derailment of a military train with forty carriages on 17 November. Thanks to the support of local residents who were willingly providing food and accommodation, the group withstood the early stages of the cold and snowy winter, and on Christmas Eve made contact with the advancing 2nd Ukrainian Front of Marshal Rodion Malinovsky.[40]

The other parts of the increasingly scattered battalion were active in rearguard action south of Zvolen. Its core was ordered to guard the Kalinka–Vígľaš road on 22 October, but three days later, under overwhelming German pressure, started retreating to the southern slopes of the Low Tatras, along with the other battalions of the brigade, and then to the north across the main ridge. On 1 November de Lannurien was able to form a unit of eighty-three men which survived from the former Foch Battalion in Magurka. Other groups became stuck in the valleys south of the Low Tatras, were caught by the Germans and in many cases were later executed. This was the fate of de Lannurien's deputy Gérard Forestier, who became one of 747 prisoners killed near Kremnička in late November.[41] In the combats of the Slovak uprising fifty-five members of Foch Battalion were killed and another forty injured.

De Lannurien's remaining forces headed to the Chočské Heights in the Low Tatras area that was assigned to the remnants of the 1st Czechoslovak Partisan Brigade of M. R. Štefánik by the leadership of the partisan units.[42] Their dugouts were attacked on 13 November, during one of the German anti-partisan raids, and sixteen members, including the battalion's interpreter Prof. Vladimír Jeršov and nurse Albína Binderová, were captured and later transported to a POW camp in north Germany. On 18 November, exposed to the cruel winter and spreading epidemic, de Lannurien decided to divide his unit into six groups, which were to find and/or fight their ways to the south. His own ten men (nine French and one Yugoslav) crossed the river Hron and got in touch with an eighty-man group of Lieutenant Želinský. Together in December they carried out several attacks on German military vehicles on the strategic Lučenec–Zvolen road. In early January 1945 they met the advancing Soviet troops near Lučenec.[43]

Some of the groups were captured, and others survived having made a remarkable contribution to Second World War transnational cooperation. Jean-Baptiste Boyer, Marcel Garrejat, André Gerverun and André Poisson joined a partisan unit of the 1st Czechoslovak Partisan Brigade of J. V. Stalin commanded by Nikolai Kalichenko in early November. They continued partisan activities in the Veporské Heights, suffering from a lack of food, clothes and ammunition. Boyer and a Slovak student were captured by a Vlasov unit while trying to get some stocked provisions and arms but, assisted by local residents, they managed to escape SS detention in Hronec. They were able to take part in a truly transnational partisan Christmas organised by Kalichenko, joined by Russians, Slovaks, French, Hungarians, Poles, Serbs, Croats, British and Dutch as well as German anti-fascists. A bunker inhabited by the four French became a model of transnational cooperation. They took care of the US pilot Jerry Saint-Hilair from Boston, whose family had come to the USA from France, and looked after an injured Hungarian Partisan. There was perhaps some symbolism in the fact that in the final passage to meet the approaching Red and Romanian Armies, in the aftermath of the failed Slovak 'national' uprising, this multinational unit even rescued two Jewish families.[44]

The second case study is provided by the special forces that came from the West and also contributed to transnational interactions during the uprising and beyond. The OSS, then based in Bari, dispatched the DAWES mission whose task was to support the insurgents and to rescue US airmen who had been shot down over Slovak territory in previous months and then liberated from POW camps at the outbreak of the uprising. The mission was sent in two waves, on 17 September and 7 October 1944, when US B-17 flying fortresses, loaded with arms and ammunition, landed at the airfield Tri duby (Three Oaks).[45] The first group, headed by the US naval officer Holt Green, had six members, of whom four were real transnationals in terms of their trajectories and identities. Jaroslav 'Jerry' Mičan was born in Prague, graduated from Charles University and moved to the USA in the 1920s. Ján Schwartz and Joe Horvát were ethnic Slovaks who had also settled down in the USA in the interwar period, while Charles Heller, born in Chicago, had Czech parents.

The second and more numerous group of OSS agents was even more transnational. It included one ethnic Pole (Edward Baranski), two Slovak citizens (Emil Tomeš and Anton Novák) and one Croatian citizen (Daniel Pavletič). Two other US agents, Tibor Keszthelyi and Steve Čatloš, were ethnic Hungarians whose task was to proceed to Hungary, while Francis

Perry, an Austrian by his origin, was told to get to Vienna. These plans, drawn up in Bari, were soon reduced in scope and ambition in view of the advancing Wehrmacht and SS troops that were gradually tightening the siege around the resisting forces.[46]

In the meantime, the uprising brought about numerous cases of transnational interactions on a daily basis. The Allied airmen headed to Banská Bystrica from all corners of Slovakia with the clear goal of getting to a plane that would carry them to safety. On their way they were repeatedly assisted by various partisan units and local inhabitants. Some airmen, such as the New Zealander Gordon Follas, indeed chose to stay longer with the partisans for 'killing Germans'.[47]

By the end of October 1944 the uprising was suppressed by the Germans. A group of these OSS agents, accompanied by Slovak resisters and the British SOE WINDPROOF mission, originally destined for Hungary and headed by John Sehmer (whose father was German), retreated to the Slovak mountains. That was the only option of all the remaining military forces who wished to continue fighting the Germans.[48] The odyssey of this transnational group lasted for two months. Most of its members were captured on 26 December 1944 and then interrogated in Bratislava. Fourteen Americans and three British were transferred to Mauthausen, where they were executed in January and February 1945 on the orders of Ernst Kaltenbrunner. Only a minority of the group, including four Americans, escaped from the siege and survived the winter in the mountains, eventually making contact with the Red Army.[49]

While the Soviets themselves dispatched a number of paratroops of truly multinational character to Slovakia, they were much less enthusiastic about supporting cooperation with combatants from the West. The Red Air Force failed to airlift the OSS team from Tri duby towards the end of October, despite their repeated pleas – at the time when the Germans were already pressing hard while the Soviet aircraft were landing at the airfield every night.

The Soviet treatment of the SOE special COURRIER 5 mission represented the peak of Soviet maltreatment of Western agents. The party of three Slovaks, commanded by First Lieutenant Imrich Eröš, was equipped with wireless set and tasked to contact the commanders of the uprising and establish radio connection with the SOE/OSS south Italian base. Dropped near Liptovský Mikuláš on 6 September, they fulfilled their orders and set up a radio base in a mountain chalet called Na Trangoške. From there they transmitted a good deal of important intelligence to their superiors and negotiated the sending of military and medical supplies from Bari. However, during the night of 25–6 September the two radio operators with their transmitter were kidnapped by an NKVD commando led by a

Soviet officer, Katrushchin. One of them, František Holý, was later shot as an alleged German spy.[50]

This episode suggests that transnational cooperation in the final stages of the war was often superseded by the emergence of Cold War dynamics. The Soviets distrusted any agents coming from the West and sought to establish their own sphere not only of operations but also of influence. Indeed, the orders and instructions that the Soviet commanders of the partisan brigades were receiving from the leadership of the partisan movement in the months after the uprising were only partly operational. They were also given political tasks such as creating communist cells in the partisan brigades and proper 'progressive' agitation.[51]

Conclusion

Beyond the specificities of each of these three uprisings, all of them can be seen as a privileged moment when people from various countries and backgrounds combined their experiences and skills to defeat the Nazis. A key role was played by foreigners, whether economic migrants or political exiles, who had been living in the three countries studied here before the Second World War. They were on an equal footing with the other actors. Some of them had a solid military formation. Others had a strong political background and did not need to be informed of what was at stake politically from Nazi domination. A small number of migrants or refugees played a leading role in these uprisings, as attested by the cases of Lieutenant Mirosław Iringh, August Agbola O'Brown and Georges Szekeres.

Prisoners of war who escaped from camps during the chaotic last year of the war were also crucial. They brought qualities of military leadership to local insurgents who were often much less trained. They often learned other languages in POW camps and were able to communicate directly or via interpreters with people of other nationalities. Equally important were the special agents of SOE such as Sergeant John Ward and the American OSS agents, whose families were all of East-Central European origin. They brought expertise, arms and, in the case of the *Cichociemni*, paratroopers themselves. They transmitted intelligence back to the Allies and broadcast messages. Their main problems were not transnational, in that generally, because of their backgrounds, they related well to local fighters, but international, as when in Slovakia they came up against the NKVD, which was trying to develop a Soviet sphere of interest. Transnational assistance was also provided by deserters from Wehrmacht auxiliary units, although these tended to stand by rather than to become directly involved against German forces, and from former inmates from concentration camps, although they acted as supporters rather than as fighters.

The transnational dimension of these interventions was soon forgotten. It was immediately overlaid by narratives of national liberation, as the Gabonese Georges Dukson discovered very clearly on 26 August 1944. General de Gaulle's assertion that the French had liberated themselves was subscribed to by non-communists and communists alike. The PCF wished to underline its patriotic credentials and sidelined the memory of the thousands of Polish and Romanian Jews, Italian anti-fascists or Spanish republicans who had resisted in the FTP-MOI or the *milices patriotiques*. The onset of the Cold War eliminated these transnational connections even more. Although August Agbola O'Brown was accorded some recognition in Communist Poland, perhaps because he represented the struggle of colonised peoples against imperialism, Mirosław Iringh was not. During the Cold War those who had resisted with communists in Eastern Europe were *non grata* in the West, while those who had resisted in the West were *non grata* in Eastern Europe. It was not until the end of the Cold War and the rise of East European nationalism in the 1990s that non-communist foreign resisters such as Mirosław Iringh and the *Cichociemni* were recognised. Likewise it was not until the weakening of the political influence of the PCF in the 1980s that the story of foreign resisters in the French Resistance was properly told.

10

Afterlives and memories

Robert Gildea and Olga Manojlović Pintar with Mercedes Yusta Rodrigo, Jorge Marco, Diego Gaspar Celaya, Roderick Bailey, Jason Chandrinos, Cristina Diac, Zdenko Maršálek, Franziska Zaugg, Bojan Aleksov, Yaacov Falkov and Megan Koreman

In 1993 an elderly Frenchman, Jean-Baptiste Boyer, travelled to a ceremony in Slovakia which was recognising the role of foreign fighters in the Slovak national uprising. In 1944 he had been sent under Vichy's STO scheme to work for the Third Reich's war economy in a factory at Dubnica. As the Soviets advanced and the Reich collapsed, he escaped with a group of eighteen and joined the French Partisans of the Stefanik Brigade under Captain Georges Barazer de Lannurien, fighting to liberate Slovakia.[1]

The final chapter explores how, when and where transnational experiences of resistance were acknowledged, whether in national, political or private communities, and how they changed over time. This may help us understand why people with experiences in transnational resistance did not easily became part of the public understanding of the war. Two strands will be followed. The first traces the afterlives of resisters with transnational experiences, that is, what direction their lives took after the Second World War. Clearly the historical context changed very quickly, as national liberation and victory in Europe gave way to the Cold War and wars of decolonisation. Resisters clearly had to navigate these challenges, some reinventing themselves in order to do so and some falling foul of changing circumstances. The second strand explores how transnational resistance was remembered over the period from the war down to the present. These memories are found at three different levels: at the level of the individual's own memory, articulated in memoirs or testimonies; at the level of the group or association to which they belonged and at some stage began again to remember their past as a group; and at the level of the collective memory of the society or country as a whole. This memory operated independently of the resisters themselves and may also be called the dominant narrative of the society or country. Such memories are in dialogue with each other but also in a power struggle. Group memories contest each other and seek to impose themselves as the dominant narrative of society, which then seeks to eclipse other memories.[2] This struggle takes place over time, articulated by associations of resistance veterans, by resistance foundations that took over from them as they died out, by journalists, historians, publishers and filmmakers, by political activists and by politicians themselves, all of them in turn shaped by new conflicts, new circumstances and new paradigms. Dominant narratives were forged by the national liberations of 1944–45, the onset of the Cold War and wars of decolonisation. These were challenged and modified by East–West détente after 1956, the Six Day War of 1967, the events of 1968, the eruption of Holocaust memory in the 1970s and 1980s and the end of the Cold War which accelerated both globalisation and the rise of populist nationalism in post-Cold War Europe. The memory of transnational resistance, which for a long while was buried by these dominant narratives, gradually but unevenly broke once again into the public sphere.

The nationalisation of resistance narratives, 1944–48

In countries that had been defeated by the Axis, occupied and often fragmented during the war, the authorities that assumed power at the liberation wanted to create a narrative of national resistance and liberation that would legitimate the new regimes and bring unity to their divided peoples. In some countries, such as France, the contribution of 'national' resistance fighters was highlighted at the expense of 'transnational' ones, who were swept to one side or silenced. In other countries, notably the People's Democracies of Eastern Europe, the official anti-fascist and communist ideology for a time at least incorporated transnational' resisters who had fought under those ideologies in order to build a new socialist society.

The liberation of Paris in August 1944 was an international moment, with the involvement of transnational fighters both as regulars and irregulars. Spanish republicans of 'La Nueve', the 9th Company of the 3rd Chad Regiment, were the first to arrive in occupied Paris, and foreign fighters were prominent in the FTP-MOI.[3] Their presence and their story, however, were of no interest to General de Gaulle, returning from four years' exile in London and Algiers, who was keen immediately to building a founding national myth of French liberation. To crowds massed outside the Paris Hôtel de Ville on 25 August 1944 he declared, 'Paris liberated! Liberated by its own efforts, liberated by its people with the help of the armies of France, with the help of all of France, that is France in combat. The one France, the true France, eternal France.'[4] According to this narrative, France had been liberated by the Free French, supported by the French people, restoring an eternal France that was independent of changing political regimes. This account marginalised the efforts of the foreigners in the internal and external resistance and even the contribution of the Allies. Three weeks later, on 16 September 1944, de Gaulle was in Toulouse, which was reputed to be the capital of a 'red republic' in the south of France, for its liberation ceremonies. Reviewing a parade of FFIs, he was incensed by the presence of Spanish republicans, who had no uniforms and wore German helmets repainted blue. 'Why have these Spaniards come to bother us', he demanded, 'marching with the FFIs?'[5] Two days later, in the Dordogne, the General reviewed FFIs who with SOE support were conducting operations against German forces holed up in the port of Royan and on the Île d'Oléron. The General summoned the British SOE Captain Peter Lake, who called himself Jean-Pierre. His report to his SOE bosses in London ten days later related the brutal interrogation:

> De Gaulle: Jean-Pierre, that's a French name.
> Lake: My *nom de guerre*, mon Général.
> De Gaulle: What are you doing here?
> Lake: I belong to the Inter-Allied Mission for Dordogne and I am at the moment with Dordogne troops at Marenne, mon Général.
> De Gaulle. You have no business here, I say. You have no right to exercise a command ... We don't need you here. It only remains for you to leave. I have already told one, Aristide [the SOE agent Captain Roger Landes], who was indulging in politics, to get out ... Return, return quickly. Au revoir.[6]

The Spanish republicans parading in Toulouse had taken part in the liberation of France, but their ultimate goal for the previous five years was the liberation of their homeland from the dictatorship of General Franco, which had cost the lives of perhaps 230,000 of their comrades and families. Their ambition was to rewrite the national narrative and reverse the outcome of the Civil War by a *reconquista* of Spain, this time by communists, socialists and anarchists. They considered that since the Allies had liberated Italy, France and Germany from Mussolini and Hitler their next task was to liberate Spain. For the British and Americans, and even for de Gaulle's French Provisional Government, there was a problem. Franco had remained neutral during the war, resisting blandishments to join the Axis, while the Spanish republicans were, if not anarchists, then communists. There was no enthusiasm to see them take power.

On 19 October 1944 Colonel Vincente Lopez Tovar, who had spent nearly five years fighting in France, led an attack by five thousand men, many of them former *guerrilleros*, over the Pyrenees through the Val d'Aran, hoping to raise a revolt in Spain.[7] After these attacks from abroad failed, the PCE under Santiago Carrillo decided to encourage guerrilla activity inside Spain. Many experienced fighters, veterans of the French resistance and members of the Communist Party, were sent to reinforce existing groups and to stir up the civilian population, especially peasants. The PCE leadership hoped to see an insurrection, which they envisioned along the lines of the last stages of the war in France.[8] However, Carrillo and the PCE leadership were suspicious of transnational resisters such as Domingo Ungría, who had fought in a guerrilla unit with the Red Army and might challenge them. Ungría was subsequently found dead in circumstances that have not been explained.[9]

Other guerrilla groups returning to Spain were quickly infiltrated and betrayed. This was also the fate of Ramón Via. In November 1944 Via took part in a small attack across the sea from Oran to organise a guerrilla group in Malaga on the French model of the FTP-MOI.[10] He was soon betrayed and arrested. But from Malaga prison he wrote a Zola-inspired letter 'to accuse the Francoist regime and denounce their barbarous policy of terror' that was translated into French and widely distributed.[11] On 1 May 1946 he and twenty-five other political prisoners managed to escape, but three weeks later he was cornered by police and died in a shoot-out. In the French and Spanish resistance, communist, socialist and labour press Via was acclaimed as a transnational hero of the anti-fascist struggle, but not outside these circles.[12]

Eastern Europe showed a different picture. Transnational resisters, often former members of the International Brigades, had been key players in the struggle to liberate fascist-occupied Central and Eastern Europe and the Balkans. They now played a leading role in the construction of the so-called People's Democracies which emerged in those areas and in which – as a result of the advance of the Red Army – communist parties were dominant.

In liberated Yugoslavia anti-fascism was considered not only as an uncompromised struggle but also as an emancipatory practice that constructed an ideology of 'brotherhood and unity' to transcend the wartime legacy of inter-ethnic and international conflicts. Veterans of the International Brigades and of resistance outside Yugoslavia were hailed as the bearers of this new gospel. Sixty-four 'Spaniards' were proclaimed People's Heroes of Yugoslavia, and four of them became the most influential generals of the postwar Yugoslav People's Army. Other transnational veterans were promoted to the diplomatic service which defined Yugoslav foreign policy after 1945. Ljubo Ilić became the chief of the Yugoslav military mission in the West and the Yugoslav ambassador in several countries.[13] In 1946 a Belgrade street was named after the International

Brigades, and the Association of Yugoslav Volunteers of the Spanish Republican Army, now formed, propagated its memory to a wider public.[14]

In liberated Poland, similarly, 'Spaniards' were drafted into key positions in the Provisional Government of National Unity's state security office, ministries of defence and foreign affairs, the trade unions and leading communist media. This was the case for Poles of both non-Jewish and Jewish origin who had bonded in the XIII International Brigade.[15] In May 1945 Henryk Toruńczyk, a veteran of the XIII Dąbrowski Brigade, who had founded the Polish Independent Special Battalion with the Soviet military intelligence to fight behind German lines, was appointed first commander of the Internal Security Corps. This corps reported to the Ministry of Public Security and was designed to continue the war against Communist Poland's enemies.[16]

Romanian fighters, who were often of Jewish as well as communist backgrounds and had served with the International Brigades and then with the French Resistance or in Moscow, were able to return to their homeland, sometimes after an exile of ten years, when the country left the Axis and sided with the Allies on 23 August 1944. They participated in the communist takeover of power and were active in both state and party institutions. 'Spaniards' who had spent the war in the Soviet Union were particularly successful. Galia Sincari and Mihail Burcă returned to Romania from Moscow in 1946, and Mihail became deputy to the minister of the interior.[17] Those who had been active in France tended to acquire more mundane jobs. Mihail Patriciu, who had escaped from Le Vernet and fought with the FTP-MOI, returned to Romania in 1945, and became a police inspector in Cluj, in his native Transylvania. Boris Bruhman, later known as Boris Holban, a Jewish-communist Bessarabian who was too young to fight in Spain but directed the FTP-MOI in Paris, became a general director in the Ministry of Foreign Affairs in 1947 and a major-general in the Ministry of Defence in 1948.[18]

Cold War purges of transnational resisters, 1947–54

The Cold War froze over in 1947–48 and divided Eastern from Western Europe. It had a deleterious effect on resisters with transnational backgrounds. In the first place the Iron Curtain severed their connections. It was now barely possible for them to meet former comrades-in-arms, publicly and privately. Secondly, the very concept of a 'transnational' fighter took on the meaning of a probable fifth columnist, spy or traitor. The ambiguous and shifting identities assumed by transnational resisters were no longer tolerable; identities had to be clear-cut, 'with us' or 'against us'. In the West, which developed an ideology of the free world that was threatened by global communism, any resister with a communist background became suspect and might be blacklisted. In the Stalinist East, anyone who had connections with the West during the Second World War risked being denounced as an imperialist or capitalist agent. If they had been a POW in Germany or inmate of a concentration camp in the German Reich they were easily accused of collaborating with Nazism. If they disagreed with Stalin they might be labelled a Trotskyist. Being Jewish meant the risk of being denounced as a Zionist, especially after the formation of the state of Israel in 1948. Many transnational fighters who had achieved positions of power in the state and military were now purged, not only losing their jobs but also jailed, deported or executed.

Yugoslavia, which had served as a bridge between West and East, tried to develop a strategy of non-alignment in the Cold War. It soon found itself, however, rejected by both sides. From 1943 Tito's partisans had been favoured by the Allies because they were seen as more effective in the struggle against the Axis while the 'national' resistance fighter Draža Mihailović and his Četniks were exposed as collaborating with the Italians and the Germans. Mihailović was executed by the Titoist regime in 1946, but then the Cold War arrived. In March 1948 the US president, Harry Truman, withdrew support from Tito by posthumously decorating Mihailović with the Legion of Merit for being 'instrumental in obtaining a final Allied victory'.[19] On the other hand, the Soviets now regarded Yugoslavia as the weakest link in the communist chain and an entry-point for Western influence. The Yugoslav communist leadership was accused of claiming that the Yugoslav people had liberated themselves without the help of the Red Army, for supporting Greek and the Albanian communists against the orders of Moscow and making plans for a Balkan federation with the Bulgarians. Yugoslavia was duly expelled from the Cominform in June 1948, and for the Soviets the crime of Titoism was added to the familiar ones of Trotskyism and being a Gestapo agent.[20]

The Yugoslav regime, which had initially embraced its transnational fighters and offered them key posts in the state and military, now turned on them as spies and traitors. In the so-called Dachau trials held in Ljubljana in 1947–49 thirty-seven people were convicted for being Gestapo spies or Western agents.[21] Among them were nine 'Spaniards' – the International Brigaders from Yugoslavia and Austria who had survived the Dachau and Buchenwald concentration camps.[22] Meanwhile twenty-four Yugoslavs who had fought in the Spanish Civil War were detained in Goli Otok prison and were condemned as Soviet spies. They included Emilijan (Milan) Kalafatić, who had fought in Spain and France, escaped from Castres with Ilić, resisted in the FTP-MOI and, back in Yugoslavia, become assistant chief of the Yugoslav secret police and minister for industry.

In 1949, however, he was expelled from the Yugoslav Communist Party as an NKVD agent and tortured in Goli otok.[23] Another victim was the Jewish communist painter Boro Baruh, who had studied in Paris, where he recruited volunteers for the International Brigades and later joined the partisans in Yugoslavia.[24] Considered suspect for a whole range of reasons, he too was sent to Goli otok.

In Poland, the communist-dominated United Polish Workers Party run by the hardline Stalinist Bolesław Bierut took full power in 1948. The International Brigaders of the XIII Dąbrowski Brigade who had helped to found the new Polish regime became suspect because of their contacts with the West. Henryk Toruńzyck, for example, was demoted from the Internal Security Corps in May 1945 and sent as an adminstrator first to the German lands now annexed by Poland, then to the Ministry of Light Industry. He died in 1966, aged fifty-seven, and with him the 'Dąbrowszczacy' lost all influence in the regime.[25]

In Czechoslovakia, former International Brigaders played a part both in the short-lived multi-party era of 1945–48 and in the coup d'état of February 1948 which gave a monopoly of power to the Czechoslovak Communist Party. Ferdinand Otto Miksche, an International Brigader who had fought with Czechoslovak army in France in 1940 and then joined the Free French, returned to join the Czechoslovak army and was appointed a military attaché to France. In the autumn of 1947, sensing the upcoming communist coup, he defected and remained in France.[26] Meanwhile, on the other side, Josef Pavel, known in Spain by his *nom de guerre* Franz Schuster and commander of the Dimitrov Battalion, organised and secretly armed workers' militias which took a key part in the 1948 coup. Artur London, who was sent to Spain from the Soviet Union in 1937, became one of the leaders of the MOI in France, survived Mauthausen and became Czechoslovak deputy foreign minister in 1948. At the same time Osvald Závodský, who had been political commissar in the Masaryk Battalion in Spain, fought with the Czechoslovak forces in France in 1940, was also active in the FTP-MOI and survived Mauthausen, became chief of the State Security.[27]

This situation did not last. Czechoslovakia was the only East-Central European country apart from Yugoslavia where Soviet troops were not stationed and Stalin feared a replication of the 'Yugoslav model'. As the Cold War intensified, agents of the communist state with an Interbrigadist past fell under suspicion, particularly if they were Jewish in origin. This was intensified because of Israel's integration into the Western military camp in 1952. Many of the architects of the 1948 coup who were tainted as Spanish fighters or French resisters were now accused of being American agents and Zionists and became the victims of the system of terror they had helped to create. Rudolf Slánský, Artur London and Osvald Závodský were arrested and tried in November 1952, accused of Titoism and Zionism. Slánský was hanged almost at once, and Závodský in March 1954, while Artur London was sentenced to life imprisonment.[28]

As in other communist states of East-Central Europe, former Interbrigadists in Romania were both the architects of the new state and, in the Cold War, among its first victims. A control commission was set up by the Party in 1949 to investigate the pasts of ninety-six members of the International Brigades. Mihail Patriciu was under suspicion because he had come back to Romania from Marseilles, via Yugoslavia, and was dismissed from the Securitate.[29] Mihail Burcă lost his post in the Interior Ministry and in 1991 recalled, 'It was in '52. I was thrown out of my job then. I was in a desperate situation and even contemplated suicide, right here in this house.'[30] He and his wife, Galia Sincari, were nevertheless to reinvent themselves as loyal communists. In 1956 she told the Institute for the Party History of the Central Committee of the Romanian Communist Party that her decision to go to Spain was not accidental but the ultimate, and necessary, result of a life spent in service to the Party, both in Spain and in the Soviet Union. She aligned herself perfectly with the ideology of postwar Communist Romania.[31]

In the DDR there was a similar tension between those who had been active in Spain and those who had been based in Moscow. Franz Dahlem, who had been a political commissar in Spain and survived Mauthausen, was a founder of the Sozialistische Einheitspartei Deutschlands, or Socialist Unity Party (SED), and entirely committed to building a Communist East Germany. He was, however, pitted against Walter Ulbricht, who had spent the war in Moscow. Removed from the politburo of the SED, he was banished to the Berlin suburbs.[32]

In the West the Cold War intensified suspicion of communists, especially foreign communists, as potential traitors. In the USA, even home-grown communists were suspect. Veterans of the Lincoln Brigade (VALB) who had been in the OSS and the key to OSS success in Italy because of previous relations with Italian communists in Spain, were recalled in 1945. As the 'red scare' of anti-communism intensified and the USA drew closer to the Franco regime, so the Lincolns became the target of witch-hunts. Meeting a former OSS comrade who had been wounded in North Africa, Irving Goff quipped, 'Here we are, a handful of nobody.'[33] Milton Wolff, who had led a battalion at the Battle of the Ebro and seen action in Burma, was hauled in 1953 before the Subversive Activities Control Board, which condemned the Veterans as a communist organisation.[34]

In France, communist ministers who had served in the early governments of the French Fourth Republic were sacked in May 1947. Attacked as a fifth column within France, the PCF responded by developing its own brand of national communism. The Party had been divided since 1939 between those like Maurice Thorez, who accepted the Nazi–Soviet Pact and spent the war in Moscow, and those like Charles Tillon, who had served in the International Brigades, rejected the pact and begun to resist in France from 1940, building and commanding the FTP largely independently of Party control. Thorez imposed on the Party both loyalty to Moscow and a certain French patriotism. In 1952 Charles Tillon was purged from the Party's central committee, and he later published a denunciation entitled *A 'Moscow Trial' in Paris*.[35]

In 1950 the PCE was banned in France and a vast police operation, called 'Bolero-Paprika', rounded up Spanish communists in exile. Even though many of them had fought in the French Resistance they were considered a danger to the French state. Even Lopez Tovar, who had received the Legion of Honour in 1946, was now placed under house arrest. He complained that he received no support from the PCF.[36] The leadership of the PCE was no more welcoming of former International Brigaders and guerrillas. The few guerrilla fighters who managed to reach France from Spain after the PCE called off guerrilla action in Spain in 1951 were considered suspects, interrogated and then dispersed in France and other countries in Eastern Europe, especially the DDR, in order to prevent contact between them.[37] In 1956 the PCE publicly renounced the armed struggle and opted for the policy of 'national reconciliation'. From that moment, the memory of the resistance was obliterated within the PCE, since it contravened the new strategy of peaceful struggle against Franco's dictatorship. In this way 'old heroes became troubling shadows of the past'.[38]

Wars of decolonisation and the suppression of transnational resisters, 1944–57

In Western Europe, liberation from Axis power was transformed almost immediately into efforts to recover colonies that had all but been lost in order to rebuild imperial power. In the French case, the platform for liberation had been its empire in Africa, and liberation of the metropolis was followed by the recovery of the rest of its empire in the Near East and Vietnam. At an imperial conference held in Brazzaville in French Congo in January 1944, de Gaulle announced, 'the goals of the work of civilisation undertaken by France eliminate any idea of autonomy, any possibility of development outside the French imperial bloc; there can be no question even of a distant self-government in the colonies'.[39]

The impact on former transnational resisters was dual. Some, having worked with anti-fascist and communist rebels, now reinvented themselves as soldiers of empire. Maurice Bigeard was a French army officer trained by SOE in England and dropped back into the Pyrenees region in 1944, and worked closely with Spanish republicans who were at the forefront of the French Resistance. Sent out to Indochina after the war in Europe to save the French empire from the Viet Minh, who were seeking their own liberation from the French, he was taken prisoner and witnessed the 1954 defeat of Dien Bien Phu that ended the French empire in Indochina. He resolved that this defeat would not be repeated in Algeria, where nationalists rose in revolt against the French in 1954. Bigeard recalled that in Algeria 'Every evening we sat around under the light of a few paraffin lamps, talking about Dien Bien Phu and our dead comrades, how we felt at the time. We also spoke of the present war and how we needed to win it very quickly.'[40] In January 1957 he commanded one of the parachute regiments that was sent into the labyrinth of the Algiers Casbah to eliminate terrorism in what became known as 'the Battle of Algiers'. Bodies of suspects dropped from helicopters into the Bay of Algiers became known as 'Bigeard prawns'.[41]

Other transnational resisters, however, took a different path and found themselves confronting the might of the British Empire. For the British, domination of the Mediterranean and the Middle East was vital from the imperial point of view, and in July 1944 British military planners concluded that 'potentially, Greece is the cornerstone of British influence in the Balkans'.[42] They invaded Greece in September 1944, bringing the government-in-exile, and did everything they could to ensure that the communist-controlled ELAS did not take power. When ELAS refused to lay down its arms the British military declared martial law and bombed working-class suburbs of Athens. When demonstrations broke out in Athens on 3 December 1944 in favour of the partisans Greek police opened fire, killing twenty-eight and wounding many more. British forces, reinforced from Italy, fought ELAS for two months until an agreement allowed elections to be held and a plebiscite, which restored the monarchy.[43]

ELAS was fighting for Greek liberation but included many foreign fighters, including Polish escapees from German camps, Soviet deserters from Wehrmacht military and auxiliary working units and even anti-Nazi German soldiers.[44] One of these was Gerhard Reinhardt, who had deserted from a German punishment battalion in 1943 to join ELAS and co-founded a branch of the AKFD in August 1944. As the Germans retreated, the British became the new enemy, equally opposed to communism. Reinhardt denounced 'English capitalism infiltrating Greece ... joining arms with Hitler's collaborators, security battalions and Greek fascist scum to massacre the real democrats of this country'.[45] The fifty-two-man core of the AKFD crossed the border into Yugoslav Macedonia in January

1945. Most of them, including Reinhardt, joined the II.Österreichisches Freiheit Bataillon of the III Yugoslav Army Corps and reached Vienna in August 1945.[46] But whereas the Yugoslav Partisans worked well enough with deserters from the Italian army, they were unable to see the German anti-Nazis as trustworthy comrades-in-arms rather than as oppressors. Thirteen members of the AKFD were assassinated in Veles, Macedonia, in circumstances that remain unclear.

Britain's imperialist ambitions in the Mediterranean alienated Greeks not only in their homeland but also from those who had worked with them during the war in SOE. As Britain's hold on Egypt weakened, her grip on Cyprus became strategically more important. Faced by Greek Cypriot nationalist guerrillas, Britain declared a state of emergency in December 1955 and hanged two Cypriot rebels. Sylvia Apostolidou, who had been decorated by the British for her SOE work, sent back her George Medal, protesting that British liberators had become imperialists. 'It is useless, dishonoured, I told them. These two boys did what you and we did in wartime: fought for their own homeland. Then, you said "well done"; now you hang them.'[47]

In their bid to control the Mediterranean the British also tried to prevent Jewish concentration camp survivors from reaching their mandate in Palestine. Even after the Holocaust they adhered to their 1939 White Paper limiting Jewish migration to Palestine. Tens of thousands of Jewish survivors, however, with the help of Jewish rescue organisations, were aiming to claim Palestine for the Jews. One of those organisations was the Armée Juive, based in Toulouse, which had taken part in *maquisard* fighting on behalf of the French Resistance and had renamed itself the Organisation Juive de Combat (OJC) in the hope of being recognised as part of the resistance. Its main aim, however, was to resume its primary work of taking Holocaust survivors, especially young people, to Palestine. In the knowledge that their work might now involve conflict with the British, Abraham Polonski, head of the OJC, was appointed by the Haganah in April 1946 leader of that organisation in France and French North Africa, which had a substantial Jewish population.[48] The OJC moved Jewish children from refugee camps to the south of France, where between March 1946 and April 1948 sixteen thousand migrants, including large numbers of children, sailed in fifteen ships. Still more Jewish camp survivors made their way across the Alpine passes to Italy, sometimes with the help of the Jewish Brigade, getting to Bari, from where ships were also leaving for Palestine.[49] The main obstacle to their flight was the British, and the Mediterranean battle culminated in the *Exodus* affair of June–August 1947, when a ship carrying over four thousand Jewish refugees was rammed and boarded by the British navy off the Palestine coast on 18 July, and sent back to France.[50]

Some members of the OJC decided that they would go to Palestine themselves and reinvent themselves in what in 1948 became the state of Israel. Kania Geiger, a Polish Jew exiled to France, had already given herself a French identity as Anne-Marie Bonnard and, marrying the Strasbourg Jew Ernest Lambert, became Anne-Marie Lambert. They worked for the Armée Juive from Lyons, ferrying Jewish children to the Swiss frontier, but Ernest was arrested by the Gestapo and shot on 8 July 1944. Anne-Marie went to Palestine with their baby, and Jacques Lazarus, another Strasbourg Jew recruited to the Armée Juive by Lambert, described in his 1947 history of Jewish resistance how they set out to make a new simple life away from war and massacre:

> They left one fine morning from old Europe. They lead a tough existence as Palestinian pioneers on a collective farm ... In this country of Hope she wants to forget the terrible things that afflict her spirit. But she will raise her daughter in the memory of her father, a hero shot one day in July.[51]

Meanwhile Ginette and Pierrot Mouchenik, Paris Jews who had been in the Armée Juive, took different decisions. Pierrot decided to stay in France while Ginette took a new identity in Palestine. In 1947 she wrote to Polonski, her former boss, from her kibbutz of Sdot Yam, near the ruins of Caesaria on the coast between Tel Aviv and Haifa. There were two hundred people in her kibbutz, she said, with fifty children. Only twenty of them were French and she was learning Hebrew, 'a very pretty language and one which, fortunately, is not as complicated as I thought'. She gave herself a new name, Shulamith, or 'Peace'. 'Life on the kibbutz', she reflected, 'is in truth the realisation of an ideal that when young I did not think would be possible ... the renewal of the old Jewish people.'[52] As with Anne-Marie Lambert, resistance had led to a new life in a Palestine that in 1948 would become the state of Israel.

The resurgence of transnational memory, (i): Cold War détente, 1956–64

Gradually, erratically, and with many contradictions, transnational links between former transnational resisters and their associates were re-established, and transnational memories and identities were reconfigured. This was not a linear or simple process. Encounters between resisters from different countries could just as easily produce misunderstanding and conflict as joyful communion. New identities shaped in different circumstances after the war had an impact on individual and collective memories. The breakthrough of transnational encounters and memories at one moment and in one sphere could be checked at other moments and at other times. Rather than tracing a single thread of the emergence of transnational encounters and memories, we will open a series of windows onto those developments, between the Cold War détente of 1956 and the globalised world of the 2000s.

Khrushchev's Secret Speech of 25 February 1956, distancing the Soviet regime from some of the crimes of Stalinism, introduced a period of détente in East–West relations. Resisters who had been condemned and sometimes executed for spying and treachery were rehabilitated. Others were able gradually to escape from the pall of suspicion and to remake connections across the Iron Curtain with comrades with whom they had fought fifteen or twenty years earlier.

In Slovakia, on 29 August 1956, a group of French veterans joined their former Slovak fellow combatants to witness the unveiling of the Memorial to French Partisans on Zvonica Hill, where fifty-six French Partisans were buried. In Belgrade, on 28 October 1956, a public ceremony was held for the first time to mark the formation of the International Brigades, twenty years on. The trials of International Brigaders in 1947–49 were set aside, and once again Yugoslavia became the mecca of transnational resistance. More than three hundred veterans of the Spanish Civil War came together from all over Europe, invited and welcomed by Aleksandar Ranković, vice president of the Yugoslav government and the president of the Union of the Associations of the People's Liberation War Fighters (SUBNOR).[53] The event was attended by the legendary General Enrique Lister and representatives of the Spanish government-in-exile, including Juan Negrín, the last prime minister of the republic. The current president of the Spanish government-in-exile, Diego Martines Bari, sent a message to the people of Yugoslavia saying that 'the goals of social equality, justice and freedom we held yesterday are equally important today for the liberation of peoples'.[54] Guests were introduced to the Yugoslav president, Tito, at his residency at Brioni Island, and a monument to the International Brigadiers was unveiled in Belgrade.

These events had echoes across Europe. In the wake of the foundation of the European Economic Community (EEC), two international conferences on European resistance movements were convened organised by the Belgian Federation of History Teachers and the French Committee for the History of the Second World War, the first in Liège and Brussels in 1958, the second in Milan in 1961. Former resisters and historians from East and West were brought together, although the ongoing Cold War set limits to the understanding that could be achieved. Soviet and Polish communist camps boycotted the first conference because of the presence of the AK General Tadeuz Bór-Komorovski.[55] At the second conference Professor Boltine of the Moscow Institute of Marxism-Leninism argued that 'the progressive nature of the resistance was explained by the leading role in each country of the working class and its avant-garde, the communist parties'. The Czech delegate claimed that 'American commanders failed to aid the Slovak uprising in 1944'. In response, the US delegate Norman Kogan and the British delegate William Deakin admitted that their governments had been reluctant to support politically inspired resistance movements, by which they meant communists. Pointedly, Deakin said that he had opposed Munich but also the Nazi–Soviet Pact.[56]

Increasingly, the DDR became something of a hub for transnational resistance exchanges. Franz Dahlem, who was rehabilitated in 1956, set up a Solidarity Committee for the Spanish People in 1963 in order to support the struggles of workers against the Franco regime and to 'continue the work of the International Brigades'. Many former fighters wrote personally to Dahlem, and Spanish political refugees were welcomed in the DDR.[57] In 1965 Edith Zorn, a former German anti-Nazi resister in France, sent Dahlem the first fruits of her research on anti-Nazi comrades now living in both Germanies, entitled 'Some Research Findings on the Activities of German Anti-Fascists who Fought with the French Resistance'.[58] A representative of the French Resistance, the FTP leader Albert Ouzoulias, went to East Berlin in 1964 to take part in festivities to honour victims of the Nazi regime. He paid homage to the DDR by citing the last words of the metalworker Pierre Timbaud before being shot by the Germans at Châteaubriant in 1941: 'Long live the German Communist Party!'[59] Eastern Europe rather than West was taking the lead in the commemoration of transnational resistance as a sign of its revived commitment to anti-fascism.

The resurgence of transnational memory, (ii): the Six Day War of 1967

The story of transnational Jewish resistance was interrupted by the desire of many Jewish resisters to integrate fully into European or American society while others became Israeli citizens. The Six Day War of 1967, which set Israel against its neighbouring Arab states, rekindled interest in Jewish resistance. It showed that Jews had struggled for survival by a great variety of means, including fighting in Allied armies, ghetto uprisings and partisan warfare. A conference was organised in Jerusalem in April 1968 by Yad Vashem, the institution that promoted Holocaust memory, on 'Jewish Resistance during the Holocaust'. Welcoming the delegates, the Israeli minister of social welfare said that 'only a Jew who believed profoundly in the future of the Jewish people could make a transition in our generation from self-sacrificing Kiddish Hashem [sanctification of God's name] to the

Kiddish Hashem of armed resistance'.[60] This conference opened a framework in which Jewish resistance could be articulated alongside Jewish suffering.

Important accounts now appeared chronicling the role of Jewish fighters both in Allied armies and in internal resistance movements. The Czech historian Erich Kulka, who had survived Auschwitz and left Czechoslovakia for Israel after the Soviet invasion of 1968, published a work on Jews in Swoboda's army in the Soviet Union which appeared in Hebrew and as a samizdat in Czechoslovakia in 1977 before being published in the USA in 1987 and Prague in 1990.[61] Anny Lévy, who had resisted with the OJC in Toulouse under Abraham Polonski, using a French *nom de guerre*, Anny Latour, wrote from Paris in December 1967 to Polonski, who had moved to Israel, hoping to come and see him. She wrote again in March 1968 saying that she had interviewed eighteen former Armée Juive/OJC resisters in France, and she flew to Israel in October 1968 to interview Polonski himself and Albert Cohen, who had provided the liaison between Polonski in Toulouse and the Lamberts in Lyons.[62]

Latour's book on Jewish resistance in France, published in 1970, dealt only with the Zionist resisters of the OJC.[63] The story of the Polish-Jewish and communist resisters of the FTP-MOI was entirely different. It was undertaken among others by David Erlich, who called himself David Diamant in France. He was an engineer who had left Poland in 1930 because of persecution, and was involved in a network called Solidarity which was rescuing Jews from the 1942 round-ups. He published a number of works on the foreign Jewish contribution to the French Resistance and organised a conference in 1974 on 'Jews in the French Resistance and the Jewish Resistance in France'.[64] He pointed out that the whole Jewish community was at risk and had to go underground: 'to survive meant to fight. The mission of active resistance organisations was to lead the Jewish masses to safety either alongside French organisations or within them.'[65] Although all Jews in France had been at risk, French Jews such as Robert Aron, a right-winger who enjoyed protection from Vichy, were less so. His 1944 *Histoire de Vichy* defended the regime's record before 1942, and in his 1967 history of the postwar purges, he denounced FTP-MOI commandos as 'murderers'.[66] This triggered a war between French Jews and Jews of foreign origin. Claude Lévy, himself of Polish-Jewish origin, who had been involved at the age of eighteen in the 35th FTP-MOI Brigade in Toulouse, with Polish Jews and Italian anti-fascists, and survived deportation, wrote an account of their activity in his 1970 *Les pariahs de la Résistance*.[67] The story of transnational resistance in France was returning to the agenda.

The resurgence of transnational memory, (iii): the 'long 1968'

The events of 1968 had powerful but often contradictory influences on the afterlives of transnational resisters and the memories of their deeds. On the one hand, in Czechoslovakia, the weakening of 'Stalinist' communism opened a space for reconsidering the role of those who had resisted abroad but were labelled 'dissident' communists. On the other hand, in Poland, Polish-Jewish resisters came in for criticism as Jewish, because anti-Semitism was cranked up after the Six Day War as a way to purging the Communist Party of those 'cosmopolitan' communists who had been prominent in it since 1945.[68]

The younger generation who made 1968 were in part inspired by the example of Second World War resisters. The more radical among them prized the exploits of foreign communists in the FTP-MOI, especially the Manouchian Group, who had been used by the German authorities in the notorious *Affiche Rouge* to discredit the resistance as the work of communists, foreigners and Jews in the French Resistance.[69] The young Polish-Jewish Marcel Rayman, who was among those executed on 21 February 1944, was a particular icon. Pierre Goldman, a communist student activist whose Polish-Jewish father had been an activist in the Union des Juifs pour la Résistance et l'Entr'aide (Jewish Union for Resistance and Mutual Aid) in Lyons, recalled that 'I grew up around memories of the resistance, of a certain resistance – that of communist Jews – and before I even knew the meaning of the words Alésia, Saint-Louis, Napoleon and Verdun, I knew of Marcel Rayman and his comrades.'[70]

In Czechoslovakia, during the 1960s, there was a slow return of former International Brigaders to important positions. During the Prague Spring of 1968, Josef Pavel (Schuster) became a minister of the interior, while František Kriegel, a doctor of medicine serving in the International Brigades as well as in the Chinese and US army in Burma during the war, became a member of the Central Committee of the Czechoslovak Communist Party and the so-called National Front. Both strongly opposed the Soviet invasion of 21 August 1968, which led to another dip in the commemoration of the legacy of the International Brigades in Czechoslovakia. That said, many former Interbrigadists took the opposite view, defending the existing communist rule in Czechoslovakia and supporting the Soviet intervention.

Poland's March 1968 was marked by a return of anti-Semitism, encouraged by the Gomulka government. Louis Gronowski called the outbreak a 'dry pogrom' and returned from Poland to France in August 1968.[71] Roman Krakus, another Polish-Jewish Interbrigadist and commander of the Carmagnole FTP-MOI group in Lyons, who had returned to Poland after the war to build socialism, came back to France in 1969 and died the following year. Jan Gerhard, who had fought in the Polish army in Poland in 1939 and in France in 1940, but felt shamed because of his Jewish origin, became head of the 35th FTP-MOI Brigade in Toulouse in 1943. He returned with the Allied armies in a Polish battalion composed mainly of International Brigaders, but was murdered in Warsaw in 1970. It is unclear whether this was a political killing or an ordinary murder, but Gerhard was clearly not *persona grata* in the new Poland.[72]

The reconnection of former resisters with a transnational past and the elaboration of an intergenerational memory of transnational resistance around 1968 made possible challenges to dominant national myths of resistance. In France this was facilitated by the fall of de Gaulle in 1969 and his death the following year. In 1969 Franz Dahlem recontacted Georges Marrane, who had first welcomed him as an exile in 1934, and André Tollet, who had chaired the PCL in 1944, who were setting up a Musée de la Résistance at Ivry sur-Seine.[73] In 1971 Franz and Käthe Dahlem returned in to Ivry to seek recognition for their role in the French Resistance and to pursue their research.[74] Franz reinvented himself as an international resister who was neither purely German nor purely French. In a handwritten memoir sent to Albert Ouzoulias in 1974 he called himself 'an internationalist of Lorraine origin, fighting for the freedom of both the German and French peoples'.[75] Käthe, who died that year, received numerous tributes to her role as a transnational resister, whether as Franz's secretary in his Valencia base, 'the mother of the International Brigaders' in Spain, listening to the concerns of young combatants far from home with her 'big heart and Rhineland humour', or as one of the promoters of the Comité Allemagne Libre pour l'Ouest (Free Germany Committee in the West), the French branch of the AKFD.[76]

Franz Dahlem died in 1981. He received a brief obituary in *Der Spiegel*, but as communism struggled in the Eastern bloc he was already a man out of his time.[77] He presented himself less as a transnational resister than as an international resister, shaped by the Comintern. He remained a communist hardliner who accepted the 1939 Nazi–Soviet Pact and faithfully supported the authoritarian communist regime of East Germany. More modern, playful and seductive in retelling the transnational resistance story was Gerhard Leo, who had come to France with his family as a young German-Jewish exile, and had worked for the Comité Allemagne Libre pour l'Ouest in Toulouse to encourage soldiers to desert from the Wehrmacht. Arrested by the German authorities and sent for trial and almost certain execution in Paris, he was in a train which was ambushed by an FTP *maquis* as it crossed the Corrèze, and joined the *maquisards*, nicknamed 'the Survivor'. He became a journalist for *Neues Deutschland* in the

DDR but returned to Paris as its correspondent between 1973 and 1985. In 1986 he persuaded the municipality of Uzerche to erect a monument to pay generous tribute to 'my liberator and friend', his FTP commander in the Corrèze who had saved him from the train but later been hanged by the SS.[78] In 1988 he published his memoirs, *Frühzug nach Toulouse*, which were translated for a French audience in 1997.[79]

The resurgence of transnational memory, (iv): the fall of the Colonels and the death of Franco

Elsewhere in Europe, the deaths of dictators and the coming to power of more left-wing governments offered openings to transnational resistance connections and memories. Further activism by former resisters was also stimulated. In 1963 Gerhard Reinhardt, who had resisted with ELAS in Greece, became secretary of the Committee of Anti-Fascist Resistance Fighters of the DDR. His close friends used his guerrilla nickname Manolis, and he jokingly signed letters 'Germanolis'. From 1965 he was senior research assistant of the Institute of Marxism-Leninism of the central committee of the SED and edited books on the history of the 999 'parole' battalions of the Wehrmacht and their anti-fascist struggle.[80] After the military coup of 21 April 1967 he used his base as secretary of the Solidarity Committee with Greek Patriots in the DDR to organise protests, petitions and campaigns there and was a key activist of the anti-dictatorial movement abroad.[81] He called this combat 'the second round of fighting for Greece's freedom', this time against the Colonels. On 10 August 1974, after the collapse of the Greek military dictatorship, he organised a celebration of thirty years of the AKFD in an emotional Greek-German gathering of former resistance veterans in the village of Ansprung.[82]

The death of Franco in 1975 and the transition to democracy in Spain released the memories of the Spanish republican struggle and the International Brigades. These were expressed more in France than in Spain, where the new democratic regime under King Juan Carlos was keen to lay to rest Civil War antagonisms by means of the Pacto del Olvido, the Pact of Forgetting. Any exaltation of anti-fascist memory was considered a threat to the stability of the country. The first movements for recognition of the Spanish guerrillas and their contribution to the French Resistance came from an association of former Spanish guerrillas based in Toulouse, authorised by the French government in May 1976. This made possible the re-emergence of a group memory of this episode of transnational resistance. On 24 April 1977 the association held a ceremony to honour the Spanish *maquisards* who had fallen in battles of Castelnau-Durban and Rimont in the Ariège in 1944.[83] It also launched a subscription for a national monument to the memory of Spanish guerrillas who had died for France, sculpted by the Spanish republican Manolo Valiente. The election of the French socialist François Mitterrand in May 1981 opened the way to a major commemoration which brought together the ambitious French and more cautious Spanish governments. Together, at Prayols near Foix in June 1982, Mitterrand and the socialist Spanish premier Felipe Gonzalez unveiled the monument to the Spanish guerrillas in France.[84] It would be some time, though, before they achieved recognition in their own country.

It was not only Spanish republican fighters who were now recognised. The fact that Mitterrand's socialist government enjoyed communist support in the period 1981–83 opened the way to a wider recognition of the role of foreign resisters, not least those of Jewish origin. At the same time the growing threat of the Front National after the defeat of the mainstream right in 1981 and its hostility to foreigners and Jews gave an added incentive to former resisters to make contact with each other, form associations and promote the memory of their transnational resistance in the public sphere. One of the Polish-Jewish leaders of the Carmagnole FTP-MOI group in Lyons, Henri Krisher, explained in a 2000 interview the foreignness of their organisation:

> No generation of people were beaten as they were. Trained in the hard school of Polish illegality, they were the *Yiddishland* revolutionaries ... and if they were internationalists the fate of the Jewish people was their main pre-occupation. The destruction of fascism, but also the coming of a messianic time, of a socialism that would free the Jewish people.[85]

Despite or because of this revolutionary Jewish heritage, they now wished to be written into the story of the *French* Resistance, which could no longer be purely national. Krisher and the Italian anti-fascist Carmagnole resister Léon Landini used the fortieth anniversary of their foundation in 1982 and the influence of their local deputy, the war minister Charles Hernu, to secure medals for former members and have streets named after their martyrs. They also made contact with the historian Annette Wieviorka, who wrote a book on the exploits of the 'generation of the round-ups', the young Jews who had taken to resistance after their parents were arrested in the summer of 1942 and sent to the death camps.[86]

After the communists were removed from the government in 1983, the debate between national communism and transnational resistance finally erupted. Transnational resisters were able to contest the national narrative of resistance imposed by the PCF. The 1985 film *Des terroristes à la retraite*, directed by Mosco Boucault, focused on the FTP-MOI and in particular the Manouchian Group. It claimed that the Party had sent foreign communists on the most dangerous resistance missions, sacrificed them and then claimed their glory. These claims were undoubtedly exaggerated, but they dramatised a settling of scores with hardline communists. The Party attempted to have the film banned, then blamed Boris Holban, a Romanian communist and former military commander of FTP-MOI, for betraying the group, but to no avail. In an accompanying debate on *Les dossiers de l'écran* Annette Kamieniecki accused the PCF of Frenchifying the names of foreign resisters and attributing the deeds of the FTP-MOI to French communists.[87] The event provoked a rewriting of the French national resistance narrative by historians. Denis Peschanski, a researcher with the Conseil National de Recherche Scientifique (CNRS) whose parents were resisters of Polish-Jewish origin, organised a conference on the role of Central European immigrants and refugees in the resistance and in 1989 published the influential *Le sang de l'étranger* with Stéphane Courtois and a former resister of Polish-Jewish origin, Adam Rayski.[88] Boris Holban published his memoirs detailing his trajectory as a transnational resister the same year.[89] The story of transnational resistance was making inroads into both the Gaullist and communist narratives of national resistance.

The importance of the specifically Jewish dimension of foreign transnational resistance was asserted by the foundation in 2005 by the Union des Juifs pour la Résistance et l'Entr'aide of an Association for the Memory of the Jewish Resisters of the MOI (MRJ-MOI). It was set up by the last survivors of the 'generation of the round-up', mostly of Polish-Jewish origin, such as Georges Weinstein, and the children of those resisters, such as Claudie Bassi Lederman, the daughter of the FTP-MOI activist Charles Lederman. Also represented were Jewish children who had been hidden from the Nazis, the so-called 'enfants cachés'. Meeting at 14 rue de Paradis, near the Gare du Nord, which had been a base during the occupation, it gave a new lease of life to the story of foreign Jewish resistance.[90]

Holocaust memory and the resurgence of memories of transnational Jewish rescue and resistance

The trajectories and memories of resisters with a transnational past were not only those with Spanish, International Brigades, communist or Jewish backgrounds. There were also the trajectories and memories of resisters with very different backgrounds who had helped to rescue Allied servicemen, resisters and also Jews in flight from deportation and death. These were not the 'scum of the earth' but very proper businesspeople, clergy and nurses.

The stories of these rescuers came increasingly to the fore with a renewed interest in the Holocaust in the 1980s. This was stimulated by the American television series *Holocaust* in 1978 and Claude Lanzmann's epic

Shoah in 1985. The scandal around the Nazi past of the former secretary general of the United Nations and Austrian president Kurt Waldheim in 1986 and the 1987 trial of the Lyons Gestapo chief Klaus Barbie in France brought responsibility for the Holocaust to the centre of public debate in Europe and North America. In 1993 the United States Holocaust Memorial Museum (USHMM) was founded in Washington, DC, while Yad Vashem in Jerusalem set up an International School for Holocaust education. An International Holocaust Remembrance Alliance was set up on Swedish initiative 1998, leading to the Stockholm Declaration 2000 on mandatory Holocaust education in schools and the institution of Holocaust Memorial Day in 2001.

Yad Vashem had been recognising Gentiles who saved persecuted Jews, known as the Righteous among Nations, for many years, but the numbers of those recognised rose sharply from the 1980s. Among these were 'transnational' figures such as the Dutchman Abbe John aan de Stegge, a priest at a parish in Toulouse. Meanwhile Jean Henry Weidner, founder of the escape line Dutch-Paris, was honoured as one of the Righteous among Nations in 1978 and invited as one of only nine individuals to hold candles at the opening of the USHMM. The appeal of the idea of the rescuer was such that around 1980 a group of resistance veterans who had not belonged to Dutch-Paris claimed to have run the line and even contrived to have stamps issued with their images as its leaders.[91]

As the Holocaust was debated, pressure grew on governments in Europe to recognise their responsibility in the wartime deportation of Jews from their countries. In France, in the wake of the Barbie trial and using the fiftieth anniversary in 1992 of the round-up and deportation of 13,000 Jews from Paris, a campaign was mounted to require the French government to take this step. François Mitterrand refused to acknowledge this, arguing that these were the crimes of Vichy, not of the republic. In 1995, however, the newly elected president Jacques Chirac recognised the role of the French state in the deportation of 76,000 Jews from France. At the same time he cited the statistic established by Serge Klarsfeld that three-quarters of the 330,000 Jews living in wartime France had been saved. Thus he suggested that while the Vichy state had betrayed the Jews, the French people had hidden, fed and spirited them away.[92] This may be seen as a sort of reverse transnational resistance in that the French were rescuing (mainly) foreign Jews.

This recognition was formalised in 2007, when the role of rescuers, many of whom were women, was commemorated at a ceremony of recognition of the Righteous of France at the Panthéon in Paris presided over by Jacques Chirac and the Auschwitz survivor and former president of the European Parliament, Simone Veil. Recognition of the Righteous among

Nations was thus repatriated from Jerusalem to Paris and endeavoured to nationalise the story of rescue. From now on the narrative of French resistance supported by the French people was accompanied by that of rescue of foreign Jews by the generosity and humanity of the French people themselves.[93]

The end of the Cold War, internationalism and the rise of nationalism

The end of the Cold War in 1989–90 brought about a tectonic shift in geopolitics. The Berlin Wall fell, and soon after that the Soviet empire crumbled in Eastern Europe. There was a boost to globalisation in terms of the global movement of ideas, technologies, capital and people, and the triumph of neo-liberal political economics. At the same time, however, the breakup of the Soviet empire and the collapse of communism worldwide which was partly caused by a surge in nationalist movements now intensified a populist surge in Eurasia, Europe and North America.

These conflicts and changing paradigms had a huge impact on the later lives of transnational resisters and on the politics of transnational resistance memory. The shifts and impacts, however, played out in very different ways. In the first place, connections were re-established between East and West, and there was a greater recognition of the contribution of transnational resistance in a more global environment. This, for example, made it possible for Jean-Baptiste Boyer to travel to Slovakia in 1993 to take part in celebrations of the Slovak uprising. On the other hand, the collapse of international communism and the rise of nationalist movements, leading among other things to the breakup of Yugoslavia, led to an eclipse of transnational resisters and their memories.

Ken Loach's 1995 film *Land and Freedom*, offering a sensitive analysis of the role of International Brigaders in the Spanish Civil War and reaffirming the values of international labour solidarity, attracted international attention. It received several prestigious awards and was nominated for the Palme d'Or at the Cannes Film Festival. It called for a wider consideration of the transnational role of Spanish republicans in the long resistance to Axis Europe and placed on the agenda recognition of the International Brigaders by countries who had hitherto rejected a story that challenged their national myths. The story of the International Brigaders, however, was far from being universally acclaimed and was received very differently in different countries than in others, depending on their current relationship with their wartime past. Here we will look at the cases of Spain, France, Israel and the former Yugoslavia.

Because of the long shadow of Franco and the Pact of Forgetting, the Spanish authorities were slow to pay tribute to Spanish republican fighters. It was not until twenty years after Franco's death and fifty years after the end of the Second World War, on 20 May 1995, that the socialist Spanish minister of defence, Julián García Vargas, unveiled a monument in Madrid's Fuencarral cemetery to the Spaniards who had fought Hitler. The following year, sixty years after the beginning of the Spanish Civil War, the Spanish government granted Spanish citizenship to the last survivors of the International Brigades. On 31 May 2006 King Juan Carlos decorated Lazar Latinović, president of the Association of Spanish Fighters and the last living Yugoslav who fought in Spain, with the Order of Civil Merits.[94] Two years earlier, in 2004, National Day in Spain was celebrated by including in the traditional military parade a veteran from 'La Nueve', the 9th Company of the 3rd Chad Regiment, composed mainly of Spanish republicans, which had been first into occupied Paris in August 1944. It was nevertheless considered vital for national unity in a country still scarred by the Civil War to invite a veteran from the Blue Division of Spanish soldiers who fought with Nazi troops against the Soviet Union on the Eastern Front. The socialist defence minister, José Bono, argued that the celebration, inviting veterans from both sides, was a 'tribute to peace, concord and the understanding of all Spaniards'.[95]

In France, meanwhile, International Brigaders were not formally recognised as war veterans. They were not formally recognised as war veterans (*anciens combattants*) by the French state until 1996, sixty years after the International Brigades were formed. To perpetuate their memory the Friends of the Spanish Republican Fighters was set up that year. Its secretary was Claire Rol-Tanguy, whose father had fought in Spain and then with the FTP and who died in 2002.[96] Meanwhile, to mark the sixtieth anniversary of the liberation of Paris in 2004, the socialist mayor Bertrand Delanoë unveiled a series of plaques along the route taken into the capital by the Spanish republicans of 'La Nueve'.

Even in Israel, which had never been overly sympathetic to the story of the International Brigades, no doubt because they had largely fought for a communist utopia rather than a Zionist one, an exhibition dedicated to 'No Pasaran: The International Brigades and their Jewish Fighters in the Spanish Civil War 1936–1939' was held at the Jewish National and University Library in Jerusalem in 2003.[97] This marked a significant advance from the Vad Vashem conference of 1968, which had included many kinds of Jewish resister, all struggling against the Shoah, but had left aside Jewish International Brigaders. The communist past of the former Palestinian International Brigader Jona Brodkin was conveniently forgotten as he became a symbol of Israeli national resistance.[98]

The emerging cult of the International Brigades opened a door to a more international or transnational understanding of resistance. But the door was not opened very far. The rise of nationalism in post-Cold War Europe made sure that national narratives of resistance were both hard to overwrite and indeed experiencing a revival. In France the Barbie trial had called into question the good reputation of the French Resistance, as one leading resister, Raymond Aubrac, was accused of betraying de Gaulle's emissary, Jean Moulin, to Barbie. Defenders of the French Resistance responded in 1992 by setting up the Resistance Foundation to 'combat the falsifyers' of the resistance story and to pass on 'the common heritage championed by all resisters'.[99] This was reinforced in 1997 when Raymond Aubrac and his wife Lucie, also a famous resister, both communists, were hauled in front of a tribunal of French historians to face renewed accusations of betrayal. This may be seen as a reassertion of the unblemished orthodoxy of the mainstream, non-communist French Resistance.[100]

Elsewhere in Europe, the remaining veterans with transnational pasts and their memories found themselves confronted by the upsurge of nationalism that followed the end of the Cold War. In Poland, just after Solidarity swept to victory in the elections of 4 June 1989, a monument to the Warsaw uprising was unveiled on 1 August. This was a tribute above all to the heroes of the non-communist AK who felt that they had been betrayed by the Red Army, which held back from the city, allowing the Nazis to crush the uprising. Significantly, the English-language 1950 memoirs of the AK general Bór-Komorowski, a leader of the uprising, were republished in 2011.[101] Increasingly, the story of Polish resistance was told as a story of resistance against the Soviets, not against the Germans, and as a national story rather than a transnational one.[102]

Meanwhile in Yugoslavia, resisters with a transnational background who had fought in Spain issued warnings about the rise of nationalism. The influential Association of Yugoslav Volunteers of the Spanish Republican Army, meeting in Sarajevo in 1984, sent an open letter to the Central Committee of the Union of the Communists of Yugoslavia. The Brigaders were invited to talk to the highest Party leaders and were told that their initiative was disturbing. Resistance fighters with transnational experience were defamed throughout the 1980s because the dominant narrative was increasingly nationalist. Gojko Nikoliš, a Spanish fighter and leader of the partisans' medical corps, was publicly attacked in a leading Belgrade journal.[103] This marked an important moment in the rise to power as Serbian president in 1989 of Slobodan Milošević. From the 1970s there had been a slow process of historiographical revision in favour of the 'national' resistance fighter Draža Mihailović and his Četniks.[104] The rise of Serbian nationalism enshrined a new legitimacy based on the rehabilitation of the royalist, anti-communist collaborators during the Second

World War. These were presented as anti-fascist, victims of communism and the new national heroes, while the transnational partisan movement was criminalised as responsible for war crimes and the postwar repression of non-communists.[105] As the transnational actors died out their memory was attacked. They were held responsible for the civil war in Yugoslavia in the 1990s, and streets named after them were renamed. This revision of the national past reached its peak when in 2004 the Serbian parliament rehabilitated Mihailović. A year later a delegation of American veterans handed over the Legion of Merit awarded by US President Truman to Draža Mihajlović in 1948 to his daughter Gordana. Finally, in 2015 the Serbian High Court confirmed the parliament's decision of 2004.

These developments were facilitated by the changing European view of fascism and communism. On 2 April 2009 the European Parliament resolution on European Conscience and Totalitarianism condemned the totalitarian crimes of communism, Nazism and fascism as a shared legacy of the European societies. This equalisation of the 'two totalitarianisms' strongly influenced historical interpretations. In post-socialist states transnational activism was associated with now 'doomed' ideas of communism and socialism while the new nationalist actors were presented and legitimated as the victims of communism. They were rehabilitated, and the crimes for which they had been tried were forgotten.[106]

The contested memory of transnational resistance has nevertheless continued. There was a pushback by institutions committed to telling the story of transnational resistance. In 2006, 2011 and 2016 the Museum of Yugoslavia, the Archive of Serbia, the Yugoslav Film Archive in Belgrade and several museums in Serbia, Montenegro and Bosnia and Herzegovina hosted exhibitions that revived the memory of the people who fought in the Spanish war and in the Yugoslav Partisan movement. The Association of Spanish Fighters (1936–1939) supported a public dialogue on the process of the historical revisionism of history and established contacts between historians and activists from Serbia and Spain.[107] These initiatives, however, were scarcely enough to undermine national narratives of resistance.

Conclusion

Transnational experiences of resistance had a long afterlife and shaped individual and group memories. Initially, the trajectories of resisters with a transnational background were closed down by national liberation, the onset of the Cold War and struggles around the end of empire. Their memories struggled to make an impact in the face of myths of national liberation, Cold War narratives of heroes and traitors, and the dominant Holocaust account of Jewish victimhood. Later on it became easier to reconnect between East and West and to develop these memories. Key moments in these breakthroughs were the post-1956 period of Cold War détente, the Six Day War which highlighted Jewish resistance, events around 1968, the death of Franco and the election of a left-wing government in France in 1981. The growth in Holocaust memory took the spotlight away from Jewish resistance and focused it on the memory of the rescue of persecuted Jews by Gentiles, although a sub-memory of foreign Jewish resistance saw a revival. The end of the Cold War in 1989–90 had profound but contradictory effects. On the one hand, the demolition of the Berlin Wall and the globalisation of the economy and society opened the way to the recovery of transnational links and transnational stories. This was seen in recognition accorded to the International Brigades and Spanish republicans in Spain, France and Israel. On the other hand, however, collapse of communism in Central and Eastern Europe and the breakup of the multinational Soviet Union, of Czechoslovakia and especially of Yugoslavia brought to power political parties strongly rooted in the nationalist ideology which told a completely different story of national resistance that was more opposed to communism than to Nazism.

There is now a memory war between a nationalist, anti-communist and essentialist narrative and a rival transnational, progressive narrative that allows for people having multiple and changing identities. In society and politics, the former is dominant, but in the scientific world the transnational approach is much more influential. This project on transnational resistance has contributed to this approach by recovering stories of transnational trajectories, encounters and transformations in order to rethink the history of resistance in Europe's long Second World War.

Conclusion

Ismee Tames and Robert Gildea

This transnational approach to individuals and groups resisting fascism outside their countries of origin has highlighted two things: first, the importance of space, borders and the transgression of borders, and second, the importance of ways in which individual and group ideas, beliefs and even identities changed over time depending on the shift of events.

It is clear from this study that we cannot understand transnational trajectories, encounters and experiences – and therefore people's behaviour during and after the period under scrutiny – if we remain locked into national narratives and frameworks. A 'national' approach obfuscates experiences beyond borders and retells them in narrow and distortive frameworks of 'being away' or even being 'disloyal' or a 'deserter to the national cause'. We need to look at Europe as an 'open' or interconnected space. These connections take us across Europe but also to North Africa, to other parts of the world then tied to Europe because of the existence of colonial empires and to the USA, which had a powerful but ambivalent relationship with Europe.

The transnational approach has led us to concentrate on individuals and networks rather than institutions, organisations, political parties or (again) nation-states. Transnational approaches highlight 'transnational lives' and 'the new microhistory of connected lives' because they allow the historian to trace individual pathways over time. They encourage us to explore encounters which gave rise to cooperation but also to misunderstanding and to conflict. They also encourage us to examine, in so far as the sources allow, the development over time of the beliefs, experiences and even identities of individuals and groups.

Many of the people we have met in this book took part in combat against fascist forces, in irregular and regular armies and armed groups.

This underscores that resistance is not only (or not merely) a moral standpoint, as may be believed in many European countries because of the ways in which the Second World War (and the Holocaust) are taught in school and re-presented in the public sphere: as a struggle between good and evil and a lesson in 'the right values', be they democracy and human rights or national pride and identity. For many contemporaries, rather, the Second World War meant outright warfare in the hope of survival, to be on the winning side or to prevent an unlivable world. This means that studying resistance against fascism does not propose clear 'lessons' for the future. We need to study and contextualise the people we are interested in and allow them to change through time, to be contradictory in their behaviour or statements, to fall apart, to become somebody completely different, to be marvellously inspiring or equally to be treacherous.

Illuminating these contradictions on the part of those who resisted is one of the contributions of this book. It does not in any way make the horrendous crimes of the Nazis less awful: it only shows what war and mass violence do to people, how it makes them behave, adapt and transform. It shows how 1945 was not the end of pain and violence for many but only the beginning of the next episode of seeking to reinvent themselves.

The scale and ambition of the approach required that this study be a collective project. No single historian could access all the archives and master all the languages required to make sense of them. Often we have followed individuals who had left traces in archives in countries across Europe, the USA and Israel, from France to Yugoslavia or from Spain to Russia, and were studied from different perspectives or periods of their lives by different historians.

The archives used were extremely challenging when it came to trying to better understand individual experiences, subjectivities and identities. Only through following the individual through a wide variety of sources – official state, military, police and party archives, ego-documents created during or after the conflict, postwar memory cultures – could we get closer to an individual. Following individual people themselves helps us to focus and to stay clear of writing the histories of organisations or nation-states: endeavours that are worthy of research but not what this book intended to achieve.

How people present themselves in the sources or how they are being (re-)presented gives us an idea of which parts of their experiences and identities were deemed relevant to record (and keep) and in what wording and categories. Thus we can trace how stories change when the context changes: from a context of war and secrecy surrounding resistance groups, to the postwar resettlement and framing of new political contexts, to a greater focus on topics like the Holocaust or the end of the Cold War, to a commitment to 'keeping the memory alive' that resulted in oral history projects and documentaries.

How people changed or felt changed by resistance activities obviously differed from case to case and was influenced by myriad factors. However, this study does make clear that in order to get an idea of how people changed, how they (re-)told their stories or how they were perceived in public can never be a question of 'getting closer to the ultimate truth'. How they are represented in the archives and how they told and retold their lives is always an indication of how they negotiated what was deemed possible to say and what was too dangerous, too painful or simply a nuisance at that specific time and place.

Studying transnational resistance can never use representative groups or be based on equal and standardised data; that is simply not how lived reality is reflected in the surviving sources. We cannot and shall never be able to conduct historical research as if we are working in a laboratory environment. The history of war and mass violence especially leaves us with sources as shattered and damaged as the people who lived through them. In future, digitised archives and collections may make other approaches possible – for instance making it easier to trace people and connecting information about them from various archives. Today, however, this kind of research is still in its infancy and not yet able to address the kind of wide and complex questions proposed in this book. The book may, however, hopefully be a stepping stone in an exploration of digitised and automated ways of extracting, analysing and presenting data on the trajectories of individuals.[1]

The study has tried to show that transnational resistance did not spring fully armed from the European soil in 1939 or 1940. It had a long prehistory in the interwar period and even before the First World War. Its context was that of mass migration, usually from east to west, for reasons of economic or intellectual betterment, or the flight of political or religious refugees, or a combination of both. Many migrants or refugees used existing family connections, economic ties or organisational pathways. Some of the illegal routes they took across frontiers had been trodden for many years by smugglers who were happy to be paid for trafficking people as well as goods. Political commitment to fight fascism also had a history. Many of the resisters had already espoused communism in their own country, inspired by the Bolshevik Revolution of 1917, or were affiliated to the international communist movement or Comintern. Many had begun to fight fascism and Nazism from the 1920s in Italy or 1933 in Germany and volunteered in 1936 or 1937 to join the International Brigades in Spain to support their work. Nationalist regimes which excluded national minorities, communists, socialists and Jews came to power across Europe in the interwar period and intensified their exile along familiar escape routes. After the *Anschluss* and *Kristallnacht* in 1938 the flight of Jews from Austria and Germany – going either south and east or north and west – became a flood. The outbreak of war in 1939 and the steady advance of the Axis powers reduced Europe to a 'shatter zone' in which boundaries established in 1918–19 were bulldozed, occupation regimes and puppet states were established, and the persecution of 'foreigners', communists and Jews reached new levels. The Nazi campaign to destroy the European Jews became a 'war within the war' which provoked only two responses: fight or flight. The Jewish minority thus played a central role in many of the networks and movements of rescue and resistance that have been a focus of this study.

Trajectories

For this project, the point at which prehistory became history was 1936, in what the Austrian-Jewish writer Franz Borkeneau called 'the Spanish cockpit'.[2] The Spanish Civil War, which in many ways marked the beginning of the Second World War, attracted volunteers from all over Europe and beyond to fight not only Franco's bid to destroy the Republic but also against the intervention of Mussolini's Italy and Hitler's Germany in support of Franco. Some, like the French metalworker and communist trade unionist Henri Tanguy, later known as Rol-Tanguy, only had to cross the Pyrenees. Others, such as Henryk Toruńczyk, came from Poland, although he was already 'on the move', studying in Belgium. Mendel Langer came from Palestine although his family had fled there from Austrian Galicia, and, expelled as a communist trade unionist from the Palestine Mandate had come to live and work in France, changing his name to Marcel. Irving Goff came from New York to fight in Spain as one of the Lincoln Brigade, but his Jewish family had fled from pogroms in Odessa at the turn of the century.

Those hardened by the anti-fascist struggle in Spain fanned out after the defeat of the Spanish Republic in 1939, often via French internment camps along the Pyrenees or in North Africa, to take leadership roles in many resistance movements that developed in different parts of Axis-occupied Europe, from France and Germany to the Balkans, Poland and Russia. One of the key findings of this book has been the central formative role of former International Brigaders and exiled Spanish republicans at the head of European resistance movements. They brought military knowhow, political sophistication and membership of networks that could be redeployed in many theatres – especially theatres where partisan activities were possible, such as Central Europe and the Balkans. Their role was less in north-western parts of the continent like the Low Countries, where geography made these kinds of irregular warfare hardly possible. Henri Tanguy took on his Catalan aide-de-camp in Spain, Conrado Miret i Musté, to set up the FTP-MOI in France and then, after the latter's arrest, took on another veteran from Spain, the Transylvanian-Jewish Francisc (Ferenz) Wolf, otherwise known as József Boczor. Henryk Toruńczyk, who had worked with the Soviet intelligence chief Ilya Starinov in Spain, found his way to the Soviet Union and with Starinov founded the Polish Independent Special Battalion to undertake guerrilla action behind the German lines in occupied Poland. The Spanish republican Domingo Ungría, who had also discovered Starinov in Spain, likewise reappeared in the Soviet Union and with Starinov masterminded a remote-controlled bomb attack on German forces that had just occupied Kharkov. Meanwhile the Yugoslav Interbrigadist Ljubo Ilić went on, via French internment camps and prisons, to become one of the national leaders of the FTP in France.

The defeat of states and the breakdown of borders in the 'shatter zone' of occupied Europe made for very complicated pathways between combat zones. Józef Maciąg, a Pole with a Dalmatian mother and brought up in Bosnia, fought for the Polish army in 1939 and was traumatised by its destruction. He found his way to the Middle East, where he joined an Independent Carpathian Brigade which fought with the French in Syria and the British in North Africa, before being taken on by SOE and parachuted into Serbia, close to where he had come from, to work with the partisans. His movements were assisted by the Allies, but most resisters had to improvise their own escape routes across occupied Europe or between occupied and unoccupied Europe. Former Polish International Brigaders of the XIII Dąbrowski Brigade now in France, led by Bolesław Mołojec and Józef Mrozek, established an underground railway back to Poland by posing as volunteers to work in German factories. Escape lines such as Dutch-Paris used pre-existing business, diplomatic and religious contacts in the occupied Netherlands, Belgium and France to send downed Allied airmen and others to safety in neutral countries Spain and Switzerland. Other escape lines, such as the so-called Außenministerium, organised by Dutch youth to secretly bring home comrades who had been recruited as forced labour to work in German war factories, had much shorter ranges, exploiting former smuggling routes between the Netherlands and Germany.

The activity of these escape lines was intensified by the need to resist the Nazi persecution and deportation of Jews, which was assisted by puppet regimes in countries such as Vichy France and Ustaša-run Croatia. Routes through France to Switzerland and Spain, especially for Jewish youth destined eventually for Palestine, were organised by the OSE and Armée

Juive, which operated from Toulouse and Lyons. Meanwhile the Jewish community of Trieste helped with the transfer of Central European Jews fleeing into the Balkans and to Mediterranean ports. Unfortunately, the way out of these ports was blocked after the outbreak of war.

For a long time, these trajectories were followed by relatively few people. As the Axis powers headed for defeat, however, many more took their turn, deserting from Axis armies or escaping from Axis prisons, POW camps or labour camps. The surrender of Italy to the Allies was a turning point. Italian soldiers were faced by the dilemma of either being taken prisoner by their former German allies, who did not forgive their betrayal, or making common cause with partisans who were fighting the Germans. Thus Italians deserted to Albanian, Yugoslav or Greek partisans, Yugoslavs held in Italian POW camps and prisons escaped to join Italian Partisans, and even German anti-Nazis such as Gerhard Reinhardt deserted to join the Greek communist resistance and co-founded an Anti-Nazi Freedom Committee.

Encounters

A second dimension of the study has been to explore sites of transnational encounter where transnational resistance was in different ways generated, incubated or sustained. The first of these sites were internment camps, prisons and POW camps, which we have characterised as 'crucibles of transnational resistance'. Despite or because of the segregation by political or national group and the repression to which they were subject, internees were often able to overcome differences and to educate themselves politically. The German communist cadre Franz Dahlem reflected that 'The French government made the mistake of concentrating the cadres of the International Brigades and the apparatchiks of central committees of communist parties in countries with fascist regimes or occupied by the Nazis in the Le Vernet camp.' Of course, they often remained divided nationally or politically, inheriting conflicts between communists and anarchists which had been carried over from their experiences in the Spanish Civil War. Camps were sites of rivalry and conflict as much as they were of connection. Hospitals in the camp, however, provided an opportunity for individuals of different nationalities and political backgrounds to meet in a relatively protected space. There were also moments when transnational solidarity was dramatically realised. One of these was when the camp authorities, backed by force, attempted to remove internees to fight in armies they regarded as ideologically hostile or for deportation to a worse camp. Ljubo Ilić remembered that at Gurs in April 1940 'everyone was outside, up against the barbed wire, singing Spanish Civil War songs, the

Marseillaise and shouting slogans ... One of the Brigadists struck up the *Internationale*, which carried across the camp with the speed of an explosion.' Internees were sometimes able to make links with resistance movements outside, such as the underground Communist Party organisation or – in the case of POWs – forced workers in German factories. If they escaped, like Ilić, they were often in a position, because of their political education and contacts, to take leadership roles in resistance movements.

Escape lines were a second site of transnational encounters. On the Pyrenean border between France and Spain José Gistau was an old-time smuggler of cattle and goods. During the Spanish Civil War he worked with 'a lot of leftists, especially teachers', to get weapons to Spain in spite of the arms blockade. After the defeat of the republic he helped Spanish republican refugees and International Brigaders across the mountains to France and then, when the Dutch-Paris escape line was set up, worked with university students such as Simone Calmels, who was based in Toulouse. For this clandestine work he called himself Barranco. Meanwhile the Spanish republican Francisco Ponzán, who had fled Spain in 1939 and worked with a group of exiled Spanish anarchists in France, worked for the Belgian-based Pat O'Leary line to exfiltrate back to Spain a galaxy of international agents – British, Italian, Swiss, German, Polish and Russian. These escape lines involved far more people than International Brigaders, because escape was for many not for military purposes but to flee the Holocaust, the 'war within the war'. Thus Jean Weidner changed himself and many around him from involvement in business networks or religious ministry into smuggling out of occupied Europe those on the run from the Nazis. Networks of Protestants and Catholics as well as of Jews played an important role in saving Jews, and here – more than in military escape lines, especially when it came to saving children – women had a leading role to play. In the Armée Juive, for example, the Polish-born Kania Geiger, going in France under the name of Anne-Marie Bonnard, negotiated routes to and funding from Switzerland, and women couriers guided children to safety at risk to their own lives. Mila Racine, born in Moscow in 1921, was arrested by the Germans in October 1943 and later deported to Ravensbrück, where she died in March 1945. Marianne Cohn, born in Mannheim in 1922, left to her own devices after her parents were interned in Gurs, was arrested at Annemasse while taking a convoy of children in May 1943. In July 1944 she was taken from prison by the Gestapo and brutally murdered.[3]

A third site of encounter were regular armies that were notionally national but inevitably multinational, drawing on servicemen from many nationalities. Non-nationals were generally not allowed to serve in national armies, such as the French army or remnants of the Polish or Czechoslovak armies fighting on French soil in 1940. They were, however, drafted into the Foreign Legion, foreign volunteer regiments or work battalions. Joining one of these was often a way for former International Brigaders or Spanish republicans to escape from internment camps in 1940, when the French were desperate for manpower. Some, like the interned Spanish republican soldier Antonio Soriano, refused to be drafted, saying: 'we are not legionnaires, we are an army with an ideology'. Other Spaniards, however, who joined the 13th Half Brigade of the Foreign Legion and were sent to Narvik in April 1940, were praised by their French commander: 'the reds or ex-reds fought like lions in the snowy mountains of Norway'.

After the defeat of France, when Britain became the base of the continuing war against the Axis, many international soldiers joined the Free French or special services of the British army that would accept them. Ferdinand Otto Miksche, an Austro-Hungarian who became a Czechoslovak citizen after 1918, was ill at ease in the Czechoslovak army and went to fight in Spain. Evacuated to Britain in 1940, he preferred to leave the Czechoslovak army once again to join the Free French of General de Gaulle, and was promoted to their general staff. Meanwhile the British army set up the 10th Inter-Allied Commando, which included French, Belgians, Dutch, Norwegians, Poles and Yugoslavs and which, among other actions, attacked Walcheren Island in November 1944. Within the commando the lingua franca of the 3rd Miscellaneous troop, composed mainly of German, Austrian and Jewish anti-fascists, was German. Meanwhile in North Africa, after Operation Torch, a new wave of foreign internees was released from Vichy's camps and work battalions or deserted from the Foreign Legion to join the Corps Français d'Afrique. Composed of Spanish republicans, Yugoslavs, Dutch Jews and indigenous Muslims, it was initially deployed not with the French army but with the British and US armies, and later mostly joined the Free French.

Very often foreigners were not happy in these regiments, chafing against the discipline, the sense of being mercenaries and the anti-Semitism of many in the officer class. When they left the ranks, as they often did, they brought military expertise and political sophistication that they put to good use as they transferred to partisan or guerrilla units. These units were a fourth site of transnational encounter in their own right. In the early days they were fed by individual escapes from camps or prisons, using existing communist or other networks. They also included foreign Jews, helped from their own escape organisations or retreating from their urban centres to the mountains and forests when repression and the round-up of Jews became intense. In the Soviet Union, communists who had fled into exile before the war from other countries could be recruited to fight. Thus the OMSBON, set up in October 1941, included German,

Austrian, Polish, Czechoslovak, Romanian, Chinese and Vietnamese communists. The German communist Karl Kleinjung and the Latvian communist Imants Sudmalis were both involved with Soviet Partisans in the Belarussian forest, the former often disguised as a German officer. Meanwhile the Jewish Soviet officer Leonid Berenshtein led a partisan unit in south-east Poland and Slovakia which included Bessarabian Jews, Poles, Slovaks, Hungarians and German deserters. In the Balkans the complement was reversed as escaping Soviet POWs joined the Greek communist resistance. The lieutenant of engineers Ivan Barsukov, taken prisoner near Moscow, commanded a 'Ruski company' within the Xth Division of ELAS which included Bulgarians, Italians and Greeks. Later he entered Yugoslav territory with three thousand 'Russian' troops, including escaped Russian POWs and Todt Organisation forced labourers, fighting with Tito's partisans, in order to liberate Macedonia.

The uprisings of 1944 in Warsaw, Paris and Slovakia, which have often been presented as moments of national liberation, were a fifth site of transnational encounter. In Warsaw, for example, a British RAF sergeant who had escaped from a German POW camp and became a SOE officer worked with a Slovakian platoon that included Georgians who were escaped Soviet POWs, escapees from a Jewish concentration camp and a Nigerian jazz musician, August Agbola O'Brown. In Paris, which was always a cosmopolitan city, exiles and refugees who had lain low during the German occupation came out of the shadows to join in resistance activity alongside local Parisians. Among the insurgents was a French colonial soldier from Gabon, Georges Dukson, who had escaped from a German POW camp in 1943 and joined the FFIs, earning the nickname 'the Black Lion of the XVIIème [*arrondissement*]'. In Slovakia, meanwhile, French POWs under Captain Georges de Lannurien who had escaped from a German POW camp in Silesia joined up with Czechoslovak Partisans to take part in the Slovak uprising. Supporting the rising were agents of the US OSS, who were themselves Americanised migrants from Czechoslovakia whose parents had settled in the USA in the 1920s.

Experiences

These transnational encounters often – but not always – gave rise to transnational experiences which – for this project at least – were the touchstone of the crystallisation of transnational resistance. A focus on individual 'reinvention', however, may evoke too many positive associations for the twenty-first-century reader. We should be aware that transnational resistance against fascism was about war and persecution, about trying to sustain oneself and to survive, about dealing with violence experienced

– in camps, in prison, in combat, in extremely vulnerable positions when on the run – and about dealing with acts of violence committed by the resisters themselves. How to deal with the experience of often extreme violence may even be the most pressing aspect when it comes to the need to reshape and reinvent oneself when involved in transnational resistance. This is something to which the archives, and also postwar memoirs, do not usually give clear-cut answers. We have to read these sources 'against the grain' and be aware of their silences.

Encounters did not always give rise to dramatic reinventions or transformations. Far from it. Encounter with the 'other' could trigger misunderstanding, hostility or conflict. On occasion, however, these encounters did cause a resister to change their thinking or beliefs, for example to espouse communism or Zionism. They might encourage them to change their practice, perhaps from activity that was basically about rescue to one that privileged armed resistance. They might, finally, persuade resisters to change their identity – at least outwardly – in order to blend more successfully into their new environment, something that might be betrayed by a change of name or nickname.

Limits to transnational experiences were often heavily shaped by a shared language, or conversely by not being able to clearly communicate. Many rescuers and resisters grew up in borderland areas, such as Galicia (Austrian before 1918, then Polish) or Bessarabia (Russian before 1918, then Romanian), which were multi-ethnic, multi-religious and multilingual. Those who came from these regions grew up speaking several languages, and if, as often happened, they were driven out or fled, they learned the language or languages of the country in which they finished up. In many military situations there was a lingua franca, less official than improvised. Thus the Latvians who joined the Slavic Heavy Artillery Group in Spain did not speak any Slavic languages but got by in German. Much of the resistance in France, particularly in the south-west, spoke Spanish. Some transnational resisters nevertheless had difficulty learning languages and had to rely on translators. Ramón Vía, who after the Spanish Civil War fled from Spain to Oran in French Algeria, found himself in a largely Spanish-speaking community. To liaise with the French, he relied on the schoolteacher-resister Lisette Vincent and the communist activist Remedios Martínez. Similarly the French POW leader de Lannurien, who became involved in the Slovak uprising, relied on the wife of a local landowner, Countess Martha Himmler, to liaise with the Soviets. Women, it should be underlined, often played a liaison and networking role in resistance activity and here provided links between transnational and local resistance.

In many cases, bringing together many different nationalities provoked as easily antagonism as transnational cooperation. Within the International

Brigades there was a resentment that too many leadership posts were dominated by Germans or Poles or that the Serbs stuck together like a veritable clan. After the end of the Spanish Civil War the Poles who had dominated the XIII Dąbrowsky Brigade went on almost as a unit to dominate much of the Polish resistance behind enemy lines. On the other hand, a shared 'Spanish' past brought together very disparate nationalities in later phases of resistance. Resisters from many nationalities in south-west France had been together in the XIV Guerrilla Corps of the Spanish army. The Albanian guerrilla leader Mehmet Shehu was able to work easily with Italian deserters because he had fought in Spain with the XII Garibaldi Brigade. Meanwhile in Italy after the Allied landings the OSS relied on contacts between the former Lincoln Brigade combatant Irving Goff and Italian communists working behind German lines, for which trust was based on a shared odyssey in Spain.

Fighting with different national groups was often made easier if a non-national adopted a national identity. The Czechoslovak army that fought in France in 1940 found it difficult to integrate soldiers from the Sudeten German minority of their state, even though these might be German-Jewish Czech citizens fleeing Nazism. One of these, Fritz Beer, changed his name from Fritz to the Czech Bedřich, but this was not enough to endear him to other Czechoslovak soldiers, and he remained in Britain after 1945. More successfully, another Sudeten German of Jewish origin, Jan Theilinger, joined the 10th Inter-Allied Commando based in Britain and changed his name to the very British John Robert Taylor.

It was perhaps easier to adopt another national identity while in exile in Prague or London. On the ground tensions between nationalities often came back into play. The idea of a Balkan federation made it possible to hold together resisters of Yugoslav and Bulgarian communist origin, but at the same time their conflict over which country was to have Macedonia drove them apart. Similarly, the Slav-speaking population of Greece was divided from the Greek communist resistance by disputes over Macedonia and found it easier to resist alongside Yugoslav Partisans.

Many resistance groups were in effect multinational rather than transnational. With the help of SOE the Italian General Gino Piccini defected with his men to the Albanian communist partisans and formed a Comando Italiano Truppe alla Montagna, but he and they never really integrated in the Albanian resistance. Likewise the Polish resistance group named after Tadeusz Kościusko, hero of the Polish uprising of 1794, led by Czesław Klim, who had fought the Soviets in 1919–21 and in 1939, understandably kept itself at arm's length from the Soviet Pinsk Brigade, while a Hungarian Partisan group under a Soviet major which intervened in Slovakia in the autumn of 1944 was in reality led by two Hungarian officers.

Jews, we have argued, were often at the heart of transnational resistance. They adapted to many different forms of resistance, national, communist or Zionist. Lew Goldenberg, born in Paris to parents who fled Russia after the failed 1905 revolution, was already part of the French legal establishment under the name Leo Hamon when the French Resistance called him. By contrast Albert Cohen, who was born in Argentina and served in the French Levant army in 1940, did not discover Zionist resistance until he was deprived of his non-commissioned officer status by the Vichy regime. He attended a synagogue in Toulouse and there, he remembered, 'I discovered a whole Jewish world that I scarcely knew, for though I was a foreigner I was French in my heart.'[4] Another conversion experience was undergone by the German-Jewish Fritz Cahn, who was certainly no communist when he fled Munich but was protected by Yugoslav Partisans, changed his name to Fric Kan and eventually espoused communism.

There are myriad examples of Jews joining resistance organisations and being fully accepted. For example, Slovene officers and trade unionists together with Jews, both interned by Italians on the island of Rab, escaped together in September 1943 and together formed a Rab Battalion in the mountains of Croatia, both dedicated to the fight against fascism. Anti-Semitism, however, was often as present in resistance movements as it was in society. The Polish resistance leader Stefan Kilanowicz (also known as Grzegorz Korczyński), commander of the communist People's Guard, recruited escaped Soviet POWs and even Holocaust survivors, but was also accused of extreme brutality towards non-communists and Jews in Poland. Likewise, Jews of the Armée Juive in Toulouse who retreated to the mountain *maquis* in the resistance summer of 1944 and formed the Trumpeldor platoon of the Montagne Noire *maquis* were told by a French officer, 'Your Jewish problem gets up our noses. Change your names, marry some Christian girls, and in a generation there will be no Jewish problem.'

Transnational resistance was also confronted by the tension between communism and anti-communism. This was attenuated after Germany invaded the Soviet Union in 1941 and communism and anti-fascism once again aligned, but the advance of the Red Army and onset of the Cold War politics caused those tensions to recur. For example, Poles who escaped from labour camps to fight with the Greek communist resistance in the so-called Battalion of Death were told by ELAS that the only Polish government was based in Moscow. Then Adam Kula, a Polish officer working closely with SOE, who was parachuted into Greece in September 1943, told them about the Polish government in London, the AK and the Soviet massacre of Polish officers at Katyn. This changed their attitude to the Greek communists in a moment. Meanwhile, at a higher level, the Soviets became increasingly suspicious of Spanish republicans working with Soviet Partisans and refused to airlift out an American OSS mission in difficulty during the Slovak uprising. The Americans were similarly suspicious of OSS agents with a communist past in the Lincoln Brigade in Spain and demanded in 1945 that OSS rest such people rather than send them to China, where work was yet to be done against the Japanese.

A final question is whether transnational resistance finished where the colonial sphere began. That is, were colonial subjects who often served in the armies of imperial powers such as Britain or France welcomed into the ranks of resistance fighters or indeed into those armies once they moved out of the colonial sphere to liberate Europe? The underlying question was whether resistance against the tyranny of the Axis translated into resistance against colonialism or whether liberation from the Axis simply confirmed the return of the imperial and colonial power of the Allies.

There are some instances of colonial subjects being involved in resistance activity. In 1940 about seventy Somalians, Eritreans and Ethiopians were brought to Naples for an exhibition dedicated to Italy's overseas empire. Because of the outbreak of the war they were unable to return home. They were moved to central Italy for greater safety, but from there about twenty-five joined the Italian resistance in October 1943, and at least three of these were killed. In North Africa, however, indigenous Muslims were subjects, not citizens, and were subjected to a brutal legal code, the Code de l'Indigénat. The PCA, which was active underground, was dominated by French settlers, many of whom were naturalised Spaniards. It expelled the indigenous Muslim Ahmed Smaïli in 1941 for challenging their authority and allegedly denouncing them to the Vichy police. Muslim Algerians were allowed to serve in the French army and indeed, with sub-Saharan Africans, provided what was known as the *Force noire* of the French army. But there were many reservations about transferring black and North African troops to France in the armies of liberation, which underwent a process of *blanchiment* either before they landed in the south of France in August 1944 or else before the invasion of Germany in the winter of 1944–45. Ironically, this process opened the ranks for more Spanish republicans to be included in the French armies that liberated Paris on 25 August 1944. Moreover, on the following day, 26 August, Georges Dukson, who came to join the liberation parade on the Champs-Élysées, was unceremoniously bundled away from de Gaulle and out of camera shot.

The transnational approach also points to the fact that liberating a certain geographic space from fascism held different meanings and promises for the various resisters and fighters involved. The promises expected by resisters from abroad were often overlooked, not listened to or simply unwanted by local populations and by (new) local or national authorities.

The defeat of Germany in 1945 did not mark the end of the story for many transnational resisters. The new enemy could now be the imperial powers, above all the British and the French. The French were keen to re-impose their authority in Algeria, where the provisional government had been based in 1943–44 and which was regarded as part of metropolitan France. After the imperial setbacks suffered in the war France and Britain looked to re-establish their colonies in Africa, the Middle East and Asia. Britain was also minded to establish Greece, liberated from the Axis, as a semi-colony and to hold onto its Palestine Mandate as a key to its influence in the Middle East. This meant that it found itself at odds with the Greek communist resistance, with which it had worked but which it now fought to prevent it taking power, using force if necessary. Britain also attempted to prevent Jewish Holocaust survivors from making their way to Palestine to build up their Jewish homeland, and found its authority contested by members of the Armée Juive, now the OJC, who saw their ongoing task as to extend their escape line from now-liberated Europe to a Palestine that they now claimed.

This study does not conclude in 1945 and concludes only formally in 1948, with the foundation of the state of Israel and the onset of the Cold War. We follow the trajectories of some of the resisters we have been following into the postwar world, to see how they fared in the rebuilding of liberated nation-states, which for many was the ultimate goal of their struggle against fascism. In the postwar period it was much easier to brush aside the memories of transnational experiences in some areas of Europe than in other parts. People returning to for instance Belgium or the Netherlands were simply not heard when they referred to their transnational experiences because the troubled national recovery focused on other things and could get away easily with ignoring these experiences. In countries like Romania, Yugoslavia or Czechoslovakia, however, the transnational experiences were easier for many people to relate to because they had seen them happening on their own doorstep. This did not mean that these experiences were better acknowledged: far from it. The fact that people had been abroad or had come into contact with people of very different and diffuse backgrounds often strongly connected to fears and ideas about potential disloyalty or untrustworthiness to the new Moscow-backed communist regimes. This meant that many had to manoeuvre extremely carefully when relating to transnational experiences.

Some former resisters reached positions of influence and authority in those new states, especially in the People's Democracies of Eastern Europe and above all in Yugoslavia. Others were regarded as threats to the national cause that was now the dominant agenda. We examined their fate at the beginning of the Cold War, when transnationalism became shorthand for cosmopolitanism, and for being fifth columnists and even downright traitors. Communist parties in both East and West became national communist parties, and purged and even executed individuals who had distinguished careers in the International Brigades and as leaders of European resistance movements. Henryk Toruńczyk, for example, was hanged, while in order to survive Galia Sincari, who had been a nurse with the International Brigades and an accidental communist, had to invent a past for herself as a lifelong member of the Party.

These examples shed a new light on the statement that the Second World War and fascist occupation nearly destroyed the pre-war European states. We know from previous research how the (new) ruling elites in practically all postwar states needed the story of resistance against fascism in order to legitimate their own (often contested) rule. This study shows how regimes and societies used and abused the stories of people involved in resistance against fascism in Europe. Especially in the early post-1945 communist regions of Europe, not only fascism was deemed something that needed to be crushed forever, but also many people beyond the grip of Moscow were targeted. However anti-fascist their credentials may have been, they were deemed suspicious by the new rulers and put at severe risk. This resulted in the seemingly contradictory persecution of precisely those who had been among some of the most arduous resisters against fascism.

Wars of decolonisation also had a divisive effect on transnational resisters. Some, like Marcel Bigeard, continued his military career in defence of the crumbling French Empire, first in Indochina, then in Algeria, and resorted to brutal methods against indigenous peoples who had learned lessons of resistance and national liberation from the French Resistance itself. Others supported those wars of national liberation both in formal parts of the empire and in semi-colonies, such as Greece. The anti-Nazi resister Gerhard Reinhardt, who had joined ELAS in Greece, became a strong critic of British colonialism, while Sylvia Apostolidou, who had worked for SOE, sent back her George Medal in 1955 when the British government declared a state of emergency and hanged two Cypriot rebels.

Finally, the study explores the memory of transnational resisters. This memory includes their individual memory, accessible through the ego-documents which have been a principal source for this book, and the collective memory of associations of resistance veterans to which they might have belonged and which spoke for them. We have explored how these individual and collective memories both struggled against what might be called the societal memory or dominant narrative of the countries in which they have lived. These dominant narratives were shaped by the historical developments we have mentioned – national liberation, the Cold War, wars of decolonisation – which tended to eclipse the memory of transnational resistance as well as affecting the individuals themselves. Subsequent events, such as East–West détente, the Six Day War of 1967, the events of 1968, the death of Franco and the fall of the Colonels in Greece, opened spaces for the memory of transnational resistance to be articulated and debated. This process was not, however, linear. While on the one hand the end of the Cold War and globalisation expanded the space for memories of transnational resistance to be heard, the surge in nationalism in Central and Eastern Europe had the effect of marginalising and even discrediting the contribution of transnational resistance. In Western Europe too, a surge in nationalism since the crisis of 2008 resulted in transnational dimensions in Second World War memories being downplayed in favour of national memories.

Highlighting how these 'big history' developments about fascist occupation and state legitimacy link with and are tied into the real-life experiences of people who had in one capacity or another resisted fascist domination gives us a new awareness of the uncertainties and unexpected shifts in fate they had to confront. Whereas popular culture in Western Europe now easily speaks of 'resistance heroes' when referring to those involved in resistance against Nazi Germany, in the early postwar years it was never self-evident who was deemed a hero or indeed a dangerous, transgressive and uncontrollable individual. These might also be dangerous in a moral sense: people involved in transnational resistance activities usually had transgressed more than just geographical borders. The necessity of reinventing oneself in a completely different and often violent context made people resort to behaviour that for many would have been unthinkable in their 'old lives'. Just think of the importance of creating new identities – a new name, family history or background. Not only did this imply a high level of lying and pretending; it also meant that social and religious norms suddenly were put into perspective, contested or even turned upside down. Resisting fascist rule opened up spaces in which previously marginalised people could reinvent themselves as combat heroes; or women could claim a role outside the family that previously would have been unimaginable to them. The postwar regimes were usually suspicious of such transgressive potential.

The story of transnational resistance to fascism is not, fortunately, dependent on the memory of it in different European societies. Historians have their say too, and this project was enabled by a combination of a transnational approach, refined by twenty years of historiography, and the collective work of an international team of twenty-three historians of fourteen nationalities – British, Dutch, French, Spanish, Italian, Swiss, German, Latvian, Czech, Serb, Romanian, Greek, Israeli and American – who crossed many frontiers to research in archives and to meet in workshops in Belgrade, Dublin and Oxford. In a way, in time of peace, they re-embodied and re-enacted the trajectories, encounters, experiences and indeed transformations of the transnational resisters they were studying seventy years later. This is a scholarly work, with no political agenda, but it is perhaps not without significance that this project, conceived in 2011, has evolved in a period of rising nationalisms and at a time when Europe has been searching for new stories and new legitimacy. We do not provide a new story or base for political legitimacy. Looking for 'the lessons' of resistance against fascism through the prism of transnational experiences, we see that these lessons may partly be about upholding beliefs in a shared humanity and definitely are about how the experiences of war force us to radically reinvent ourselves, and that these changes cannot be understood as somehow an expression of the 'true identity' of the nation or nation-state coming to the fore.

A last contribution of this research is an awareness that in 1948 Europe was still in ruins with millions of people in displaced persons' camps, European powers were caught up in civil war or colonial wars, the Middle East was contested between Arabs and Jews, fascism still in place in Spain, and Moscow communism was strengthening its grip on Central and Eastern Europe. The military defeat of fascism and Nazism thus did not bring peace and prosperity automatically, nor did it end the urge felt by many, either to return to their country of origin or to live in completely new places, to keep fighting for a better world. The years 1936–48 are not a 'best practice' when we seek how to respond to dehumanising and totalitarian systems and worldviews, but they are an extreme historical example of the challenges with which we are confronted and which also shape us.

Notes

Introduction

1 Arthur Koestler, *The Scum of the Earth* (London: Jonathan Cape, 1941), 85.
2 Kevin McDermott and Jeremy Agnew, *The Comintern: A History of International Communism from Lenin to Stalin* (Basingstoke: Macmillan, 1996); Tim Rees and Andrew Thorpe, *International Communism and the Communist International* (Manchester: Manchester University Press, 1998); and Serge Wolikow, *Histoire de l'Internationale communiste* (Paris: L'Atelier, 2010).
3 Hugo García, Mercedes Yusta, Xavier Tabet and Cristina Clímaco, *Rethinking Antifascism: History, Memory and Politics, 1922 to the Present* (Oxford and New York: Berghahn, 2016).
4 Gordon East, 'The Concept and Political Status of the Shatter Zone', in Norman J. G. Pounds (ed.), *Geographical Essays on Eastern Europe* (Bloomington: Indiana University Press, 1961), 1–27; Timothy Snyder, *Bloodlands: Europe between Hitler and Stalin* (London: Bodley Head, 2010).
5 Philip Burrin, *Living with Defeat: France under the German Occupation, 1940–1944* (London: Arnold, 1996); Robert Gildea, *Marianne in Chains: In Search of the German Occupation, 1940–1945* (London: Macmillan, 2002).
6 Geraldien von Frijtag Drabbe Kunzel, 'Resistance, Reprisals and Reactions', in Robert Gildea, Anette Warring and Olivier Wieviorka (eds), *Surviving Hitler and Mussolini: Daily Life in Occupied Europe* (Oxford and New York: Berg, 2006), 182–3.
7 Robert Gildea, *Fighters in the Shadows: A New History of the French Resistance* (London: Faber & Faber, 2015), 231.
8 Robert Gildea, Dirk Luyten and Juliane Fürst, 'To Work or Not to Work?', in Gildea, Warring and Wieviorka (eds), *Surviving Hitler and Mussolini*, 42–87.
9 Desley Deacon, Penny Russell and Angela Wollacott (eds), *Transnational Lives: Biographies of Global Modernity, 1700–Present* (Basingstoke: Palgrave Macmillan, 2010).
10 Sanjay Subrahmanyam, 'Connected Histories: Notes towards a Reconfiguration of Early Modern Eurasia', *Modern Asian Studies*, 31.3 (1997), 735–62; Sanjay Subrahmanyam, 'Holding the World in Balance: The Connected Histories of the Iberian Overseas Empires, 1500–1640', *American*

Historical Review, 112.5 (2007), 1359–85; Margrit Pernau, *Transnationale Geschichte* (Göttingen: Vandenhoeck & Ruprecht, 2011), 37–42.

11 Jürgen Osterhammel, 'Global History and Historical Sociology', in James Belich, John Darwin, Margret Frenz and Chris Wickham (eds), *The Prospect of Global History* (Oxford: Oxford University Press, 2016), 34.

12 Emma Rothschild, *The Inner Life of Empires: An Eighteenth-Century History* (Princeton, NJ, and Oxford: Princeton University Press, 2011), 279.

13 Michael Werner and Bénédicte Zimmermann, 'Penser l'histoire croisée: entre empirie et réflexivité', *Annales: histoire, sciences sociales*, 58.1 (2003), 7–36; Michael Werner and Bénédicte Zimmermann, 'Beyond Comparison: *Histoire croisée* and the Challenge of Reflexivity', *Theory and History*, 45 (2006), 30–50.

14 Pieter Lagrou, *The Legacy of Nazi Occupation: Patriotic Memory and National Recovery in Western Europe, 1945–1965* (Cambridge: Cambridge University Press, 2000).

15 Amir Weiner, *Making Sense of War: The Second World War and the Fate of the Bolshevik Revolution* (Princeton and Oxford: Princeton University Press, 2001).

16 M. R. D. Foot, *SOE in France: An Account of the Work of the British Special Operations Executive in France, 1940–1944* (London: HMSO, 1968; rev. edn, 2004).

17 Raul Hilberg, *The Destruction of the European Jews* (Chicago: Quadrangle, and London: W. H. Allen, 1961).

18 *European Resistance Movements, 1939–1945: First International Conference on the History of the Resistance Movements, Held at Liège-Bruxelles-Breendonk, 14–17 September 1958* (Oxford and New York: Pergamon Press, 1960); *European Resistance Movements, 1939–1945: Proceedings of the Second International Conference on the History of the Resistance Movements, Held at Milan 26–29 March 1961* (Oxford and New York: Pergamon Press, 1964).

19 Lucien Steinberg, *La révolte des justes: les juifs contre Hitler* (Paris: Fayard, 1968), trans. as *Not as a Lamb: The Jews against Hitler* (Farnborough: Saxon House, 1970); Yuri Suhl, *They Fought Back: The Story of Jewish Resistance in Nazi Europe* (London: London: MacGibbon & Kee, 1968).

20 *Jewish Resistance During the Holocaust, Proceedings of the Conference on Manifestations of Jewish Resistance, Jerusalem, 7–11 April 1968* (Jerusalem: Yad Vashem, 1971), 15–16.

21 Florimond Bonte, *Les antifascistes allemands dans la Résistance française* (Paris: Éditions Sociales, 1969); G. Vasilichi (ed.), *Les Roumains dans la Résistance française au cours de la Seconde Guerre mondiale* (Bucharest: Meridiane, 1971); F. W. D. Deakin, *Embattled Mountain* (London and New York, Oxford University Press, 1971).

22 Jacques Delperrie de Bayac, *Les Brigades internationales* (Paris: Fayard, 1968), 78–83; Verle B. Johnston, *Legions of Babel: The International Brigades in the Spanish Civil War* (University Park and London: Pennsylvania State University Press, 1967).

23 Henri Michel, *La guerre de l'ombre: la Résistance en Europe* (Paris: Grasset, 1970); trans. as *The Shadow War: Resistance in Europe, 1939–1945* (London: Deutsch, 1972).

24 *Resistance in Europe, 1939–1945: An Introduction* (Salford: University of Salford, 1973).

25 Jørgen Haestrup, *Europe Ablaze: An Analysis of the History of the European Resistance Movements, 1939–1945* (Odense: Odense University Press, 1978); Werner Rings, *Leben mit dem Feind: Anpassung und Widerstand in Hitlers Europa, 1939–1945* (Munich: Kindler, 1979), trans. as *Life with the Enemy. Collaboration and Resistance in Europe, 1939–1945* (London: Weidenfeld and Nicolson, 1982).

26 See for example Kirk Ford, *OSS and the Yugoslav Resistance, 1943–1945* (College Station, TX: Texas A&M University Press, 1992), and Heather Williams, *Parachutes, Patriots and Partisans: The Special Operations Executive and Yugoslavia, 1941–1945* (London: Hurst & Co., 2003).

27 Mart Laar, *War in the Woods: Estonia's Struggle for Survival, 1944–1956* (Washington, DC: Compass Press, 1992); Arvydas Arušaujas, *Anti-Soviet Resistance in the Baltic States* (Vilnius: Du Ka, 1999); Marek Ney-Krwawicz, *The Polish Home Army, 1939–1945* (London: PMST, 2001); Marek Jan Chodakiewicz, *Between Nazis and Soviets: Occupation Politics in Poland, 1937–1947* (Lanham, MD: Lexington Books, 2004).

28 Michael Alfred Peszke, *Battle for Warsaw, 1939–1944* (Boulder, CO: East European Monographs, 1995); Ney-Krwawicz, *The Polish Home Army*; Norman Davies, *Rising '44: The Battle for Warsaw* (London: Macmillan, 2003); Peter D. Stachura (ed.), *The Warsaw Uprising, 1944* (Stirling: Centre for Research in Polish History, 2007); Alexander Richie, *Warsaw 1944: The Fateful Uprising* (London: HarperCollins, 2013).

29 Claudio Pavone, *Une guerra civile: saggio storico sulla moralità nella resistenza* (Turin: Bollati Boringhieri, 1991), trans. as *A Civil War: A History of the Italian Resistance* (London and New York: Verso, 2013).

30 Tony Judt (ed.), *Resistance and Revolution in Mediterranean Europe 1939–1948* (London: Routledge, 1989); Jean-Marie Guillon and Robert Mencherini (eds), *La Résistance et les Européens du Sud: actes du colloque tenu à Aix-en-Provence, 20–22 mars* 1997 (Paris: L'Harmattan, 1999); Bob Moore (ed.), *Resistance in Western Europe* (Oxford and New York: Berg, 2000).

31 Rab Bennett, *Under the Shadow of the Swastika: The Moral Dilemmas of Resistance and Occupation in Hitler's Europe* (Basingstoke: Macmillan, 1999); Tim Kirk and Anthony McElligott (eds), *Opposing Fascism: Community, Authority and Resistance in Europe* (Cambridge: Cambridge University Press, 1999).

32 Stéphane Courtois, Denis Peschanski and Adam Rayski, *Le sang de l'étranger: les immigrés de la MOI dans la Résistance* (Paris: Fayard, 1989); Karel Bartosek, René Gallissot and Denis Peschanski (eds), *De l'exil à la Résistance: réfugiés et immigrés d'Europe centrale en France, 1933–1945* (Paris: Presses Universitaires de Vincennes, 1989); Philippe Joutard and François Marcot

(eds), *Les étrangers dans la Résistance en France* (Besançon: Université de Franche-Comté, 1992); Denis Peschanski, 'La Résistance immigrée', in Jean-Marie Guillon and Pierre Laborie (eds), *Mémoire et histoire: la Résistance* (Toulouse: Privat, 1995).

33 Mark Wyman, *DPs: Europe's Displaced Persons, 1945–1951* (Ithaca and London: Cornell University Press, 1989, 1998); Richard Bessel (ed.), *Life after Death: Approaches to a Cultural and Social History of Europe during the 1940s–1950s* (Cambridge: Cambridge University Press, 2003); Bob Moore, *Prisoners of War, Prisoners of Peace: Captivity, Homecoming and Memory in World War II* (Oxford and New York: Berg, 2005); Frank Biess, *Homecomings: Returning POWs and the Legacy of Defeat in Postwar Germany* (Princeton and Oxford: Princeton University Press, 2006).

34 Margaret Keck and Kathryn Sikkink, *Activists beyond Borders: Advocacy Networks in International Politics* (Ithaca, NY: Cornell University Press, 1998); Sidney Tarrow, *The New Transnational Activism* (Cambridge and New York: Cambridge University Press, 2005).

35 Josie McLellan, *Antifascism and Memory in East Germany: Remembering the International Brigades, 1945–1989* (Oxford: Clarendon Press, 2004).

36 Philippe Lejeune, *On Autobiography* (Minneapolis, MN: University of Minnesota Press, 1989); Daniel Bertaux, *Le récit de vie* (Paris: Nathan, 1997; 2nd edn, Armand Colin, 2006).

37 Zdenka Novak, *When Heaven's Vault Cracked: Zagreb Memories* (Brauton, Devon: Merlin Books, 1995); Gerhard Léo, *Un Allemand dans la Résistance: le train pour Toulouse* (Paris: Éditions Tirésias, 1997); Damira Titonel Asperti, *Écrire pour les autres: mémoires d'une résistante: les antifascistes italiens en Lot-et-Garonne sous l'occupation* (Bordeaux: Presses Universitaires de Bordeaux, 1999); Jolande Withuis, *Weest mannelijk, zijt sterk: Pim Boellaard (1903–2001), het leven van een verzetsheld* (Amsterdam: De Bezige Bij, 2008); Imre Rochlitz, *Accident of Fate: A Personal Account, 1938–1945* (Waterloo, Ont.: Wilfrid Laurier University Press, 2011).

38 Rémi Skoutelsky, *L'espoir guidait leurs pas: les volontaires français dans les Brigades internationales, 1936–1939* (Paris: Grasset, 1999); Antonio Arévalo, *La guerra en singular: testimonios de combatientes españoles en la liberación de Francia, 1939–1945* (Madrid: Ediciones El Cruce, 2004); Paul Arrighi, *Silvio Trentin: un Européen en résistance, 1919–1943* (Poret-sur-Garonne: Loubatières, 2007); Andrea Martocchia, *I partigiani jugoslavi nella Resistenza italiana* (Rome: Odradek, 2011); Enrico Acciai, *Antifascismo, volontariato e guerra civile in Spagna: le sezione italiana della Colona Ascaso* (Milan: Unicopli, 2016) Gerben Zaagsma, *Jewish Volunteers, the International Brigades and the Spanish Civil War* (London and New York: Bloomsbury Academic, 2017).

39 García, Yusta, Tabet and Clímaco (eds), *Rethinking Antifascism.*

40 Jochen Böhler and Robert Gerwarth, *The Waffen-SS: A European History* (Oxford: Oxford University Press, 2017); Arnd Bauerkämper and Grzegorz Rossolinski, *Fascism without Borders: Transnational Connections and*

Cooperation between Movements and Regimes in Europe from 1918 to 1945 (New York: Berghahn Books, 2017).

41 Philip Cooke and Ben H. Shepherd (eds), *European Resistance in the Second World War* (Barnsley: Pen & Sword Military, 2013).

42 Gildea, *Fighters in the Shadows*, 205–39, 360–72, 385–91, 401–2, 410–16, 426–32, 437–8, 458–64, 471–9.

43 Olivier Wieviorka, *The Resistance in Western Europe, 1940–1945* (New York: Columbia University Press, 2019).

1 'For your freedom and ours!': transnational experiences in the Spanish Civil War, 1936–39

1 Gabriel Colomé, *La Olimpiada Popular de 1936: deporte y política* (Barcelona: Institut de Ciències Polítiques i Socials, 2008), 14–19.

2 For an up-to-date overview of the background of the uprising, see Francisco J. Romero Salvadó, *The Spanish Civil War: Origins, Course and Outcomes* (Basingstoke and New York: Palgrave Macmillan, 2008), 1–59.

3 Antony Beevor, *The Battle for Spain: The Spanish Civil War, 1936–1939* (London: Phoenix, 2007), 55–80, 106–7; Paul Preston, *The Spanish Civil War: Reaction, Revolution and Revenge* (London: William Collins, 2016), 66–103; Michael Alpert, *The Republican Army in the Spanish Civil War, 1936–1939* (New York: Cambridge University Press, 2013), 17–44, 56–9.

4 Michael Jabara Carley, 'Caught in a Cleft Stick: Soviet Diplomacy and the Spanish Civil War', in Gaynor Johnson (ed.), *The International Context of the Spanish Civil War* (Cambridge: Cambridge Scholars Publishing, 2009), 159–61; Stanley G. Payne, *The Spanish Civil War, the Soviet Union, and Communism* (New Haven, CT: Yale University Press, 2004), 124–44. For Operation X, see Yuri Rybalkin, *Stalin y España: la ayuda militar soviética a la República* (Madrid: Marcial Pons, 2008); Frank Schauff, *Der verspielte Sieg: Sowjetunion, Kommunistische Internationale und Spanischer Bürgerkrieg 1936–1939* (Frankfurt am Main and New York: Campus Verlag, 2005).

5 Rémi Skoutelsky, *L'espoir guidait leurs pas: les volontaires français dans les Brigades internationales, 1936–1939* (Paris: Grasset, 1999), 44–62, 119–34; Michel Lefebvre-Peña and Rémi Skoutelsky, *Les Brigades internationales: images retrouvées. catalogue de l'exposition 'No pasaran, images des Brigades internationales dans la guerre d'Espagne'* (Paris: Seuil, 2003), 15–17.

6 Citation from Eric Hobsbawm, *Age of Extremes: The Short Twentieth Century, 1914–1991* (London: Michael Joseph, 1994), 160. For an overview of historiographical debates, see e.g. Ruth MacKay, 'The Good Fight and Good History: The Spanish Civil War', *History Workshop Journal*, 70.1 (2010), 199–206; Richard Baxell, 'Myths of the International Brigades', *Bulletin of Spanish Studies*, 91.1–2 (2014), 11–24; Helen Graham, 'Spain Betrayed? The New Historical McCarthyism', *Science & Society*, 68.3 (2004), 364–9; Tony Judt, 'Rehearsal for Evil', *New Republic*, 225.11 (2001), 29–35; Robert Stradling,

History and Legend: Writing the International Brigades (Cardiff: University of Wales Press, 2002).

7 See, e.g., Pedro Mateo Merino, *Por vuestra libertad y la nuestra. andanzas y reflexiones de un combatiente republicano* (Madrid: Disenso, 1986).

8 Archivio di Stato di Firenze (ASF), Aureliano Santini, Quaderno Nero Completo, pp. 3–20, and Quaderni die Aureoliano Santini alias Silvio Morelli, pp. 22–5. For Santini's missions to Italy and a postwar account of his political reliability, see Russian State Archive of Socio-Political History, Moscow (RGASPI), 545/6/499, report on Morelli Silvio, 23 Aug. 1940.

9 See e.g. ASF, QF Cat. A/8, letter from Santini to Paolina Corsinovi, 24 March 1937.

10 Archives of Yugoslavia, Belgrade (AoY), fond 724, Yugoslav Volunteers in the Spanish Civil War, file VIII, unit I/1, M.F. 115/450 (70–3), Ljubo Ilić, personal file. See also Hervé Lemesle, 'Des Yougoslaves engagés au XXe siècle: itineraires de volontaires yougoslaves en Espagne républicaine' (PhD dissertation, University Paris I, Pantheon-Sorbonne, 2011), 332–3.

11 Latvian National Archives, Riga (LNA), LVA, 2161-1-84, 'Žanis Grīva', 4 Feb. 1967; 'Trīsdesmito gadu ...', 18 Feb. 1953. See also LNA, LVA, 2161-1-49, Žanis Grīva, 'Jānis Beniķis', n.d., and 'Manas dzīves fragmenti', March 1966.

12 National Archives of Romania (NAR), Bucharest, Collection no. 53, file B/276, vol. II, p. 31, statement by David Iancu, 28 June 1950.

13 NAR, Bucharest, Collection no. 60, file 96, pp. 167–8, statement by Galia Sincari, n.d. [1956].

14 Ibid.

15 Clara Thalmann and Paul Thalmann, *Revolution für die Freiheit: Stationen eines politischen Kampfes. Moskau / Madrid / Paris* (Grafenau: Trotzdem Verlag, 1987), 48–90. On her falling-out with mainstream communism, see Albert Uttiger, 'In Gedenken an Clara Thalmann: Die Landkommune Hinter Nizza', *Berner Tagwacht*, 5 Feb. 1987. See also Clara Thalmann and Paul Thalmann, 'Von der Schwierigkeit, nach Spanien zu Reisen', in Erich Hackl and Cristina Timón Solinís (eds), *Geschichten aus der Geschichte des Spanischen Bürgerkriegs* (Darmstadt: Hermann Luchterhand, 1986), 75–80.

16 Joel Beinen, 'The Palestine Communist Party 1919–1948', *MERIP Reports*, 55 (1977), 3–17.

17 RGASPI, 545/6/646, fols 33–8; Yaacov Falkov, personal collection (by courtesy of Brodkin's niece, Mrs Addie Markuze-Haas), untitled Brodkin autobiography, n.d.

18 Museum of Dutch Literature (Stichting Nederlands Literatuurmuseum en Literatuurarchief), The Hague (MDL), L 00255–1259, folder 'Seksualiteit', autobiographical notes by Jef Last, n.d., 6–7; L 00255–1260, Jef Last, 'Dagboek van een Veroordeelde' [Diary of a condemned man], 49–52.

19 Jef Last, *Mijn vriend André Gide* (Amsterdam: Contact, 1937), 137.

20 He was far from alone in this. See Lisa A. Kirschenbaum, *International Communism and the Spanish Civil War: Solidarity and Suspicion* (New York: Cambridge University Press, 2015), 135.

21 Letters to Gide detail Last's state of mind and his trip to France: C. J. Greshoff (ed.), *André Gide–Jef Last: correspondance, 1934–1950* (Lyons: Presses Universitaires de Lyon, 1985), 4–5, 31.

22 See e.g. Enrico Acciai, *Antifascismo, volontariato e guerra civile in Spagna: le sezione italiana della Colona Ascaso* (Milan: Unicopli, 2016).

23 Skoutelsky, *L'espoir guidait leurs pas*, 61–2.

24 Maria Tagangaeva, '"Socialist in Content, National in Form": The Making of Soviet National Art and the Case of Buryatia', *Nationalities Papers*, 45.3 (2017), 393–409, https://doi.org/10.1080/00905992.2016.1247794. For more on the early organisation of the International Brigades, see Kirschenbaum, *International Communism and the Spanish Civil War*, 85–7.

25 Samuël Kruizinga, 'Struggling to Fit In: The Dutch in a Transnational Army, 1936–1939', *Journal of Modern European History*, 16.2 (2018), 192–4.

26 Skoutelsky, *L'espoir guidait leurs pas*, 61–3; Richard Baxell, *Unlikely Warriors: The British in the Spanish Civil War and the Struggle against Fascism* (London: Aurum, 2012), 118–25. For an eye-witness account, see William Rust, *Britons in Spain: The History of the British Battalion of the XVth International Brigade* (London: Lawrence and Wishart, 1939), 20–2.

27 See the chart on the organisation of the International Brigades on 1 September 1938 in League of Nations Report C34.M.18.1939.IX, 'Retrait d'Espagne des combattants non espagnols: rapport provisoire de la commission militaire internationale chargee de constater le retrait des combattants non espagnols en Espagne', 15 Jan. 1939, League of Nations and United Nations Office Archives, Geneva, R3662/1/17950/35667.

28 Francisco J. Romero Salvadó, *The Spanish Civil War: Origins, Course and Outcomes* (Basingstoke and New York: Palgrave Macmillan, 2008), 1–59, 157–83.

29 See Jacques Delperrie de Bayac, *Les Brigades internationales* (Paris: Fayard, 1968), 78–83; Verle B. Johnston, *Legions of Babel: The International Brigades in the Spanish Civil War* (University Park and London: Pennsylvania State University Press, 1967), 36–7, 83–8.

30 'An Account by M. Fred on Work in Spain', 14 December 1937, in Ronald Radosh, Mary R. Habeck and Grigory Sevostianov (eds), *Spain Betrayed the Soviet Union in the Spanish Civil War* (New Haven, CT: Yale University Press, 2001), 295–368. For an example of 'national' units set up for propagandistic reasons, see Gerben Zaagsma, *Jewish Volunteers, the International Brigades and the Spanish Civil War* (London and New York: Bloomsbury Academic, 2017), 36–57.

31 Kirschenbaum, *International Communism and the Spanish Civil War*, 85, 95–100; Peter N. Carroll, *The Odyssey of the Abraham Lincoln Brigade: Americans in the Spanish Civil War* (Stanford, CA: Stanford University Press, 1994), 57–9. See also 'Walter', 'Notes on the Situation in the International Units in Spain', 14 January 1938, in Radosh, Habeck and Sevostianov (eds), *Spain Betrayed*, 436–60.

32 Citations from Medienwertstatt Freiburg, *Die lange Hoffnung: Erinnerungen*

an ein anderes Spanien mit Clara Thalmann und Augustin Souchy (Grafenau: Trotzdem Verlag, 1985), 38.

33 Thalmann and Thalmann, *Revolution für die Freiheit*, 135–75; Thomas Pampuch and Erich Rathfelder, 'Von der Courage, die Freiheit zu Leben', *Die Tageszeitung*, 30 Jan. 1987. Details on Thalmann's time in Spain can also be found in Schweizerisches Sozial Archiv, Zürich, Organisation für die Sache der Frau Schweiz: Dossier Clara Thalmann 1908–1987. For more on Thalmann's release, see Peter Huber, *Die schweizer Spanienfreiwilligen: biografisches Handbuch* (Zürich: Rotpunktverlag, 2009), 390.

34 Greshoff (ed.), *André Gide–Jef Last*, 32.

35 Jef Last, *Brieven uit Spanje* (Amsterdam: Contact, 1936); Jef Last, *In de loopgraven voor Madrid: 2e serie brieven van het Spaansche Front* (Amsterdam: Contact, 1937); Jef Last, *Over de Hollanders in Spanje* (Amsterdam: Contact, 1937).

36 André Gide, *Retour de l'U.R.S.S., suivi de Retouches à mon retour de l'U.R.S.S.* (Paris: Gallimard, 1937); trans. as *Back from the USSR and Afterthought: A Sequel to Back from the USSR* (London: Martin Secker and Warburg, 1937); Jef Last, *De Spaanse tragedie*, 2nd edn (Amsterdam: Contact, 1962), 101–3, 125, 128–41 (citation on 103).

37 See Kruizinga, 'Struggling to Fit In'.

38 Nico Rost, *Het geval Jef Last: iver Fascisme en Trotzkisme* (Amsterdam: Pegasus, 1938). On Last's mission for the ITWF: Greshoff (ed.), *André Gide–Jef Last*, 51–69.

39 Archivio Fondazione Gramsci, Rome, PFCdI, f. 513.1.1480, radio address by 'Silvio Morelli', Santini's *nom de guerre*, 26 March 1937.

40 ASF, Fondo di Questura Cat. A/8 Santini Aureliano, Aureliano to Paolina Corsinovi, 24 March 1937.

41 Archivio Famiglia Santini, Arezzo, Quaderni di Aureliano Santini alias Silvio Morelli, pp. 29–31; RGASPI, 545/6/499, Morelli Silvio (Santini Aureliano), 23 Aug.1940.

42 Ivan Hariš-Gromovnik, *Diverzant* (Zagreb, 2007), 35, www.slobodnajugoslavija.com/literatura/Diverzant_Ivan_Haris_Gromovnik.pdf (last accessed 1 July 2018).

43 AoY, 724-VIII-I/1, 115/450 (70–3), personal file of Ljubo Ilić; Ljubo Ilić, 'Interbrigadisti u francuskim logorima', in Čedo Kapor (ed.), *Španija 1936–1939: zbornik sećanja jugoslovenskih dobrovoljaca u španskom ratu* (Belgrade: Vojnoizdavački Zavod, 1971), vol. 4, 7–8. See on Yugoslavs during the Spanish Civil War more generally Lemesle, 'Des Yougoslaves engagés au XXe siècle'; Vjeran Pavlaković, *Yugoslav Volunteers in the Spanish Civil War* (Belgrade: Rosa Luxemburg Stiftung Southeast Europe, 2016); Vjeran Pavlaković, *The Battle for Spain is Ours: Croatia and the Spanish Civil War 1936–1939* (Zagreb: Srednja Europa, 2014).

44 For information on the medical services of the International Brigades, see Nicholas Coni, *Medicine and Warfare: Spain, 1936–1939* (New York: Routledge, 2008), 121–140. Some medical services were provided by

Brigadiers with medical experience, while others were sent out by organisations which were not (formally) affiliated with the belligerents, such as the International Committee of the Red Cross and the International Red Aid. See Martin F. Shapiro, 'Medical Aid Provided by American, Canadian and British Nationals to the Spanish Republic during the Civil War, 1936–1939', *International Journal of Health Services*, 13.3 (1983), 443–58.

45 NAR, Bucharest, Collection no. 60, file 96, Galia Burcă, statement, pp. 168–9; 53, file 276, Bucur Clejan, statement, 29 June 1950, vol. 2, p. 33; 60, file 95, p. 72.

46 RGASPI, 545/6/646, fols 33–8; Yaacov Falkov, personal collection, untitled Brodkin autobiography.

47 Helen Graham, *The Spanish Republic at War, 1936–1939* (Cambridge and New York: Cambridge University Press, 2002), 321–2, 383; Beevor, *The Battle for Spain*, 383; Angela Berg, *Die Internationalen Brigaden im spanischen Bürgerkrieg, 1936–1939* (Essen: Klartext, 2005), 47–8.

48 See Nic Ulmi and Peter Huber, *Les combattants suisses en Espagne républicaine (1936–1939)* (Lausanne: Antipodes, 2001), 220–32; Baxell, *Unlikely Warriors*, 397–400. For the situation in the Republican Army generally, see James Matthews, *Reluctant Warriors: Republican Popular Army and Nationalist Army Conscripts in the Spanish Civil War, 1936–1939* (Oxford: Oxford University Press, 2012), 151–4, 188, 218–22.

49 Žanis Grīva, 'Spānija Liesmās', in Rūdolfs Lācis (ed.), *Viva Republica! Vospominanija Učastnikov Antifašistskoj Vojny v Ispanii* (Riga: Latvijskoe Gosudarstvennoe Izd-vo, 1957), 53–61; S Ziemelis, *Latvijas cīnītāji Spānijā, 1936–1939: atminas un dokumenti* (Rīga: Liesma, 1966), 214–16, 242–3, 248–50.

50 NAR, Bucharest, Collection no. 60, file 96, Galia Burcă, statement, pp. 168–9; 53, file 276, Bucur Clejan, statement, 29 June 1950, vol. II, p. 33; B/276, vol. II, p. 14/v; 60, file 95, p. 72.

51 Archivio Famiglia Santini, Quaderni di Aureliano Santini alias Silvio Morelli, pp. 29–31; RGASPI, 545/6/499, Morelli Silvio (Santini Aureliano), 23 Aug. 1940.

52 RGASPI, Ljubo Ilić, personal files, 495–277–630–2. See below, pp. 217–18.

53 See the biographical entry in Petar Kačavenda and Dušan Živković (eds), *Narodni heroji Jugoslavije*, vols 1–2 (Belgrade: Partizanska Knjiga, Narodna Knjiga; Titograd: Pobjeda, 1982), 295–6.

54 ASF, Aureliano Santini, Quaderno Nero Completo, pp. 30–1, and Quaderni di Aureliano Santini alias Silvio Morelli, pp. 34–41; QF Cat. A/8/Santini Aureliano: Mandato di arresto contro Santini Aureliano, Comunista Schedato, 26 Dec. 1942.

55 LNA, LVVA, 2575-6-1724, Folmanis to Latvian legation in Paris, 23 May 1939, p. 19; ibid., Latvian consul Paris to Folmais, 11 Dec. 1939, p. 2.

56 Grīva, 'Spānija Liesmās', 61–5; LNA, LVA, 2161-1-42, Žanis Grīva, 'Manas dzīves fragmenti', March 1966, pp. 8–9.

57 NAR, Bucharest, Collection no. 60, file 95, pp. 72–9. For corroborating

statements given later, see NAR, Collection no. 53, file B276, vol. II, pp. 29–30; Fund Central Committee of the RCP-Central Control Commission (CCP), file B/3309, pp. 7–8. For testimony given by Sincari at the 1956 meeting, see NAR, Bucharest, Collection no. 60, file 96, p. 166.

58 Kirschenbaum, *International Communism and the Spanish Civil War*, 213; George H. Hodos, *Show Trials: Stalinist Purges in Eastern Europe, 1948–1954* (New York: Praeger, 1987).

59 RGASPI, 545/6/646, fols 33–8; Yaacov Falkov, personal collection, untitled Brodkin autobiography.

60 Zaagsma, *Jewish Volunteers*, 125–6, 159–64.

61 Jeanne Weiss-Rykart, 'Erinnerungen an Clara Thalmann', *Emanzipation*, 13.3 (1987), 8–9.

62 Els Winand and Axel Wagener, 'Interview mit Clara Thalmann, Teil I: "Dem Unterdrücker ans Genick"', *Schwarzer Faden: Vierteljahreszeitschrift für Lust und Freiheit*, 2 (1985), 24–34; Pampuch and Rathfelder, 'Von der Courage, die Freiheit zu Leben'.

63 MDL, L 00255–1260, Last, 'Dagboek van een Veroordeelde', 77–93 (quotation on p. 80); Greshoff (ed.), *André Gide–Jef Last*, 108–9.

2 The 'Spanish matrix': transnational catalyst of Europe's anti-Nazi resistance

1 Ilya Starinov, *Zapiski diversanta* (Moscow: Al'manakh 'Vympel', 1997), 209.

2 RGASPI, 49512/93, fols 3–4, 'Iz "Eko de Pari" ot 19.IV.1937 g.', 3 May 1937.

3 RGASPI, 545/6/1519, fol. 12, Vasil Vesov, 'Perechen' voprosov kasaiushiisia instr. TsK Roberta', 1 Sept. 1938.

4 RGASPI, 495/12/9, fols 122–48, 'Resolution der Interbrigaden vom 15.11.40 zur Einschätzung der Lage, der Arbeit und der Aufgaben der Interbrigaden in der Zeit der Internierung in den französischen Lagern. (Erhalten am 19.3.41. durch Friedrich Wolf.)'

5 Ibid.

6 Robert Gildea, *Fighters in the Shadows: A New History of the French Resistance* (London: Faber & Faber, 2015), 215; see below, Chapter 3.

7 NAR, Collection no. 60, file 135, pp. 15, 19.

8 Ibid., p. 72.

9 RGASPI, 545/6/1414, fols 3–5, 'Extraits de la biografia écrite le 22/3/38'; 'Tanguy Georges Henri René', n.d.; 'Apreciacion sobre el camarada: Tanguy René', 20 July 1938; 545/6/33, fol. 68, 'Biografias', n.d.

10 RGASPI, 545/6/1414, fol. 12, Partido Comunista de España (PCE), Comisión Central de Cuadros, 'Biografia de militantes. Tanguy Georges Henri René', 22 March 1938.

11 RGASPI, 545/6/1414, fol. 9, Lucien Bigouret to the IB Military Commissariat, 'Apreciacion sobre el camarada: Tanguy Rene', 28 Aug. 1938.

12 Roger Bourderon, *Rol-Tanguy* (Paris: Tallandier, 2004).

13 Phryné Pigenet, *Catalans malgré tout: l'exil catalan en France au XXe siècle.*

Histoire et mémoire (Perpignan: Trabucaire, 2017), 10–103, 122–3, 128 n. 65; Jorge Torres Hernández, 'Los hermanos Miret-i-Musté: los catalanes Conrado y Josep, organizadores de la Résistance en Francia', in Josep Sánchez Cervelló and Sebastià Agudo (eds), *Las Brigadas Internacionales: nuevas perspectivas en la historia de la Guerra Civil y del exilio* (Tarragona: Universitat Rovira i Virgili, Publicacions Universitat Rovira i Virgili, 2015), 349–53.

14 Hernández, 'Los hermanos Miret-i-Musté', 365.

15 RGASPI, 545/6/59, fol. 51, 'Condemnados politicos. Grupo Balcanico', undated document, spring 1939; 545/6/839, fol. 97, untitled short biography of Francics Wolf signed by 'Edo' (Bolesław Molojec), 1 March 1941.

16 RGASPI, 545/6/36, fol. 41; on Wolf's arrival in Spain via Massanet, see 'Entradas de voluntarios del dia 27 Enero 1938.-', 27 Jan. 1938; 545/6/30, fol. 159, Lista alfabetica de los dosarios existentes hecha segun la cartoteca, n.d.; 545/6/31, fol. 142, 'Rumanos', n.d., Feb. 1939.

17 RGASPI, 545/6/839, fol. 97, untitled short biography of Francics Wolf signed by 'Edo' (Bolesław Molojec), 1 March 1941.

18 RGASPI, 545/6/839, fol. 142, 'Rumanos', n.d., Feb. 1939.

19 RGASPI, 545/6/59, fol. 51, list of the Balkan prisoners at Argelès-sur-Mer, including Wolf's name, 'Condemnados politicos. Grupo Balcanico', n.d., spring 1939; David Diamant, *Combattants, héros et martyrs de la Résistance: biographies, dernières lettres, témoignages et documents* (Paris: Éditions Nouveau, 1984), 172–4; 'Francisc Wolf-Boczor in lagărul de concentrare din Gurs – Franța. 1940', Institutul de Studii Istorice și Social-Politice de pe Linga C.C. al P.C.R., Fototeca, Numarul de Clișeu 21515, in Biblioteca Digitala de Castilla-La Mancha, Fondo Fotográfico de las Brigadas Internacionales, 'Francisc Wolf Boczor', ES.2003AHP.

20 Henri Rol-Tanguy and Roger Bourderon (eds), *Libération de Paris: les cent documents* (Paris: Hachette, 1994), 44.

21 Geneviève Dreyfus-Armand, 'Celestino Alfonso', in *La Résistance en Île-de-France*, DVD-ROM, AERI, 2004.

22 Scott Soo, *The Routes to Exile: France and the Spanish Civil War Refugees, 1939–2009* (Manchester: Manchester University Press, 2017), 2.

23 Sebastian Agudo, 'Los republicanos españoles en la resistencia francesa de la zona Sur: siguiendo el ejemplo de las Brigadas Internacionales', in Sánchez Cervelló and Agudo (eds), *Las Brigadas Internacionales*, 257.

24 Sixto Agudo, 'Yo fui testigo ...', in Irene Abad et al., *Historias de maquis en el Pirineo aragonés* (Jaca: Pirineum Editorial, 1999), 115–17.

25 'Testimonio de Vicente López Tovar, coronel de guerrilleros', in Biblioteca Virtual Miguel de Cervantes, www.cervantesvirtual.com/obra-visor/espanoles-en-la-liberacion-de-francia-19391945--0/html/ffdeef08-82b1-11df-acc7-002185ce6064_8.html (last accessed 15 Sept. 2019).

26 Gildea, *Fighters in the Shadows*, 226.

27 'Historique de l'état-major des guerrilleros espagnols en france', typed report, n.d., in personal archive of Luis Fernández, in Agudo, 'Yo fui testigo...', 117.

28 Jan Ciechanowski, *The Warsaw Rising of 1944* (Cambridge: Cambridge University Press, 1974).

29 Gérard Noiriel, *Le creuset français: histoire de l'immigration, XIXe–XX siècles* (Paris: Seuil, 1988), 'Annexe statistique'; Janine Ponty, *Polonais méconnus: histoire des travailleurs immigrés en France dans l'entre-deux-guerres* (Paris, Publications de la Sorbonne, 2005), 7–76; Anna Nowakowska-Wierzchoś, 'Życie codzienne polskich emigrantek w okupowannej Francji 1940–1944', in Piotr Chruścielski and Marcin Owsiński (eds), *Konferencja 'Od Westerplatte do Norymbergi: II woja światowa we współczesnej historiografii, muzealnictwie i edukacji'* (Sztutowo: Muzeum Stutthof, 2010); 'Francja: Polonia i Polacy', in Barbara Szydłowska-Ceglowa (ed.), *Polonia w Europie: Praza zbiorowa* (Poznań: Ośr. Inform. Nauk. PAN, 1992), 365–410, at 378.

30 Jacek Pietrzak, 'Polscy uczestnicy hiszpańskiej wojny domowej', *Acta Universitatis Lodziensis*, Folia Historica, 97 (2016), 65–86.

31 Kazimierz Sobczak (ed.), *Encyklopedia II wojny światowej* (Warsaw: Wydawnictwo Ministerstwa Obrony Narodowej, 1975), 443; Józef Urbanowicz (ed.), *Mała encyklopedia wojskowa*, vol. 2 (Warsaw: Wydawnictwo Ministerstwa Obrony Narodowej, 1971), 658.

32 RGASPI, 545/6/771, fols 75–80, 'Information Sobre el Cuadro', XIII Brigada International, 'RUTKOWSKI Szymon, Capitan Jefe de la Intendencia', Barcelona, 1 July 1938; fol. 86, '2.843. RUTKOWSKI Jan (Polonais) (Simon)', attestation file signed by 'Edo', 31 July 1940.

33 RGASPI, 545/6/771, fols 75–94, 'Information Sobre el Cuadro', XIII Brigada International, 'RUTKOWSKI Szymon, Capitan Jefe de la Intendencia', Barcelona, 1 July 1938; 'Averiguaciones sobre les Cuadros', Comisariado de Guerra de las Brigadas Internationales, 23 Aug. 1938; 'RUTKOWSKI Jan (Polonais) (Simon)', attestation file signed by 'Edo', 31 July 1940; 'Rutkovskii Ian Antonovich', 29 March 1941; 'Upoważnienie', authorisation letter signed by Daniel Abramowicz, 7 September 1937; 'Spravka', strictly secret note signed by Belov and Kasman, 20 March 1943.

34 Jan Rutkowski, *Czas walki, klęsk i zwycięstwa: wspomnienia dąbrowszczaka: 1936–1945* (Warsaw: Zakład Narodowy im. Ossolińskich, 1980), 362.

35 Piotr Gontarczyk, *Polska Partia Robotnicza: droga do władzy 1941–1944* (Warsaw: Fronda, 2003), 31–3; Mikołaj Iwanow, 'Bolesław Mołojec – zaufany człowiek Stalina?', lecture given during the International Science Conference in Gdańsk, 'Dąbrowszczacy w trzech odsłonach: Wojna Domowa, II Wojna Światowa, PRL', Muzeum II Wojny Światowej, 27 June 2018; Vladimir Piatnitskii, *Zagovor protiv Stalina* (Moscow: Sovremennik, 1998), 341–2.

36 RGASPI, 545/6/33, fol. 69, 'Biografias', n.d.

37 RGASPI, 545/3/781, fols 81–2. See for example El Comisario del Acantonamiento, 'Parte Diario – Del Acantonamiento de la 13. B.I.', 8 Dec. 1938.

38 Ibid., fol. 97, Dowodca Obozu Molojec, Komisarz Obozu Szyr, 'Rozkaz nadzwyczajny na dzien 12 grudnia 1938 roku', Oboz Miedzynarodowy XIII Brygady, Sztab, n.d.

39 Ibid., fols 87–9, Centro de desmobilizacion de las B. I. Brigada 'Dombrowski', Estado Mayor, 'Orden del dia de la Brigada para el dia 10 de Diciembre 1938'; 'Instructiones para el oficial de servicio del batallon', 10 December 1938.

40 Ibid., fol. 110, El Jefe del Centro 'Edward', El Comisario Politico del Centro Szyr, 'Orden solemne para el dia 15 de Diciembre de 1938', Centro de desmovilizacion de las B. I. Brigada 'Dombrowski', Acantonamienro no. 6, Estado Mayor, 15 Dec. 1938.

41 Mikołaj Iwanow, 'Bolesław Mołojec – zaufany człowiek Stalina?'

42 Gontarczyk, *Polska Partia Robotnicza*, 47–52, 82, 91–9; Iwanow, 'Bolesław Mołojec – zaufany człowiek Stalina?'

43 RGASPI, 545/3/781, fol. 10, Centro de desmobilizacion de la XIII Brigada. Al Comisario Inspector de las B.I., 'En contestacion a la carta del 2. De Noviembre remito a Vd. la lista de los estudiantes existentes en el batallon', n.d., Nov. 1938.

44 Gontarczyk, *Polska Partia Robotnicza*, 169–70; Kazimierz Sobczak, Eugeniusz Kozłowski and Lech Wyszczelski, *Hiszpańska wojna narodoworewolucyjna 1936–1939* (Warsaw: WPH, 1986), 56–7.

45 Gontarczyk, *Polska Partia Robotnicza*, 168; Iwanow, 'Bolesław Mołojec – zaufany człowiek Stalina?'

46 Franciszek Księżarczyk, *Droga w ogniu* (Warsaw: Wydawnictwo Ministerstwa Obrony Narodowei, 1965), 176–9.

47 RGASPI, 545/6/663, fol. 83, 'Edo', '1.512. KILANOWICZ Stefan (Polonais)', 17 June 1940; 545/6/714, fols 104–6, Komisariat Wojenny Brygad Miedzynarodowych, Barcelona, 'Kilanowicz Stefan Jan', n.d.

48 Gontarczyk, *Polska Partia Robotnicza*, 190.

49 Władysław Góra, 'Sotrudnichestvo pol'skikh I sovetskikh partisan na pol'skikh zemliakh v gody Vtoroi Mirovoi voiny', in Iurii Novopashin (ed.), *Sovetskie voennoplennye i dvizhenie soprotivleniia na pol'skikh zemliakh v gody Vtoroi Mirovoi voiny (sbornik statei)* (Moscow: AN SSSR, Institut Slavianovedeniia i Balkanistiki, 1991), 146–7.

50 Gontarczyk, *Polska Partia Robotnicza*, 178–82; Piotr Gontarczyk, 'Z genealogii elit PZPR: przypadek Stefana Kilianowicza vel Grzegorza Korczyńskiego', *Glaukopis*, 1 (2003), 214–29; Stanisław Okęcki (ed.), *Polish Resistance Movement in Poland and Abroad 1941–1945* (Warsaw: PWN, 1988), 146–9; Andrzej Werblan, *Władysław Gomułka: pamiętniki*, vol. 2 (Warsaw: BGW, 1994), 134.

51 Gontarczyk, *Polska Partia Robotnicza*, 44; Ryszard Nazarewicz, *Armii Ludowej dylematy i dramaty* (Warsaw: Oficyna Drukarska, 1998), 14–20, 35.

52 Pietrzak, 'Polscy uczestnicy hiszpańskiej wojny domowej', 65–86.

53 Jorge Marco, 'Transnational Soldiers and Guerrilla Warfare from the Spanish Civil War to the Second World War', *War in History*, 20 Sept.2018, https://doi.org/10.1177/0968344518761212.

54 Ilya Starinov, *Miny zamedlennogo deistviia: razmyshleniia partizana-diversanta* (Moscow: Al'manakh 'Vympel', 1999), 24.

55 RGASPI, 545/6/33, fol. 70, 'Biografias. Torunczyk Henryk', n.d.; 545/6/793, fols 87–117, Informacion Sobre El Cuadro, XIII Brigada Internacional, 'Torunczyk Henryk. Capitan Jefe de Estado Mayor', Barcelona, 1 July 1938; Bartłomiej Różycki, 'Dąbrowszczacy i pamięć o hiszpańskiej wojnie domowej w Polsce Ludowej', *Pamięć i Sprawiedliwość*, 1.21 (2013), 199–200.

56 Michael Alpert, *The Republican Army in the Spanish Civil War, 1936–1939* (Cambridge: Cambridge University Press, 2007), 265–7; Francisco Javier López-Brea Espiau and José Ramón Soler Fuensanta, *Soldados sin rostro: los servicios de información, espionaje y criptografía en la guerra civil española* (Barcelona: Inédita Ediciones, 2008), 83–7; Barton Whaley, *Guerrillas in the Spanish Civil War* (Cambridge, MA: Center for International Studies, Massachusetts Institute of Technology, 1969), 61.

57 Daniel Arasa, *Los españoles de Stalin* (Barcelona: Belacqua, 2005), 108–15, 127–8, 162–4; Anna K. Starinov, *Behind Fascist Lines: A Firsthand Account of Guerrilla Warfare during the Spanish Revolution* (New York: Ballantyne Press, 2001), 273–6.

58 Archivo Histórico del Partido Comunista de España, Madrid (AHPCE), Emigracion política, Caja 100/2, Domingo Ungría to Dolores Ibárruri, 30 March 1942.

59 Arasa, *Los españoles de Stalin*, 302–3.

60 Ferran Sánchez i Agustí, *Maquis a Catalunya: de la invasió de la Vall d'Aran a la mort de Caracremada* (Lleida: Pagès Editors, 1999), 153, 158–9; Mario Martín Gijón, *La Resistencia franco-española (1936–1950): una historia compartida* (Badajoz: Diputación de Badajoz, Área de Cultura, 2014), 427; Hartmut Heine, *La oposición política al franquismo: de 1939 a 1952* (Grijalbo: Crítica, 1983), 213–16; Bartosz Kaczorowski, *Franco i Stalin: związek Sowiecki w polityce Hiszpanii w okresie drugiej wojny światowej* (Łódź and Cracow: Wydawnictwo Uniwersytetu Łódźkiego, 2016), 245–9, 262–3; Esther Rodríguez, *Els Maquis* (Barcelona: Cossetània Edicions, 2005), 70; Geoffrey Swain, 'Stalin and Spain, 1944–1948', in David J. Dunthorn and Christian Leitz (eds), *Spain in an International Context* (New York: Berghahn Books, 1999), 245–7.

61 AHPCE, Emigracion política, Caja 99/2.1, list of comrades N'X.

62 AHPCE, Equipo de Pasos, Informes sobre Camaradas, jacquet 639. Informe de 'Manso' sobre Ricardo en la AGL; Salvador J. Cava, *Los guerrilleros de Levante y Aragón*, vol. 2: *El cambio de estrategia* (Cuenca: Tomebamba, 2007), 659; Fernando Hernández Sanchez, *Los años de plomo: la reconstrucción del PCE bajo el primer franquismo (1939–1953)* (Barcelona: Editorial Crítica, 2015), 191–7; Mercedes Yusta, *Guerrilla y resistencia campesina: la resistencia armada contra el franquismo en Aragón* (Saragossa: Prensas Universitarias de Zaragoza, 2003), 178–81, 183, 186, 202.

63 Ilya Starinov, *Soldat stoletiia* (Moscow: Geroi Otechestva, 2002), http://lib.ru/MEMUARY/STARINOW/soldat.txt (last accessed 4 June 2018).

3 Camps as crucibles of transnational resistance

1 Musée de la Résistance Nationale, Champigny-sur-Marne, Fonds Ouzoulias, carton 2, dossier 2, Résistance allemande, Dahlem, handwritten memoirs [1974], 5. See also Sibille Hinze, *Antifaschisten im Camp Le Vernet* (Berlin: Militärverlag des Deutschen Demokratischen Republik, 1988), 30–2, 44.

2 Eugen Kogon, *The Theory and Practice of Hell: The German Concentration Camps and the System behind Them* (New York: Farrar, Strauss and Giroux, 2006), 253–7.

3 Geoffrey Megargee (ed.), *Encyclopedia of Camps and Ghettos 1933–1945*,vol. 1: *Early Camps, Youth Camps and Concentration Camps and Subcamps under the SS-Business Administration Main Office*; vol. 2: *Ghettos in German-Occupied Eastern Europe*; vol. 3: *Camps and Ghettos under European Regimes Aligned with Nazi Germany* ((Bloomington and Indianapolis: Indiana University Press in association with the United States Holocaust Memorial Museum, 2009, 2012, 2018). See also *Verzeichnis der Haftstätten unter dem Reichsführer-SS (1933–1945: Konzentrationslager u. deren Aussenkommandos sowie andere Haftstätten unter d. Reichsführer-SS in Deutschland und deutsch besetzten Gebieten*, vol. 1 (Bad Arolsen: Internationaler Suchdienst, 1979).

4 Camilla Poesio, *Il confino fascista: l'arma silenziosa del regime* (Rome and Bari: Laterza, 2011).

5 Carlo Spartaco Capogreco, *I campi del duce: l'internamento civile nell'Italia fascista (1940–1943)* (Turin: Einaudi, 2004); Costantino Di Sante, *I campi di concentramento in Italia: dall'internamento alla deportazione (1940–1945)* (Milan: Franco Angeli, 2001).

6 Denis Peschanski, *La France des camps: l'internement, 1938–1946* (Paris: Gallimard, 2002), 39–42; 'Rapport du Docteur Weissmann-Netter', in Comité International de Coordination et d'Information pour l'Aide à l'Espagne Republicane (ed.), *Deux missions internationales visitent les camps de réfugiés espagnols* (Paris: Comité International de Coordination et d'Information pour l'Aide à l'Espagne Republicane, 1939), 20; Juan Bautista Vilar, 'El exilio español de 1939 en el Norte de África', *Historia del presente*, 12 (2008), 19, 21; Lucio Santiago, Rafael Barrera and Gerónimo Lloris, *Internamiento y resistencia de los republicanos españoles en África del Norte durante la Segunda Guerra mundial* (San Cugat del Vallés: Imprenta El Pot, 1981), 17.

7 Archivo del Comité Central del Partido Comunista de España, Madrid (ACCPCE), Caja 44, Carpeta 19, 'Datos de Ramón Via Fernández', 1944; 'Ramón Via. Síntesis biográfica'; Juan Martínez Leal, 'El Stanbrook: un barco mítico en la memoria de los exiliados españoles', *Pasado y memoria*, 4 (2005), 65–81.

8 Jules Dumont, 'Rapport de la délégation envoyée en Algérie pour visiter les camps de réfugiés espagnols', in Comité International de Coordination et d'Information pour l'Aide à l'Espagne Republicane (ed.), *Deux missions internationales visitent les camps de réfugiés espagnols*, 16; Santiago, Barrera and Lloris, *Internamiento y resistencia*, 31–3.

9 ACCPCE, 'Algunos datos sobre la actividad de Ramón Via', 1945, Informes Camaradas, Jacq 1944–1945.
10 Carlos Jiménez Margalejo, *Los que teníamos dieciocho años* (Madrid, Incipit Editores, 2000), 103; Cipriano Mera, *Guerra, exilio y cárcel de un anarco-sindicalista* (Madrid: La Malatesta Editorial, 2011), 337.
11 ACCPCE, 'Algunos datos sobre la actividad de Ramón Via', 1945; Santiago, Barrera and Lloris, *Internamiento y resistencia*, 31–2; Margalejo, *Los que teníamos dieciocho años*, p. 123.
12 Santiago, Barrera and Lloris, *Internamiento y resistencia*, 31–2.
13 Jiménez Margalejo, *Los que teníamos dieciocho años*, 105–9; Mera, *Guerra, exilio y cárcel*, 337–8.
14 ACCPCE, Caja 44, Carpeta 19, 'Algunos datos sobre Ramón Via', 1944; Santiago, Barrera and Lloris, *Internamiento y resistencia*, 113; testimony of Santiago Lucio and Lisette Vincent in J. Làszlo Nagy, 'Les activités communistes en Algérie sous le régime de Vichy', *Cahiers d'histoire de l'Institut de Recherches Marxistes*, 11 (1982), 99; Jean-Luc Einaudi, *Un rêve algérien: histoire de Lisette Vincent, une femme d'Algérie* (Paris: Presses Universitaires de France, 2001), 190–3.
15 ACCPCE, 'Algunos datos sobre la actividad de Ramón Via', 1945; Allison Drew, *We Are No Longer: Communists in Colonial Algeria* (Manchester: Manchester University Press, 2014), 121; Santiago, Barrera and Lloris, *Internamiento y resistencia*, 121–2; Charles-Robert Ageron, 'Le Parti Communiste Algérien de 1939 à 1943', *Vingtième siècle: revue d'histoire*, 12 (1986), 43.
16 Jorge Marco, 'Genre, ethnicité, classe: colonialisme et invisibilité des femmes dans la résistance transnationale en Algérie (1939–1942)', in Laurent Douzou and Mercedes Yusta (eds), *La Résistance à l'épreuve du genre: hommes et femmes dans la résistance antifasciste en Europe du Sud* (Rennes: Presses Universitaires de Rennes, 2018), 155–73.
17 RGASPI, 545/6/1405, personal file of Ahmed Smaïli; André Moine, *Deportation et résistance: Afrique du Nord, 1939–1944* (Paris: Éditions Sociales, 1972), 206–27; Emmanuel Sivan, *Communisme et nationalisme en Algérie, 1920–1962* (Paris: Presses de la Fondation Nationale des Sciences Politiques, 1976), 117–19; Drew, *We Are No Longer in France*, 118.
18 Archives Départementales, Haute-Garonne, 16J199, Ljubomir Ilić, 'Interbrigadistes dans les camps français' [1986], 1–8; full text of shorter version published in Karel Bartosek, René Gallissot and Denis Peschanski (eds), *De l'exil à la Résistance: réfugiés et immigrés d'Europe centrale en France, 1933–1945* (Saint-Denis: Presses Universitaires de Vincennes, 1989), 131–42.
19 RGASPI, 545/4/62.
20 Gilbert Badia, *Les barbelés de l'exil* (Grenoble: Presses Universitaire de Grenoble, 1979), 252–5.
21 Archives Départementales, Haute-Garonne, 16J199, Ilić, 'Interbrigadistes dans les camps français', 11.

22 Tamiment Library, New York University, Comintern Archives, Moscow, Fond 545, International Brigades Records, OPIS 4, file 60.

23 Hinze, *Antifaschisten im Camp Le Vernet*; Kelsey William McNiff, 'The French Internment Camp Le Vernet d'Ariège. Local Administration, Collaboration and Public Opinion in Vichy France' (PhD dissertation, Princeton University, 2004).

24 Bundesarchiv, Berlin-Lichterfelde (BArchB), NY 4072/45; Musée de la Résistance Nationale, Fonds Ouzoulias, carton 2, dossier 5, report of commissaire special Bernheim to prefect of Ariège, 18 November 1939; Dahlem to minister of the interior, 20 Aug. 1940.

25 Arthur Koestler, *The Scum of the Earth* (London: Jonathan Cape, 1941), 111; Arthur Koestler, *Dialogue with Death* (London: Penguin, 1942).

26 Archives Départementales (AD), Ariège, 5W282, dossier 4274, Luigi Longo, and dossier 4294, Alessandro Vaia; Alexander Höbel, *Luigi Longo: una vita partigiana, 1900–1945* (Rome, Carocci, 2013), 236–81.

27 Interview with Cristobal Robles, Elnes (Pyrénées Orientales), 1998, in F. Guilheim, *L'obsesion du retour: les républicains espagnols, 1939–1975* (Toulouse: Presses Universitaires de Toulouse Le Mirail, 2005), 140.

28 Archives Départementales, Haute-Garonne, 16J199, Ilić, 'Interbrigadistes dans les camps français', 16.

29 Bundesarchiv, Berlin-Lichterfeld, NY 4072/245, 'Lebensbeschreibung von Käthe Dahlem', 1–10.

30 Dora Schaul, *Résistance: Erinnerungen deutscher Antifascisten* (Berlin: Dietz Verlag, 1973), 27–9. On the MOI see above, pp. 35, 37.

31 AD, Ariège, 5W367, commandant du camp to prefect, 19 Aug. 1940.

32 AD, Ariège, 5W374, chef de camp to prefect, 24 Feb. 1941; prefect to minister of the interior Admiral Darlan, 25 Feb. 1941; Captain Boutonnet to minister of war, 28 Feb. 1941.

33 AD, Ariège, 5W397, prefect to Darlan, 18 April 1941.

34 Ibid.; AD, Ariège, 5W375, prefect to regional prefect, 29 Aug. 1941.

35 AD, Ariège, 5W373, report of Commissaire Special Ludman, Camp du Vernet, 20 July 1941.

36 Höbel, *Luigi Longo*, 290.

37 Tamiment Library, New York University, Comintern Archives, Moscow, Fond 545, International Brigades Records, OPIS 4, file 1-3, 232–3, letter of Semion Kramskoi from Camp de Bossuet, Algeria, 14 April 1941.

38 NAR, Central Committee of the RCP-Central Control Commission, file A/49, p. 6.

39 See above, pp. 36–7.

40 Jorge Marco, *Guerrilleros and Neighbours in Arms: Identities and Cultures of Anti-Fascist Resistance in Spain* (Brighton: Sussex Academic Press, 2016), 3, 49–57; Jorge Marco, 'Transnational Soldiers and Guerrilla Warfare from the Spanish Civil War to the Second World War', *War in History*, 20 September 2018, https://doi.org/10.1177/0968344518761212. See below, pp. 217, 249.

41 AD, Ariège, 5W366, lists of chef du camp, 19 Nov. 1941, 16 Feb. 1942.

42 Jonny Granzow, *16 septembre 1943: l'évasion de la prison de Castres* (Portet-sur-Garonne: Loubatières, 2009), 80–113.
43 Robert Gildea, *Fighters in the Shadows: A New History of the French Resistance* (London: Faber & Faber, 2015), 233–9.
44 Granzow, *16 septembre 1943*, 128–222; Alessandro Vaia, *De Galeotto a generale* (Rome: Teti, 1977), 177–8; Bettina Giersberg, 'Die Arbeit des Schriftstellers Rudolf Leonhard im französischen Exil 1933 bis 1945' (PhD dissertation, University of Potsdam, 2005).
45 Altiero Spinelli, Ernesto Rossi and Eugenio Colorni, *Il manifesto di Ventotene* (Milan: Mondadori, 2006).
46 Franco Giannantoni and Ibio Paolucci, *Giovanni Pesce 'Visone', un comunista che ha fatto l'Italia: l'emigrazione, la guerra di Spagna, Ventotene, i Gap, il dopoguerra* (Varese: Arterige, 2005), 81–9.
47 Ibid.
48 Spinelli, *Come ho tentato di diventare saggio* (Bologna: Il Mulino, 1984), 264–5.
49 Paolo Finzi, *Insuscettibile di ravvedimento: l'anarchico Alfonso Failla (1906–1986). Carte di polizia/scritti/testimonianze* (Ragusa: La Fiaccola, 1993), 246.
50 Ibid., 247.
51 Höbel, *Luigi Longo*.
52 Finzi, *Insuscettibile di ravvedimento*, 324.
53 Alvaro Tacchini, *Guerra e resistenza nell'Alta Valle del Tevere (1943–1944)* (Castello: Petruzzi, 2015), 321.
54 Ivo Barić, *Zbornik radova sa skupa, Kampor – polje sjećanja*, Rab, 2011 (Rab: Grad Rab, Udruga Antifašista Raba and SABA RH, 2012); Franc Potočnik, *Il campo di sterminio fascista: l'isola di Rab* (Turin: Anpi, 1979); Alessandra Kersevan, *Lager italiani: pulizia ethnica e campi di concentramento fascisti per civili jugoslavi 1941–1943* (Rome: Nutrimenti, 2008).
55 Jaša Romano, *Jevreji Jugoslavije 1941–1945: žrtve genocida i učesnici narodnooslobodilačkog rata* [Jews of Yugoslavia 1941–1945: victims of genocide and participants in the war of people's liberation] (Belgrade: Jevrejski Istorijski Muzej, Saveza Jevrejskih Opština Jugoslavije, 1980), 383.
56 Fredi Kramer, 'Viktor Hajon: Zvijezda nepobjedivog "Juga"' [Viktor Hajon:star of the invincible 'south'], *Ha-Kol*, 118 (2011), 44.
57 Imre Rochlitz, *Accident of Fate: A Personal Account 1938–1945* (Waterloo, Ont.: Wilfrid Laurier University Press, 2011), 116.
58 Ibid., 117.
59 The transcript of the interview with Elvira Kohn for the Centropa database of Jewish memory is available at www.centropa.org/biography/elvira-kohn (last accessed 28 Oct. 2019). See also Lucija Benyovsky, 'Fašistički logor kampor na Rabu prema sačuvanim bilješkama Elvire Kohn' [Fascist camp on Rab according to Elvira Kohn's diary], in Ognjen Kraus and Ivo Goldstein (eds), *Antisemitizam, Holokaust, antifašizam* (Zagreb: Židovska Općina, 1996), 214–23.
60 Emil Kerenji, '"Your Salvation is the Struggle against Fascism": Yugoslav

Communists and the Rescue of Jews, 1941–1945', *Contemporary European History*, 25.1 (2016), 57–74; Slavko Goldstein, 'Kakva sreća, otići u smrt uzdignuta čela' [What fortune to die with your head held high], *Jutarnji list*, 8 May 2010. All figures based on Jaša Romano, 'Jevreji u logoru na Rabu i njihovo uključivanje u Narodnooslobodilački rat' [Jews interned on Rab and their joining of the People's Liberation War], *Zbornik Jevrejskog istorijskog muzeja*, 2 (1973), 1–69.

61 For a testimony of those who paid for individual escape to Italy see oral history interview with Dorrit L. Ostberg, The Jeff and Toby Herr Oral History Archive, https://collections.ushmm.org/search/catalog/irn506644 (last accessed 1 Sept. 2019).

62 Romano, 'Jevreji u logoru na Rabu'. The Italian researcher Anna Pizzuti identified 3,331 Jewish refugees on Rab. See 'Gli ebrei internati nel campo di RAB – identificazione e destino', Ebrei stranieri internati in Italia durante il periodo bellico, www.annapizzuti.it/public/dbrab.pdf (last accessed 1 Sept. 2019).

63 The testimonies of Rab survivors are to be found in the five volumes of Aleksandar Goan (ed.), *Mi smo preživeli: Jevreji o Holokaustu* [We survived: Jews on the Holocaust] (Belgrade: Savez Jevrejskih Opština Srbije, 2001–05), and interviews at the USC Shoah Foundation Institute for Visual History and Education, Los Angeles. See also Rochlitz, *Accident of Fate*, 139–53.

64 Rochlitz, *Accident of Fate*, 127–38.

65 K. M. Mallmann, 'Kreuzritter des antifaschistischen Mysteriums – zur Erfahrungsperspektive des Spanischen Bürgerkrieges', in H. Grebing and C. Wickert (eds), *Das 'andere' Deutschland im Widerstand gegen den Nationalsozialismus: Beiträge zur politischen Überwindung der nationalsozialistischen Diktatur im Exil und im Dritten Reich* (Essen: Klartext Verlag, 1994), 32–55; U. Eumann, 'Nach Francos Sieg: Leidenswege Kölner Spanienkämpfer', *Geschichte im Westen*, 28 (2013), 119–39.

66 B. Distel, 'Widerstand der Verfolgten', in Wolfgang Benz und Walter H. Pehle (eds), *Lexikon des deutschen Widerstandes*, 3rd edn (Frankfurt am Main: Fischer Taschenbuch Verlag, 2008), 120.

67 'Vospominaniia Adama Stena', in Iakov Aizenshtadt (ed.), *V plenu u Gitlera i Stalina: kniga Pamiati Maksa Grigorievicha Mintza* (Jerusalem: Verba Publishers, 1999), 57.

68 'Beseda v Tsk KPSS' in Aizenshtadt (ed.), *V plenu u Gitlera i Stalina*, 125.

69 E. Brodsky, *Vo imia pobedy nad fashizmom* (Moscow: Nauka, 1970), 149–13; Iakov Aizenshtadt, 'Ocherk o zhizni i podvigakh Maksa Mintza', in Aizenshtadt (ed.), *V plenu u Gitlera i Stalina*, 21–4; Max Mintz, 'Pis'mo boevomu drugu', in Aizenshtadt (ed.), *V plenu u Gitlera i Stalina*, 200–4.

70 Alexander Dallin, *German Rule in Russia, 1941–1945* (Basingstoke: Palgrave Macmillan, 1981), 452–3; Robert Gildea, Dirk Luyten and Juliane Fürst, 'To Work or Not to Work?', in Robert Gildea, Olivier Wieviorka and Anette Warring (eds), *Surviving Hitler and Mussolini: Daily Life in Occupied Europe* (Oxford: Berg, 2006), 58–60.

71 'Vospominaniia M. G. Mintza', in Aizenshtadt (ed.), *V plenu u Gitlera i Stalina*, 54–5.

72 J.-L. Bellanger, 'Détenus soviétiques en Résistance', *Le Patriote Résistant*, 922 (Sept. 2017), 14; Brodsky, *Vo imia pobedy*; Rolf Keller and Silke Petry, *Sowjetische Kriegsgefangene im Arbeitseinsatz 1941–1945: Dokumente zu den Lebens- und Arbeitsbedingungen in Norddeutschland. Schriftenreihe der Stiftung niedersächsische Gedenkstätten* (Göttingen: Wallstein Verlag, 2013), 53–7.

73 Aizenshtadt (ed.), *V plenu u Gitlera i Stalina*, 22–5; 'Vospominaniia Adama Shtena', ibid., 57.

74 Brodsky, *Vo imia pobedy*, 149–53.

75 BArchB, R 58/213, Reichssicherheitshauptamt, Amt IV, Meldung wichtiger staatspolizeilicher Ereignisse Nr. 2, 11 Aug. 1944, p. 134; Brodsky, *Oni ne propali bez vesti*, 74; Silke Petry, 'Im Kampf gegen den Faschismus' – organisierter Widerstand sowjetischer Kriegsgefangener in Norddeutschland', in 'Tagung: Widerstand, Verweigerung und Selbstbehauptung 1933–1945', 20 June 2014, www.radio-uebrigens.de/?p=1339 (last accessed 20 June 2014).

76 I. Bauz, S. Brüggemann and R. Maier (eds), *Die deheime Staatspolizei in Württemberg und Hohenzollern* (Stuttgart: Schmetterling Stuttgart, 2013), 366–7; Jürgen Zarusky, 'Brüderliche Zusammenarbeit der Kriegsgefangenen (BSW)', in Benz und Pehle (eds), *Lexikon des deutschen Widerstandes*, 183–4.

77 K. Drobisch, 'Antinazistische Deutsche Volksfront(ADV)', in Benz and Pehle (eds), *Lexikon des deutschen Widerstandes*, 163–4; BArchB, R 58/213, Reichssicherheitshauptamt, Amt IV, Meldung wichtiger staatspolizeilicher Ereignisse Nr. 5, 29 Sept. 1944, pp. 192–3; Hans Schafranek, 'Die "Anti-Hitler Bewegung Österreichs" und die "Anti-Hitler Bewegung der Ostarbeiter" im Widerstand gege das NS-Regime 1942–1944', in Christine Schindler (ed.), *Feindbilder* (Vienna: Dokumentationsarchiv des Österreichischen Widerstandes, 2015), 253–8.

78 Zarusky, 'Brüderliche Zusammenarbeit', 183–4.

79 BArchB, R 58/213, Reichssicherheitshauptamt, Amt IV, Meldung wichtiger staatspolizeilicher Ereignisse Nr. 2, 12 May 1944, p. 43; Nr. 5, 30 June 1944, p. 82.

4 From regular armies to irregular resistance (and back)

1 Vojenský Ústřední Archiv – Vojenský Historický Archiv, Prague (VÚA–VHA), personal materials of Zdeněk Přibyl.

2 Anna Pravdová, *Zastihla je noc: čeští výtvarní umělci ve Francii 1938–1945* (Prague: Národní Galerie, 2009), 24–7.

3 VÚA–VHA, card index of International Brigades members, Zdeněk Přibyl.

4 Musée de la Résistance en Ligne, http://museedelaresistanceenligne.org/personne.php?id=17465 (last accessed 20 June 2018).

5 See below, pp. 216–17.

6 VÚA–VHA, applications for resistance fighter status under Act no. 255/1946, no. 17120/56, Zdeněk Přibyl; Pravdová, *Zastihla je noc*, 128.

7 Regina M. Delacor, 'From Potential Friends to Potential Enemies: The Internment of Hostile Foreigners in France at the Beginning of the Second World War', *Journal of Contemporary History*, 35.3 (2000), 361–8. See above, pp. 52–5.

8 Service Historique de la Défense, Vincennes (SHD), GR, 7 N 2475–2, 3, Étrangers volontaires pour s'engager dans l'armèe française. The issue had been mentioned already in 1947: Alfred Vagst, 'Foreigner as Soldier in the Second World War', *Journal of Politics*, 9.3 (1947), 392–416. On internment camps see above, Chapter 3.

9 André-Paul Comor, *L'épopée de la 13éme Demi-brigade*, (Paris: NEL, 1988), 27.

10 A. D. Printer, 'Spanish Soldiers in France', *Nation*, 155 (1943), 489–90, quoted by Douglas Porch, *The French Foreign Legion: A Complete History of the Legendary Fighting Force* (Toronto: HarperCollins Canada, 1991), 449.

11 Testimony of Enrique Ballester Romero, in Antonio Vilanova Fuentes, *Los olvidados: los exiliados espagñoles en la Segunda Guerra mundial* (Paris: Ruedo Ibérico, 1969), 319.

12 Testimony of Manuel Fernández, in *La Nueve ou les oubliés de la victoire*(-documentary film), dir. Alberto Marquardt, France, Point du Jour, 2009, at 19:10–19:40 minutes.

13 For details, see Diego Gaspar Celaya, '"Premature Resisters": Spanish Contribution to the French National Defence Campaign in 1939/1940', *Journal of Modern European History*, 16.2 (2018), 203–24.

14 Diego Gaspar Celaya, *Republicanos argoneses en la Segunda Guerra mundial: una historia de exilio, trabajo y lucha, 1939/1945* (Saragossa: Rolde de Estudios Aragoneses, 2010), 115–22; Diego Gaspar Celaya, *La guerra continúa: voluntarios españoles al servicio de la Francia libre (1940–1945)* (Madrid: Marcial Pons, 2015), 145–54; Vincent Parello, 'Les compagnies de travailleurs étrangers (CTE) en France à la fin de la Troisième République', *Bulletin Hispanique*, 118.1 (2016), 233–50.

15 See '11ème Regiment Étranger d'Infanterie', Nederlanders in het Franse Vreemdelingenlegioen, www.kwaak99.demon.nl/11%20REI.htm (last accessed 20 June 2018).

16 See Union des Engagés Volontaires, Anciens Combattants Juifs leurs Enfants et Amis, www.combattantvolontairejuif.org (last accessed 20 June 2018); François Szulman, 'Septembre 1939 – septiembre 2009: 70 ans après l'engagement massif des juifs étrangers dans la Seconde Guerre mondiale', *Notre volonté (UEVACJEA)*, 36 (2009), 2–5.

17 Zosa Szajkowski, *Jews and the French Foreign Legion* (New York: KATV, 1975), quoted by Douglas Porch, *The French Foreign Legion: A Complete History of the Legendary Fighting Force* (New York: Skyhorse, 2010), 449.

18 Jiří Friedl, '"Španěláci" z tábora Gurs (ke vstupu čs. interbrigadistů do naší armády ve Francii 1939–40)', *Historie a vojenství*, 49.4 (2000), 813.

19 VÚA–VHA, Depot of the Czechoslovak units in Great Britain 1939–1947, box 1, file 1, chronicle of the depot, p. 30, 4 June 1940.
20 VÚA–VHA, applications for resistance fighter status under Act no. 255/1946, no. 3403/65, Alois Samec; RGASPI, 545/6/1471. For details of the action, see Jorge Marco, 'Transnational Soldiers and Guerrilla Warfare from the Spanish Civil War to the Second World War', *War in History*, 20 Sept. 2018, https://doi.org/10.1177/0968344518761212.
21 VÚA–VHA, Czechoslovak units in France 1939–40, box 41, file 359, personal order of Technical Depot Company no. 31/40, 1 June 1940.
22 For distributing leaflets, four soldiers were sentenced to two years' imprisonment in February 1940. VÚA–VHA, Czechoslovak units in France 1939–40, box 15, file 130, Daily Order of the 1st Division no. 21/40, 6 Feb. 1940.
23 Vincenc Kocman, *Boj bez slávy* (Brno: Krajské Nakladatelství v Brně, 1962), passim; VÚA–VHA, International Brigades 1936–69, boxes 1–22, personal memories of individual Interbrigadists (mainly from 1950s and 1960s).
24 SHD, GR, 1N 70, summary of the colonel commanding the 1st Foreign Infantry Regiment, on the state of mind of the legion, March 1939.
25 Comor, *L'épopée de la 13éme Demi-brigade.*
26 Marie Émile Antoine Béthouart, *Cinq années d'espérance: mémoires de guerre, 1939–1945* (Paris: Plon, 1968), 77.
27 VÚA–VHA, Czechoslovak units in France 1939–40, various personal orders of particular units.
28 Jérémy Guedj, 'Les juifs français face aux juifs étrangers dans la France de l'entre deux guerres', *Cahiers de la Méditerrannée*, 78.2 (2009), 43–73.
29 Toman Brod and Eduard Čejka, *Na západní frontě: historie československých vojenských jednotek na Západě v letech druhé světové války* (Prague: Naše Vojsko, 1965), appendix 11, 556, declaration of Czechoslovak democratic soldiers in Cholmondeley, 26 July 1940; Fritz Beer, *... a tys na Němce střílel, dědo? Českoněmecký Žid mezi komunismem a nacismem* (Prague: Paseka, 2008), 234.
30 Beer, *... a tys na Němce střílel, dědo?*, 148–9, 235.
31 Ibid., 249.
32 'Fritz Beer', Arco Verlag, www.arco-verlag.com/autoren/autor/9-fritz-beer.html (last accessed 4 March 2019).
33 C. Levisse-Touzé, 'Les Espagnols dans la Résistance extérieure et dans l'Armée de la Libération', in Roger Bourderon (ed.), *La guerre d'Espagne: l'histoire, les lendemains, la mémoire* (Paris: Tallandier, 2007), 167.
34 SHD, GR, 12P 84, 'Bureau des statistiques de la Légion Étrangère', 'Dépôts de la Légion Étrangère', 'Dépôt commun des régiments étrangers de Sidi-Bel-Abbes'.
35 VÚA–VHA, Applications for resistance fighter status under Act no. 255/1946, no. 117738/47, Osvald Závodský; RGASPI, 545/6//1467; Jan Kalous, 'Osvald Závodský – aktér i oběť politických procesů', *Paměť a dějiny*, 8.3 (2013), 85–95.
36 Avgust Leśnik, 'Les volontaires yugoslaves/slovènes dans la Guerre Civile

espagnole (1936–1939): analyse structurelle et la liste', *Annales*, 17.1 (2007), 107–38.

37 Andrejka Novakovič, 'Slovenci v španski državljanski vojni in njihova vloga po njej v domovini', in Jože Hočevar (ed.), *Slovenci v španski državljanski vojni: zbornik referatov znanstvenega simpozija v Kopru, 12. februarja 2010* (Koper: Združenje Borcev za Vrednote NOB, 2010), 51–70, at 57.

38 VÚA–VHA, Czechoslovak units in France 1939–40, box 40, file 357, personal orders of Artillery Depot Battery nos. 1, 2, 15, 19, 30.

39 Gojko Berić and Ivo Vejvoda, *Zbogom XX. stoljeće: sjećanja Ive Vejvode* (Zagreb: Profil Knjiga, 2013), 89–90.

40 Ibid., 88.

41 VÚA–VHA, applications for resistance fighter status under Act no. 255/1946, no. 3403/65, Alois Samec.

42 SHD, GR, 11P 249-1, 1e Brigade de Légion Française (FFL), 'Organisation et effectifs'; GR, 11p 249-2, Brigade Française d'Orient, 'notes d'organisation', 'effectifs'; Jean-François Muracciole, *Les Français libres: l'autre Résistance* (Paris: Tallandier, 2009), 144; Celaya, *La guerra continúa*, 322–7.

43 Zdenko Maršálek, *'Česká', nebo 'československá' armáda? Národnostní složení československých vojenských jednotek v zahraničí v letech 1939–1945* (Prague: Academia, 2017), 148–53; Zdenko Maršálek, 'Českoslovenští interbrigadisté jako příslušníci zahraničních vojenských jednotek v letech druhé světové války', in Zdenko Maršálek and Emil Voráček (eds), *Interbrigadisté: Československo a španělská občanská válka* (Prague: Historical Institute of the Czech Academy of Sciences, 2017), 195–221.

44 Brod and Čejka, *Na západní frontě*, appendix 11, 556, declaration of Czechoslovak democratic soldiers in Cholmondeley, 26 July 1940.

45 VÚA–VHA, personal materials of F. O. Miksche; The Liddell Hart Military Archives, King's College, London, GB0099 KCLMA, F. O. Miksche; RGASPI, 545/6/1469.

46 The National Archives, Kew (TNA), DEFE 2/977, Activities of 10th Inter-Allied Commando, June 1942 – October 1945. See also Jeremy Monk, 'Forgotten Heroes? The Czechs of X-Troop, No. 10 Commando', *Prague Post*, 30 July 2017.

47 A thorough overview of plans of and reports on the amphibious attack on the island of Walcheren is located in TNA, DEFE 2/307–311.

48 VÚA–VHA, collection 24, Jan Theilinger.

49 TNA, HO 334/169/21552, naturalisation certificate, John Robert Taylor, 31 Dec. 1946; War Office (WO) 106/6155, Pioneer Corps records.

50 Peter N. Carroll, *The Odyssey of the Abraham Lincoln Brigade: Americans in the Spanish Civil War* (Stanford, CA: Stanford University Press, 1994); Anthony Cave Brown, *The Last Hero: Wild Bill Donovan* (New York: Times Books, 1982).

51 Studs Terkel, *An Oral History of World War Two* (London: Hamish Hamilton, 1985), 491.

52 Ibid., 492.

53 See above, p. 58.
54 Terkel, *An Oral History*, 494.
55 Ibid.
56 Carroll, *The Odyssey*, 272–3; Cave Brown, *The Last Hero*, 708–20.
57 See above, p. 58.
58 Christine Levisse-Touzé, 'Les Espagnols dans la Résistance extérieure et dans l'Armée de la Libération', in Bourderon (ed.), *La guerre d'Espagne*, 161–76.
59 Mohamed Sahia Cherchari, 'Indigènes et citoyens ou l'impossible universalisation du suffrage', *Revue française de droit constitutionnel*, 60.4 (2004), 741–70; Éric Deroo and Antoine Champeaux, 'Panorama des troupes coloniales françaises dans les deux guerres mondiales', *Revue historique des armées*, 271 (2013), 72–88.
60 Centre des Archives du Personnel Militaire, Pau (CAPM), CFA, 11/1. CFA was commanded on the ground by Gen. Monsabert (1942) and Gen. Magnan (1943).
61 CAPM, CFA, 22/1/2/3, 'Note du Gen. Giraud (n° 1634/EM-INA)', 24 May 1943; CFA, 22/1/2/3, 'Note de service (n° 6/59/4)' of CFA War Depot colonel in chief, 6 June 1943; CFA, 11/6, 'Note de service (n° 51/c)' of Col. Bryere, CFA North Morocco commander.
62 CAPM, CFA, 11/6, Putz recruitment campaign authorisation; Col. Bryere (CFA North Morocco commander), confidential report about foreigners' recruitment in North Africa concentration camps, 21 Jan. 1943; CFA, 11/3, secret letter addressed by Gen. Monsabert to Gen. Commander in Chief of General Staff, 22 May 1943. *Indigénes* recruitment campaign instructions in CAPM, CFA, 11/6, 'Note de service (n° 51/c)' of Col. Bryere, CFA North Morocco commander, and CFA, 11/6, 'Note de service 240' of col. in charge of CFA recruitment campaign at Fez.
63 SHD, GR, 16P 494000, Joseph Putz personal records; GR, 16P 96926, Miguel Buiza personal records.
64 SHD, GR, 11P 257–, 'Journal des marches et opérations du corps franc d'Afrique (25 novembre 1942–31 mai 1943'; GR, 11P 258, 'Journaux des marches et opérations du corps franc d'Afrique au Maroc (1 décembre 1942–8 juin 1943'; Jean-Louis Crémieux-Brilhac, *La France libre: de l'appel du 18 juin à la Libération* (Paris: Gallimard, 1996), 451; Romain Durand, *De Giraud à de Gaulle: le Corps franc d'Afrique* (Paris: L'Harmattan, 1999), 32; Jean-François Muracciole, *Les Français libres*, 153.
65 SHD, GR, 11P 257-8; GR, 16P 65869, Harry Bober personal records.
66 Celaya, *La guerra continua*, 384–5; also quoted in Evelyn Mesquida, *La Nueve: los españoles que liberaron París* (Barcelona: Ediciones B, 2008), 172–3.
67 Durand, *De Giraud à de Gaulle*, 160; Crémieux-Brilhac, *La france libre*, 631; Muracciole, *Les Français libres*, 156.
68 Eduardo Pons Prades, *Republicanos españoles en la Segunda Guerra mundial* (Barcelona: La Esfera de los Libros, 2002), 374–5.
69 Celaya, *La guerra continua*, 375–88; Muracciole, *Les Français libres*, 218–23.
70 Manuel Fernández, testimony, in Mesquida, *La Nueve*, 245.

71 Ibid., 246–7.
72 Eric Jennings, *La France libre fut africaine* (Paris: Perrin, 2014), 169.
73 Quoted by Mike Thompson, 'Paris Liberation Made "Whites Only', BBC Radio 4, 6 April 2009, http://news.bbc.co.uk/1/hi/world/europe/7984436.stm (last accessed 10 April 2020).
74 For more on this *blanchiment* process see Celaya, *La guerra continua*, 410–15; Daniel Hernandez, testimony, in Mesquida, *La Nueve*, 192.

5 Inherently transnational: escape lines

1 Jiří Friedl, *Na jedné frontě: vztahy československé a polské armády (Polskie Siły Zbrojne) za druhé světové války* (Prague: Ústav pro Soudobé Dějiny AV ČR, 2005), 42–70.
2 Ludvík Svoboda, *Cestami života*, vol. 1 (Prague: Naše Vojsko, 1971), 247–56.
3 Toman Brod, *Tobrucké krysy* (Prague: Naše Vojsko, 1967), 23. See also VÚA–VHA, military administration of the Czechoslovak National Committee in France, box 10, file 88, overview of Beirut transports; VÚA–VHA, Depot of the Czechoslovak Units in Great Britain 1939–47, box 50, file 165, statistical overviews of manpower for the year 1941.
4 Zdenko Maršálek, *'Česká', nebo 'československá' armáda? Národnostní složení československých vojenských jednotek v zahraničí v letech 1939–1945* (Prague: Academia, 2017), 26.
5 Bob de Graaff, *Stepping Stones to Freedom: Help to Allied Airmen in the Netherlands during World War II*, trans. Dee Wessels Boer-Stallman (Marceline, MO: Walsworth, 1995); Sherri Greene Ottis, *Silent Heroes: Downed Airmen and the French Underground* (Lexington, KY: University of Kentucky Press, 2001).
6 See Chapter 2 above. See also Ryszard Nazarewicz, 'Dąbrowszczacy w walce z okupantem w kraju' in Ryszard Nazarewicz (ed.), *Dąbrowszczacy w wojnie hiszpańskiej 1936–1939* (Warsaw: Akademia Nauk Społecznych PZPR, 1989), 142–56.
7 Haganah Archives, Tel Aviv, A. Polonski papers, D7/9, report on OJC by Jacques Lazarus, end 1944; Jacques Lazarus, *Juifs au combat: témoignage sur l'activité d'un mouvement de résistance* (Paris: Éditions du Centre, 1947); Yehuda Bauer, *American Jewry and the Holocaust. The American Jewish Joint Distribution Committee, 1939–1945* (Detroit, MI: Wayne State University Press, 1981), 153, 244. See Chapter 3 above.
8 Bo Lidegaard, *Countrymen: The Untold Story of How Denmark's Jews Escaped the Nazis* (London: Atlantic Books, 2013).
9 Carlo De Maria, *Lavoro di comunità e ricostruzione civile in Italia* (Rome: Viella, 2014), 46–9; Carlo Musso, *Diplomazia partigiana; gli alleati, I rifugiati italiani e la delegazione del CLNAI in Svizzera (1943 – 1945)* (Milan: Franco Angeli, 1983), 00–25; Carlo Vallauri (ed.), *Le repubbliche partigiane: esperienze di autogoverno democratico* (Rome and Bari, 2013), 117–47.
10 Hoover Institution Library and Archive, Stanford, CA, Weidner Collection,

WA WC, 23 Smit; TNA, WO 208/5454; Verzetsmuseum, Amsterdam, interview with van der Heijden; Eugène van der Heijden, 'Oorlogsherinneringen', *Escape*, 80 (March 1994), 31–4, and 81 (June 1994), 26–30.

11 Sergio Sanchez, 'José Gistau, paquetero de suerte', *El mundo de los Pirineos*, 3 (May 1998).

12 Ibid.

13 Guy Hermet, *Les Espagnols en France* (Paris: Les Éditions Ouvrières, 1967), 23–4; Javier Rubio, *La emigración de la guerra civil de 1936 a 1939*, vol. 1 (Madrid: Ediciones San Martín, 1977); Geneviève Dreyfus-Armand, *L'exil des Espagnols républicains en France: de guerre civile à la mort de Franco* (Paris: Albin Michel, 1999).

14 Émilienne Eychenne, *Les Pyrénées de la liberté: le franchissement clandestin des Pyrénées pendant la Seconde Guerre mondiale, 1939–1945* (Paris: Éditions France-Empire, 1983); Robert Belot, *Aux frontières de la liberté: Vichy, Madrid, Alger, Londres, s'évader de France sous l'Occupation* (Paris: Fayard, 1998); Josep Calvet, *Las montañas de la libertad: el paso de refugiados por los Pirineos durante la Segunda Guerra mundial, 1939–1944* (Madrid: Alianza Editorial, 2010).

15 Calvet, *Las montañas de la liberdad*, 32; Eychenne, *Les Pyrénées de la liberté*, 55–82. This collaboration made possible the capture of the Spanish Republic's minister of the interior Julian Zugazagoitia and the president of the Generalitat of Catalonia, Lluis Companys; Julián Casanova, *A Short History of the Spanish Civil War* (London and New York: I. B. Tauris, 2014), 187–8.

16 Ramón J. Campo, *El oro de Canfranc* (Saragossa: Obra Social y Cultural, 2002), 100–1.

17 SHD, GR, 16P 358760, Albert Le Lay personal records.

18 Campo, *El oro de Canfranc*, 119.

19 SHD, GR, 16P 30824, Honoré Baradat personal records; Honoré Baradat, personal records of escapes by Canfranc and Portalet, in Louis Poullenot, *Basses Pyrénées: ocupation, libération, 1940–1945* (Paris: J & D Éditions, 1995).

20 Interview with Victor Alberto Fairen Le Lay, Albert Le Lay's grandson, and Le Lay's family spokesperson, recorded by Diego Gaspar Celaya, Madrid, 11 May 2018.

21 The Germans did not pay attention to his activities as long as the transit of goods was not affected until late September 1943, when the Gestapo's suspicions forced Le Lay and his family to flee. SHD, GR, 16P 358760.

22 SHD, GR, 16P 358760, Albert Le Lay personal records.

23 SHD, GR, 16P 189803, Henri Dorfsman personal records; Lucien Henrion, *Le commandant Alexandre Lofi* (Metz: Académie Nationale de Metz, 1994), 155–6; Robert Paxton, *L'armée de Vichy: le corps des officiers français 1940–1944* (Paris: Tallandier, 2004), 42–3.

24 Calvet, *Las montañas de la libertad*, 261–3. Josep Calvet, *Évades: 29 décembre 1943. Fotografies de Jacques Léonard*, catalogue of exhibition, Museu

Memorial de l'Exili, La Jonquera, 24 March –1 July 2018). Monsignor André Boyer-Mas organised the convoy from Malaga.

25 'Article 160, Ordonnance n° 45/2447, du 19 octobre 1945, portant code de la nationalité française', *Journal Officiel de la République Française*, 20 October 1945, p. 6711; Dreyfus-Armand, *L'exil des républicains*, 177–82.

26 Secundino Serrano, *Maquis: historia de la guerrilla antifranquista* (Madrid: Temas de Hoy, 2001). See also Chapters 2 and 10.

27 Interview with Martín Arnal Mur, Angües, Huesca, Spain, recorded by Diego Gaspar Celaya, 2 March 2018.

28 SHD, GR, 17P 187, Pat O'Leary line homologation file. See also Vincent Brome, *The Way Back: The Story of Lieut.-Commander Pat O'Leary* (London: Companion Book Club, 1958); Donald Caskie, *The Tartan Pimpernel* (London: Fontana Books, 1960); Greene Ottis, *Silent Heroes*, 76–118.

29 SHD, GR, 17P 187, Pat O'Leary line homologation file.

30 Ibid.; Pilar Ponzán, *Lucha y muerte por la libertad: memoria de 9 años de guerra 1936–1945* (Barcelona: Tot, 1996); Antonio Téllez Solà, *La red de evasión del grupo Ponzán: anarquistas en la guerra secreta contra el franquismo y el nazismo (1936–1944)* (Barcelona: Virus, 1996); Dreyfus-Armand, *L'exil des républicains*, 156–8.

31 Robert Terres, *Double jeu pour la France 1939–1944* (París: Grasset et Fasquelle, 1977).

32 Claude d'Abzac-Epezy, 'Armée et secrets, 1940–1942: le contre-espionnage de l'armée de Vichy', *Bulletin de l'Institut Pierre Renouvin*, 36.2 (2012), 45–56.

33 SHD, GR, 17P 187, Pat O'Leary line homologation file.

34 For the full story of Dutch-Paris see Megan Koreman, *The Escape Line: How the Ordinary Heroes of Dutch-Paris Resisted the Nazi Occupation of Western Europe* (New York: Oxford University Press, 2018); originally in Dutch as *Gewone helden: de Dutch-Paris ontsnappingslijn* (Amsterdam: Boom, 2016).

35 See Federico Varese and Meir Yaish, 'The Importance of Being Asked: The Rescue of Jews in Nazi Europe', *Rationality and Society* 12.3 (2000), 307–34.

36 For Dutch-Paris in Belgium see Nationaal Archief, The Hague, 2.13.71 (MvOL) 413, and Hoover Institution Library and Archive, Weidner Collection, Belgian Resistance (all files in series).

37 Hoover Institution Library and Archive, Weidner Collection 3, Biographical Information.

38 Abbé John aan de Stegge, Jacques Rens and Paul Veerman, Simone Collomb, Ernest Bouchet.

39 Hoover Institution Library and Archive, Weidner Collection 26, Segers; Weidner Collection 4, Chait 1; Centre de l'Histoire de la Résistance et de la Déportation, Lyons, testimony, Mme Raymonde Perrier neé Pillot, 11 March 1992.

40 *Nieuw Israelitisch Weekblad*, 6 Jan. 1950.

41 On *Zwangsarbeit* in general see Ulrich Herbert, *Hitler's Foreign Workers: Enforced Foreign Labour under the Third Reich* (Cambridge: Cambridge University Press, 1997); Winfried Meyer and Klaus Neitmann (eds),

Zwangsarbeit während der NS-Zeit in Berlin und Brandenburg: Formen, Funktionen und Rezeption (Berlin: Berliner Wissenschafts-Verlag, 2001); Christine Glauning and Andreas Nachama (eds), *Alltag Zwangsarbeit 1938–1945: Katalog zur gleichnamigen Dauerausstellung* (Berlin: Stiftung Topographied.Terrors,2013);RimcoSpanjer,DieteOudesluijsandJohanMeijer (eds),*ZurArbeitgezwungen:ZwangsarbeitinDeutschland1940–1945*(Bremen: Edition Temmen, 1999); B. A. Sijes, *De arbeidsinzet: de gedwongen arbeid van NederlandersinDuitsland, 1940–1945*(TheHague:MartinusNijhoff,1966).

42 See the archives of the JOC-KAJ at the Centre d'Études et de Documentation Guerre et Sociétés Contemporaines/Studie- en Documentatiecentrum Oorlog en Hedendaagse Maatschappij, Brussels; Frans Govers, *Stemmen uit Dachau: 'Ter eren van de doden en ter waarschuwing van de levenden'* (Hapert: Kenmpen, 1990).

43 It is almost impossible to estimate the number of forced labourers, particularly *Ostarbeiter*, who managed to escape from their workplaces in the Third Reich.

44 Testimony of I. A. M. Schmutzer, 19 May 1948, in *Enquetecommissie Regeringsbeleid 1940–1945*, vol. 6c (The Hague: State Printing and Publishing Company, 1952).

45 A. F. M. Cammaert, 'Het verborgen ront: geschiedenis van de georganiseerde illegaliteit in de provincie Limburg tijdens de Tweede Wereldoorlog' (PhD dissertation, University of Groningen, 1994), 524–6; Instituut voor Oorlogs-, Holocaust- en Genocidestudies, Amsterdam, 251a, Stichting Landelijke Organisatie voor Hulp aan Onderduikers en Landelijke Knokploegen, 134; Jeroen Kemperman, *Oorlog in de collegebanken: studenten in verzet, 1940–1945* (Amsterdam: Boom, 2018), 184–99.

46 Instituut voor Oorlogs-, Holocaust- en Genocidestudies, 251a, 134.

47 Estimates vary from 200 to 750 people but Cammaert, 'Het verborgen front', thinks a conservative estimate is nearer the truth.

48 Lennert Savenije, *Nijmegen, collaboratie en verzet: een stad in Oorlogstijd* (Nijmegen: Vantilt, 2018).

49 Gjalt van Wijk, 'Der Widerstand und die illegale Rückführung der niederländischen zwangsverpflichteten Studenten während des Zweiten Weltkrieges', in Spanjer, Oudesluijs and Meijer (eds), *Zur Arbeit gezwungen*, 239–53.

50 Instituut voor Oorlogs-, Holocaust- en Genocidestudies, 251a, 134.

51 Ruth Aliav and Peggy Mann [Klüger], *The Last Escape: The Launching of the Largest Secret Rescue Movement of All Time* (London: Gollancz, 1974); Alan Swarc, 'Illegal Immigration to Palestine, 1945–1948: The French Connection' (PhD dissertation, University College London, 2005).

52 For the consequences of helping the persecuted see Rab Bennett, *Under the Shadow of the Swastika: The Moral Dilemmas of Resistance and Occupation in Hitler's Europe* (Basingstoke: Macmillan, 1999), and Jacques Semelin, Claire Andrieu and Sarah Gensburger (eds) *Resisting Genocide: The Multiple Forms of Rescue*, trans. Emma Bentley and Cynthia Schoch (New York: Columbia University Press, 2011).

6 Transnational perspectives on Jews in the resistance

1 Sidney Tarrow, *The New Transnational Activism* (Cambridge and New York: Cambridge University Press, 2005), 1–2.

2 Ibid., 41–3.

3 Gabriele Anderl and Walter Manoschek: *Gescheiterte Flucht: Der jüdische 'Kladovo-Transport' auf dem Weg nach Palästina 1939–42* (Vienna: Verlag für Gesellschaftskritik, 1993).

4 There are two biographies of Altmaier: Christoph Moss, *Jakob Altmaier: Ein jüdischer Sozialdemokrat in Deutschland (1889–1963)* (Cologne: Böhlau, 2003), and Werner Schiele, *An der Front der Freiheit: Jakob Altmaiers Leben für die Demokratie* (Flörsheim: H. Lauck, 1991).

5 Wolfgang Wilhelmus, 'rthur Becker: Agrarier-Sozialdemokrat-Jude', in Irene Diekmann (ed.), *Wegweiser durch das jüdische Mecklenburg-Vorpommern* (Potsdam: Verlag für Berlin-Brandenburg, 1998), 429–47.

6 Peter Pirker, 'Transnational Resistance in the Alps-Adriatic-Area in 1939/40', *Acta Histriae*, 20.4 (2012), 849–51.

7 For more on Kornweitz's activities in Yugoslavia see Hans Schafranek, 'Julius Kornweitz und Leo Gabler – Auslandsemissäre der KPÖ im Visier der Gestapo', in Dokumentationsarchiv des Österreichischen Wiederstandes (ed.), *Jahrbuch 2011* (Vienna, 2011), 185–208.

8 Franz Theodor Csokor, *Zeuge einer Zeit: Briefe aus dem Exil 1930–1950* (Munich: Georg Müller, 1964), 308.

9 Henriette Mandl, *Cabaret und Courage: Stella Kadmon, eine Biographie* (Vienna: WUV Universitaetsverlag, 1993). See also Kay Weniger, *Zwischen Bühne und Baracke: Lexikon der verfolgten Theater-, Film- und Musikkünstler 1933 bis 1945. Mit einem Geleitwort von Paul Spiegel* (Berlin: Metropol, 2008); Peter Berger, 'The Gildemeester Organisation for Assistance to Emigrants and the expulsion of Jews from Vienna, 1938–1942', in Terry Gourvish (ed.), *Business and Politics in Europe, 1900–1970: Essays in Honour of Alice Teichova* (Cambridge, Cambridge University Press, 2003), 215–45.

10 USC Shoah Foundation Testimonies, Los Angeles, https://sfi.usc.edu/full-length-testimonies, interview with Fritz Cahn, conducted by Milica Mihajlovic, Belgrade, Serbia, 23 April 1998.

11 AoY, Ministarstvo Unutrašnjih Poslova, Državni Sud za Zaštitu Države, AJ, MUP (DSZD), fond 135.

12 Dr Teodor Kovač, 'Something about Ha-shomer Ha-Za'ir and its "Nest" in Novi Sad', in Milica Mihalovic, *Jewish Youth Societies in Yugoslavia, 1919–1941* (Belgrade: Jewish Historical Museum, 1995), 73. See also interview with Dordje Hajzler, USHMM collection, https://collections.ushmm.org/search/catalog/irn513556 (last accessed 1 September 2009).

13 Ernst Pawel, *Life in Dark Ages: A Memoir* (New York: Fromm International, 1995), 52, 71.

14 Joseph Schwarzberg, *Dangerous Measures* (Toronto: Azrieli Foundation, 2018), 29.

15 Pierre Birnbaum, *Anti-Semitism in France: A Political History from Léon Blum to the Present* (Oxford: Blackwell, 1992); Pierre Birnbaum, *The Jews of the Republic: A Political History of State Jews in France from Gambetta to Vichy* (Stanford, CA: Stanford University Press, 1996)
16 Archives Nationales, Paris (AN), 72AJ126B1, testimony of Leo Hamon, 7 March 1946, cited by Robert Gildea, *Fighters in the Shadows: A New History of the French Resistance* (London: Faber & Faber, 2015), 46–7.
17 Jean Jérôme (Michał Feintuch), *La part des hommes: souvenirs d'un témoin* (Paris: Acropole, 1983), 245–6.
18 Ibid., 65.
19 Ibid., 153.
20 Claude Lévy, *Les parias de la Résistance* (Paris: Calmann-Lévy, 1970), 61, cited by Gildea, *Fighters in the Shadows*, 214.
21 RGASPI, 545/6/731, 'Biografia de Militantes. Langer Marcel', Partido Comunista de España, Comision Central de Cuadros, Barcelona, 19 March 1938, fol. 54a. See Zachary Lockman, *Comrades and Enemies – Arab and Jewish Workers in Palestine, 1906–1948* (Berkeley: University of California Press, 1996), 111–47.
22 RGASPI, 545/6/731, 'Biografia de Militantes. Langer Marcel', fol. 54a.
23 RGASPI, f545/ 6/665, 'Langer Marcel', Cervicio de Personal, Seccion Polaca, Albacete, 28 Jan. 1938, fol. 58.
24 RGASPI, 545/6/665, '1.883. Langer arcel (Polonais)', fol. 4a, brief account signed by 'Edo', 29 June 1940; Marc Brafman, 'Les origines, les motivations, l'action et les destins des combattants juifs (parmi d'autres immigrés) de la 35e Brigade FTP-MOI de Marcel Langer, Toulouse 1942–1944', *Le monde juif*, 152 (1994), 79–95.
25 Mémorial de la Shoah, Paris, Centre de Documentation Juive Contemporaine (CDJC), DLXI-77, interview with Abraham Polonski, conducted by Anny Latour, Tel Aviv, 1968.
26 Renée Poznanski, *Jews in France during World War II* (Hanover and London: University Press of New England, 2001).
27 Ray Moseley, *Reporting War: How Foreign Correspondents Risked Capture, Torture, and Death to Cover World War Two* (New Haven, CT: Yale University Press, 2017), 80–9.
28 Csokor, *Zeuge einer Zeit*, 298.
29 Moseley, *Reporting War*, 80–9.
30 After the war Franjo Spitzer changed his German name to Ervin Šinko and switched to writing in Serbo-Croatian; he defended Tito's Yugoslavia in polemics against the Soviet line following the 1948 split in the Cominform.
31 Alexander Sacher-Masoch, *Beppe und Pule: Roman einer Insel* (Vienna: W. Verkauf, 1948). The subtitle states that these stories were written on Korčula between 1941 and 1943. In 1956 Sacher-Masoch published a novel, *Die Ölgärten brennen*, based on his wartime experience in Yugoslavia. The final work in the Korčula triology is *Plaotina: Geschichten vor einer Dalmatinischen Insel* (Basel: Gute Schriften, 1963).

32 Csokor lived in Rome and worked for the BBC before returning to Vienna in 1946 in a British uniform. He described his refugee years in Yugoslavia in his novel *Als Zivilist im Balkankrieg*, in the book of memoirs *Auf fremden Strassen*, a 1946 tragedy in four acts on the Yugoslav Partisans, *Der verlorene Sohn*, and in a collection of his letters from exile, *Zeuge einer Zeit*.

33 Walter Manoschek, *'Serbien ist judenfrei!' Militärische Besatzungspolitik und Judenvernichtung in Serbien 1941/42* (Munich: Verlag Oldenbourg, 1995).

34 Ivo and Slavko Goldstein, *Holocaust in Croatia* (Pittsburgh: University of Pittsburgh Press, 2016).

35 For more on Novi Sad raid see Zvonimir Golubović, *Racija u Južnoj Bačkoj 1942. godine* (Novi Sad, 1992); Randolph L. Braham, *The Politics of Genocide. The Holocaust in Hungary* (New York: Columbia University Press, 1981), chapter 'The Délvidék Massacres', 207–15. Ilza's name is in the list of 4,628 victims of the massacre compiled by the USHMM: https://www.ushmm.org/online/hsv/source_view.php?SourceId=28982 (last accessed 1 Sept. 2019).

36 USC Shoah Foundation Testimonies, Los Angeles, https://sfi.usc.edu/full-length-testimonies, interview with Fritz Cahn, conducted by Milica Mihajlovic, Belgrade, Serbia, 23 April 1998.

37 TNA, WO 202/293, AC/A/8050.

38 For more on the legendary Baruh family see Mirjana Belić-Koročkin, Radivoje Davidović, *Bora Baruh: 1911–1942* (Belgrade: Interprint, 2001).

39 For more detailed account on this network of Jewish resisters including Oskar Davičo, Marko Čelebonović, Eli Finci, Moša Pijade and others see Radivoje Davidović, *Od Daviča do Čelebonovića – ulice beogradskih Jevreja* (Belgrade: Čigoja, 2010).

40 Romano, *Jevreji Jugoslavije 1941–1945* is the most comprehensive volume to date on the participation of Yugoslav Jews in the anti-fascist resistance.

41 Daniel Lee, *Pétain's Jewish Children: French Jewish Youth and the Vichy Regime, 1940–1942* (Oxford: Oxford University Press, 2014).

42 Georges Loinger and Kathy Hazan, *Aux frontières de l'espoir* (Paris: Le Manuscrit, 2006), 25.

43 Ibid., 29.

44 Gildea, *Fighters in the Shadows*, 194–5.

45 On the Secours National see Jan Kulok, 'Trait d'union: The History of the French Relief Organisation Secours National/Entr'aide Française under the Third Republic, the Vichy Regime and the Early Fourth Republic, 1939–1949' (D.Phil. dissertation, University of Oxford, 2003) and Jean-Pierre Le Crom, *Au secours, Maréchal! L'instrumentalisation de l'humanitaire, 1940–1944* (Paris: Presses Universitaires de France, 2013).

46 About a thousand according to the statistics established by Ruth Fivaz-Silbermann, 'La fuite en Suisse: migrations, strategies, fuite, accueil, refoulement et destin des réfugiés juifs durant la Seconde Guerre' (Ph.D. dissertation, University of Geneva, 2017).

47 Renée Poznanski, *Propagandes et persécutions: la Résistance et le 'problème juif'* (Paris: Fayard, 2008).

48 AN, 72AJ220/II, testimony of Georges Boris, 27 May and 3 June 1947; Geoffroy de Courcel in Georges Boris, *Servir la France: textes et témoignages* (Paris: Julliard, 1963), 286; Jean-Louis Crémieux-Brilhac, *Georges Boris: trente ans d'influence. Blum, de Gaulle, Mendès France* (Paris, Gallimard, 2010), 20–1, 27–85; Gildea, *Fighters in the Shadows*, 25–6.

49 Jean-Louis Crémieux-Brilhac, 'La France libre et 'le problème juif', *Le débat*, 162 (Nov.–Dec. 2010), reprinted in Jean-Louis Crémieux-Brilhac, *L'étrange victoire: de la défense de la République à la liberation de la France* (Paris, Gallimard, 2016), 155–85.

50 Georges Zérapha, at the Congrès National de la Ligue Internationale contre le Racisme et l'Antisémitisme (LICRA), 15–16 Dec. 1945 quoted by David Knout, *Contribution à l'histoire de la Résistance juive en France* (Paris: Éditions du Centre, 1947), 82.

51 Gildea, *Fighters in the Shadows*, 68–9, 95, 143.

52 On these disagreements see Bernard Comte, 'Mounier sous Vichy: le risque d'une présence en 'clandestinité publique', in Guy Cocq (ed.), *Emmanuel Mounier: l'actualité d'un grand témoin* (Paris: Éditions Parole et Silence, 2003), 63, and Robert Salmon, *Chemins faisant (*Paris: Éditions LBM, 2004).

53 Léo Hamon, *Vivre ses choix* (Paris: Robert Laffont, 1991), 90.

54 For this report and the whole story of this trip, see Renée Poznanski and Léo Hamon (eds), *Avant les premières grandes rafles: les juifs à Paris sous l'Occupation (juin 1940–avril 1941)*, Cahiers de l'Institut d'Histoire du Temps Présent, 22 (Paris: CNRS, 1992).

55 Georges Wellers, André Kaspi and Serge Klarsfeld (eds), *La France et la question juive* (Paris: Éditions Sylvie Messinger, 1981), 386.

56 Poznanski, *Jews in France during World War II*, 406–7.

57 Testimony of Irma Mico, July 2007, in Claude Collin, *Le Travail allemand: une organisation de résistance au sein de la Wehrmacht* (Paris: Les Indes Savantes, 2013), 55–78.

58 Abraham Lissner, *Un franc-tireur juif raconte ...* (Paris: n. pub., 1969), 45.

59 Boris Holban, *Testament: après 45 ans de silence* (Paris: Calmann-Lévy, 1989), 122.

60 On the role of Jewish women in the French Resistance, see Renée Poznanski, 'Women in the French Jewish Underground: Shield-Bearers of the Resistance?', in Lenore J. Weizman and Dalia Ofer (eds), *Women in the Holocaust* (New Haven, CT: Yale University Press, 1998), 234–52.

61 Brafman, 'Les origines, les motivations', 79–95; Lévy, *Les parias de la Résistance*; Gildea, *Fighters in the Shadows*, 221, 236–7; David Tidhar, *Entsiklopedyah le-halutsei ha-yishuv u-bonav*, vol. 11 (Tel Aviv: Sifriyat Rishonim, 1961), 3807; Okęcki (ed.), *Polish Resistance Movement*, 243; Rolande Trempé, 'Le rôle des étrangers: MOI et guérilleros', in *La Libération dans le Midi de la France* (Toulouse: Eché Editeur et Service de Publications de l'UTM, 1986), 63–78, at 69.

62 Interview with Claude Lévy, conducted by Renee Poznanski, Paris, 1987.

63 See Catherine Varlin's testimony, 'Une ville engloutie: la résistance des femmes juives', in Association pour la Recherche sur l'Histoire Contemporaine des Juifs (RHICOJ), *Les juifs dans la Résistance et la Libération: histoire, témoignages, débats* (Paris: Éditions du Scribe, 1985), 101–3.
64 Damira Titonel Asperti, *Ecrire pour les autres: mémoirs d'une résistante. Les anti-facistes italiens en Lot-et-Garonne sous l'Occupation* (Bordeaux: Presses Universitaires de Bordeaux, 1999).
65 Schwarzberg, *Dangerous Measures*, 48, 80, 89.
66 Mémorial de la Shoah, Paris, CDJC, DLXI-66, interview with Pierre Loeb, n.d., p. 13.
67 André Carrel, *Mes humanités: itinéraire d'un homme engagé* (Paris: L'Œil d'Or, 2009), 12–84.
68 AN, 72AJ42, 'L'insurrection parisienne. Extrait des souvenirs inédits de Léon Hamon', 11–17; Gildea, *Fighters in the Shadows*, 397–8.

7 SOE and transnational resistance

1 Imperial War Museum Sound Archive, London, interview no. 9812, Peter Lake, 1987.
2 For the best general introduction to SOE, see W. J. M. Mackenzie, *The Secret History of SOE: Special Operations Executive 1940–1945* (London: St Ermin's, 2000). Other published studies of note include a series of official histories on SOE operations in individual countries and theatres, written, like Mackenzie's, with privileged access to original files: the first was M. R. D. Foot's *SOE in France: An Account of the Work of the British Special Operations Executive in France 1940–1944* (London: HMSO, 1966); the last was this author's *Target: Italy. The Secret War against Mussolini, 1940–1943: The Official History of SOE Operations in Fascist Italy* (London: Faber & Faber, 2014). Although written without access to SOE's records, David Stafford's *Britain and European Resistance, 1940–1945: A Survey of the Special Operations Executive, with Documents* (Toronto: University of Toronto Press, 1980) remains an important study of SOE's relationship vis-à-vis the British War Cabinet and chiefs of staff. There are also two edited collections of essays: M. Seaman (ed.), *The Special Operations Executive* (London: Routledge, 2005) and N. Wylie (ed.), *The Politics and Strategy of Clandestine War: Special Operations Executive, 1940–46* (London: Routledge, 2007).
3 Well-received recent monographs on SOE include K. J. V. Jespersen, *Med hjælp fra England: Special Operations Executive og den danske modstandskamp 1940–1945* (Odense: University Press of Southern Denmark, 2000), published in English as *No Small Achievement: Special Operations Executive and the Danish Resistance, 1940–1945* (Odense: University Press of Southern Denmark, 2002); Roderick Bailey, *The Wildest Province: SOE in the Land of the Eagle* (London: Jonathan Cape, 2008), a study of SOE operations in Albania and Kosovo; D. Stafford, *Mission Accomplished: SOE and Italy 1943–1945* (London: Bodley Head, 2011); P. Pirker, *Subversion deutscher*

Herrschaft: Der britische Kriegsgeheimdienst SOE und Österreich (Vienna: Vienna University Press, 2012); Bailey, *Target: Italy*; and R. Duckett, *The Special Operations Executive in Burma: Jungle Warfare and Intelligence Gathering in World War II* (London: I. B. Tauris, 2018). Although the historiography remains shaped by studies of SOE operations in individual countries, less conventional approaches have included Juliette Pattinson's *Behind Enemy Lines: Gender, Passing and the Special Operations Executive* (Manchester: Manchester University Press, 2009), an examination of gender relations pertaining to SOE and its operations in France, and C. J. Murphy's *Security and Special Operations: SOE and MI5 during the Second World War* (London: Palgrave Macmillan, 2006).

4 TNA, HS 8/281, Armistice and Post-War Committee, Lord Selborne to the prime minister, 27 April 1944.

5 D. Hamilton-Hill, *SOE Assignment* (London: William Kimber, 1973), 79.

6 Imperial War Museum Sound Archive, interview no. 26754, Ronald Turnbull, 1994.

7 Imperial War Museum Sound Archive, interviw no. 12270, Frank Griffiths, 1991.

8 Air and naval support to SOE possessed its own transnational features. For example, Czech and Polish crews flew alongside British and Commonwealth ones on operations to drop stores and agents into Europe, while Polish-manned boats were used to put them ashore in southern France.

9 TNA, HS 9/987/2, 'Application for Engagement', 24 Dec. 1943.

10 TNA, HS 9/978/2, comments on Captain S. Makowski, 7 Jan. 1944.

11 Ibid., comments on Captain S. Makowski, 30 Dec. 1944.

12 Ibid., comments on Captain S. Makowski, 12 Jan. 1944.

13 TNA, HS 9/978/2., F Section Pro-Forma no. 228: Makowski, Stanislaw, T/Captain, 19 Dec. 1945.

14 TNA, HS 9/1156/7, 'Curriculum Vitae of W/S Capt. W. Petro-Pavlovsky (Known as Petro)', 1943; 'Form C.R.1: Petro-Pavolvsky, Wladimir, W.S Captain', 19 April 1943; Captain (T/Major) W. Petro-Pavolvsky, 'Request to Straighten out my Record in W.O.', 1944; W. Petro [sic], *Triple Commission* (London: John Murray, 1968), 178–247.

15 TNA, HS 9/1156/7, telegram, SOE New York to SOE London, 26 Jan. 1943. In his memoirs, Petro-Pavlovsky offers a different explanation. After he arrived in London from his liaison post in Washington, DC, SOE had 'suggested' to him that he should work for its French Section. He was then given 'all the files' but concluded from these 'that the situation in the Resistance was extremely complex ... I did not feel that I would fit into such a picture and [so] declined the offer.' Petro, *Triple Commission*, 213.

16 D. Hamson, *We Fell among Greeks* (London: Jonathan Cape, 1946), 53.

17 E. C. W. Myers, *Greek Entanglement* (London: Rupert Hart-Davis, 1955), 49–50.

18 These were the Military Medal and Bar. For more details of Khouri's awards, see his citations in TNA, WO 373/46/98 and WO 373/46/1267.

19 TNA, HS 5/484; interview with Sylvia Apostolidou, conducted by R. Bailey and A. Kakissis, Athens, Dec. 2017.

20 TNA, HS 5/345, 'Recommendation for the Award of the M.B.E. [sic]: Miss Sylvia Apostolides [sic]', 1945.

21 TNA, HS 5/484, interview with Sylvia Apostolidou, conducted by R. Bailey and A. Kakissis, Athens, Dec. 2017.

22 TNA, HS 5/345, 'Recommendation for the Award of the M.B.E. [sic]: Miss Sylvia Apostolides[sic]', 1945.The award was approved and upgraded to the George Medal.

23 Imperial War Museum Sound Archive, interview no. 9331, Selwyn Jepson, 1986.

24 See, for example, S. Lahiri, 'Clandestine Mobilities and Shifting Embodiments: Noor-un-Nisa Inayat Khan and the Special Operations Executive, 1940–44', *Gender & History*, 19.2 (2007), 307–9.

25 For more on SOE–OSS relations, see, for example, J. Jakub, *Spies and Saboteurs: Anglo-American Collaboration and Rivalry in Human Intelligence Collection and Special Operations, 1940–45* (New York: St Martin's Press, 1999).

26 For more on SOE's dealings with the NKVD, see, for example, D. O'Sullivan, *Dealing with the Devil: Anglo-Soviet Intelligence Cooperation during the Second World War* (New York: Peter Lang, 2010).

27 TNA, HS 5/889, 'Brief for Harbourne', 26 May 1943.

28 TNA, HS 5/141, Major H. Perkins (SOE London) to Major Rawicz (Polish VI Bureau), 5 Feb. 1943.

29 I am grateful to Anna Maciąg, niece of Józef Maciąg, for most of these details about her uncle and his family. The detail about the broken leg comes from P. Korczyński, 'Po dwóch stronach barykady: Za waszą wolność, a nasze przetrwanie, czyli polscy bohaterowie Jugosławii'. *Polska Zbrojna*, 12 (2016), 110. For a short biography of Józef Maciąg based on Polish military records, see Krzysztof A. Tochman, *Cichociemni na Bałkanach we Wloszech i Francji: Słownik biograficzny* (Ostoja: Miękka, 2016), 55–8. I am grateful to Magda Thomas for bringing Tochman's book to my attention.

30 TNA, HS 4/291, Lt. Col. Marian Utnik (Polish VI Bureau) to Major Pickles (SOE London), 27 Sept. 1944.

31 Why 'John Nash' was chosen seems not to be recorded, but, as noted below, SOE routinely encouraged non-British agents to change their names on grounds of safety.

32 J. Rootham, *Miss Fire: The Chronicle of a British Mission to Mihailovitch 1943–1944* (London: Chatto & Windus, 1946), 64.

33 TNA, HS 2/277, SOE War Diary: Poland and Czechoslovakia, July 1942 to March 1944.

34 See, for example, Korczyński, 'Po dwóch stronach barykady', 111.

35 TNA, HS 4/291, Lt. Col. Marian Utnik (Polish VI Bureau) to Major Pickles (SOE London), 27 Sept, 1944. Józef Maciąg is buried today in plot 1.D.1 of the British War Cemetery in Belgrade. His headstone bears his real name. Cecil

Maurice Ridewood, the British wireless operator whom he helped to escape, died in 2009.

36 What followed was a voyage, soon notorious, of fifty-seven days in which the transportees endured appalling conditions, including brutal treatment from their guards. For a recent account of the *Dunera*, see K. Inglis, S. Spark and J. Winter, *Dunera Lives: A Visual History* (Melbourne: Monash University Press, 2018).

37 Interview with Eric Sanders, conducted by R. Bailey, June 2004.

38 Imperial War Museum Sound Archive, interview no. 14582, Stephen Dale, 1994.

39 TNA, HS9/389/5, SOE personnel file; S. Dale, *Spanglet: Or by Any Other Name* (privately published, 1993).

40 TNA, HS 9/9/3, report by Sergeant P. Garvin, 19 Feb. 1942, 6 March 1942.

41 TNA, HS 9/9/3, note by Major C. Roseberry to Major-General J. H. F. Lakin, 23 Nov.1942.

42 For a detailed account of Gabor Adler's SOE service and fate, see Bailey, *Target: Italy*, 222–52, 338–53.

43 Rootham, *Miss Fire*, 114–15.

44 TNA, HS 7/70, 'History of the Allied Military Mission, Albania, 1942–1945'.

45 TNA, HS 5/142, report by Major R. E. Riddell and Captain R. A. Hibbert, 1944; see also M. Coltrinale, *L'8 settembre in Albania: la crisi armistiziale tra impotenza, errori ed eroismo (8 settembre–7 ottobre 1943)* (Rome: Nuova Cultura, 2009), 238.

46 TNA, HS 7/70, 'History of the Allied Military Mission, Albania, 1942–1945'.

47 TNA, HS 5/137, report by Captain J. D. Dumoulin, RAMC, 25 June 1944.

48 E. F. Davies, *Illyrian Venture: The Story of the British Military Mission to Enemy-Occupied Albania 1943–44* (London: The Bodley Head, 1952), 74.

49 TNA, HS 9/1644, report by I. Toptani, 1944.

50 TNA, HS 5/124, report by Major J. A. Field, 1943.

51 R. Bailey, 'La Missione Britannica per la resistenza Albanese: un punto di vista degli alleati sull'esperienza degli Italiani in Albania, 1943–1944', in L. Tosi (ed.), *Caro nemico: soldati pistoiesi e toscani nella resistenza in Albania e Montenegro 1943–1945* (Pisa: Edizione ETS, 2018), 315–25.

52 TNA, HS 9/877/5, Captain P. I. Lake, report, 11 Oct. 1944. On the leader of the Spanish 'Grupo Carlos', see Jean-Pierre Tardieu, 'Testimonios: Carlos Ordeig Fontanals (1913–1998)', in Paul Estrade (ed.), *El trabajo forzado de los espagñoles en la Francia de Vichy: los grupos de Trabadojes Extranjeros en Corrèze (1940–1944)* (Madrid: UNED, 2016), 285–97.

53 See above, p. 38.

54 TNA, 9/150/6, Major W. R. Probert, 'Report on Activities of the Mission "Aube" in the Ariège Department', 27 Sept. 1944.

55 Peter Lieb, 'Repercussions of Eastern Front Experiences on Anti-Partisan Warfare in France, 1943–1944', *Journal of Strategic Studies*, 31.5 (2008), 806.

56 TNA, 9/150/6, Major W. R. Probert, 'Report on Activities of the Mission "Aube" in the Ariège Department', 27 Sept. 1944.

57 Ibid.
58 Ibid.
59 TNA HS 4/208, 'Report on Activities in Greece of Lieut. Kula (Translated from Polish)', sent under covering note, Major P. Howarth (SOE Cairo) to SOE London, 30 Jan. 1944.
60 Ibid.
61 TNA, HS 4/208, 'Report by Wladyslaw Malanowski', n.d. but *c.* Nov. 1943.
62 TNA, HS 7/154, Colonel C. M. Woodhouse, 'History of the Allied Military Mission in Greece, September 1942 to December 1944', 1945.
63 S. Sarafis, *ELAS: Greek Resistance Army* (London: Merlin Press, 1980), 230.
64 Ibid.
65 TNA, HS 9/755/6, report by Major W. S. Jordan, 1944.

8 Transnational guerrillas in the 'shatter zones' of the Balkans and Eastern Front

1 Denis Mack Smith, *Mussolini's Roman Empire* (London: Longman, 1976); Davide Rodogno, *Fascism's European Empire: Italian Occupation during the Second World War* (Cambridge: Cambridge University Press, 2006).
2 H. James Burgwyn, *Empire on the Adriatic: Mussolini's Conquest of Yugoslavia 1941–1943* (New York: Enigma Books, 2005), 19–20.
3 Jozo Tomasevich, *War and Revolution in Yugoslavia 1941–1945: Occupation and Collaboration* (Stanford, CA: Stanford University Press, 2001), 47.
4 The Ustaša were responsible for more than 500,000 deaths between 1941 and 1945. See Alexander Korb, *Im Schatten des Weltkriegs: Massengewalt der Ustaša gegen Serben, Juden und Roma in Kroatien 1941–1945* (Hamburg: Hamburger Edition, 2013), 12.
5 Tomasevich, *War and Revolution in Yugoslavia*, 61–4; Antony Beevor, *Crete 1941: The Battle and the Resistance* (London: Penguin Books, 2014).
6 After April 1941 only the 704th, 714th, 717th and 718th Infantry divisions remained in the Balkans.
7 Bundesarchiv-Militärarchiv, Freiburg (BArchF), RH 19-XI/86, 'Die große Absetzbewegung im Südosten', Oberbefehlshaber Südost (Heeresgr. F) Generalfeldmarshall Maximilan von Weichs, H.Q., Jan. 1945, p. 1.
8 B. Petranović, *Istorija Jugoslavije*, vol. 2 (Belgrade: Nolit, 1988), 52–153.
9 Mari-Janine Calic, *Geschichte Jugoslawiens im 20. Jahrhundert* (Munich: C. H. Beck, 2010), 142–3. The Germans were afraid that 'a civilian embittered by initial injustice remains a foe forever'. BArchF, RS 3-8/92, Gen. Kdo. LXIX. Res .Korps, Abt. Ic, 1 Nov. 1944, p. 6.
10 Carl Bethke, 'Von der "Umsiedlung" zur " Aussiedlung": Zur destruktiven Dynamik "ethnischer Flurbereiningung" am Beispiel der Deutschen in Bosnien und Kroatien 1941–1948', in Mariana Hausleitner (ed.), *Vom Faschismus zum Stalinismus: Deutsche und andere Minderheiten in Ostmittel- und Südosteuropa 1941–1953* (Munich: IKGS Verlag, 2008), 23–39.
11 Walter Manoschek, *'Serbien ist judenfrei!' Militärische Besatzungspolitik*

und Judenvernichtung in Serbien 1941/42 (Munich: Verlag Oldenbourg, 1993), 66–9, 75–9, 169–84; Tomasevich, *War and Revolution in Yugoslavia*, 587–9.

12 Franziska Zaugg, *Albanische Muslime in der Waffen-SS, von 'Großalbanien' zur Division 'Skanderbeg'* (Paderborn: Schöningh Verlag, 2016), 199–205.

13 BArchF, RH 19-XI/9, Abschrift, 'Kontrolle des Ein- und Durchreiseverkehrs im Kosovogebiet', Div. Kdr. Schmidhuber, 15 June 1944 (Anlage 10 zu DGA Nr. 3046/44 g.v. 6/23/1944), p. 24.

14 Robert Elsie, *Historical Dictionary of Kosova* (Lanham, MD: Scarecrow Press, 2004), 252, and Sara Berger et al., *Besetztes Südosteuropa und Italien*, vol. 14 of Sara Berger, Sanela Schmid, Erwin Lewin and Maria Vassilikou (eds), *Die Verfolgung und Ermordung der europäischen Juden durch das nationalsozialistische Deutschland 1933–1945* (Berlin: De Gruyter; Boston: Oldenbourg, 2017), 719.

15 On the evolution of the idea see Leften Stavros Stavrianos, *Balkan Federation: A History of the Movement toward Balkan Unity in Modern Times* (Hamden, CT: Archon Books, 1964).

16 Archivio Ufficio Storico dello Stato Maggiore dell'Esercito, Rome (AUSSME), I3/b13/f1, 'Situazione politica-militare dell'Albania a tutto, il 19 ottobre 1943', p. 1.

17 Pal Markovits, *Stets bei Verstand sein* (Konstanz: Hartung-Gorre, 2006), 76–8.

18 Ibid., 72.

19 Ibid., 78–9. On Jews in the partisan units see Romano, *Jevreji Jugoslavije 1941–1945*.

20 Reginald Hibbert, *Albania's National Liberation Struggle: The Bitter Victory* (London: Printer Publisher, 1991), 11–28.

21 Archivio Storico Diplomatico, Rome, Gabinetto Albania, B. 148, F. 23/1, 'Attività comunista', 14 April 1942.

22 Paulin Kola, *The Search for Greater Albania* (London: Hurst & Co., 2003), 24–6.

23 Jane Degras (ed.), *The Communist International 1919–1943*, vol. 3: *1929–1943* (London: Oxford University Press, 1965), 471.

24 Dragoljub Petrović, *Saradnja antifašističkih pokreta u Srbiji i Bugarskoj* (Belgrade: Institut za Noviju Istoriju Srbije, 1996), 93.

25 Boro Mitrovski, Venceslav Glišić and Tomo Ristovski: *Bugarska vojska u Jugoslaviji 1941–1944* (Belgrade: Međunarodna Politika, 1971), 158–77.

26 Jamila Andjela Kalonomos, *Monastir without Jews: Recollections of a Jewish Partisan in Macedonia* (New York: Foundation for the Advancement of Sephardic Studies and Culture, 2008), 79–90. The Mirche Acev Battalion, formed on 18 Aug. 1943 in the Karaorman mountains after the merger of the three detachments, Damyan Gruev, Goce Deltchev and Pitu Goli, was joined by a battalion of Kosovo Serbs and a group of Slovenes who had been recently liberated from a German camp in Greece to form the I Macedonian-Kosovo Brigade.

27 Svetozar Voukmanovitch-Tempo, *Le Parti Communiste de Grèce dans la lutte de libération nationale* (Le Livre Yougoslave, 1949), 21–4, 27–36.
28 Raymondos Alvanos, 'Social Conflicts and Political Behaviour in the Area of Kastoria (1922–1949)' (PhD diss., Aristotle University of Thessaloniki, 2005), 290 (in Greek).
29 Jochen Böhler and Robert Gerwarth (eds), *The Waffen-SS: A European History* (Oxford: Oxford University Press, 2017), 3–7.
30 Hans Peter Klausch, *Die 999er: Von der Brigade 'Z' zur Afrika-Division 999. Die Bewährungsbataillone und ihr Anteil am antifaschistischen Widerstand* (Frankfurt am Main: Röderberg-Verlag, 1986), 17–20, 121–31.
31 BArchB, NY 4306, Carton 23, Gerhard Reinhardt, 'Hinweise zum Lebenslauf von Bruno Reinhardt', 10 March 1971.
32 Gerhard Reinhardt, 'Komme ich hier zur Leoforos Alexandras?', in *Strafdivision 999: Erlebnisse und Bericht aus dem antifaschistischen Widerstandskampf* (Berlin: Deutscher Militärverlag, 1966), 70–86.
33 BArchB, NY 4306, Carton 23, Gerhard Reinhardt to the Central Secretariat of the Socialist Unity Party (SED), 21 March 1948.
34 Horst Duhnke, *Die KPD von 1933 bis 1945* (Cologne: Kiepenheuer & Witsch, 1972), 463–79.
35 Gerhard Reinhardt, 'Als Partisan im ELAS-54.Regiment', in *Strafdivision 999*, 96–8.
36 BArchB, SGY 5/1287, 'Erinnerungen des Genossen Gerhard Reinhard', 1 July 1964, 41–2.
37 Ivan Barsukov, 'The Rooski Company', *Ethiniki Antistasi*, 3 (Dec. 1962) 270–5 (in Greek).
38 Ibid., 272.
39 Radnja, Nr 85, report of Borko Temelkovski, Head of Operational Zone III, to Dobrivoje Radosavljević, 26 June 1944. See also Jovan Vujošević et al., *Proceedings of Documents and Data on the National Liberation War of the Yugoslav Peoples*, vol. 7, book 3 (Belgrade: Vojnoizdavački Zavod 'Vojno Delo', 1954), 248–50.
40 T. S. Bushueva, 'Russkie roty i batal'ony v Narodno osvoboditel'noy armii Yugoslavii', *Sovetskoe slavyanovedenie*, 3 (1972), 11–21; Aleksej Timofejev, *Rusi I Drugi svetski rat u Jugoslaviji, uticaj SSSR-a I ruskih emigranata na događaje u Jugoslaviji 1941–1945* (Belgrade: Institut za Noviju Istoriju Srbije, 2011).
41 Franjo Bavec-Branko, 'Anatoliy Diachenko and his Comrades in Slovenia', in *Bazoviška brigada* (Ljubljana: Knjižnica NOV in POS, 1970).
42 David R. Stone, 'Operations on the Eastern Front, 1941–1945', in John Ferris and Evan Mawdsley (eds), *The Cambridge History of the Second World War*, vol. 1 (Cambridge: Cambridge University Press, 2015), 337.
43 J. V. Stalin, radio roadcast, 3 July 1941. https://www.marxists.org/reference/archive/stalin/works/1941/07/03.htm (last accessed 5 May 2019).
44 Yaacov Falkov, *Meragle ha-ye'arot: pe'ilutam ha-modi'init shel ha-parṭizanim ha-Sovyeṭim 1941–1945* (Jerusalem: The Hebrew University

Magness Press and Yad Vashem Press, 2017), 27–30; Alexander Statiev, 'The Soviet Union', in Philip Cooke and Ben H. Shepherd (eds), *Hitler's Europe Ablaze: Occupation, Resistance, and Rebellion during World War II* (New York: Skyhorse Publishing, 2014), 191–7.

45 Aleksandr Zevelev et al. (eds), *Nenavist', spressovannaia v tol* (Moscow: Mysl', 1991), 35. See above, pp. 43–6.

46 Zevelev et al. (eds), *Nenavist'*, 329–30; Valentin Tomin (ed.), *Oni srazhalis' s fashizmom* (Moscow: Politizdat, 1988), 332.

47 A. Kiknadze, 'Ispytanie. Ivan Vinarov', in I. Vasilevich (ed.), *Bessmertie: ocherki o razvedchikakh. Liudi molchalivogo podviga* (Moscow: Izdatel'stvo Politicheskoi Literatury, 1987), 394.

48 Nikola Altnkov, 'Svetskata shpionska mrezha v Blgariia', *Fakel*, 19 June 2018, https://www.fakel.bg/index.php?t=6398 (last accessed 30 May 2018); Vania Georgieva, 'Blgarskiyat Richard Sorge', *Epitsentr*, 30 March 2015, http://epicenter.bg/article/Balgarskiyat-Rihard-Zorge/69638/3/74 (last accessed 30 May 2018); Aleksandr Kolpakidi, *GRU v Velikoi Otechestvennoi voine* (Moscow: Iauza, 2010), 5, 162–3, 194–5; Ivan Vinarov, *Boitsi na tikhiia front: spomeni na razuznavacha* (Sofia: Partizdat, 1988).

49 Falkov, *Meragle ha-ye'arot*, 30–4, 106–20, 156–66, 177–202.

50 Audronė Janavičienė, 'Sovietiniai diversantai Lietovuje (1941–1944)', *Genocidas ir rezistencija*, 1 (2007), 98–121.

51 Jens Gieseke, *Wer war wer im Ministerium für Staatssicherheit (MfS-Handbuch)* (Berlin: Hg. BStU, 2012), 41; Vladimir Lapskii, 'Poslednee srazhenie generala Kliainiunga', *Izvestiia*, 22 Sept. 2009, https://iz.ru/news/353316.

52 Daina Bleiere, Ilgvars Butulis, Inesis Feldmanis, Aivars Stranga and Antonijs Zunda, *Latvija Otrajā Pasaules Karā* (Riga: Jumava, 2008), 325–6; Marģers Vestermanis, *Vēstules nākamībai: Latvijas partizāņu kustības un komunistiskās pagrīdes cīnītāju pirmsnāves atvadas* (Riga: Liesma, 1965), 23–6.

53 Lithuanian Special Archives, Vilnius, f. 1, ap. 1, b. 26, l, 'On the situation in occupied Latvia', undated report signed by 'Sudmal', summer 1942, pp. 4–8.

54 Bleiere et al., *Latvija Otrajā Pasaules Karā*, 325–6.

55 Vestermanis, *Vēstules nākamībai*, 25.

56 Mikhail Semiriaga, *Sovetskie liudi v evropeiskom soprotivlenii* (Moscow: Nauka, 1970), 40; Stanisław Supruniuk, *Z Polesia do Warszawy* (Warsaw: Agencja ATM, 2009), 98; Pavel Zhilin (ed.), *Boevoe sodruzhestvo sovetskogo i pol'skogo narodov* (Moscow: Mysl', 1973), 240–1.

57 David Berlinskii and Mordukh Pogrebinskii, *Podvig Iana Nalepki* (Moscow: Voenizdat, 1959); Viliam Šalgovič, *Ján Nálepka – učiteľ, partizan, hrdina* (Martin: Osveta, 1962).

58 Elena Aga Rossi, *A Nation Collapses: The Italian Surrender of September 1943* (Cambridge: Cambridge University Press, 2000).

59 Mario De Prospo, 'Reconstructing the Army of a Collapsed Nation: The Kingdom of the South of Italy (September 1943 – March 1944)', *Journal of Modern Italian Studies*, 18.1 (2013), 1–2.

60 AUSSME, I3/b13/f1, report by Sottotenente Nazzareno Garat Crema, 27 Oct. 1943. Cf. also Avagliano Palmieri, *Gli internati militari italiani: diari e lettere dai lager Nazisti 1943–1945* (Turin: Einaudi, 2009), 3.

61 Elena Aga Rossi and Maria Teresa Giusti, *Guerra a parte: i militari italiani nei Balcani 1940–1945* (Bologna: il Mulino, 2011), 310.

62 Ibid., 309.

63 Ilio Muraca, 'I partigiani all'estero: la Resistenza fuori d'Italia', in Enzo Collotti, Renato Sandri and Frediano Sessi (eds), *Dizionario della Resistenza* (Turin: Einaudi 2006), 173; Rossi and Giusti, *Guerra a parte*, 322–37.

64 AUSSME, I3/b14/f2, Collective interrogation reports by Marco de Ferrari, D'Ulivo, Fabbri, Sacchelli, Santi, De Vita, n.d., p. 2.

65 AUSSME, I3/b13/f3, Report by Aldo Carta, pp. 1–2.

66 Ibid., p. 4.

67 AUSSME, I3/b13/f1, Report of the situation in Albania, 8–15 Sept. 1943.

68 AUSSME, I3/b13/f1, Report by Guido Tecchi, 23 Oct. 1943.

69 Roderick Bailey, *The Wildest Province: SOE in the Land of the Eagle* (London: Jonathan Cape, 2008), 82.

70 On 7 July 1945, Piccini reported that 16,289 Italian soldiers had been repatriated from Durrës to Italy between 11 September 1944 and 7 July 1945, and still about 1,200 Italian soldiers remained in Albania. AUSSME, I3/b14/f2, Report Piccini to the Ministry of War, 7 July 1945, p. 1.

71 AUSSME, 6, Piccini, Gino, 12 June 1944.

72 e.g. AUSSME, I3/b14/1, 'Les Italiens en Albanie après le 8 septembre 1938'.

73 TNA, HS 5/65, 'List of the most important guerrillas', Aug. 1943; TNA, HS 5/68, 'Daily situation', Report no. 206, 14 March 1944.

74 Buno Brunetti, *Da oppressori a combattenti per la libertà* (Lucca: Istituto Storico della Resistenza in Provincia di Lucca, 1990), 28–9.

75 Mario Fantacci, 'L'armistizio e la mia partecipazione dalla guerra di liberazione in Albania', in B. Dradi Maraldi and Pieri R. Milano (eds), *Lotta armata e resistenza delle forze armate all'estero* (Milan: Franco Angeli, 1990), 160.

76 Ioannis Nioutsikos, 'The EAM-ELAS Resistance to the Axis Occupation of Greece 1941–1944: A Case Study in the Theory and Practice of Guerilla Warfare' (PhD dissertation, King's College London, 2015), 118–20.

77 TNA, FO 371/43691/R13508, Boxshall to Laskey, 28 Aug. 1944.

78 'The ELAS Battalion of Death', *Rizospastis*, 20 Oct. 1943.

79 Carlo Ferrari, e-mail to Jason Chandrinos, 23 Nov. 2017.

80 Hermann Frank Meyer, *Blutiges Edelweiß: Die 1. Gebirgs-Division im Zweiten Weltkrieg* (Berlin: Ch. Links Verlag, 2008), 566–82.

81 Klaus Schmider, *Partisanenkrieg in Jugoslawien 1941–1944 (*Hamburg: Mittler & Sohn, 2002), 417–20, 505–8.

82 Bailey, *The Wildest Province*, 3.

83 National Archives and Records Administration, College Park, MD, T314/664, Report operation 'Draufgänger', 18–28 July 1944, Schmidhuber, Lagebeurteilung 22.7.44, 283; Schmider, *Partisanenkrieg*, 505.

84 Miloš Vuksanović, *Prva proleterska brigada* (Belgrade-Titograd: Narodna Knjiga, ISI, Pobjeda 1981), 380.
85 Antonio Roasio, *Figlio della classe operaia* (Milan: Vangelista, 1977), 219.
86 Maurizio Antonioli, *Dizionario biografico degli anarchici italiani*, vol. 1: *A–G* (Pisa: BFS, 2003), 312–14.
87 Claudio Pavone, *A Civil War: A History of the Italian Resistance* (London and New York: Verso, 2013), 368.
88 Santo Peli, *Storie di GAP: terrorismo urbano e resistenza* (Turin: Einaudi, 2017), 16 and 40. See also Luigi Borgomaneri, *Li chiamavano terroristi: storia dei GAP Milanesi* (Milan: Unicopli, 2015).
89 Era Barontini, *Dario: Ilio Barontini* (Livorno: Editrice Nuova Fortezza, 1988), 208; Fabio Baldassarri, *Ilio Barontini: fuoriuscito, internazionalista e partigiano* (Rome: Robin Edizioni, 2013), 104.
90 Peli, *Storie di GAP*, 63.
91 Roger Absalom, 'Allied Escapers and the *Contadini* in Occupied Italy (1943–1945)', *Journal of Modern Italian Studies*, 10.4 (2005), 413.
92 Rodogno, *Fascism's European Empire*, 357–8.
93 Archivio Storico Diplomatico, Rome, Gabinetto Albania, B. 181, F. 54, Confinati albanesi, 29 March 1942.
94 Petro Marko, *Intervistë me vetveten (retë dhe gurët)* (Tirana: Omsca, 2000), 365.
95 Marita Sauku Bruci and Vittorio Bruno Stamerra, *Il Cristo Rosso e il suo Apostolo: storie di confinati politici ad Ustica, Vincenzo Gigante nei ricordi di Petro Marko* (Brindisi: Hobos, 2015), 10.
96 Luigi Centra, *I deportati: internati civili nel campo di concentramento Le Fraschette di Alatri* (Casamari: La Monastica, 1998).
97 On Svetozar Laković Tozo and his experience in the Italian resistance see Svetozar Laković ('Toso'), *Memorie di un comandante partigiano montenegrino* (Perugia and Foligno: Isuc-Editoriale Umbra, 2010).
98 John Cowtan, *From the Gazala Line to Behind the Lines: Wartime Memories of John Cowtan* (London: AuthorHouse, 2011), 95; Matteo Petracci, 'La liberazione interrotta: lettere dal carcere di un partigiano etiopico', *Mondo contemporaneo*, 1 (2017), 71 and 93.
99 Matteo Petracci, 'I neri della Pai: dalla Mostra delle Terre italiane d'Oltremare alla Resistenza', in Chiara Donati and Tommaso Rossi (eds), *Guerra e resistenza nell'Appennino umbro-marchigiano: problematiche e casi di studio* (Foligno: Editoriale Umbra, 2017), 238–41. See also Gianni Dore, 'Ideologia coloniale e senso comune etnografico nella Mostra delle terre italiane d'Oltremare', in Nicola Labanca (ed.), *L'Africa in vetrina. Storie di musei e di esposizioni coloniali in Italia* (Treviso: Pagus, 1992), 47–65.
100 RGASPI, 545/6/498, Pietro Pavanin, 'Latini Guido', 26 April 1940, fols 23–4; Petracci, 'La liberazione interrotta', 95–6.
101 Petracci, 'I neri della Pai', 245–9. On the participation of African fighters in the Italian resistance see also Carlo Costa and Lorenzo Teodino, *Razza*

partigiana: storia di Giorgio Marincola, 1923–1945 (Rome: Iacobelli Editore, 2008).

102 Falkov, *Meragle ha-ye'arot*, 50–1.

103 Ibid., 92–101.

104 Ibid., 56, 59.

105 Interview with Leonid Berenshtein, recorded by Yaacov Falkov, Kiryat Haim, Israel, 7 April 2006.

9 Transnational uprisings: Warsaw, Paris, Slovakia

1 See Chapter 7.

2 Jan Ciechanowski, *The Warsaw Rising of 1944* (Cambridge: Cambridge University Press, 1974).

3 Włodzimierz Borodziej, *Der Warschauer Aufstand 1944* (Frankfurt am Main: S. Fischer Verlag, 2001); Norman Davies, *Rising '44: The Battle for Warsaw* (London: Macmillan, 2003); Halik Kochanski, *Eagle Unbowed: Poland and the Poles in the Second World War* (London: Penguin Books, 2013); Philip Cooke and Ben Shepherd (eds), *Hitler's Europe Ablaze: Occupation, Resistance and Rebellion during World War II* (New York: Skyhorse Publishing, 2014).

4 Stanisław Okęcki, *Cudzoziemcy w polskim ruchu oporu: 1939–45* (Warsaw: Interpress, 1975), a censored communist-era book, can hardly be called an 'academic monograph'.

5 'Hołd dla Słowaków', Muzeum Powstania Warszawskiego, 10 June 2005, www.1944.pl/o_muzeum/news/hold_dla_slowakow/?q=iringh (last accessed 27 April 2020); 'Obcokrajowcy w Powstaniu', Muzeum Powstania Warszawskiego, n.d., www.1944.pl/o_muzeum/ekspozycja/1_pietro/39_obcokrajowcy_w_powstaniu/?q=iringh (last accessed 27 April 2020). See also the insufficient historical attention paid to the uprising's foreign participants in the interview with Katarzyna Utracka, a historian at the Warsaw Rising Museum: 'Nieodkryta karta', *Polska Zbrojna*, 14 Aug. 2012, www.polska-zbrojna.pl/home/articleinmagazineshow/4732?t=ZA-WOLNOSC-WASZA (last accessed 27 April 2020). On schools, see Rafał Dolecki, Krzysztof Gutowski and Jędrzej Smoleński, *Po prostu historia: podręcznik szkoły ponadgimnazjalne* (Warsaw: Wydawnictwa Szkolne i Pedagogiczne, 2013), 200–54.

6 Norman Davies briefly mentions the participation in the uprising of the British sergeant John Ward and the SOE Polish paratroopers called *Cichociemni*, drawing on a book published in communist Poland in 1985. Davies, *Rising '44*, 191, 288, 324–5, 464–6; Kochanski, *Eagle Unbowed*, 228, 286, 364.

7 'Obcokrajowcy w Powstaniu'.

8 Andrzej Sowa and Dorota Truszczak, 'Powstanie styczniowe: obcy też walczyli za naszą wolność', *Polskie Radio*, 24 July 2013, www.polskieradio.pl/7/2612/Artykul/895066,Powstanie-styczniowe-obcy-tez-walczyli-za-nasza-wolnosc (last accessed 27 April 2020).

9 Waldemar Ireneusz Oszczęda, 'Udiał Słowaków w Powstaniu Warszawskim', *Almanach Muszyny dla Małej Ojczyzny* (2008), 87–92,

www.almanachmuszyny.pl/spisy/2008/UDZIAL%20SLOWAKOW.pdf (last accessed 27 April 2020).

10 'Mirosław Iringh', Muzeum Powstania Warszawskiego, n.d., www.1944.pl/historia/powstancze-biogramy/Miroslaw_Iringh (last accessed 27 April 2020).

11 'Obcokrajowcy w Powstaniu'.

12 'August Agbola O'Brown', Muzeum Powstania Warszawskiego, n.d., www.1944.pl/historia/powstancze-biogramy/August_OBrown (last accessed 27 April 2020); Ed Keazor, 'August Agboola Browne Nigerian Pioneer of Jazz Music and World War 2 Hero', *Music in Africa Magazine*, 29 May 2015, http://musicinafrica.net/august-agboola-browne-nigerian-pioneer-jazz-music-and-world-war-2-hero (last accessed 27 April 2020).

13 Davies, *Rising '44*, 191; Kochanski, *Eagle Unbowed*, 228, 268, 364; Grzegorz Korcziński, *Polskie oddziały specjalne w II wojnie światowej* (Warsaw: Bellona, 2006), 60; Jan Szatsznaider, *Cichiociemni: z Polski do Polski* (Wrocław: Krajowa Agencja Wydawnicza, 1985).

14 Brian Lett, *SOE's Mastermind. An Authorised Biography of Major General Sir Colin Gubbins, KCMG, DSO, MC* (Barnsley: Pen & Sword Military, 2016).

15 Davies, *Rising '44*, 268, 324–5, 464–6; Stefan Karbonski, *Fighting Warsaw* (London: George Allen & Unwin, 1956), 358–62; Jonathan Walker, *Poland Alone: Britain, SOE, and the Collapse of the Polish Resistance 1944* (London: The History Press, 2011), 40, 53, 76.

16 'Missing Men from 1945', *National Ex-Prisoner of War Association* (Autumn 2013), 9, www.prisonerofwar.org.uk/ AUTUMN%202013%20NEWSLETTER.pdf (last accessed 27 April 2020).

17 Piotr Wróblewski, 'Waleczny Francuz na murach Warszawy. Znacie jego historię?', *Warszawa Naszemiasto*, 23 June 2016, http://warszawa.naszemiasto.pl/artykul/waleczny-francuz-na-murach-warszawy-znacie-jego-historie,3451335,artgal,t,id,tm.html (last accessed 27 April 2020).

18 Roman Vol'nodumov, 'Russkie i varshavskoe vosstanie', *Petr I mazepA*, 1 Aug. 2015, http://petrimazepa.com/warsaw.html (last accessed 27 April 2020).

19 Bogusław Kopka, *Konzentrationslager Warschau: historia i następstwa* (Warsaw: Instytut Pamięci Narodowej, 2007), 101–12; 'Obcokrajowcy w Powstaniu'; 'Za wolność waszą', *Polska Zbrojna*, 14 Aug. 2012, www.polska-zbrojna.pl/home/articleinmagazineshow/4732?t=ZA-WOLNOSC-WASZA (last accessed 27 April 2020).

20 Evelyn Mesquida, *La Nueve, 24 août 1944: ces républicains espagnols qui ont libéré Paris* (Paris: Cherche-Midi, 2011); Diego Gaspar Celaya, 'Portrait d'oubliés: l'engagement des Espagnols dans les Forces françaises libres, 1940–1945', *Revue historique des armées*, 265 (2011), 46–55, http://journals.openedition.org/rha/7345 (last accessed 6 Jan. 2018). See also above, p. 88.

21 See Diego Gaspar Celaya, *La guerra continúa: voluntarios españoles al servicio de la Francia libre (1940–1945)* (Madrid: Marcial Pons, 2015), 409–15.

22 The desegregation was to be decided by Truman in 1948.

23 See Sylvie Lindeperg, *La voie des images: quatre histoires de tournage au printemps–été 1944* (Paris: Éditions Verdier, 2013); René Dunan, *'Ceux' de Paris: août 1944* (Genea: Éditions du Milieu du Monde, 1945). See also Eric Lafon, 'Photographie de Dukson, "un oublié de l'histoire" de la Libération', www.fondationresistance.org/pages/rech_doc/dukson-oublie-histoire-liberation_photo10.htm (last accessed 20 Feb. 2018).

24 René Dunan, *'Ceux' de Paris*, entitles his chapter 14, dedicated to Georges Dukson, 'La magnifique et lamentable histoire de Dukson "héros du XVIIe"'. See also Matthew Cobb, *The Resistance: The French Fight against the Nazis* (London: Simon & Schuster, 2009), 269–70.

25 Gaston Laroche, colonel FTPF Boris Matline, *On les nommait des étrangers: les immigrés dans la Résistance* (Paris: Les Éditeurs Français Réunis, 1965), gave the general figure of 40.000 foreigners fighting in the FFIs in August 1944, which is perhaps overstated but suggests the importance of the phenomenon.

26 See, for example, Karel Bartosek, René Gallissot and Denis Peschanski, *De l'exil à la Résistance: réfugiés et immigrés d'Europe centrale en France, 1933–1945* (Paris: Presses Universitaires de Vincennes, 1989).

27 Robert Gildea, *Fighters in the Shadows: A New History of the French Resistance* (London: Faber & Faber, 2015), 232–3.

28 Vera Varsa-Szekeres, *Salamandre: une vie confrontée à la Gestapo française et à la police politique hongroise* (Paris: L'Harmattan, 2016).

29 La Contemporaine (formerly Bibliothèque de Documentation Internationale Contemporaine), Nanterre, E pièce 2601.1–2.

30 La Contemporaine, Nanterre, 4e pièce 129 Rés. 10.

31 Stéphane Courtois, Denis Peschanski and Adam Rayski, *Le sang de l'étranger: les immigrés de la MOI dans la Résistance* (Paris: Fayard, 1989), 402.

32 Dušan Halaj, Ľubomír Moncoľ and Ján Stanislav, *Francúzi v Slovenskom národnom povstaní* [The French in the Slovak national uprising] (Banská Bystrica: Grafické Štúdio Ing. Petra Jurigu., 2003), 7.

33 See Viliam Plevza, *Dejiny Slovenského národného povstania 1944* [The history of the Slovak national uprising 1944], vol. 5 (Bratislava: Pravda, 1984), 129.

34 De la Roncière himself was captured and wounded by a border guard during his eleventh crossing on 4 Sept. 1944 and was imprisoned, but then escaped and later got to Bucharest.

35 Pim Dulová and Vladimír Jeršov, *Francúzski bojovníci v Slovenskom národnom povstaní* [The French combatants in the Slovak national uprising] (Bratislava: Povereníctvo Informácií, 1947), 15.

36 Jaroslav Hrbek et al., *Draze zaplacená svoboda: osvobození Československa 1944–1945* [Dearly paid freedom: the liberation of Czechoslovakia 1944–1945], vol. 1 (Prague: Paseka, 2009), 287.

37 Halaj, Moncoľ and Stanislav, *Francúzi v Slovenskom národnom povstaní*, 47–62.

38 Ibid., 75, 80–1.

39 Central State Archives of Public Organisations of the Ukraine, Kiev

(CSAPOU), fund 112 (Supreme Headquarters of the Partisan Movement in Czechoslovakia), opis [compartment] 1, delo [file] 13, operation report of the French unit, 13 Oct. 1944; delo 10, situation report, 18 Oct. 1944.

40 Halaj, Moncoľ and Stanislav, *Francúzi v Slovenskom národnom povstaní*, 109–15.

41 See the recollections of the last days of Forestier's struggle by his companion, the nurse Pim Dul: Dulová and Jeršov, *Francúzski bojovníci v Slovenskom národnom povstaní*, 65–78.

42 On 29 Oct. 1944 the Main Staff of Partisan Units was renamed the Main Staff of the Partisan Movement.

43 See the vivid recollections by de Lannurien's aide: René Picard: René Picard, *L'ennemi retrouvé* (Conflans-Sainte-Honorine, private publication, 1953), trans. as *A znovu sme stretli nepriateľa* (Bratislava: Nakladateľstvo Pravda, 1984), 175–249.

44 See the memoirs Jean-Baptiste Boyer, *Résistants: partisans français en Slovakie* (Saint-Cloud: Atlante Éditions, 2012); Halaj, Moncoľ and Stanislav, *Francúzi v Slovenskom národnom povstaní*, 101–8, 116–23, 307–10.

45 Stanislav Kokoška, 'Americké dodávky zbraní Slovenskému národnímu povstání' [The US supplies of arms to the Slovak National Uprising], in *SNP v pamäti národa: materiály z vedeckej konferencie k 50. výročiu SNP. Donovaly 26.–28. apríla 1994* [The Slovak national uprising in the nation's memory: materials from the conference commemorating the fiftieth anniversary of the SNU. Donovaly, 26–28 April 1994] (Bratislava: NKV International, 1994), 361–71. The Slovak sources mention slightly lower figures: Vilém Prečan (ed.), *Slovenské národné povstanie: dokumenty* [The Slovak national uprising: documents] (Bratislava: VPL, 1965), no. 561, p. 875.

46 For further details see National Archives and Records Administration, College Park, MD, entry 146, box 36, folder 485; entry 154, box 42, folder 642; entry 141A, box 12, folder 89.

47 Jim Downs, *Druhá svetová vojna: tragédia OSS na Slovensku* [The Second World War: the OSS tragedy in Slovakia] (Bratislava: Magnet Press, 2004), 403, 67–8.

48 On the WINDPROOF mission see TNA, HS 4/49, HS 4/54.

49 National Archives and Records Administration, College Park, MD, entry 190, box 22, folder 1; entry 124, box 28, folder 221; entry 136, box 34, folders 375, 376.

50 Jiří Šolc, *Bylo málo mužů* [There were not enough men] (Prague: Merkur, 1991), 250–1; Zlatica Zudová-Lešková, 'Československý výsadok Courier 5' [The Czechoslovak paratroop unit Courier 5]', *Soudobé dějiny*, 8.4 (2001), 718–31.

51 See e.g. the multiple orders by the Main Staff of the Partisan Movement in CSAPOU, fund 112, op. 1, delo 4. The file covers the period from 14 Nov. 1944 to 17 Feb. 1945.

10 Afterlives and memories

1 Jean-Baptiste Boyer, *Résistants: partisans français en Slovakie* (Saint-Cloud: Atlante Éditions, 2012), 7. See above, p. 210.

2 Robert Gildea, 'The Long March of Oral History: Around 1968 in France', *Oral History*, 38.1 (2010), 70.

3 See above, p. 88.

4 Charles de Gaulle, *Discours et messages*, vol. 1 (Paris: Plon, 1970), 439–40.

5 Robert Gildea, *Fighters in the Shadows: A New History of the French Resistance* (London: Faber & Faber, 2015), 411–12.

6 TNA, HS9/877/5, report by Captain Peter Lake, 27 Sept. 1944.

7 See above, p. 46.

8 Mercedes Yusta, *Guerrilla y resistencia campesina:la resistencia armada contra el franquismo en Aragón* (Saragossa: Prensas Universitarias de Zaragoza, 2003), 180–6; Mercedes Yusta, 'Les guerillas et le prolongement de la Guerre civile', in Roger Bourderon (ed.), *La guerre d'Espagne: l'histoire, les lendemains, la mémoire* (Paris: Tallandier, 2007), 231–40; Guy Pernet, *Pour que vive la République. 'Sebastian': son combat face au fascisme, face au franquisme* (Toulouse: Cap Bear, 2013).

9 See above, pp. 46–7.

10 Jorge Marco, *Guerrilleros and Neighbours in Arms: Identities and Cultures of Anti-Fascist Resistance in Spain* (Brighton: Sussex Academic Press, 2016), 3, 49–57. See also above, Chapter 2.

11 Ramón Via Fernández, 'Yo acuso: escrito en la cárcel de Málaga' (clandestine leaftet, 1946); Ramón Via Fernández, *J'accuse ... paroles confiées par Ramon Via Fernández a un prisonnier sorti de la prison de Malaga* (Paris: Secours Populaire Français et le Comité France-Espagne, 1946).

12 *L'Humanité*, 5 and 7 July 1946; *Cili-Soir*, 5 July 1946; *Franc-Tireur*, 7 July 1946; *España Popular*, 9 July 1946; *Mundo Obrero*, 11 July 1946; *Combat*, 13 July 1946; *Le Populaire*, 13 July 1946.

13 RGASPI, 495/277/, 639, Ilich Lyubomir.

14 The work of the association is available in AoY, fond 674, Association of Yugoslav Volunteers of the Spanish Republican Army.

15 See above, Chapter 2.

16 See above, pp. 44–5.

17 Biographical data about Mihail Burcă in Galia Burcă's personal file in NAR, Bucharest, Collection no. 53, file B/276, vols 1–2, passim, and Andrei Siperco (ed.), *Confesiunile elitei comuniste. România 1944–1965: rivalități, represiuni, crime ... Arhiva Alexandru Șiperco* (Bucharest: Institutul Național Pentru Studiul Totalitarismului, 2015), 388–92.

18 Arhiva Consiliului Național Pentru Studierea Arhivelor Securității, Bucharest, Information fund, file no. 187872, 4; Gildea, *Fighters in the Shadows*, 218, 224.

19 United States Department of State, *Foreign Relations of the United States, 1948*, vol. 4: *Eastern Europe, the Soviet Union* (Washington, DC: US Govt. Print. Off., 1972–76), 1066, document 691 860H.00/3–3148, telegram from

the Ambassador in Yugoslavia (Cannon) to the Secretary of State, secret, Belgrade, 31 March 1948, 4 p.m., 362.

20 Ivo Banac, *With Stalin against Tito: Cominformist Splits in Yugoslav Communism* (Ithaca, NY, and London: Cornell University Press, 1988).

21 Boro Krivokapić, *Dahauski procesi* (Belgrade: Prosveta, and Ljubljana: Partizanska Knjiga, 1986); Martin Ivanič and Branko Ziherl (eds), *Dahauski procesi: Reziskovalno poročilo za dokumenti* (Ljubljana: Komunist, 1990).

22 The official number of the detained includes 16,090 names. See Dragoslav Mihailović et al. (eds), *Zatočenici Golog otoka: registar lica osuđivanih zbog Informbiroa, dokument Uprave državne bezbednosti FNR Jugoslavije* (Belgrade: Arhiv Srbije, 2016).

23 AoY, fond 724, Yugoslav volunteers in the Spanish Civil War, personal files, group Šp, VIII-K/48, Emilijan Kalafatić; RGASPI, 495/ 277/639, Kalafatich Milan 1841.

24 See above, p. 121.

25 Różycki, 'Dąbrowszczacy i pamięć', 201–9.

26 See above, pp. 81–2.

27 Jan Kalous, 'Osvald Závodský – aktér i oběť politických procesů', *Paměť a dějiny*, 8.3 (2013), 85–95. See also Stéphane Courtois, *Le livre noir du communisme: crimes, terreur, répression* (Paris: Laffont, 1999).

28 Artur London, *On Trial* (London: Macdonald & Co., 1970), 11; Jan Gerber, *Ein Prozess in Prag: Das Volk gegen Rudolf Slánský und Genossen* (Göttingen: Vandenhoeck & Ruprecht, 2016).

29 Full details of the Party investigation conducted In Patriciu's case in his personal file at NAR, Bucharest, fund C.C. of R.C.P.-P.C.C., file P/37, passim.

30 Interview with Mihail Burcă, 5 July 1991, in Robert Levy, *Ana Pauker: The Rise and Fall of a Jewish Communist* (Berkeley: University of California Press, 2001), 160.

31 See above, pp. 27–8.

32 Gregory Sandford, *From Hitler to Ulbricht: The Communist Reconstruction of East Germany, 1945–1946* (Princeton, NJ: Princeton University Press, 1983); Josie McLellan, *Antifascism and Memory in East Germany: Remembering the International Brigades, 1945–1989* (Oxford: Clarendon Press, 2004), 46–8, 60–1.

33 Studs Terkel, *An Oral History of World War Two* (London: Hamish Hamilton, 1985), 493.

34 Peter N. Carroll, *The Odyssey of the Abraham Lincoln Brigades: Americans in the Spanish Civil War* (Stanford, CA: Stanford University Press, 1994), 293–309.

35 Gildea, *Fighters in the Shadows*, 449; Charles Tillon, *Un procès de Moscou à Paris* (Paris: Seuil, 1971).

36 AD Haute-Garonne, 16J222, Lopez Tovar, Autobiography, 1991, pp. 146–8; Aurélie Denoyer, *L'exil comme patrie: les réfugiés communistes espagnols en RDA (1950–1989)* (Rennes: Presses Universitaires de Rennes, 2017).

37 José Aurelio Romero Navas, '1952: huida de los seis últimos guerrilleros a Francia', *Jábega*, 88 (2001), 96.

38 Marco, *Guerrilleros and Neighbours in Arms*, 17; Jorge Marco, 'Ecos partisanos: la memoria de la resistencia como memoria conflictiva', *Historia del presente*, 17 (2011), 84–6.

39 *La Conférence Africaine Française, Brazzaville (30 janvier–8 février 1944)* (Algiers: Commissariat aux Colonies, 1944), 27, 35. See also Paul Isoart, 'Les aspects politiques, constitutionnels et administratifs des recommendations', in Institut Charles de Gaulle/IHTP, *Brazzaville, janvier–février 1944: aux sources de la decolonisation* (Paris: Plon, 1988), 81.

40 Jacques Bigeard, *Pour une parcelle de gloire* (Paris: Plon, 1975), 229–30.

41 Robert Gildea, *Empires of the Mind: The Colonial Past and the Politics of the Present* (Cambridge: Cambridge University Press, 2019), 92.

42 Report of Joint Planning Staff, 11 July 1944, cited by Lars Baerentzen, 'The German Withdrawal from Greece in 1944 and British Naval "Inactivity"', *Journal of Modern Greek Studies*, 5.2 (Oct. 1987), 255–6.

43 John Campbell and Philip Sherrard, *Modern Greece* (London: Ernest Benn Ltd, 1968), 180–3.

44 See above, pp. 150–4.

45 BArchB, NY 4306, Karton 2, G. Reinhardt, letter to the Central Secretariat of the Socialist Unity Party (SED), 21 March 1948.

46 H. Kühnrich and F. K. Hitze, *Deutsche bei Titos Partisanen 1941–1945: Kriegsschicksale auf dem Balkan in Augenzeugenberichte und Dokumenten* (Cologne: GNN Verlag, 1997), 174–7, 215–24.

47 Sylvia Apostolidou, quoted in G. Apostolidou, 'Antistasi genous thilikou', *Έθνος* [Nation], 1 June 2008.

48 Haganah Archives, A. Polonski, D 11bis-VI/6, agreement of 9 April 1946.

49 Thomas Albrich and Ronald W. Zweig (eds), *Escape through Austria: Jewish Refugees and the Austrian Route to Palestine* (London and Portland: Frank Cass, 2002), 43–6, 89–95.

50 Haganah Archives, A. Polonski, D 14-VII/3, report of Pierrot Mouchenik, n.d., and report by Arthur Epstein, 17 Aug. 1947; Alan Swarc, 'Illegal Immigration to Palestine, 1945–1948: The French Connection' (PhD dissertation, University College London, 2005), 126–46.

51 Jacques Lazarus, *Juifs au combat: témoignage sur l'activité d'un mouvement de résistance* (Paris: Éditions du Centre, 1947), 112–13, 149.

52 Haganah Archives, A. Polonski, D 14-I/25, Ginette Mouchenik to Polonski, 21 July 1947.

53 'Bili smo u Španiji dostojni predstavnici naših naroda', *Politika*, 28 Oct. 1956, p. 2.

54 'Narodi sveta preko svojih dobrovoljaca zbratimili su se sa španskim narodom', *Politika*, 28 Oct. 1956, p. 6.

55 *European Resistance Movements, 1939–1945: Proceedings of the First International Conference on the History of the Resistance Movements, Held at*

Liège-Bruxelles-Breendonk, 14–17 September 1958 (Oxford and New York: Pergamon Press, 1960), xv.

56 *European Resistance Movements, 1939–1945: Proceedings of the Second International Conference on the History of the Resistance Movements Held at Milan 26–29 March 1961* (Oxford and New York: Pergamon Press, 1964), 10, 94, 118, 642–4.

57 McLellan, *Antifascism and Memory*, 68–70.

58 Edith Zorn, 'Einige Forschungergebnisse zur Taetigkeit deutscher Antifaschisten, die an der Seite der franzoesischen Résistance kaempften', *Beitraege zur deutschen Arbeiterbewegung*, 7.2 (1965), 155–65. See also BArchB, Franz Dahlem papers, NY 4072/151, pp. 155–65, and Franz Kuhn, 'Edith Zorn', in Nicole Colin, Corinne Defrance, Ulrich Pfeil and Joachim Umlauf (eds), *Lexikon deutsch-französischer Kuturbeziehungen* (Tübingen: Narr Verlag, 2015), 490.

59 Musée de la Résistance Nationale, Fonds Ouzoulias. carton 21, dossier 5, Résistance allemande, speech of Ouzoulias, Berlin, 7 Sept. 1964, cited in Gildea, *Fighters in the Shadows*, 460.

60 *Jewish Resistance during the Holocaust: Proceedings of the Conference on Manifestations of Jewish Resistance, Jerusalem, 7–11 April 1968* (Jerusalem: Yad Vashem, 1971), 15–16.

61 Erich Kulka, *Jews in Svoboda's Army in the Soviet Union* (Lanham, MD: University Press of America, 1987); in Czech as *Židé v československé Svobodově armádě* (Prague: Naše Vojsko, 1990).

62 Haganah Archives, A. Polonsky, D 11bis IX-A/1, Latour to Polonsky, 20 Dec. 1967, 30 March and 21 Sept. 1968; Memorial de la Shoah, Centre de Documentation Juive Contemporaine, Paris, DL XI-17, interview with Albert Cohen; DL X1–77, interview with Abraham Polonski.

63 Anny Latour, *La Résistance juive en France, 1940–1944* (Paris: Stock, 1970).

64 David Diamant, *Héros juifs de la Résistance* (Paris: Éditions Renouveau, 1962); *Les juifs dans la Résistance française, 1940–1944: avec armes ou sans armes* (Paris: Le Pavillon, 1971); AD Seine Saint-Denis 335J7, Fonds David Diamant, Symposium, 23 Nov. 1974, 'Les juifs sans la Résistance française ou la Résistance juive en France'.

65 AD Seine Saint-Denis 335 J5, Fonds Diamant, 'Les juifs de France dans la guerre contre le Nazisme', MS, n.d. but 1960s, p. 18, cited by Gildea, *Fighters in the Shadows*, 220–1. Memorial de la Shoah, Paris, DLXI-84, interview with Adam Rayski, conducted by Anny Latour.

66 Robert Aron, *Histoire de Vichy, 1940–1944* (Paris: Fayard, 1954); Robert Aron, *Histoire de l'Épuration I: de l'indulgence aux massacres, nov. 1942–sept. 1944* (Paris: Fayard, 1967).

67 Aron, *Histoire de l'Épuration I*, 453–4; Claude Lévy, *Les parias de la Résistance* (Paris: Calmann-Lévy, 1970).

68 Leszek W. Głuchowski and Antony Polonsky (eds), *1968: Forty Years After* (Oxford: Littman Library of Jewish Civilization, 2009).

69 Interview with Tiennot Grumbach, conducted by Robert Gildea, Paris, 18 April 2008.
70 Pierre Goldman, *Souvenirs obscurs d'un juif polonais né en France* (Paris: Broché, 1975), 33. Alésia was the site of a great battle between the Gauls and Julius Caesar; Louis IX or Saint-Louis was a great crusading king of France.
71 Louis Gronowski, *Le dernier grand soir: un juif de Pologne* (Paris: Seuil, 1980), 289.
72 Gildea, *Fighters in the Shadows*, 431.
73 BArchB, NY 4072/147, Dahlem to Beling, 2 May 1969; Niebergall to Marrane and Tollet, 20 Jan. 1971; Musée de la Résistance Nationale, Liquidation OS-FN-FTP. Allemagne, Dahlem to 'camarade Georges [Marrane]', 3 April 1971; Gildea, *Fighters in the Shadows*, 455.
74 Musée de la Résistance Nationale, Liquidation OS-FN-FTP, Allemagne, Dahlem to 'camarade Georges [Marrane], 3 April 1971.
75 Musée de la Résistance Nationale, Fonds Ouzoulias, carton 2, dossier 2, Résistance allemande, Dahlem, handwritten memoirs, 1974, p. 2.
76 BArchB, NY 4072/242, 'Lebensbeschreibung von Käthe Dahlem'; NY 4072/245, Lotte Spangenberg, 'Käthe – de Mütter der Interbrigade'.
77 *Der Spiegel*, 28 Dec. 1981, www.spiegel.de/spiegel/print/d-14354570.html (last accessed 30 May 2019).
78 Musée de la Résistance Nationale, Liquidation OS-FN-FTP, Allemagne, Michel Lissansky to Rouquet, 14 and 15 Aug. 1984; Floriane Benoît and Charles Silverstre (eds), *Les inconnus de la Résistance* (Paris: L'Humanité/Messidor, 1984), 170; Gerhard Leo, *Frühzug nach Toulouse: Ein Deutscher in der französischen Résistance 1942–1944* (Berlin: Nation, 1988); David Knout, *Contribution à l'histoire de la Résistance juive en France* (Paris: Éditions du Centre, 1947).
79 Leo, *Frühzug nach Toulouse*, trans. as *Un Allemand dans la Résistance: le train pour Toulouse* (Paris: Éditions Tirésias, 1997).
80 *Strafdivision 999: Erlebnisse und Berichte aus dem antifaschistischen Widerstandskampf* (Berlin: Deutscher Militärverlag, 1966); H. Burkhardt, G. Erxleben and K. Netball (eds), *Die mit dem blauen Schein: Über den antifaschistischen Widerstand in den 999er Formationen der faschistischen deutschen Wehrmacht (1942 bis 1945)* (Berlin: Militärverlag der Deutschen Demokratischen Republik, 1982).
81 BArchB, NY 4306, Kartons 2, 6, 14, 16, 19, 25 and 26, contain a vast archive of the committee in the collection of Gerhard Reinhardt's personal documents.
82 Gerhard Reinhardt, 'Das Dokument des "Germanos Manolis"', 713 pp., covering the period Nov. 1942–Jan. 1945, unpublished.
83 AD Haute-Garonne, 16J184, Daniel Latapie, Guerrilleros Espagnols, Documents, vol. V (1990), 93.
84 *La Dépêche du Midi*, 3 June 1982; Serge Barcellini and Annette Wieviorka, *Passant, souviens-toi: les lieux du souvenir de la Seconde Guerre mondiale en France* (Paris: Plon, 1995), 279.
85 Association pour la Recherche sur l'Histoire Contemporaine des Juifs

(RHICOJ), *Les juifs dans la Résistance et la Libération* (Paris: Scribe, 1985), 174–84.

86 Annette Wieviorka, *Ils étaient juifs, résistants, communistes* (Paris: Denoël, 1986), 140–59; Gildea, *Fighters in the Shadows*, 461–2.

87 Institut National de l'Audiovisuel, Paris, *Les dossiers de l'écran*, 2 July 1985.

88 Stéphane Courtois, Denis Peschanski and Adam Rayski, *Le sang de l'étranger: les immigrés de la MOI dans la Résistance* (Paris: Fayard, 1989).

89 Boris Holban, *Testament: après 45 ans de silence* (Paris: Calmann-Lévy, 1989).

90 Mémoire des Résistants Juifs de la MOI, www.mrj-moi.com; Gildea, *Fighters in the Shadows*, 475–6.

91 See Megan Koreman, *The Escape Line: How the Ordinary Heroes of Dutch-Paris Resisted the Nazi Occupation of Western Europe* (New York: Oxford University Press, 2018), and Bob de Graaff, *Stepping Stones to Freedom: Help to Allied Airmen in the Netherlands during World War II*, trans. Dee Wessels Boer-Stallman (Marceline, MO: Walsworth, 1995). On the false Dutch-Paris stamp issue see Hoover Institution Library and Archive, Weidner Collection, WA WC 31 Veerman, folder 3.

92 Rebecca Clifford, *Commemorating the Holocaust. Dilemmas of Remembrance in France and Italy* (Oxford: Oxford University Press, 2013), 194–200.

93 Sarah Gensburger, *Les Justes de France: politiques publiques de la mémoire* (Paris: FNSP, 2010), 80.

94 Diego Gaspar Celaya, 'D'un mythe à l'autre: mémoire et histoire des Espagnols dans la Résistance', *Conserveries mémorielles*, 20 (2017), http://journals.openedition.org/cm/2441 (last accessed 1 May 2019); José Riera Siquier, Spanish ambassador in Belgrade, 'Presentation', in Muzej Istorije Jugoslavije, *U čast španskih boraca: Jugoslovenski dobrovoljci u Španskom građanskom ratu 1936–1939. Arhivski materijal, svedočenja sećanja, Katalog izložbe / Homenaje a los brigadistas yugoslavos: los voluntarios yugoslavos en la Guerra Civil 1936–1939. Documentación de archivo, testimonios, memorias* (Belgrade: Muzej Istorije Jugoslavije/Museo de Historia de Yugoslavia, 2006), 3.

95 'Un desfile rodeado de polémica conmemora la Fiesta Nacional', *El Mundo*, 12 Oct. 2004.

96 Les Amis des Combattants en Espagne Républicain, www.acer-aver.fr/.

97 https://www.scribd.com/document/41917821/No-Pasaran-English (last accessed 1 July 2019).

98 See above, pp. 17–18, 24, 25.

99 Gildea, *Fighters in the Shadows*, 467.

100 Ibid., 471.

101 Tadeuz Bór-Komorowski, *The Secret Army: The Memoirs of General Bór-Komorowski* (Barnsley: Frontline Books, 2011).

102 Marek Jan Chodakiewicz, *Between Nazis and Soviets: Occupation Politics in Poland, 1939–1947* (Langham, Maryland, Lexington Books, 2004).

103 'Vojko i Savle', *Politika*, 18 Jan. 1987.

104 Walter R. Roberts, *Tito, Mihailovic and the Allies, 1941–1945* (New Brunswick, NJ: Rutgers University Press, 1973); Phyllis Auty and Richard Glogg (eds), *British Policy toward Wartime Resistance in Yugoslavia and Greece* (London: Macmillan Press, 1975); Jozo Tomasevich, *The Chetniks: War and Revolution in Yugoslavia 1941–1945* (Stanford, CA: Stanford University Press, 1975); Veselin Djuretić, *Saveznici i jugoslovenska ratna drama*, vols 1–2 (Belgrade: SANU, 1985).

105 Todor Kuljić, *Prevladavanje prošlosti: uzroci i pravci promene slike istorije krajem XX veka* (Belgrade: Helsinški Odbor za Ljudska Prava u Srbiji, 2002), 449–93.

106 Kristen Ghodsee, 'A Tale of "Two Totalitarianisms": The Crisis of Capitalism and the Historical Memory of Communism', *History of the Present: A Journal of Critical History*, 4.2 (2014), 115–42.

107 Milo Petrović (ed.), *Preispitivanje prošlosti i istorijski revizionizam (Zlo)upotrebe Španskog građanskog rata i Drugog svetskog rata na prostoru Jugoslavije* (Belgrade: Association of the Yugoslav Volunteers of the Spanish Republican Army; Politics Faculty of Belgrade University; Rosa Luxemburg Stiftung Southeast Europe, 2014). https://www.rosalux.rs/sites/default/files/publications/Preispitivanje_pro%C5%A1losti_i_istorijski_revizionizam.pdf (last accessed 5 July 2019).

Conclusion

1 See for instance European Holocaust Research Infrastructure (https://ehri-project.eu) and Tribunal Archives as a Digital Research Facility (Triado; https://www.niod.nl/en/news/tribunal-archives-digital-research-facility).

2 Franz Borkenau, *The Spanish Cockpit: An Eye-Witness Account of the Political and Social Conflicts of the Spanish Civil War* (Ann Arbor, MI: University of Michigan Press, 1963).

3 Robert Gildea, *Fighters in the Shadows: A New History of the French Resistance* (London: Faber & Faber, 2015), 199–200.

4 Mémorial de la Shoah, Paris, CDJC DLXI-17, interview with Albert Cohen, conducted by Anny Latour, 1973.

Bibliography

Archives

Belgium

Centre d'Études et de Documentation Guerre et Sociétés Contemporaines/Studie- en Documentatiecentrum Oorlog en Hedendaagse Maatschappij, Brussels.

Croatia

Hrvatski Državni Arhiv, Zagreb.

Czech Republic

Vojenský Ústřední Archiv – Vojenský Historický Archiv, Prague.

France

Archives Départementales, Ariège.
Archives Départementales, Haute-Garonne.
Archives Départementales de la Seine, Saint-Denis.
Archives Nationales, Paris.
Bibliothèque Nationale, Inathèque.
Bureau des Anciens de la Légion Étrangère, Aubagne.
La Contemporaine (formerly La Bibliothèque de Documentation Internationale Contemporaine), Nanterre.
Centre des Archives du Personnel Militaire, Pau.
Centre d'Histoire de la Résistance et de la Déportation, Lyons.
Mémorial de la Shoah, housing the Centre de Documentation Juive Contemporaine, Paris.
Musée de la Résistance Nationale, Champigny-sur-Marne.
Service Historique de la Défense, Fonds de l´Armée de Terre, Vincennes.

Germany

Bundesarchiv, Berlin-Lichterfelde.
Bundesarchiv-Militärarchiv, Freiburg.

Israel

Haganah Archives, Tel Aviv.

Italy
Archivio Centrale dello Stato, Rome.
Archivio dell'Instituto Nazionale per la Storia del Movimento di Liberazione in Italia, Milan.
Archivio di Stato di Firenze.
Archivio Famiglia Santini, Arezzo.
Archivio Fondazione Gramsci, Rome.
Archivio Storico Diplomatico, Rome.
Archivio Ufficio Storico dello Stato Maggiore dell'Esercito, Rome.

Latvia
Latvian National Archives, Riga.

Lithuania
Lithuanian Special Archives, Vilnius.

Netherlands
Instituut voor Oorlogs-, Holocaust- en Genocidestudies, Amsterdam.
Nationaal Archief, The Hague.
Museum of Dutch Literature/Stichting Nederlands Literatuurmuseum en Literatuurarchief, The Hague.
Verzetsmuseum, Amsterdam.

Romania
Arhiva Consiliului Național Pentru Studierea Arhivelor Securității, Bucharest.
Arhivele Naționale Istorice Centrale, Bucharest.

Russia
Russian Centre for the Storage of Documents of Contemporary History, Moscow.
Russian State Archive of Socio-Political History, Moscow.

Serbia
Arhiv Jugoslavije, Belgrade.

Spain
Archivo del Comité Central del Partido Comunista de España, Madrid.
Archivo Histórico del Partido Comunista de España, Madrid.
Archivo Histórico Provincial de Albacete.

Switzerland
League of Nations and United Nations Office Archives, Geneva.
Schweizerisches Sozial Archiv, Zürich.

United Kingdom
Archives of the Royal Pioneer Corps Association, Bicester, Oxfordshire.

Imperial War Museum Sound Archive, London.
The Liddell Hart Centre for Military Archives, King's College, London.
The National Archives, Kew.

United States of America
Hoover Institution Library and Archive, Stanford, CA.
National Archives and Records Administration, College Park, MD.
Tamiment Library, New York University.
United States Holocaust Memorial Museum, Washington, DC.
USC Shoah Foundation, Los Angeles.

Ukraine
Central State Archives of Public Organisations of Ukraine, Kiev.

Printed sources

Newspapers
Berner Tagwacht
Cili-Soir
Combat
Der Spiegel
Deutsche Welle
Die Tageszeitung
El Mundo
Emanzipation
España Popular
Έθνος [Nation]
Franc-Tireur
Izvestiia
L'Humanité
La Dépêche du Midi
Le Patriote Résistant
Le Populaire
Mundo Obrero
Nieuw Israelitisch Weekblad
Politika
Prague Post
Rinascita
Rizospastis

Official papers
'Article 160, Ordonnance n° 45/2447, du 19 octobre 1945, portant code de la nationalité française', *Journal Officiel de la République Française*, 20 October 1945.
United States Department of State, *Foreign Relations of the United States, 1948,*

vol. 4: *Eastern Europe, the Soviet Union* (Washington, DC: US Govt. Print. Off., 1972–76).

Books

Abad, Irene, et al., *Historias de maquis en el Pirineo aragonés* (Jaca: Pirineum Editorial, 1999).

Acciai, Enrico, *Antifascismo, volontariato e guerra civile in Spagna: le sezione italiana della Colona Ascaso* (Milan: Unicopli, 2016).

Aizenshtadt, Iakov (ed.), *V plenu u Gitlera i Stalina: kniga Pamiati Maksa Grigorievicha Mintza* (Jerusalem: Verba Publishers, 1999).

Albrich, Thomas, and Ronald W. Zweig (eds), *Escape through Austria: Jewish Refugees and the Austrian Route to Palestine* (London and Portland: Frank Cass, 2002).

Aliav, Ruth, and Peggy Mann, *The Last Escape: The Launching of the Largest Secret Rescue* Movement of All Time (London: Gollancz, 1974).

Alpert, Michael, *The Republican Army in the Spanish Civil War, 1936–1939* (New York: Cambridge University Press, 2013).

Anderl, Gabriele, and Walter Manoschek, *Gescheiterte Flucht: Der jüdische 'Kladovo-Transport' auf dem Weg nach Palästina 1939–1942* (Vienna: Verlag für Gesellschaftskritik, 1993).

Antonioli, Maurizio, *Dizionario biografico degli anarchici italiani*, vol. 1: *A–G* (Pisa: BFS, 2003).

Arasa, Daniel, *Los españoles de Stalin* (Barcelona: Belacqua, 2005).

Arévalo, Antonio, *La Guerra en singular: testimonios de combatientes españoles en la liberación de Francia, 1939–1945* (Madrid: Ediciones El Cruce, 2004).

Arielle, Nir, *From Byron to Bin Laden: A History of Foreign War Volunteers* (Cambridge, MA: Harvard University Press, 2018).

Aron, Robert, *Histoire de l'Épuration I: de l'indulgence aux massacres, nov. 1942–sept. 1944* (Paris: Fayard, 1967).

Arrighi, Paul, *Silvio Trentin: un Européen en résistance, 1919–1943* (Portet-sur-Garonne: Loubatières, 2007).

Arušaujas, Arvydas, *Anti-Soviet Resistance in the Baltic States* (Vilnius: Du Ka, 1999).

Association pour la Recherche sur l'Histoire Contemporaine des Juifs (RHICOJ), *Les juifs dans la Résistance et la Libération: histoire, témoignages, débats* (Paris: Éditions du Scribe, 1985).

Auty, Phyllis, and Richard Glogg (eds), *British Policy toward Wartime Resistance in Yugoslavia and Greece* (London: Macmillan Press, 1975).

Badia, Gilbert, *Les barbelés de l'exil* (Grenoble: Presses Universitaires de Grenoble, 1979).

Bailey, Roderick, *Target: Italy. The Secret War against Mussolini, 1940–1943: The Official History of SOE Operations in Fascist Italy* (London: Faber & Faber, 2014).

Bailey, Roderick, *The Wildest Province: SOE in the Land of the Eagle* (London: Jonathan Cape, 2008).

Baldassarri, Fabio, *Ilio Barontini: fuoriuscito, internazionalista e partigiano* (Rome: Robin Edizioni, 2013).

Banac, Ivo, *With Stalin against Tito:* Cominformist Splits in Yugoslav Communism (Ithaca, NY, and London: Cornell University Press, 1988).

Barcellini, Serge, and Annette Wieviorka, *Passant, souviens-toi: les lieux du souvenir de la Seconde Guerre mondiale en France* (Paris: Plon, 1995).

Barić, Ivo, *Zbornik radova sa skupa, Kampor – polje sjećanja*, Rab, 2011 (Rab: Grad Rab, Udruga Antifašista Raba and SABA RH, 2012).

Barontini, Era, *Dario: Ilio Barontini* (Livorno: Editrice Nuova Fortezza, 1988).

Bartosek, Karel, René Gallissot and Denis Peschanski (eds), *De l'exil à la Résistance: réfugiés et immigrés d'Europe centrale en France, 1933–1945* (Saint-Denis: Presses Universitaires de Vincennes, 1989).

Bauer, Yehuda, *American Jewry and the Holocaust: The American Jewish Joint Distribution Committee, 1939–1945* (Detroit, MI: Wayne State University Press, 1981).

Bauerkämper, Arnd, and Grzegorz Rossoliński-Liebe (eds), *Fascism without Borders: Transnational Connections and Cooperation between Movements and Regimes in Europe from 1918 to 1945* (New York: Berghahn Books, 2017).

Bauz, Ingrid, S. Bruggemann and R. Maier (eds), *Die geheime Staatspolizei in Württemberg und Hohenzollern* (Stuttgart: Schmetterling Stuttgart, 2013).

Bavec-Branko, Franjo, *Bazoviška brigada* (Ljubljana: Knjižnica NOV in POS, 1970).

Baxell, Richard, *Unlikely Warriors: The British in the Spanish Civil War and the Struggle against Fascism* (London: Aurum, 2012).

Beer, Fritz, *... a tys na Němce střílel, dědo? Českoněmecký Žid mezi komunismem a nacismem* (Prague: Paseka, 2008).

Beevor, Antony, *The Battle for Spain: The Spanish Civil War, 1936–1939* (London: Phoenix, 2007).

Beevor, Antony, *Crete 1941: The Battle and the Resistance* (London: Penguin Books, 2014).

Belić-Koročkin, Mirjana, and Radivoje Davidović, *Bora Baruh: 1911–1942* (Belgrade: Interprint, 2001).

Belot, Robert, *Aux frontières de la liberté: Vichy, Madrid, Alger, Londres, s'évader de France sous l'Occupation* (Paris: Fayard, 1998).

Bennett, Rab, *Under the Shadow of the Swastika: The Moral Dilemmas of Resistance and Occupation in Hitler's Europe* (Basingstoke: Macmillan, 1999).

Benoît, Floriane, and Charles Silverstre (eds), *Les inconnus de la Résistance* (Paris: L'Humanité/Messidor, 1984).

Benz, Wolfgang, and Walter H. Pehle (eds), *Lexikon des deutschen Widerstandes*, 3rd edn (Frankfurt am Main: Fischer Taschenbuch Verlag, 2008).

Berg, Angela, *Die Internationalen Brigaden im spanischen Bürgerkrieg, 1936–1939* (Essen: Klartext, 2005).

Berger, Sara, et al., *Besetztes Südosteuropa und Italien*, vol. 14 of Sara Berger, Sanela Schmid, Erwin Lewin and Maria Vassilikou (eds), *Die Verfolgung und Ermordung der europäischen Juden durch das nationalsozialistische Deutschland 1933–1945* (Berlin: De Gruyter; Boston: Oldenbourg, 2017).

Berić, Gojko and Ivo Vejvoda, *Zbogom XX. stoljeće: sjećanja Ive Vejvode* (Zagreb: Profil Knjiga, 2013).

Berlinskii, David, and Mordukh Pogrebinskii, *Podvig Iana Nalepki* (Moscow: Voenizdat, 1959).

Bermejo, B., and S. Checa, *Libro memorial: Españoles deportados a los campos nazis, 1940–1945* (Madrid: Ministerio de Cultura, 2007).

Bertaux, Daniel, *Le récit de vie* (Paris: Nathan, 1997; 2nd edn, Paris: Armand Colin, 2006).

Bertaux, Pierre, *Libération de Toulouse et de sa région* (Paris: Hachette, 1973).

Bessel, Richard (ed.), Life after Death: *Approaches to a Cultural and Social History of Europe during the 1940s–1950s* (Cambridge: Cambridge University Press, 2003).

Béthouart, Marie Émile Antoine, *Cinq années d'espérance: mémoires de guerre, 1939–1945* (Paris: Plon, 1968).

Biess, Frank, *Homecomings: Returning POWs and the Legacy of Defeat in Postwar Germany* (Princeton, NJ, and Oxford: Princeton University Press, 2006).

Bigeard, Jacques, *Pour une parcelle de gloire* (Paris: Plon, 1975).

Birnbaum, Pierre, *Anti-Semitism in France: A Political History from Léon Blum to the Present* (Oxford: Blackwell, 1992).

Birnbaum, Pierre, T*he Jews of the Republic: A Political History of State Jews in France from Gambetta to Vichy* (Stanford, CA: Stanford University Press, 1996).

Bleiere, Daina, Ilgvars Butulis, Inesis Feldmanis, Aivars Stranga and Antonijs Zunda, *Latvija Otrajā Pasaules Karā* (Riga: Jumava, 2008).

Böhler, Jochen, and Robert Gerwarth, *The Waffen-SS: A European History* (Oxford: Oxford University Press, 2017).

Bonte, Florimond, *Les antifascistes allemands dans la Résistance française* (Paris: Éditions Sociales, 1969).

Borgomaneri, Luigi, *Li chiamavano terroristi: storia dei GAP Milanesi* (Milan: Unicopli, 2015).

Boris, Georges, *Servir la France: textes et témoignages* (Paris: Julliard, 1963).

Bór-Komorowski, Tadeuz, *The Secret Army: The Memoirs of General Bór-Komorowski* (Barnsley: Frontline Books, 2011).

Borkenau, Franz, *The Spanish Cockpit: An Eye-Witness Account of the Political and Social Conflicts of the Spanish Civil War* (Ann Arbor, MI: University of Michigan Press, 1963).

Borodziej, Włodzimierz, *Der Warschauer Aufstand 1944* (Frankfurt am Main: S. Fischer Verlag, 2001).

Bourderon, Roger, *Rol-Tanguy* (Paris, Tallandier, 2004).

Bourderon, Roger (ed.), *La guerre d'Espagne: l'histoire, les lendemains, la mémoire* (Paris: Tallandier, 2007).

Boyer, Jean-Baptiste, *Résistants: partisans français en Slovakie* (Saint-Cloud: Atlante Éditions, 2012).

Braham, Randolph L., *The Politics of Genocide: The Holocaust in Hungary* (New York: Columbia University Press, 1981).

Brod, Toman, *Tobrucké krysy* (Prague: Naše Vojsko, 1967).

Brod, Toman, and Eduard Čejka, *Na západní frontě: historie československých vojenských jednotek na Západě v letech druhé světové války* (Prague: Naše Vojsko, 1965).

Brodsky, E., *Oni ne propali bez vesti: ne slomlennye fashistskoi nevolei* (Moscow: Mysl', 1987).

Brodsky, E., *Vo imia pobedy nad fashizmom* (Moscow: Nauka, 1970).

Brome, Vincent, *The Way Back: The Story of Lieut.-Commander Pat O'Leary* (London: Companion Book Club, 1958).

Brunetti, Bruno, *Da oppressori a combattenti per la libertà* (Lucca: Istituto Storico della Resistenza in Provincia di Lucca, 1990).

Buchanan, Tom, *Britain and the Spanish Civil War* (Cambridge: Cambridge University Press, 1997).

Burgwyn, H. James, *Empire on the Adriatic: Mussolini's Conquest of Yugoslavia 1941–1943* (New York: Enigma Books, 2005).

Burkhardt, H., G. Erxleben and K. Netball (eds), *Die mit dem blauen Schein: Über den antifaschistischen Widerstand in den 999er Formationen der faschistischen deutschen Wehrmacht (1942 bis 1945)* (Berlin: Militärverlag der Deutschen Demokratischen Republik, 1982).

Burrin, Philip, *Living with Defeat: France under the German Occupation, 1940–1944* (London: Arnold, 1996).

Calvet, Josep, *Las montañas de la libertad: el paso de refugiados por los Pirineos durante la Segunda Guerra mundial, 1939–1944* (Madrid: Alianza Editorial, 2010).

Calic, Mari-Janine, *Geschichte Jugoslawiens im 20. Jahrhundert* (Munich: C. H. Beck, 2010).

Campbell, John, and Philip Sherrard, *Modern Greece* (London: Ernest Benn Ltd, 1968).

Campo, Ramón J., *El oro de Canfranc* (Saragossa: Obra Social y Cultural, 2002).

Caplan, Jane, and Nikolaus Wachsman (eds), *Concentration Camps in Nazi Germany: The New Histories* (London: Routledge, 2010).

Carrel, André, *Mes humanités: itinéraire d'un homme engagé* (Paris: L'Œil d'Or, 2009).

Carroll, Peter N., *The Odyssey of the Abraham Lincoln Brigade: Americans in the Spanish Civil War* (Stanford, CA: Stanford University Press, 1994).

Casanova, Julián, *A Short History of the Spanish Civil War* (London and New York: I. B. Tauris, 2014).

Caskie, Donald, *The Tartan Pimpernel* (London: Fontana Books, 1960).

Català, Neus, *De la resistencia y la deportación: 50 testimonios de mujeres españolas* (Barcelona: Peninsula, 2000).

Cava, Salvador J., *Los guerrilleros de Levante y Aragón*, vol. 2: *El cambio de estrategia* (Cuenca: Tomebamba, 2007).

Cave Brown, Anthony, *The Last Hero: Wild Bill Donovan* (New York: Times Books, 1982).

Celaya, Diego Gaspar, *La guerra continúa: voluntarios españoles al servicio de la Francia libre (1940–1945)* (Madrid: Marcial Pons, 2015).

Celaya, Diego Gaspar, *Republicanos argoneses en la Segunda Guerra mundial: una historia de exilio, trabajo y lucha, 1939/1945* (Saragosa: Rolde de Estudios Aragoneses, 2010).

Centra, Luigi, *I deportati: internati civili nel campo di concentramento Le Fraschette di Alatri* (Casamari: La Monastica, 1998).

Chodakiewicz, Marek Jan, *Between Nazis and Soviets: Occupation Politics in Poland, 1939–1947* (Langham, MD: Lexington Books, 2004).

Chruścielski, Piotr, and Marcin Owsiński (eds), *Konferencja 'Od Westerplatte do Norymbergi: II woja światowa we współczesnej historiografii, muzealnictwie i edukacji'* (Sztutowo: Muzeum Stutthof, 2010).

Ciechanowski, Jan, *The Warsaw Rising of 1944* (Cambridge: Cambridge University Press, 1974).

Clay Large, David, *Nazi Games: The Olympics of 1936* (New York: W. W. Norton, 2007).

Clifford, Rebecca, *Commemorating the Holocaust: Dilemmas of Remembrance in France and Italy* (Oxford: Oxford University Press, 2013).

Cobb, Matthew, *The Resistance: The French Fight against the Nazis* (London: Simon & Schuster, 2009).

Cocq, Guy (ed.), *Emmanuel Mounier: l'actualité d'un grand témoin* (Paris: Éditions Parole et Silence, 2003).

Collin, Claude, *Le Travail allemand: une organisation de la résistance au sein de la Wehrmacht* (Paris: Les Indes Savantes, 2013).

Collotti, Enzo, Renato Sandri and Frediano Sessi (eds), *Dizionario della resistenza* (Turin: Einaudi, 2006).

Colomé, Gabriel, *La Olimpiada Popular de 1936: deporte y política* (Barcelona: Institut de Ciències Polítiques i Socials, 2008).

Coltrinale. M., *L'8 settembre in Albania: la crisi armistiziale tra impotenza, errori ed eroismo (8 settembre–7 ottobre 1943)* (Rome: Nuova Cultura, 2009).

Comité International de Coordination et d'Information pour l'Aide à l'Espagne Republicane (ed.), *Deux missions internationales visitent les camps de réfugiés espagnols* (Paris: Comité International de Coordination et d'Information pour l'Aide à l'Espagne Republicane, 1939).

Comor, André-Paul, *l'épopée de la 13éme Demi-brigade de Légion Étrangère 1939–1945* (Paris: NEL, 1988).

Coni, Nicolas, *Medicine and Warfare: Spain, 1936–1939* (New York: Routledge, 2008).

Cooke, Philip, and Ben H. Shepherd (eds), *European Resistance in the Second World War* (Barnsley: Pen & Sword Military, 2013).

Cooke, Philip, and Ben H. Shepherd (eds), *Hitler's Europe Ablaze: Occupation, Resistance, and Rebellion during World War II* (New York: Skyhorse Publishing, 2014).

Copeman, Fred, *Reasons in Revolt* (Chatham: W. & J. Mackay, 1948).

Costa, Carlo, and Lorenzo Teodino, *Razza partigiana: storia di Giorgio Marincola, 1923–1945* (Rome: Iacobelli Editore, 2008).

Courtois, Stéphane, *Le livre noir du communisme: crimes, terreur, répression* (Paris: Laffont, 1999).

Courtois, Stéphane, Denis Peschanski and Adam Rayski, *Le sang de l'étranger: les immigrés de la MOI dans la Résistance* (Paris: Fayard, 1989).

Cowtan, John, *From the Gazala Line to Behind the Lines: Wartime Memories of John Cowtan* (London: AuthorHouse, 2011).

Crémieux-Brilhac, Jean-Louis, *Georges Boris: trente ans d'influence. Blum, de Gaulle, Mendès France* (Paris: Gallimard, 2010).

Crémieux-Brilhac, Jean-Louis, *La France libre: de l'appel du 18 juin à la Libération* (Paris: Gallimard, 1996).

Crémieux-Brilhac, Jean-Louis, *L'étrange victoire: de la défense de la République à la libération de la France* (Paris: Gallimard, 2016).

Csokor, Franz Theodor, *Zeuge einer Zeit: Briefe aus dem Exil 1930–1950* (Munich: Georg Müller, 1964).

Dale, S., *Spanglet: Or by Any Other Name* (privately published, 1993).

Dallin, Alexander, *German Rule in Russia, 1941–1945* (Basingstoke: Palgrave Macmillan, 1981).

Davidović, Radivoje, *Od Daviča do Čelebonovića – ulice beogradskih Jevreja* (Belgrade: Čigoja, 2010).

Davies, E. F., *Illyrian Venture: The Story of the British Military Mission to Enemy-Occupied Albania 1943–44* (London: The Bodley Head, 1952).

Davies, Norman, *Rising '44: The Battle for Warsaw* (London: Macmillan, 2003).

De Gaulle, Charles, *Discours et messages*, vol. 1 (Paris: Plon, 1970).

Deacon, Desley, Penny Russell and Angela Wollacott (eds), *Transnational Lives: Biographies of Global Modernity, 1700–Present* (Basingstoke: Palgrave Macmillan, 2010).

Deakin, F. W. D., *Embattled Mountain* (London and New York: Oxford University Press, 1971).

Degras, Jane (ed.), *The Communist International*, vol. 3: *1929–1943* (London: Oxford University Press, 1965).

Delperrie de Bayac, Jacques, *Les Brigades internationales* (Paris: Fayard, 1968).

Denoyer, Aurélie, *L'exil comme patrie: les réfugiés communistes espagnols en RDA (1950–1989)* (Rennes: Presses Universitaires de Rennes, 2017).

Di Sante, Costantino, *I campi di concentramento in Italia: dall'internamento alla deportazione (1940–1945)* (Milan: Franco Angeli, 2001).

Diamant, David, *Combattants, héros et martyrs de la Résistance: biographies, dernières lettres, témoignages et documents* (Paris: Éditions Nouveau, 1984).

Diamant, David, *Héros juifs de la Résistance* (Paris: Éditions Renouveau, 1962).

Diamant, David, *Les juifs dans la Résistance française, 1940–1944: avec armes ou sans armes* (Paris: Le Pavillon, 1971).

Diekmann, Irene (ed.), *Wegweiser durch das jüdische Mecklenburg-Vorpommern* (Potsdam: Verlag für Berlin-Brandenburg, 1998).

Djuretić, Veselin, *Saveznici i jugoslovenska ratna drama*, vols 1–2 (Belgrade: SANU, 1985).

Dolecki, Rafał, Krzysztof Gutowski and Jędrzej Smoleński, *Po prostu historia: podręcznik szkoły ponadgimnazjalne* (Warsaw: Wydawnictwa Szkolne i Pedagogiczne, 2013).

Dominioni, Matteo, *Lo sfascio dell'impero: gli italiani in Etiopia 1936–1941* (Rome and Bari: Laterza, 2008).

Donati, Chiara, and Tommaso Rossi (eds), *Guerra e resistenza nell'Appennino umbro-marchigiano: problematiche e casi di studio* (Foligno: Editoriale Umbra, 2017).

Douzou, Laurent, and Mercedes Yusta (eds), *La Résistance à l'épreuve du genre: hommes et femmes dans la résistance antifasciste en Europe du Sud* (Rennes: Presses Universitaires de Rennes, 2018).

Downs, Jim, *Druhá svetová vojna: tragédia OSS na Slovensku* (Bratislava: Magnet Press, 2004).

Drew, Allison, *We Are No Longer in France: Communists in Colonial Algeria* (Manchester: Manchester University Press, 2014).

Dreyfus-Armand, Geneviève, *L'exil des républicains espagnols en France: de guerre civile à la mort de Franco* (Paris: Albin Michel, 1999).

Duckett, R., *The Special Operations Executive in Burma: Jungle Warfare and Intelligence Gathering in World War II* (London: I. B. Tauris, 2018).

Duhnke, Horst, *Die KPD von 1933 bis 1945* (Cologne: Kiepenheuer & Witsch, 1972).

Dulová, Pim, and Vladimír Jeršov, *Francúzski bojovníci v Slovenskom národnom povstaní* (Bratislava: Povereníctvo Informácií, 1947).

Dunan, René, *'Ceux' de Paris: août 1944* (Geneva: Éditions du Milieu du Monde, 1945).

Dunthorn, David J., and Christian Leitz (eds), *Spain in an International Context* (New York: Berghahn Books, 1999).

Durand, Romain, *De Giraud à de Gaulle: le Corps franc d'Afrique* (Paris: L'Harmattan, 1999).

Einaudi, Jean-Luc, *Un rêve algérien: histoire de Lisette Vincent, une femme d'Algérie* (Paris: Presses Universitaires de France, 2001).

Elsie, Robert, *Historical Dictionary of Kosova* (Lanham, MD: Scarecrow Press, 2004).

Enquetecommissie Regeringsbeleid 1940–1945, vol. 6c (The Hague: State Printing and Publishing Company, 1952).

Espagne, Michel, *Les transferts culturels franco-allemands* (Paris: Presses Universitaires de France, 1989).

Estrade, Paul, *El trabajo forzado de los espagñoles en la Francia de Vichy: los grupos de Trabadojes Extranjeros en Corrèze (1940–1944)* (Madrid: UNED, 2016).

European Resistance Movements, 1939–1945: Proceedings of the First International Conference on the History of the Resistance Movements, Held at Liège-Bruxelles-Breendonk, 14–17 September 1958 (Oxford and New York: Pergamon Press, 1960).

European Resistance Movements, 1939–1945: Proceedings of the Second International Conference on the History of the Resistance Movements, Held at Milan, 26–29 March 1961 (Oxford and New York: Pergamon Press, 1964).

Eychenne, Émilienne, *Les Pyrénées de la liberté: le franchissement clandestin des Pyrénées pendant la Seconde Guerre mondiale, 1939–1945* (Paris: Éditions France-Empire, 1983).

Falguera, Narcisse (ed.), *Guérilleros en terre de France: les républicains espagnols dans la Résistance française* (Montreuil: Le Temps des Cerises, 2004).

Falkov, Yaacov, *Meragle ha-ye'arot: pe'ilutam ha-modi'init shel ha-parṭizanim ha-Sovyeṭim 1941–1945* (Jerusalem: The Hebrew University Magness Press and Yad Vashem Press, 2017).

Ferris, John, and Evan Mawdsley (eds), *The Cambridge History of the Second World War*, vol. 1 (Cambridge: Cambridge University Press, 2015).

Finzi, Paolo, *Insuscettibile di ravvedimento: l'anarchico Alfonso Failla (1906–1986). Carte di polizia/scritti/testimonianze* (Ragusa: La Fiaccola, 1993).

Fischer, Bernd J., *Balkan Strongmen: Dictators and Authoritarian Rulers of Southeast Europe* (London: Hurst, 2007).

Foot, M. R. D., *SOE in France: An Account of the Work of the British Special Operations Executive in France, 1940–1944* (London: HMSO, 1966; rev. edn, 2004).

Ford, Kirk, *OSS and the Yugoslav Resistance, 1943–1945* (College Station, TX: Texas A&M University Press, 1992).

Friedl, Jiří, *Na jedné frontě: vztahy československé a polské armády (Polskie Siły Zbrojne) za druhé světové války* (Prague: Ústav pro Soudobé Dějiny AV ČR, 2005).

García, Hugo, Mercedes Yusta, Xavier Tabet and Cristina Clímaco (eds), *Rethinking Antifascism: History, Memory and Politics, 1922 to the Present* (Oxford and New York: Berghahn, 2016).

Gensburger, Sarah, *Les Justes de France: politiques publiques de la mémoire* (Paris: FNSP, 2010).

Gerber, Jan, *Ein Prozess in Prag: Das Volk gegen Rudolf Slánský und Genossen* (Göttingen: Vandenhoeck & Ruprecht, 2016).

Giannantoni, Franco, and Ibio Paolucci, *Giovanni Pesce 'Visone', un comunista che ha fatto l'Italia: l'emigrazione, la guerra di Spagna, Ventotene, i Gap, il dopoguerra* (Varese: Arterige, 2005).

Gide, André, *Retour de l'U.R.S.S., suivi de Retouches à mon retour de l'U.R.S.S.* (Paris: Gallimard, 1937); trans. as *Back from the USSR and Afterthought: A Sequel to Back from the USSR* (London: Martin Secker and Warburg, 1937).

Gieseke, Jens, *Wer war wer im Ministerium für Staatssicherheit (MfS-Handbuch)* (Berlin: Hg. BStU, 2012).

Gijón, Mario Martín, *La Resistencia franco-española (1936–1950): una historia compartida* (Badajoz: Diputación de Badajoz, Área de Cultura, 2014).

Gildea, Robert, *Empires of the Mind: The Colonial Past and the Politics of the Present* (Cambridge: Cambridge University Press, 2019).

Gildea, Robert, *Fighters in the Shadows: A New History of the French Resistance* (London: Faber & Faber, 2015).

Gildea, Robert, *Marianne in Chains: In Search of the German Occupation, 1940–1945* (London: Macmillan, 2002).

Gildea, Robert, Anette Warring and Olivier Wieviorka (eds), *Surviving Hitler and Mussolini: Daily Life in Occupied Europe* (Oxford and New York: Berg, 2006).

Glauning, Christine and Andreas Nachama (eds), *Alltag Zwangsarbeit 1938–1945: Katalog zur gleichnamigen Dauerausstellung* (Berlin, Stiftung Topographie d. Terrors, 2013).

Głuchowski, Leszek W., and Antony Polonsky (eds), *1968, Forty Years After* (Oxford: Littman Library of Jewish Civilization, 2009).

Goan, Aleksandar (ed.), *Mi smo preživeli: Jevreji o Holokaustu*, vols 1–5 (Belgrade: Savez Jevrejskih Opština Srbije, 2001–05).

Goldman, Pierre, *Souvenirs obscurs d'un juif polonais né en France* (Paris: Broché, 1975).

Goldstein, Ivo and Slavko, *Holocaust in Croatia* (Pittsburgh: University of Pittsburgh Press, 2016).

Golubović, Zvonimir, *Racija u Južnoj Bačkoj 1942. godine* (Novi Sad: Istorijski muzej Vojvodine, 1992).

Gontarczyk, Piotr, *Polska Partia Robotnicza: droga do władzy 1941–1944* (Warsaw: Fronda, 2003).

Gori, Francesca, and Silvio Pons (eds), *The Soviet Union and Europe in the Cold War, 1943–1953* (London and New York: Macmillan Press and St Martin's Press, 1996).

Gourvish, Terry (ed.), *Business and Politics in Europe, 1900–1970: Essays in Honour of Alice Teichova* (Cambridge, Cambridge University Press, 2003).

Govers, Frans, *Stemmen uit Dachau: 'Ter eren van de doden en ter waarschuwing van de levenden'* (Hapert: Kempen, 1990).

Graaff, Bob de, *Schakels naar de vrijheid: pilotenhup in Nederland tijdens de Tweede Wereldoorlog* (The Hague: Sdu Uitgevers, 1995); trans. as *Stepping Stones to Freedom: Help to Allied Airmen in the Netherlands during World War II*, trans. Dee Wessels Boer-Stallman (Marceline, MO: Walsworth, 1995).

Graham, Helen, *The Spanish Republic at War, 1936–1939* (Cambridge and New York: Cambridge University Press, 2002).

Grande Catalan, Antonio, *Number One Spanish Company: memorias de Antonio Grande* (Alicante: Editorial Club Universitario, 2002).

Granzow, Jonny, *16 Septembre 1943: l'évasion de la prison de Castres* (Portet-sur-Garonne: Loubatières, 2009).

Grebing, Helga, and Christl Wickert (eds), *Das 'andere' Deutschland im Widerstand gegen den Nationalsozialismus: Beiträge zur politischen Überwindung der nationalsozialistischen Diktatur im Exil und im Dritten Reich* (Essen: Klartext Verlag, 1994).

Greene Ottis, Sherri, *Silent Heroes: Downed Airmen and the French Underground* (Lexington, KY: University of Kentucky Press, 2001).

Greshoff, C. J. (ed.), *André Gide–Jef Last: correspondance, 1934–1950* (Lyons: Presses Universitaires de Lyon, 1985).

Gronowski, Louis, *Le dernier grand soir: un juif de Pologne* (Paris: Seuil, 1980).

Guerrini, Libertario, *Il movimento operaio nell'empolese: 1861–1946* (Rome: Riuniti, 1970).

Guilheim, F., *L'obsesion du retour: les républicains espagnols, 1939–1975* (Toulouse: Presses Universitaires de Toulouse Le Mirail, 2005).

Guillon, Jean-Marie, and Pierre Laborie (eds), *Mémoire et histoire: la Résistance* (Toulouse: Privat, 1995).

Guillon, Jean-Marie, and Robert Mencherini (eds), *La Résistance et les Européens du Sud: actes du colloque tenu à Aix-en-Provence, 20–22 mars 1997* (Paris: L'Harmattan, 1999).

Hackl, Erich, and Cristina Timón Solonís (eds), *Geschichten aus der Geschichte des Spanischen Bürgerkriegs* (Darmstadt: Hermann Luchterhand, 1986).

Haestrup, Jørgen, *Europe Ablaze: An Analysis of the History of the European Resistance Movements, 1939–1945* (Odense: Odense University Press, 1978).

Halaj, Dušan, Ľubomír Moncoľ and Ján Stanislav, *Francúzi v Slovenskom národnom povstaní* (Banská Bystrica: Grafické Štúdio Ing. Petra Jurigu, 2003).

Hamilton-Hill, Donald, *SOE Assignment* (London: William Kimber, 1973).

Hamon, Léo, *Vivre ses choix* (Paris: Robert Laffont, 1991).

Hamson, D., *We Fell among Greeks* (London: Jonathan Cape, 1946).

Hariš-Gromovnik, Ivan, *Diverzant* (Zagreb, 2007; first published Belgrade: Rad, 1960), www.slobodnajugoslavija.com/literatura/Diverzant_Ivan_Haris_Gromovnik.pdf (last accessed 1 July 2018).

Hausleitner, Mariana (ed.), *Vom Faschismus zum Stalinismus: Deutsche und andere Minderheiten in Ostmittel- und Südosteuropa 1941–1953* (Munich: IKGS Verlag, 2008).

Hawes, Stephen, and Ralph White (eds), *Resistance in Europe, 1939–1945* (London: Allen Lane, 1975).

Heim, Susanne, et al. (eds), *Die Verfolgung und Ermordung der europäischen Juden durch das nationalsozialistische Deutschland 1933–1945* (Berlin and Boston: De Gruyter, 2017).

Heine, Hartmut, *La oposición política al franquismo: de 1939 a 1952* (Grijalbo: Crítica, 1983).

Henrion, Lucien, *Le commandant Alexandre Lofi* (Metz: Académie Nationale de Metz, 1994).

Herbert, Ulrich, *Hitler's Foreign Workers: Enforced Foreign Labour under the Third Reich* (Cambridge: Cambridge University Press, 1997).

Hermet, Guy, *Les Espagnols en France* (Paris: Les Éditions Ouvrières, 1967).

Hibbert, Reginald, *Albania's National Liberation Struggle: The Bitter Victory* (London: Printer Publisher, 1991).

Hilberg, Raul, *The Destruction of the European Jews* (Chicago: Quadrangle, and London: W. H. Allen, 1961).

Hinze, Sybille, *Antifaschisten im Camp Le Vernet* (Berlin: Militärverlag des Deutschen Demokratischen Republik, 1988).

Höbel, Alexander, *Luigi Longo: una vita partigiana, 1900–1945* (Rome: Carocci, 2013).

Hobsbawm, Eric, *Age of Extremes: The Short Twentieth Century, 1914–1991* (London: Michael Joseph, 1994).

Hočevar, Jože (ed.), *Slovenci v španski državljanski vojni: zbornik referatov znanstvenega simpozija v Kopru, 12. februarja 2010* (Koper: Združenje Borcev za Vrednote NOB, 2010).

Hodos, George H., *Show Trials: Stalinist Purges in Eastern Europe, 1948–1954* (New York: Praeger, 1987).

Holban, Boris, *Testament: après 45 ans de silence* (Paris: Calmann-Lévy, 1989).

Hrbek, Jaroslav, et al., *Draze zaplacená svoboda: osvobození Československa 1944–1945*, vol. 1 (Prague: Paseka, 2009).

Huber, Peter, *Die schweizer Spanienfreiwilligen: biografisches Handbuch* (Zürich: Rotpunkverlag, 2009).

Inglis, Ken, Seumas Spark and Jay Winter, *Dunera Lives: A Visual History* (Melbourne: Monash University Press, 2018).

Institut Charles de Gaulle/IHTP, *Brazzaville, janvier–février 1944: aux sources de la décolonisation* (Paris: Plon, 1988).

Ivanič, Martin, and Branko Ziherl (eds), *Dahauski procesi: Reziskovalno poročilo za dokumenti* (Ljubljana: Komunist, 1990).

Jackson, M. W., *Fallen Sparrows: The International Brigades in the Spanish Civil War* (Philadelphia, PA: American Philosophical Society, 1994).

Jakub, J., *Spies and Saboteurs: Anglo-American Collaboration and Rivalry in Human Intelligence Collection and Special Operations, 1940–45* (New York: St Martin's Press, 1999).

Jennings, Eric, *La France libre fut africaine* (Paris: Perrin, 2014).

Jérôme, Jean [Michał Feintuch], *La part des hommes: souvenirs d'un témoin* (Paris: Acropole, 1983).

Jespersen, J. V., *Med hjælp fra England: Special Operations Executive og den danske modstandskamp 1940–1945* (Odense: University Press of Southern Denmark, 2000); in English as *No Small Achievement: Special Operations Executive and the Danish Resistance, 1940–1945* (Odense: University Press of Southern Denmark, 2002).

Jewish Resistance during the Holocaust: Proceedings of the Conference on Manifestations of Jewish Resistance, Jerusalem, 7–11 April 1968 (Jerusalem: Yad Vashem, 1971).

Jiménez Margalejo, Carlos, *Los que teníamos dieciocho años* (Madrid: Incipit Editores, 2000).

Johnson, Gaynor (ed.), *The International Context of the Spanish Civil War* (Cambridge: Cambridge Scholars Publishing, 2009).

Johnston, Verle B., *Legions of Babel: The International Brigades in the Spanish Civil War* (University Park and London: Pennsylvania State University Press, 1967).

Joutard, Philippe, and François Marcot (eds), *Les étrangers dans la Résistance en France* (Besançon: Université de Franche-Comté, 1992).

Judt, Tony (ed.), *Resistance and Revolution in Mediterranean Europe 1939–1948* (London: Routledge, 1989).

Kačavenda, Petar, and Dušan Živković (eds), *Narodni heroji Jugoslavije*, vols 1–2 (Belgrade: Partizanska Knjiga, Narodna Knjiga; Titograd: Pobjeda, 1982).

Kaczorowski, Bartosz, *Franco i Stalin: związek Sowiecki w polityce Hiszpanii w okresie drugiej wojny światowej* (Łódź and Cracow: Wydawnictwo Uniwersytetu Łódźkiego, 2016).

Kalonomos, Jamila Andjela, *Monastir without Jews: Recollections of a Jewish Partisan in Macedonia* (New York: Foundation for the Advancement of Sephardic Studies and Culture, 2008).

Kapor, Čedo (ed.), *Španija 1936–1939: zbornik sećanja jugoslovenskih dobrovoljaca u španskom ratu* (Belgrade: Vojnoizdavački Xavod, 1971).

Karbonski, Stefan, *Fighting Warsaw* (London: George Allen & Unwin, 1956).

Keck, Margaret, and Kathryn Sikkink, *Activists beyond Borders: Advocacy Networks in International Politics* (Ithaca, NY: Cornell University Press, 1998).

Keller, Rolf, and Silke Petry (eds), *Sowjetische Kriegsgefangene im Arbeitseinsatz, 1941–1945: Dokumente zu den Lebens- und Arbeitsbedingungen in Norddeutschland. Schriftenreihe der Stiftung niedersächsische Gedenkstätten* (Göttingen: Wallstein Verlag, 2013).

Kemperman, Jeroen, *Oorlog in de collegebanken: studenten in verzet, 1940–1945* (Amsterdam: Boom, 2018).

Kersevan, Alessandra, *Lager italiani: pulizia ethnica e campi di concentramento fascisti per civili jugoslavi 1941–1943* (Rome: Nutrimenti, 2008).

Kirk, Tim, and Anthony McElligott (eds), *Opposing Fascism: Community, Authority and Resistance in Europe* (New York: Cambridge University Press, 1999).

Kirschenbaum, Lisa A., *International Communism and the Spanish Civil War: Solidarity and Suspicion* (New York: Cambridge University Press, 2015).

Klausch, Hans Peter, *Die 999er. Von der Brigade 'Z' zur Afrika-Division 999: Die Bewährungsbataillone und ihr Anteil am antifaschistischen Widerstand* (Frankfurt am Main: Röderberg-Verlag, 1986).

Knout, David, *Contribution à l'histoire de la résistance juive en France* (Paris: Éditions du Centre, 1947).

Kochanski, Halik, *Eagle Unbowed: Poland and the Poles in the Second World War* (London: Penguin Books, 2013).

Kocman, Vincenc, *Boj bez slávy* (Brno: Krajské Nakladatelství v Brně, 1962).

Koestler, Arthur, *Dialogue with Death* (London: Penguin, 1942).

Koestler, Arthur, *The Scum of the Earth* (London: Jonathan Cape, 1941).

Kogon, Eugen, *The Theory and Practice of Hell: The German Concentration Camps and the System behind Them* (New York: Farrar, Strauss and Giroux, 2006).

Kola, Paulin, *The Search for Greater Albania* (London: Hurst & Co., 2003).

Kolpakidi, Aleksandr, *GRU v Velikoi Otechestvennoi voine* (Moscow: Iauza, 2010).

Kopka, Bogusław, *Konzentrationslager Warschau: historia i następstwa* (Warsaw: Instytut Pamięci Narodowej, 2007).

Korb, Alexander, *Im Schatten des Weltkriegs: Massengewalt der Ustaša gegen*

Serben, Juden und Roma in Kroatien 1941–1945 (Hamburg: Hamburger Edition, 2013).

Korczinski, Grzegorz, *Polskie oddziały specjalne w II wojnie światowej* (Warsaw: Bellona, 2006).

Koreman, Megan, *Gewone helden: de Dutch-Paris ontsnappingslijn* (Amsterdam: Boom, 2016); in English as *The Escape Line: How the Ordinary Heroes of Dutch-Paris Resisted the Nazi Occupation of Western Europe* (New York: Oxford University Press, 2018).

Kraus, Ognjen, and Ivo Goldstein (eds), *Antisemitizam, Holokaust, antifašizam* (Zagreb: Židovska Općina, 1996).

Kriegel, Annie, and Stéphane Courtois, *Eugen Fried: le grand secret du PCF* (Paris: Seuil, 1997).

Krivokapić, Boro, *Dahauski procesi* (Belgrade: Prosveta, and Ljubljana: Partizanska Knjiga, 1986).

Księżarczyk, Franciszek, *Droga w ogniu* (Warsaw: Wydawnictwo Ministerstwa Obrony Narodowei, 1965).

Kühnrich, Heinz, and Franz-Karl Hitze, *Deutsche bei Titos Partisanen 1941–1945. Kriegsschicksale auf dem Balkan in Augenzeugenberichte und Dokumenten* (Cologne: GNN Verlag, 1997).

Kuljić, Todor, *Prevladavanje prošlosti: uzroci i pravci promene slike istorije krajem XX veka* (Belgrade: Helsinški Odbor za Ljudska Prava u Srbiji, 2002).

Kulka, Erich, *Jews in Svoboda's Army in the Soviet Union* (Lanham, MD: University Press of America, 1987); in Czech as *Židé v československé Svobodově armádě* (Prague: Naše Vojsko, 1990).

La Conférence Africaine Française, Brazzaville (30 janvier–8 février 1944) (Algiers: Commissariat aux Colonies, 1944).

Laar, Mart, *War in the Woods: Estonia's Struggle for Survival, 1944–1956* (Washington, DC: Compass Press, 1992).

Labanca, Nicola (ed.), *L'Africa in vetrina: storie di musei e di esposizioni coloniali in Italia* (Treviso: Pagus, 1992).

Lācis, Rūdolfs (ed.), *Viva Republica! Vospominanija Učastnikov Antifašistskoj Vojny v Ispanii* (Riga: Latvijskoe Gosudarstvennoe Izd-vo, 1957).

Lagrou, Pieter, *The Legacy of Nazi Occupation: Patriotic Memory and National Recovery in Western Europe, 1945–1965* (Cambridge: Cambridge University Press, 2000).

Laković, Svetozar, *Memorie di un comandante partigiano montenegrino* (Perugia and Foligno: Isuc-Editoriale Umbra, 2010).

Laroche, Gaston, *On les nommait des étrangers: les immigrés dans la Résistance* (Paris: Les Éditeurs Français Réunis, 1965).

Last, Jef, *Brieven uit Spanje* (Amsterdam: Contact, 1936).

Last, Jef, *De Spaanse tragedie*, 2nd edn (Amsterdam: Contact, 1962).

Last, Jef, *In de loopgraven voor Madrid: 2e sierie brieven van het Spaansche front* (Amsterdam: Contact, 1937).

Last, Jef, *Mijn vriend André Gide* (Amsterdam: Van Ditmar, 1966).

Last, Jef, *Over de Hollanders in Spanje* (Amsterdam: Contact, 1937).

Latour, Anny, *La Résistance juive en France, 1940–1944* (Paris: Stock, 1970).

Lazarus, Jacques, *Juifs au combat: témoignage sur l'activité d'un mouvement de résistance* (Paris: Éditions du Centre, 1947).

Le Crom, Jean-Pierre, *Au secours, Maréchal! L'instrumentalisation de l'humanitaire, 1940–1944* (Paris: Presses Universitaires de France, 2013).

Lee, Daniel, *Pétain's Jewish Children: French Jewish Youth and the Vichy Regime, 1940–1942* (Oxford: Oxford University Press, 2014).

Lefebvre-Peña, Michael, and Rémi Skoutelsky (eds), *Les Brigades internationales: images retrouvées. Catalogue de l'exposition 'No pasarán, images des Brigades internationales dans la guerre d'Espagne'* (Paris: Seuil, 2003).

Lejeune, Philippe, *On Autobiography* (Minneapolis, MN: University of Minnesota Press, 1989).

Leo, Gerhard, *Frühzug nach Toulouse: Ein Deutscher in der französischen Résistance 1942–1944* (Berlin: Nation, 1988); trans. as *Un Allemand dans la Résistance: le train pour Toulouse* (Paris: Éditions Tirésias, 1997).

Lett, Brian, *SOE's Mastermind: An Authorised Biography of Major General Sir Colin Gubbins, KCMG, DSO, MC* (Barnsley: Pen & Sword Military, 2016).

Lévy, Claude, *Les parias de la Résistance* (Paris: Calmann Lévy, 1970).

Levy, Robert, *Ana Pauker: The Rise and Fall of a Jewish Communist* (Berkeley: University of California Press, 2001).

Lidegaard, Bo, *Countrymen: The Untold Story of How Denmark's Jews Escaped the Nazis* (London: Atlantic Books, 2013).

Lindeperg, Sylvie, *La voie des images: quatre histoires de tournage au printemps–été 1944* (Paris: Éditions Verdier, 2013).

Lissner, Araham, *Un franc-tireur juif raconte ...* (Paris: n. pub., 1969).

Lockman, Zachary, *Comrades and Enemies: Arab and Jewish Workers in Palestine, 1906–1948* (Berkeley: University of California Press, 1996).

Loinger, Georges, and Kathy Hazan, *Aux frontières de l'espoir* (Paris: Le Manuscrit, 2006).

London, Artur, *On Trial* (London: Macdonald & Co., 1970).

López-Brea Espiau, Francisco Javier, and José Ramón Soler Fuensanta, *Soldados sin rostro: los servicios de información, espionaje y criptografía en la guerra civil española* (Barcelona: Inédita Ediciones, 2008).

Louis, William Roger, *Imperialism at Bay: The United States and the Decolonization of the British Empire* (Oxford: Clarendon Press, 1977).

Mack Smith, Denis, *Mussolini's Roman Empire* (London: Longman, 1976).

Mackenzie, W. J. M., *The Secret History of SOE: Special Operations Executive 1940–1945* (London: St Ermin's, 2000).

Mandl, Henriette, *Cabaret und Courage: Stella Kadmon, eine Biographie* (Vienna: WUV Universitaetsverlag, 1993).

Manoschek, Walter, *'Serbien ist judenfrei!' Militärische Besatzungspolitik und Judenvernichtung in Serbien 1941/42* (Munich: Verlag Oldenbourg, 1995).

Maraldi, B. Dradi, and Pieri R. Milano (eds), *Lotta armata e resistenza delle forze armate all'estero* (Milan: Franco Angeli, 1990).

Marco, Jorge, *Guerrilleros and Neighbours in Arms: Identities and Cultures of Anti-Fascist Resistance in Spain* (Brighton: Sussex Academic Press, 2016).

Maria, Carlo De, *Lavoro di comunità e ricostruzione civile in Italia* (Rome: Viella, 2014).

Marko, Petro, *Intervistë me vetveten (retë dhe gurët)* (Tirana: Omsca, 2000).

Markovits, Pal, *Stets bei Verstand sein* (Konstanz: Hartung-Gorre, 2006).

Maršálek, Zdenko, *'Česká', nebo 'československá' armáda? Národnostní složení československých vojenských jednotek v zahraničí v letech 1939–1945* (Prague: Academia, 2017).

Maršálek, Zdenko, and Emil Voráček (eds), *Interbrigadisté: Československo a španělská občanská válka* (Prague: HÚ AV ČR – ÚSD AV ČR, 2017).

Martocchia, Andrea, *I partigiani jugoslavi nella Resistenza italiana* (Rome: Odradek, 2011).

Matthews, James, *Reluctant Warriors. Republican Popular Army and Nationalist Army Conscripts in the Spanish Civil War, 1936–1939* (Oxford: Oxford University Press, 2012).

Mazower, Mark, *Dark Continent: Europe's Twentieth Century* (London: Allen Lane, 1998).

McDermott, Kevin, and Jeremy Agnew, *The Comintern: A History of International Communism from Lenin to Stalin* (Basingstoke: Macmillan, 1996).

McLellan, Josie, *Antifascism and Memory in East Germany: Remembering the International Brigades, 1945–1989* (Oxford: Clarendon Press, 2004).

Medienwertstatt Freiburg (ed.), *Die lange Hoffnung: Erinnerungen an ein anderes Spanien mit Clara Thalmann und Augustin Soúchy* (Grafenau: Trotzdem Verlag, 1985).

Megargee, Geoffrey (ed.), *Encyclopedia of Camps and Ghettos 1933–1945*, vols 1–3 (Bloomington and Indianapolis: Indiana University Press and the United States Holocaust Memorial Museum, 2009–18).

Mera, Cipriano, *Guerra, exilio y cárcel de un anarcosindicalista* (Madrid: La Malatesta Editorial, 2011).

Merchán Tejero, Francisca (ed.), *Memorias del olvido: la contribución de los Republicanos españoles a la Resistencia y a la liberación de Francia, 1939–1945* (Paris: Federación de Asociaciones y Centros de Emigrantes Españoles en Francia, 1996).

Merino, Pedro Mateo, *Por vuestra libertad y la nuestra: andanzas y reflexiones de un combatiente republicano* (Madrid: Disenso, 1986).

Mesquida, Evelyn, *La Nueve: los españoles que liberaron París* (Madrid: Ediciones B, 2008); in French as *La Nueve, 24 août 1944: ces républicains espagnols qui ont libéré Paris* (Paris: Cherche-Midi, 2011).

Meyer, Hermann Frank, *Blutiges Edelweiß: Die 1. Gebirgs-Division im Zweiten Weltkrieg* (Berlin: Ch. Links Verlag, 2008).

Meyer, Winfried, and Klaus Neitmann (eds), *Zwangsarbeit während der NS-Zeit in Berlin und Brandenburg: Formen, Funktionen und Rezeption* (Berlin: Berliner Wissenschafts-Verlag, 2001).

Michel, Henri, *La guerre de l'ombre: la résistance en Europe* (Paris: Grasset, 1970);

trans. as *The Shadow War: Resistance in Europe, 1939–1945* (London: Deutsch, 1972).

Mihailović, Dragoslav, et al. (eds), *Zatočenici Golog otoka: registar lica osuđivanih zbog Informbiroa, dokument Uprave državne bezbednosti FNR Jugoslavije* (Belgrade: Arhiv Srbije, 2016).

Mihalovic, Milica, *Jewish Youth Societies in Yugoslavia, 1919–1941* (Belgrade: Jewish Historical Museum, 1995).

Mitrovski, Boro, Venceslav Glišić and Tomo Ristovski, *Bugarska vojska u Jugoslaviji 1941–1944* (Belgrade: Međunarodna Politika, 1971).

Moine, André, *Deportation et résistance: Afrique du Nord, 1939–1944* (Paris: Éditions Sociales, 1972).

Moore, Bob, *Prisoners of War, Prisoners of Peace: Captivity, Homecoming and Memory in World War II* (Oxford and New York: Berg, 2005).

Moore, Bob (ed.), *Resistance in Western Europe* (Oxford and New York: Berg, 2000).

Morača, Pero (ed.), *Narodni heroji Jugoslavije*, vol. 1 (Belgrade: Mladost, 1975).

Moseley, Ray, *Reporting War: How Foreign Correspondents Risked Capture, Torture, and Death to Cover World War Two* (New Haven, CT: Yale University Press, 2017).

Moss, Christoph, *Jakob Altmaier: Ein jüdischer Sozialdemokrat in Deutschland (1889–1963)* (Cologne: Böhlau, 2003).

Muracciole, Jean-François, *Les Français libres: l'autre Résistance* (Paris: Tallandier, 2009).

Murphy, C. J., *Security and Special Operations: SOE and MI5 during the Second World War* (London: Palgrave Macmillan, 2006).

Musso, Carlo, *Diplomazia partigiana: gli alleati, i rifugiati italiani e la delegazione del CLNAI in Svizzera (1943–1945)* (Milan: Franco Angeli, 1983).

Muzej Istorije Jugoslavije, *U čast španskih boraca: Jugoslovenski dobrovoljci u Španskom građanskom ratu 1936–1939. Arhivski materijal, svedočenja sećanja, Katalog izložbe / Homenaje a los brigadistas yugoslavos: los voluntarios yugoslavos en la Guerra Civil 1936–1939. Documentación de archivo, testimonios, memorias* (Belgrade: Muzej Istorije Jugoslavije/Museo de Historia de Yugoslavia, 2006).

Myers, E. C. W., *Greek Entanglement* (London: Rupert Hart-Davis, 1955).

Nazarewicz, Ryszard, *Armii Ludowej dylematy i dramaty* (Warsaw: Oficyna Drukarska, 1998).

Nazarewicz, Ryszard (ed.), *Dąbrowszczacy w wojnie hiszpańskiej 1936–1939* (Warsaw: Akademia Nauk Społecznych PZPR, 1989).

Ney-Krwawicz, Marek, *The Polish Home Army, 1939–1945* (London: PMST, 2001).

Noiriel, Gérard, *Le creuset français: histoire de l'immigration, XIXe–XXe siècles* (Paris: Seuil, 1988).

Novak, Zdenka, *When Heaven's Vault Cracked: Zagreb Memories* (Brauton, Devon: Merlin Books, 1995).

Novopashin, Iurii (ed.), *Sovetskie voennoplennye i dvizhenie soprotivleniia na pol'skikh zemliakh v gody Vtoroi Mirovoi voiny (sbornik statei)* (Moscow: AN SSSR, Institut Slavianovedeniia i Balkanistiki, 1991).

O'Sullivan, D., *Dealing with the Devil: Anglo-Soviet Intelligence Cooperation during the Second World War* (New York: Peter Lang, 2010).

Okęcki, Stanisław, *Cudzoziemcy w polskim ruchu oporu: 1939–45* (Warsaw: Interpress, 1975).

Okęcki, Stanisław (ed.), *Polish Resistance Movement in Poland and Abroad 1941–1945* (Warsaw: PWN, 1988).

Palmieri, Avagliano, *Gli internati militari italiani: diari e lettere dai lager Nazisti 1943–1945* (Turin: Einaudi, 2009).

Pattinson, Juliette, *Behind Enemy Lines: Gender, Passing and the Special Operations Executive* (Manchester: Manchester University Press, 2009).

Pavlaković, Vjeran, *The Battle for Spain is Ours: Croatia and the Spanish Civil War 1936–1939* (Zagreb: Srednja Europa, 2014).

Pavlaković, Vjeran, *Yugoslav Volunteers in the Spanish Civil War* (Belgrade: Rosa Luxemburg Stiftung Southeast Europe, 2016).

Pavone, Claudio, *Une guerra civile: saggio storico sulla moralità nella resistenza* (Turin: Bollati Boringhieri, 1991); trans. as *A Civil War: A History of the Italian Resistance* (London and New York: Verso, 2013).

Pawel, Ernst, *Life in Dark Ages: A Memoir* (New York: Fromm International, 1995).

Paxton, Robert, *L'armée de Vichy: le corps des officiers français 1940–1944* (Paris: Tallandier, 2004).

Payne, Stanley G., *Spain's First Democracy: The Second Republic, 1931–1936* (Madison, WI: The University of Wisconsin Press, 1993).

Payne, Stanley G., *The Spanish Civil War, the Soviet Union, and Communism* (New Haven, CT: Yale University Press, 2004).

Paynter, Will, *My Generation* (London: George Allen & Unwin, 1972).

Peli, Santo, *Storie di GAP: terrorismo urbano e resistenza* (Turin: Einaudi, 2017).

Pernau, Margrit, *Transnationale Geschichte* (Göttingen: Vandenhoeck & Ruprecht, 2011).

Pernet, Guy, *Pour que vive la République. 'Sebastian': son combat face au fascisme, face au franquisme* (Toulouse: Cap Bear, 2013).

Peschanski, Denis, *La France des camps: l'internement, 1938–1946* (Paris: Gallimard, 2002).

Peszke, Michael Alfred, *Battle for Warsaw, 1939–1944* (Boulder, CO: East European Monographs, 1995).

Petracci, Matteo, *Pochissimi inevitabili bastardi: l'opposizione dei maceratesi al fascismo. Dal biennio rosso alla caduta del regime* (Ancona: Il Lavoro Editoriale, 2009).

Petranović, B., *Istorija Jugoslavije*, vol. 2 (Belgrade: Nolit, 1988).

Petro, W., *Triple Commission* (London: John Murray, 1968).

Petrović, Dragoljub, *Saradnja antifašističkih pokreta u Srbiji i Bugarskoj* (Belgrade: Institut za Noviju Istoriju Srbije, 1996).

Petrović, Milo (ed.), *Preispitivanje prošlosti i istorijski revizionizam (Zlo)upotrebe*

Španskog građanskog rata i Drugog svetskog rata na prostoru Jugoslavije (Belgrade: Association of the Yugoslav Volunteers of the Spanish Republican Army; Politics Faculty of Belgrade University; Rosa Luxemburg Stiftung Southeast Europe, 2014), https://www.rosalux.rs/sites/default/files/publications/Preispitivanje_pro%C5%A1losti_i_istorijski_revizionizam.pdf (last accessed 5 July 2019).

Piatnitskii, Vladimir, *Zagovor protiv Stalina* (Moscow: Sovremennik, 1998).

Picard, René, *L'ennemi retrouvé* (Conflans-Sainte-Honorine: private publication, 1953); trans. as *A znovu sme stretli nepriateľa* (Bratislava: Nakladateľstvo Pravda, 1984).

Pigenet, Phryné, *Catalans malgré tout: l'exil catalan en France au XXe siècle. Histoire et mémoire* (Perpignan: Trabucaire, 2017).

Pirker, P., *Subversion deutscher Herrschaft: Der britische Kriegsgeheimdienst SOE und Österreich* (Vienna: Vienna University Press, 2012).

Plevza, Viliam, *Dejiny Slovenského národného povstania 1944*, vol. 5 (Bratislava: Pravda, 1984).

Poesio, Camilla, *Il confino fascista: l'arma silenziosa del regime* (Rome and Bari: Laterza, 2011).

Polonsky, Antony, *The Little Dictators: The History of Eastern Europe since 1918* (London: Routledge & Kegan Paul, 1975).

Pons Prades, Eduardo, *Republicanos españoles en la Segunda Guerra mundial* (Barcelona: La eEsfera de los Libros, 2002).

Ponty, Janine, *Polonais méconnus: histoire des travailleurs immigrés en France dans l'entre-deux-guerres* (Paris: Publications de la Sorbonne, 2005).

Ponzán, Pilar, *Lucha y muerte por la libertad: memoria de 9 años de guerra, 1936–1945* (Barcelona: Tot, 1996).

Porch, Douglas, *The French Foreign Legion: A Complete History of the Legendary Fighting Force* (Toronto: HarperCollins Canada, 1991; New York: Skyhorse, 2010).

Potočnik, Franc, *Il campo di sterminio fascista: l'isola di Rab* (Turin: Anpi, 1979).

Poullenot, Louis, *Basses Pyrénées: ocupation, libération, 1940–1945* (Paris: J & D Éditions, 1995).

Pounds, Norman J. G. (ed.), *Geographical Essays on Eastern Europe* (Bloomington: Indiana University Press, 1961).

Poznanski, Renée, *Jews in France during World War II* (Hanover and London: University Press of New England, 2001).

Poznanski, Renée, *Propagandes et persécutions: la Résistance et le 'problème juif'* (Paris: Fayard, 2008).

Poznanski, Renée, and Léo Hamon (eds), *Avant les premières grandes rafles: les juifs à Paris sous l'Occupation (juin 1940–avril 1941)*, Cahiers de l'Institut d'Histoire du Temps Présent, 22 (Paris: CNRS, 1992).

Pravdová, Anna, *Zastihla je noc: čeští výtvarní umělci ve Francii 1938–1945* (Prague: Národní Galerie, 2009).

Prečan, Vilém (ed.), *Slovenské národné povstanie: dokumenty* (Bratislava: VPL, 1965).

Preston, Paul, *The Spanish Civil War: Reaction, Revolution and Revenge* (London: William Collins, 2016).

Radosh, Ronald, Mary R. Habeck and Grigory Sevostianov (eds), *Spain Betrayed: The Soviet Union in the Spanish Civil War* (New Haven, CT: Yale University Press, 2001).

Rees, Tim, and Andrew Thorpe, *International Communism and the Communist International* (Manchester: Manchester University Press, 1998).

Richie, Alexander, *Warsaw 1944: The Fateful Uprising* (London: HarperCollins, 2013).

Rings, Werner, *Leben mit dem Feind: Anpassung und Widerstand in Hitlers Europa, 1939–1945* (Munich: Kindler, 1979); trans. as *Life with the Enemy. Collaboration and Resistance in Europe, 1939–1945* (London: Weidenfeld and Nicolson, 1982).

Rippon, Anton, *Hitler's Olympics: The Story of the 1936 Nazi Games* (Barnsley: Pen & Sword Military, 2012).

Roasio, Antonio, *Figlio della classe operaia* (Milan: Vangelista, 1977).

Roberts, Walter R., *Tito, Mihailovic and the Allies, 1941–1945* (New Brunswick, NJ: Rutgers University Press, 1973).

Rochlitz, Imre, *Accident of Fate: A Personal Account 1938–1945* (Waterloo, Ont.: Wilfrid Laurier University Press, 2011).

Rodogno, Davide, *Fascism's European Empire: Italian Occupation during the Second World War* (Cambridge: Cambridge University Press, 2006).

Rodríguez, Esther, *Els Maquis* (Barcelona: Cossetània Edicions, 2005).

Rol-Tanguy, Henri, and Roger Bourderon (eds), *Libération de Paris: les cent documents* (Paris: Hachette, 1994).

Romano, Jaša, *Jevreji Jugoslavije 1941–1945: žrtve genocida i učesnici narodnooslobodilačkog rata* (Belgrade: Jevrejski Istorijski Muzej, Saveza Jevrejskih Opština Jugoslavije, 1980).

Rootham, J., *Miss Fire: The Chronicle of a British Mission to Mihailovitch 1943–1944* (London: Chatto & Windus, 1946).

Rossi, Elena Aga, *A Nation Collapses: The Italian Surrender of September 1943* (Cambridge: Cambridge University Press, 2000).

Rossi, Elena Aga, and Maria Teresa Giusti, *Guerra a parte: i militari italiani nei Balcani 1940–1945* (Bologna: il Mulino, 2011).

Rost, Nico, *Het geval Jef Last: over Fascisme en Trotzkisme* (Amsterdam: Pegasus, 1938).

Rothschild, Emma, *The Inner Life of Empires: An Eighteenth-Century History* (Princeton, NJ, and Oxford: Princeton University Press, 2011).

Rubio, Javier, *La emigración de la guerra civil de 1936 a 1939* (Madrid: Ediciones San Martín, 1977).

Rust, William, *Britons in Spain: The History of the British Batallion of the XVth International Brigade* (London: Lawrence & Wishart, 1939).

Rutkowski, Jan, *Czas walki, klęsk i zwycięstwa: wspomnienia dąbrowszczaka: 1936–1945* (Warsaw: Zakład Narodowy im. Ossolińskich, 1980).

Rybalkin, Yuri, *Stalin y España: la ayuda militar soviética a la República* (Madrid: Marcial Pons, 2008).

Sacher-Masoch, Alexander, *Beppe und Pule: Roman einer Insel* (Vienna: W. Verkauf, 1948).

Sacher-Masoch, Alexander, *Die Ölgärten brennen* (Mannheim: Persona Verlag, 1994).

Šalgovič, Viliam, *Ján Nálepka – učiteľ, partizan, hrdina* (Martin: Osveta, 1962).

Salmon, Robert, *Chemins faisant* (Paris: Éditions LBM, 2004).

Salvadó, Francisco J. Romero, *The Spanish Civil War: Origins, Course and Outcomes* (Basingstoke and New York: Palgrave Macmillan, 2008).

Sánchez, Fernando Hernández, *Los años de plomo: la reconstrucción del PCE bajo el primer franquismo (1939–1953)* (Barcelona: Editorial Crítica, 2015).

Sánchez Cervelló, Josep, and Sebastià Agudo (eds), *Las Brigadas Internacionales: nuevas perspectivas en la historia de la Guerra Civil y del exilio* (Tarragona: Universitat Rovira i Virgili, Publicacions Universitat Rovira i Virgili, 2015).

Sánchez i Agustí, Ferran, *Maquis a Catalunya: de la invasió de la Vall d'Aran a la mort de Caracremada* (Lleida: Pagès Editors, 1999).

Sandford, Gregory, *From Hitler to Ulbricht: The Communist Reconstruction of East Germany, 1945–1946* (Princeton, NJ: Princeton University Press, 1983).

Santiago, Lucio, Rafael Barrera and Gerónimo Lloris, *Internamiento y resistencia de los republicanos españoles en África del Norte durante la Segunda Guerra mundial* (San Cugat del Vallés: Imprenta El Pot, 1981).

Sarafis, S., *ELAS: Greek Resistance Army* (London: Merlin Press, 1980).

Sauku Bruci, Marita, and Vittorio Bruno Stamerra, *Il Cristo Rosso e il suo Apostolo: storie di confinati politici ad Ustica, Vincenzo Gigante nei ricordi di Petro Marko* (Brindisi: Hobos, 2015).

Savenije, Lennert, *Nijmegen, collaboratie en verzet: een stad in oorlogstijd* (Nijmegen: Vantilt, 2018).

Schauff, Frank, *Der verspielte Sieg: Sowjetunion, Kommunistische Internatonale und Spanischer Bürgerkrieg, 1936–1939* (Frankfurt am Main and New York: Campus Verlag, 2005).

Schaul, Dora (ed.), *Résistance: Erinnerungen deutscher Antifascisten* (Berlin: Dietz Verlag, 1973).

Schiele, Werner, *An der Front der Freiheit: Jakob Altmaiers Leben für die Demokratie* (Flörsheim: H. Lauck, 1991).

Schindler, Christine (ed.), *Feindbilder* (Vienna: Dokumentationsarchiv des Österreichischen Widerstandes, 2015).

Schmider, Klaus, *Partisanenkrieg in Jugoslawien 1941–1944* (Hamburg: Mittler & Sohn, 2002).

Schwarzberg, Joseph, *Dangerous Measures* (Toronto: Azrieli Foundation, 2018).

Seaman, M. (ed.), *The Special Operations Executive* (London: Routledge, 2005).

Semelin, Jacques, Claire Andrieu and Sarah Gensburger (eds), *Resisting Genocide: The Multiple Forms of Rescue*, trans. Emma Bentley and Cynthia Schoch (New York: Columbia University Press, 2011).

Semiriaga, Mikhail, *Sovetskie liudi v evropeiskom soprotivlenii* (Moscow: Nauka, 1970).

Serrano, Secundino, *Maquis: historia de la guerrilla antifranquista* (Madrid: Temas de Hoy, 2001).

Sijes, B. A., *De arbeidsinzet: de gedwongen arbeid van Nederlanders in Duitsland, 1940–1945* (The Hague: Martinus Nijhoff, 1966).

Sinko, Ervin, *The Novel of a Novel: Abridged Diary Entries from Moscow, 1935–1937*, ed. and trans. George Deak (Lanham, MD: Lexington Books, 2018).

Siperco, Andrei (ed.), *Confesiunile elitei comuniste. România 1944–1965: rivalități, represiuni, crime ... Arhiva Alexandru Șiperco* (Bucharest: Institutul Național Pentru Studiul Totalitarismului, 2015).

Sivan, Emmanuel, *Communisme et nationalisme en Algérie, 1920–1962* (Paris: Presses de la Fondation Nationale des Sciences Politiques, 1976).

Skoutelsky, Rémi, *L'espoir guidait leurs pas: les volontaires français dans les Brigades internationales, 1936–1939* (Paris: Grasset, 1999).

SNP v pamäti národa: materiály z vedeckej konferencie k 50. výročiu SNP, Donovaly, 26–28 aprilla 1994 (Bratislava: NKV International, 1994).

Snyder, Timothy, *Bloodlands: Europe between Hitler and Stalin* (London: Bodley Head, 2010).

Sobczak, Kazimierz (ed.), *Encyklopedia II wojny światowej* (Warsaw: Wydawnictwo Ministerstwa Obrony Narodowej, 1975).

Sobczak, Kazimierz, Eugeniusz Kozłowski, and Lech Wyszczelski, *Hiszpańska wojna narodoworewolucyjna 1936–1939* (Warsaw: WPH, 1986).

Šolc, Jiří, *Bylo málo mužů* (Prague: Merkur, 1991).

Soo, Scott, *The Routes to Exile: France and the Spanish Civil War Refugees, 1939–2009* (Manchester: Manchester University Press, 2017).

Spanjer, Rimco, Diete Oudesluijs and Johan Meijer (eds), *Zur Arbeit Gezwungen: Zwangsarbeit in Deutschland 1940–1945* (Bremen: Edition Temmen, 1999).

Spartaco Capogreco, Carlo, *I campi del duce: l'internamento civile nell'Italia fascista (1940–1943)* (Turin: Einaudi, 2004).

Spinelli, Altiero, *Come ho tentato di diventare saggio* (Bologna: Il Mulino, 1984).

Spinelli, Altiero, Ernesto Rossi and Eugenio Colorni, *Il manifesto di Ventotene* (Milan: Mondadori, 2006).

Stachura, Peter D. (ed.), *The Warsaw Uprising, 1944* (Stirling: Centre for Research in Polish History, 2007).

Stafford, David, *Britain and European Resistance, 1940–1945: A Survey of the Special Operations Executive, with Documents* (Toronto: University of Toronto Press, 1980).

Starinov, Anna K., *Behind Fascist Lines: A Firsthand Account of Guerrilla Warfare during the Spanish Revolution* (Ballantyne Press: New York, 2001).

Starinov, Ilya, *Miny zamedlennogo deistviia: razmyshleniia partizana-diversanta* (Moscow: Al'manakh 'Vympel', 1999).

Starinov, Ilya, *Soldat stoletiia* (Moscow: Geroi Otechestva, 2002), http://lib.ru/MEMUARY/STARINOW/soldat.txt (last accessed 4 June 2018).

Starinov, Ilya, *Zapiski diversanta* (Moscow: Al'manakh 'Vympel', 1997).

Stavrianos, Leften Stavros, *Balkan Federation: A History of the Movement toward Balkan Unity in Modern Times* (Hamden, CT: Archon Books, 1964).

Stein, Louis, *Beyond Death and Exile: The Spanish Republicans in France, 1939–1955* (Cambridge, MA: Harvard University Press, 1980).

Steinberg, Lucien, *La révolte des justes: les juifs contre Hitler* (Paris: Fayard, 1968); trans. as *Not as a Lamb: The Jews against Hitler* (Farnborough: Saxon House, 1970).

Stradling, Robert, *History and Legend: Writing the International Brigades* (Cardiff: University of Wales Press, 2002).

Strafdivision 999: Erlebnisse und Berichte aus dem antifaschistischen Widerstandskampf (Berlin: Deutscher Militärverlag, 1966).

Suhl, Yuri, *They Fought Back: The Story of Jewish Resistance in Nazi Europe* (London: London: MacGibbon & Kee, 1968).

Supruniuk, Stanisław, *Z Polesia do Warszawy* (Warsaw: Agencja ATM, 2009).

Svoboda, Ludvík, *Cestami života*, vol. 1 (Prague: Naše Vojsko, 1971).

Szajkowski, Zosa, *Jews and the French Foreign Legion* (New York: KATV, 1975).

Szatsznaider, Jan, *Cichiociemni: z Polski do Polski* (Wrocław: Krajowa Agencja Wydawnicza, 1985).

Tacchini, Alvaro, *Guerra e resistenza nell'Alta Valle del Tevere (1943–1944)* (Castello: Petruzzi, 2015).

Tarrow, Sidney, *The New Transnational Activism* (Cambridge and New York: Cambridge University Press, 2005).

Téllez Solà, Antonio, *La red de evasión del grupo Ponzán: anarquistas en la guerra secreta contra el franquismo y el nazismo (1936–1944)* (Barcelona: Virus, 1996).

Terkel, Studs, *An Oral History of World War Two* (London: Hamish Hamilton, 1985).

Terres, Robert, *Double jeu pour la France 1939–1944* (Paris: Grasset et Fasquelle, 1977).

Thalmann, Clara, and Paul Thalmann, *Revolution für die Freiheit: Stationen eines politischen Kampfes. Moskau / Madrid / Paris* (Grafenau: Trotzdem Verlag, 1987).

Tidhar, David, *Entsiklopedyah le-halutsei ha-yishuv u-bonav*, vol. 11 (Tel Aviv: Sifriyat Rishonim, 1961).

Tillon, Charles, *Un procès de Moscou à Paris* (Paris: Seuil, 1971).

Timofejev, Aleksej, *Rusi I Drugi svetski rat u Jugoslaviji, uticaj SSSR-a I ruskih emigranata na događaje u Jugoslaviji 1941–1945* (Belgrade: Institut za Noviju Istoriju Srbije, 2011).

Titonel Asperti, Damira, *Écrire pour les autres: mémoires d'une résistante. Les antifascistes italiens en Lot-et-Garonne sous l'Occupation* (Bordeaux: Presses Universitaires de Bordeaux, 1999).

Tochman, Krzysztof A., *Cichociemni na Bałkanach we Wloszech i Francji: Słownik biograficzny* (Ostoja: Miękka, 2016).

Tomasevich, Jozo, *The Chetniks: War and Revolution in Yugoslavia 1941–1945* (Stanford, CA: Stanford University Press, 1975).

Tomasevich, Jozo, *War and Revolution in Yugoslavia 1941–1945. Occupation and Collaboration* (Stanford, CA: Stanford University Press, 2001).

Tomin, Valentin (ed.), *Oni srazhalis' s fashizmom* (Moscow: Politizdat, 1988).

Tosi, L. (ed.), *Caro nemico: soldati pistoiesi e toscani nella resistenza in Albania e Montenegro 1943–1945* (Pisa: Edizione ETS, 2018).

Trempé, Rolande, *La Libération dans le Midi de la France* (Toulouse: Eché Editeur et Service de Publications de l'UTM, 1986).

Ulmi, Nic, and Peter Huber, *Les combattants suisses en Espagne républicaine (1936–1939)* (Lausanne: Antipodes, 2001).

Urbanowicz, Józef (ed.), *Mała encyklopedia wojskowa*, vol. 2 (Warsaw: Wydawnictwo Ministerstwa Obrony Narodowej, 1971).

Vaia, Alessandro, *De Galeotto a generale* (Rome: Teti, 1977).

Vallauri, Carlo (ed.), *Le repubbliche partigiane: esperienze di autogoverno democratico* (Rome and Bari: Laterza, 2013).

Varsa-Szekeres, Vera, *Salamandre: une vie confrontée à la Gestapo française et à la police politique hongroise* (Paris: L'Harmattan, 2016).

Vasilevich, I. (ed.), *Bessmertie: ocherki o razvedchikakh. Liudi molchalivogo podviga* (Moscow: Izdatel'stvo Politicheskoi Literatury, 1987).

Vasilichi, G. (ed.), *Les Roumains dans la Résistance française au cours de la Seconde Guerre mondiale* (Bucharest: Meridiane, 1971).

Vestermanis, Marģers, *Vēstules nākamībai: Latvijas partizāņu kustības un komunistiskās pagrīdes cīnītāju pirmsnāves atvadas* (Riga: Liesma, 1965).

Via Fernández, Ramón, *J'accuse ... paroles confiées par Ramon Via Fernández a un prisonnier sorti de la prison de Malaga* (Paris: Secours Populaire Français et le Comité France-Espagne, 1946).

Vigée, Claude, *La lune d'hiver* (Paris: Flammarion, 1970).

Vilanova Fuentes, Antonio, *Los olvidados: los exiliados espagñoles en la Segunda Guerra mundial* (Paris: Ruedo Ibérico, 1969).

Vinarov, Ivan, *Boitsi na tikhiia front: spomeni na razuznavacha* (Sofia: Partizdat, 1988).

Volodarsky, Boris, *Stalin's Agent: The Life and Death of Alexander Orlov* (Oxford: Oxford University Press, 2015).

Voukmanovitch-Tempo, Svetozar, *Le Parti Communiste de Grèce dans la lutte de libération nationale* (Paris: Le Livre Yougoslave, 1949).

Vujošević, Jovan, et al., *Proceedings of Documents and Data on the National Liberation War of the Yugoslav Peoples*, vol. 7, book 3 (Belgrade: Vojnoizdavački Zavod 'Vojno Delo', 1954).

Vuksanović, Miloš, *Prva proleterska brigada* (Belgrade-Titograd: Narodna Knjiga, ISI, Pobjeda 1981).

Walker, Jonathan, *Poland Alone: Britain, SOE, and the Collapse of the Polish Resistance 1944* (London: The History Press, 2011).

Weiner, Amir, *Making Sense of War. The Second World War and the Fate of the Bolshevik Revolution* (Princeton, NJ: Princeton University Press, 2001).

Weizman, Lenore J., and Dalia Ofer (eds), *Women in the Holocaust* (New Haven, CT: Yale University Press, 1998).

Wellers, Georges, André Kaspi and Serge Klarsfeld (eds), *La France et la question juive* (Paris: Éditions Sylvie Messinger, 1981).

Weniger, Kay, *Zwischen Bühne und Baracke: Lexikon der verfolgten Theater-, Film- und Musikkünstler 1933 bis 1945. Mit einem Geleitwort von Paul Spiegel* (Berlin: Metropol, 2008).

Werblan, Andrzej, *Władysław Gomułka: pamiętniki*, vol. 2 (Warsaw: BGW, 1994).

Wieviorka, Annette, *Ils etaient juifs, resistants, communists* (Paris: Éditions Denoël, 1986).

Wieviorka, Olivier, *La mémoire désunie: le souvenir politique des années sombres de la Libération a nos jours* (Paris: Seuil, 2010).

Wieviorka, Olivier, *Une histoire de la Résistance en Europe Occidentale* (Paris: Perrin, 2017); trans. as *The Resistance in Western Europe, 1940–1945* (New York: Columbia University Press, 2019).

Williams, Heather, *Parachutes, Patriots and Partisans: The Special Operations Executive and Yugoslavia, 1941–1945* (London: Hurst, 2003).

Wingate Pike, David, *Spaniards in the Holocaust: Mauthausen, Horror on the Danube* (New York: Routledge, 2000).

Withuis, Jolande, *Weest mannelijk, zijt sterk: Pim Boellaard (1903–2001), het leven van een verzetsheld* (Amsterdam: De Bezige Bij, 2008).

Wolikow, Serge, *Histoire de l'Internationale communiste* (Paris: L'Atelier, 2010).

Wylie, N. (ed.), *The Politics and Strategy of Clandestine War: Special Operations Executive, 1940–46* (London: Routledge, 2007).

Wyman, Mark, *DPs: Europe's Displaced Persons, 1945–1951* (Ithaca, NY, and London: Cornell University Press, 1989, 1998).

Yusta, Mercedes, *Guerrilla y resistencia campesina: la resistencia armada contra el franquismo en Aragón* (Saragossa: Prensas Universitarias de Zaragoza, 2003).

Zaagsma, Gerben, *Jewish Volunteers, the International Brigades and the Spanish Civil War* (London and New York: Bloomsbury Academic, 2017).

Zaugg, Franziska: *Albanische Muslime in der Waffen-SS, von 'Großalbanien' zur Division 'Skanderbeg'* (Paderborn: Schöningh Verlag 2016).

Zevelev, Aleksandr, et al. (eds), *Nenavist', spressovannaia v tol* (Moscow: Mysl', 1991).

Zhilin, Pavel (ed.), *Boevoe sodruzhestvo sovetskogo i pol'skogo narodov* (Moscow: Mysl', 1973).

Ziemelis, Sigurds, *Latvijas cīnītāji Spānijā, 1936–1939 atminas un dokumenti* (Riga: Liesma, 1966).

Zlatin, Sabine, *Mémoires de la 'Dame d'Izieu'* (Paris: Gallimard, 1992).

Articles

Absalom, Roger, 'Allied Escapers and the *Contadini* in Iccupied Italy (1943–1945)', *Journal of Modern Italian Studies*, 10.4 (2005), 413–25.

Ageron, Charles-Robert, 'Le Parti Communiste Algérien de 1939 à 1943', *Vingtième siècle: revue d'histoire*, 12 (1986), 39–50.

Baerentzen, Lars, 'The German Withdrawal from Greece in 1944 and British Naval "Inactivity"', *Journal of Modern Greek Studies*, 5.2 (1987), 237–65.

Barsukov, Ivan, 'The Rooski Company', *Ethiniki Antistasi*, 3 (Dec. 1962) 270–5 (in Greek).

Baxell, Richard, 'Myths of the International Brigades', *Bulletin of Spanish Studies*, 91.1–2 (2014), 11–24.

Beinen, Joel, 'The Palestine Communist Party 1919–1948', *MERIP Reports*, 55 (1977), 3–17.

Bowd, Gavin, 'Romanians of the French Resistance', *French History*, 28.4 (2014), 541–59.

Brafman, Marc, 'Les origines, les motivations, l'action et les destins des combattants juifs (parmi d'autres immigrés) de la 35e Brigade FTP-MOI de Marcel Langer, Toulouse 1942–1944', *Le monde juif*, 152 (1994), 79–95.

Bushueva, T. S., 'Russkie roty i batal'ony v Narodno osvoboditel'noy armii Yugoslavii', *Sovetskoe slavyanovedenie*, 3 (1972), 11–21.

Celaya, Diego Gaspar, 'D'un mythe à l'autre: mémoire et histoire des Espagnols dans la Résistance', *Conserveries mémorielles*, 20 (2017), http://journals.openedition.org/cm/2441 (last accessed 1 May 2019).

Celaya, Diego Gaspar, 'Portrait d'oubliés: l'engagement des Espagnols dans les Forces françaises libres, 1940–1945', *Revue historique des armées*, 265 (2011), 46–55, http://journals.openedition.org/rha/7345 (last accessed 6 Jan. 2018).

Celaya, Diego Gaspar, '"Premature Resisters": Spanish Contribution to the French National Defence Campaign in 1939/1940', *Journal of Modern European History*, 16.2 (2018), 203–24.

Cherchari, Mohamed Sahia, 'Indigènes et citoyens ou l'impossible universalisation du suffrage', *Revue française de droit constitutionnel*, 60.4 (2004), 741–70.

D'Abzac-Epezy, Claude, 'Armée et secrets, 1940–1942: le contre-espionnage de l'armée de Vichy', *Bulletin de l'Institut Pierre Renouvin*, 36.2 (2012), 45–56.

Delacor, Regina M., 'From Potential Friends to Potential Enemies: The Internment of Hostile Foreigners in France at the Beginning of the Second World War', *Journal of Contemporary History*, 35.3 (2000), 361–8.

Deroo, Éric and Antoine Champeaux, 'Panorama des troupes coloniales françaises dans les deux guerres mondiales', *Revue historique des armées*, 271 (2013), 72–88.

'The ELAS Battalion of Death', *Rizospastis*, 20 Oct. 1943.

Eumann, Ulrich, 'Nach Francos Sieg: Leidenswege Kölner Spanienkämpfer', *Geschichte im Westen*, 28 (2013), 119–39.

Friedl, Jiří, 'Španěláci" z tábora Gurs (ke vstupu čs. interbrigadistů do naší armády ve Francii 1939–40)', *Historie a vojenství*, 49.4 (2000), 806–27.

Ghodsee, Kristen, 'A Tale of "Two Totalitarianisms": The Crisis of Capitalism and the Historical Memory of Communism', *History of the Present*, 4.2 (2014), 115–42.

Gildea, Robert, 'The Long March of Oral History: Around 1968 in France', *Oral History*, 38.1 (2010), 68–80.

Gontarczyk, Piotr, 'Z genealogii elit PZPR: przypadek Stefana Kilianowicza vel Grzegorza Korczyńskiego', *Glaukopis*, 1 (2003), 214–29.

Graham, Helen, 'Review: Spain Betrayed? The New Historical McCarthyism', *Science & Society*, 68.3 (2004), 364–9.

Guedj, Jérémy, 'Les juifs français face aux juifs étrangers dans la France de l'entre deux guerres', *Cahiers de la Méditerrannée*, 78.2 (2009), 43–73.

Heijden, Eugène van der, 'Oorlogsherinneringen', *Escape*, 80 (March 1994), 31–4, and 81 (June 1994), 26–30.

Janavičiené, Audronė, 'Sovietiniai diversantai Lietovuje (1941–1944)', *Genocidas ir rezistencija*, 1 (2007), 98–121.

Judt, Tony, 'Rehearsal for Evil', *New Republic*, 225.11 (2001), 29–35.

Kalous, Jan, 'Osvald Závodský – aktér i oběť politických procesů', *Paměť a dějiny*, 8.3 (2013), 85–95.

Keazor, Ed, 'August Agboola Browne Nigerian Pioneer of Jazz Music and World War 2 Hero', *Music in Africa Magazine*, 29 May 2015, http://musicinafrica.net/august-agboola-browne-nigerian-pioneer-jazz-music-and-world-war-2-hero (last accessed 27 April 2020).

Kerenji, Emil, '"Your salvation is the struggle against fascism": Yugoslav Communists and the Rescue of Jews, 1941–1945', *Contemporary European History*, 25.1 (2016), 57–74.

Korczyński, P., 'Po dwóch stronach barykady: Za waszą wolność, a nasze przetrwanie, czyli polscy bohaterowie Jugosławii'. *Polska Zbrojna*, 12 (2016), 110–13.

Kruizinga, Samuël, 'Struggling to Fit In: The Dutch in a Transnational Army, 1936–1939', *Journal of Modern European History*, 16.2 (2018), 183–202.

Lahiri, Shompa, 'Clandestine Mobilities and Shifting Embodiments: Noor-un-nisa Inayat Khan and the Special Operations Executive, 1940–44', *Gender & History*, 19.2 (2007), 305–23.

Leal, Juan Martínez, 'El Stanbrook: un barco mítico en la memoria de los exiliados españoles', *Pasado y memoria*, 4 (2005), 65–81.

Lemesle, Hervé, 'Des médailles et leurs revers: des anciens d'Espagne devenus "héros des peuples de Yougoslavie"', *Cahiers Balkaniques*, 38–9 (2011), 37–70.

Leśnik, Avgust, 'Les volontaires yugoslaves/slovènes dans la Guerre Civile espagnole (1936–1939): analyse structurelle et la liste', *Annales*, 17.1 (2007), 107–38.

Lieb, Peter, 'Repercussions of Eastern Front Experiences on Anti-Partisan Warfare in France, 1943–1944', *Journal of Strategic Studies*, 31.5 (2008), 797–823.

MacKay, Ruth, 'The Good Fight and Good History: The Spanish Civil War', *History Workshop Journal*, 70.1 (2010), 199–206.

Marco, Jorge, 'Ecos Partisanos: la memoria de la resistencia como memoria conflictiva', *Historia del presente*, 17.1 (2011), 79–91.

Marco, Jorge, 'Transnational Soldiers and Guerrilla Warfare from the Spanish Civil War to the Second World War', *War in History*, 20 Sept. 2018, https://doi.org/10.1177/0968344518761212.

Monk, Jeremy, 'Forgotten Heroes? The Czechs of X-Troop, No. 10 Commando', *Prague Post*, 30 July 2017.

Nagy, J. Làszlo, 'Les activités communistes en Algérie sous le régime de Vichy', *Cahiers d'histoire de l'Institut de Recherches Marxistes* 11 (1982), 87–100.

Osterhammel, Jürgen, 'Global History and Historical Sociology', in James Belich, John Darwin, Margret Frenz and Chris Wickham (eds), *The Prospect of Global History* (Oxford: Oxford University Press, 2016), 23–43.

Parello, Vincent, 'Les compagnies de travailleurs étrangers (CTE) en France à la fin de la Troisième République', *Bulletin hispanique*, 118.1 (2016), 233–50.

Perrin, Alban, 'Comment devient-on français quand on est juif et polonais?', *Bulletin du Centre de Recherche Français à Jérusalem*, 22 (2011), http://journals.openedition.org/bcrfj/6563 (last accessed 1 May 2019).

Petracci, Matteo, 'La liberazione interrotta: lettere dal carcere di un partigiano etiopico', *Mondo contemporaneo*, 1 (2017), 69–96.

Pietrzak, Jacek, 'Polscy uczestnicy hiszpańskiej wojny domowej', *Acta Universitatis Lodziensis*, Folia Historica, 97 (2016), 65–86.

Pirker, Peter, 'Transnational Resistance in the Alps-Adriatic Area in 1939/40', *Acta Histriae*, 20.4 (2012), 849–51.

Prospo, Mario De, 'Reconstructing the Army of a Collapsed Nation: The Kingdom of the South of Italy (September 1943–March 1944)', *Journal of Modern Italian Studies*, 18.1 (2013), 1–16.

Romano, Jaša, 'Jevreji u logoru na Rabu i njihovo uključivanje u Narodnooslobodilački rat', *Zbornik Jevrejskog istorijskog muzeja*, 2 (1973), 1–69.

Romero Navas, José Aurelio, '1952: huida de los seis últimos guerrilleros a Francia', *Jábega*, 88 (2001), 82–97.

Różycki, Bartłomiej, 'Dąbrowszczacy i pamięć o hiszpańskiej wojnie domowej w Polsce Ludowej', *Pamięć i Sprawiedliwość*, 1.21 (2013), 167–212.

Sanchez, Sergio, 'José Gistau, paquetero de suerte', *El mundo de los Pirineos*, 3 (May 1998).

Schafranek, Hans, 'Julius Kornweitz und Leo Gabler – Auslandsemissäre der KPÖ im Visier der Gestapo', in Dokumentationsarchiv des Österreichischen Wiederstandes (ed.), *Jahrbuch 2011* (Vienna, 2011), 185–208.

Shapiro, Martin F., 'Medical Aid Provided by American, Canadian and British Nationals to the Spanish Republic during the Civil War, 1936–1939', *International Journal of Health Services*, 13.3 (1983), 443–58.

Simonin, Anne, 'Le Comité Médical de la Résistance: un succès différé', *Le mouvement social*, 180.3 (1997), 159–78.

Slaby, Philip H., 'Dissimilarity Breeds Contempt: Ethnic Paternalism, Foreigners and the State in Pas-de-Calais Coalmining, France, 1920s', *International Review of Social History*, 60 (special issue) (2015), 227–51.

Subrahmanyam, Sanjay, 'Connected Histories: Notes towards a Reconfiguration of Early Modern Eurasia', *Modern Asian Studies*, 31.3 (1997), 735–62.

Subrahmanyam, Sanjay, 'Holding the World in Balance: The Connected Histories of the Iberian Overseas Empires, 1500–1640', *American Historical Review*, 112.5 (2007), 1359–85.

Szydłowska-Ceglowa, Barbara (ed.), *Polonia w Europie: Praza zbiorowa* (Poznań: Ośr. Inform. Nauk. PAN, 1992).

Szulman, François, 'Septembre 1939 – septiembre 2009: 70 ans après l'engagement massif des juifs étrangers dans la Seconde Guerre mondiale', *Notre volonté (UEVACJEA)*, 36 (2009), 2–5.

Tagangaeva, Maria, 'Socialist in Content, National in Form: The Making of Soviet National Art and the Case of Buryatia', *Nationalities Papers*, 45.3 (2017), 393–409, https://doi.org/10.1080/00905992.2016.1247794.

Vagst, Alfred, 'Foreigner as Soldier in the Second World War', *Journal of Politics*, 9.3 (1947), 392–416.

Varese, Federico, and Meir Yaish, 'The Importance of Being Asked: The Rescue of Jews in Nazi Europe', *Rationality and Society*, 12.3 (2000), 307–34.

Vatlin, Alexander, and Stephen A. Smith, 'The Comintern', in Stephen A. Smith (ed.), *The Oxford Handbook of the History of Communism* (Oxford: Oxford University Press, 2014), 187–202.

Verzeichnis der Haftstätten unter dem Reichsführer-SS (1933–1945: Konzentrationslager u. deren Aussenkommandos sowie andere Haftstätten unter d. Reichsführer-SS in Deutschland und deutsch besetzten Gebieten, vol. 1 (Bad Arolsen: Internationaler Suchdienst, 1979).

Vilar, Juan Bautista, 'El exilio español de 1939 en el norte de África', *Historia del presente*, 12 (2008), 19–42.

Vukliš, Vladan, 'Sarajevski dosije Helmuta Klozea: 1933–1937', *Prilozi*, 44 (2015), 181–205.

Weill, Georges, 'Andrée Salomon et le sauvetage des enfants juifs (1933–1947)', *French Politics, Culture and Society*, 30.2 (2012), 89–96.

Weiss-Rykart, Jeanne, 'Erinnerungen an Clara Thalmann', *Emanzipation*, 13.3 (1987), 8–9.

Werner, Michael, and Bénédicte Zimmermann, 'Beyond Comparison: *Histoire croisée* and the Challenge of Reflexivity', *Theory and History*, 45 (2006), 30–50.

Werner, Michael, and Bénédicte Zimmermann, 'Penser l'histoire croisée: entre empirie et réflexivité', *Annales: histoire, sciences sociales*, 58.1 (2003), 7–36.

Whaley, Barton, *Guerrillas in the Spanish Civil War* (Cambridge, MA: Center for International Studies, Massachusetts Institute of Technology, 1969).

Wieviorka, Annette, 'Manès Sperber: le juif universaliste', *L'histoire*, 417 (2015), 42–3.

Wieviorka, Olivier, 'Les avatars du statut résistant en France (1945–1992)', *Vingtiéme siècle: revue d'histoire*, 50 (1996), 55–66.

Winand, Els, and Axel Wagener, 'Interview mit Clara Thalmann, Teil I: "Dem Unterdrücker ans Genick"', *Schwarzer Faden: Vierteljahreszeitschrift für Lust und Freiheit*, 2 (1985), 24–34.

Zorn, Edith, 'Einige Forschungergebnisse zur Taetigkeit deutscher Antifaschisten, die an der Seite der franzoesischen Résistance kaempften', *Beitraege zur deutschen Arbeiterbewegung*, 7.2 (1965), 155–65.

Zudová-Lešková, Zlatica, 'Československý výsadok Courier 5', *Soudobé dějiny*, 8.4 (2001), 718–31.

Doctoral dissertations

Alvanos, Raymondos, 'Social Conflicts and Political Gehaviour in the Area of Kastoria (1922–1949)' (PhD dissertation, Aristotle University of Thessaloniki, 2005) (in Greek).

Cammaert, A. F. M., 'Het verborgen front: geschiedenis van de georganiseerde illegaliteit in de provincie Limburg tijdens de Tweede Wereldoorlog' (PhD dissertation, University of Groningen, 1994).

Fivaz-Silbermann, Ruth, 'La fuite en Suisse: migrations, strategies, fuite, accueil, refoulement et destin des réfugiés juifs durant la Seconde Guerre' (PhD dissertation, University of Geneva, 2017).

Giersberg, Bettina, 'Die Arbeit des Schriftstellers Rudolf Leonhard im französischen Exil 1933 bis 1945' (PhD dissertation, University of Potsdam, 2005).

Konopatchenkov, Alexey, 'Kontsentratsionnye lageria sistemy Mautkhausen v natsistskoi Germanii (1938–1945): istoriia, struktura, soprotivlenie' (PhD dissertation, Moscow State University, 2010).

Kulok, Jan, 'Trait d'union: The History of the French Relief Organisation Secours National/Entr'aide Française under the Third Republic, the Vichy Regime and the Early Fourth Republic, 1939–1949' (DPhil dissertation, University of Oxford, 2003).

Lemesle, Hervé, 'Des Yougoslaves engagés au XXe siècle: itinéraires de volontaires Yougoslaves en Espagne républicaine' (PhD dissertation, Université de Paris I, Panthéon-Sorbonne, 2011).

McNiff, Kelsey William, 'The French Internment Camp Le Vernet d'Ariège: Local Administration, Collaboration and Public Opinion in Vichy France' (PhD dissertation, Princeton University, 2004).

Nioutsikos, Ioannis, 'The EAM-ELAS Resistance to the Axis Occupation of Greece 1941–1944: A Case Study in the Theory and Practice of Guerilla Warfare' (PhD dissertation, King's College London, 2015).

Swarc, Alan, 'Illegal Immigration to Palestine, 1945–1948: The French Connection' (PhD dissertation, University College London, 2005).

Internet sources

Almanach Muszyny dla Małej Ojczyzny, www.almanachmuszyny.pl.

Altnkov, Nikola, 'Svetskata shpionska mrezha v Blgariia', *Fakel*, 19 June 2018, https://www.fakel.bg/index.php?t=6398 (last accessed 30 May 2018).

Biblioteca Virtual Miguel de Cervantes, www.cervantesvirtual.com.

Central Intelligence Agency Library, https://www.cia.gov/library.

Centropa Jewish Historical Institute, www.centropa.org.

Ebrei stranieri internati in Italia durante il periodo bellico, www.annapizzuti.it.

European Holocaust Research Infrastructure, https://ehri-project.eu.

Fondation de la Résistance, www.fondationresistance.org.

'Fritz Beer', Arco Verlag, www.arco-verlag.com/autoren/autor/9-fritz-beer.html (last accessed 4 March 2019).

Les Amis des Combattants en Espagne Républicain, www.acer-aver.fr/.

Mémoire des Résistants Juifs de la MOI, www.mrj-moi.com.

'Missing Men from 1945', *National Ex-Prisoner of War Association* (Autumn 2013), 9, www.prisonerofwar.org.uk/ AUTUMN%202013%20NEWSLETTER.pdf.

Musée de la Résistance en Ligne, www.museedelaresistanceenligne.org.

Muzeum Powstania Warszawskiego, www.1944.pl.

Nederlands in het Franse Vreemdelingenlegioen, www.kwaak99.demon.nl.

Polska Zbrojna, www.polska-zbrojna.pl.

Stalin, J. V, radio roadcast, 3 July 1941. https://www.marxists.org/reference/archive/stalin/works/1941/07/03.htm (last accessed 5 May 2019).

Tribunal Archives as a Digital Research Facility (Triado), https://www.niod.nl/en/news/tribunal-archives-digital-research-facility.

Union des Engagés Volontaires, Anciens Combattants Juifs, www.combattantvolontairejuif.org.

United States Holocaust Memorial Museum, https://collections.ushmm.org.

USC Shoah Foundation Testimonies, Los Angeles, https://sfi.usc.edu/full-length-testimonies.

Vol'nodumov, Roman, 'Russkie i varshavskoe vosstanie', *Petr I mazepA*, 1 Aug. 2015, http://petrimazepa.com/warsaw.html (last accessed 27 April 2020).

Warszawa Naszemiasto, http://warszawa.naszemiasto.pl.

Yad Vasham, World Holocaust Remembrance Centre, www.yadvashem.org.

Audiovisual sources

Dreyfus-Armand, Geneviève, 'Celestino Alfonso', in *La Résistance en Île-de-France*, DVD-ROM, AERI, 2004.

Institut National de l'Audiovisuel, Paris, *Les dossiers de l'écran*, 2 July 1985.

La Nueve ou les oubliés de la victoire (documentary film), dir. Alberto Marquardt, France, Point du Jour, 2009.

Sowa, Andrzej, and Dorota Truszczak, 'Powstanie styczniowe: obcy też walczyli za naszą wolność', *Polskie Radio*, 24 July 2013, www.polskieradio.pl/7/2612/Artykul/895066,Powstanie-styczniowe-obcy-tez-walczyli-za-nasza-wolnosc (last accessed 27 April 2020)

Index